Sense of the Faithful

Sense of the Faithful

How American Catholics Live Their Faith

JEROME P. BAGGETT

OXFORD

UNIVERSITY PRESS

2009

OXFORD
UNIVERSITY PRESS

Oxford University Press, Inc., publishes works that further
Oxford University's objective of excellence
in research, scholarship, and education.

Oxford   New York
Auckland   Cape Town   Dar es Salaam   Hong Kong   Karachi
Kuala Lumpur   Madrid   Melbourne   Mexico City   Nairobi
New Delhi   Shanghai   Taipei   Toronto

With offices in
Argentina   Austria   Brazil   Chile   Czech Republic   France   Greece
Guatemala   Hungary   Italy   Japan   Poland   Portugal   Singapore
South Korea   Switzerland   Thailand   Turkey   Ukraine   Vietnam

Published by Oxford University Press, Inc.
198 Madison Avenue, New York, New York 10016

www.oup.com

Oxford is a registered trademark of Oxford University Press

Library of Congress Cataloging-in-Publication Data
Baggett, Jerome P., 1963–
Sense of the faithful : how American Catholics live their faith / Jerome P. Baggett.
p. cm.
Includes bibliographical references and index.
ISBN 978-0-19-532695-6
1. Catholic Church—United States. 2. Catholics—United States.
3. Catholics—Religious life.
I. Title.
BX1406.3.B34 2009
282'.73090511—dc22
2008015623

1 3 5 7 9 8 6 4 2

Printed in the United States of America
on acid-free paper

For John A. Coleman, S.J.,
with much esteem and appreciation

Contents

Preface

THIS BOOK, TO USE A FAMILIAR EXPRESSION, IS TRULY A "CONVERSATION piece." The idea of writing it first occurred to me as a result of many conversations with people, especially my students and colleagues at the Jesuit School of Theology at Berkeley, regarding present-day American Catholicism. These exchanges made me realize just how little we actually know about the people in the pews, particularly how they, while thoroughly modern, continue to find a great deal of meaning in their two-millennia-old religious tradition.

To be sure, whatever this book might add to our knowledge about such concerns is also the product of much conversation. As I describe more fully toward the end of the first chapter, it is based primarily on extensive interviews with nearly three hundred active members of six Catholic parishes scattered throughout the San Francisco Bay Area. These have afforded me a ground-level view of American Catholicism. Rather than "official" pronouncements from church leaders, the focus of this book is on the decidedly "nonofficial" viewpoints expressed by the rank and file. Relying less on what are often very helpful, broad-based surveys, I plumb depths of meaning that are accessible only through more prolonged discussion. And, in resistance to simplistic and all-too-ubiquitous punditries *about* the American laity, my purpose has been to engage laypeople in dialogue in order to take stock of what they actually say for themselves.

This in itself is a worthwhile undertaking. Nevertheless, I hope that what I have recorded here will stimulate still more conversation. When I reflect on the remarkable candor and seriousness that parishioners brought to these interviews, I cannot help but think they model the very sort of open conversation about faith, doubt, and religious community that is too often lacking in the current discourse on such topics. In the face of the myriad complexities and tensions that mark their religious lives, it is even more blatantly obvious that the pious platitudes, anachronistic verities, and "holier than thou" accusations that frequently speckle this discourse simply do not suffice. The fitting response is surely additional and equally nuanced discussion. In short, I hope this book will indeed become a conversation piece for readers, especially Catholic ones, because I am convinced that the parishioners introduced here have important things to say about discerning some connection to the sacred within our fast-paced, modern society. As we will see, their religious lives defy easy summation, and thus they truly merit the consideration and forthright deliberation that only further conversation can ensure.

In an effort to facilitate this, I provide in this book, as its title denotes, a "sense of the faithful." This term has a long history, and, within theological circles, it bears particular meanings, some of which I address in the concluding chapter. Yet here I employ the term more loosely to refer, as suggested earlier, to what Catholics say about themselves, how they understand their faith, and how they draw upon it to find purpose in their daily lives. Wrought of careful listening, this book offers an account of one segment of the Catholic faithful as presented largely in their own voices and on their own terms.

If my sampling of the faithful consists of Bay Area parishioners, what exactly does it mean to acquire a sense of them beyond simply listening? Certainly it is not to record the details of their everyday existence. Famed writer W. H. Auden's astute observation that a day in the life of a single person could fill an entire novel should make us wary of such an unwieldy enterprise. Rather, for the present purposes, it means to address certain unsettled topics—those that require Catholics to explicitly reflect upon their tradition and often negotiate with components of it. Even if they do not always engage one another in conversation about them, these topics are nevertheless disparately interpreted, frequently contested and, in any case, very much up for grabs. They are nodal points at which Catholics more intentionally do the cultural work of thinking through how or to what extent the religious meanings familiar to them might contribute to their greater understanding of the world and their place in it. It is at these points that one can best witness people's improvisational use of the symbols and meanings embedded within the Catholic tradition to produce a version of the faith that best resonates with their personal experience.

Getting a sense for this kind of cultural work is not wholly unlike viewing other cultural productions, which is why I employ the metaphor of observing a painting as a means of organizing the chapters ahead. Thus, in part I, I assist the reader in getting situated, much as an art lover prepares to view an exhibit featuring a favorite painting. I do this in the first chapter by introducing readers to the dramatic changes in American Catholicism that have occurred within the past century and then detailing the rationale and research methods I used. In the second chapter

I explain what it means to view people's religious lives through the lens of cultural analysis. Social scientists who are already accustomed to this approach may want to bypass this explanation, which appears in the first half of the chapter before the thumbnail descriptions of the six parishes. However, most readers are likely to gain considerable insight from being introduced to religious culture construed as: available to individuals to an unprecedented degree; appropriated by them as their needs require; and allocated to them through the distinct parish cultures in which they participate. This may apply especially to those who, perhaps because they are so close to the Catholic faith, find that they particularly appreciate the analytical distance this approach affords them.

Like a museumgoer closely examining a painting of acute interest, in part II, I lean in closer to investigate contemporary American Catholicism and, in doing so, accentuate four areas in which the nuances of parishioners' cultural work are particularly evident. In chapter 3 I address the topic of the religious self and point to various "conversational shards" indicative of Catholics' negotiation with their tradition on the basis of what feels authentic to them. In chapter 4 the focus turns to parishioners' awareness of the various institutional dilemmas that encumber their church, as well as to the ways in which these influence their perceptions of themselves as members of the broader institution. Important to note is that, while parishioners tend to be quite critical and self-conscious in their use of Catholic symbols when thinking about themselves as both individuals and members of a hierarchical institution, this is significantly less true with respect to the next two areas. In other words, they are less aware that their conceptions of religious community reflect their social locations and are largely derived from longstanding notions of community carried within American culture more generally (I treat this topic in chapter 5). Nor, as chapter 6 illustrates, are they typically aware of the ways their parish cultures often delimit the role the church's social justice teachings might otherwise play in influencing Catholics' sense of obligation and contributions to civil society.

Finally, I step back a bit in part III. To recapitulate the major themes, here I reflect on an inherent paradox of religious traditions. Characterized by both stasis and flux, traditions conserve cultural meanings for new generations of people who, in reinterpreting these as novel situations require, ultimately alter those very meanings. To comprehend this is to more fully grasp the perennial and dynamic nature of religious faith. It also, I contend, pushes us to acknowledge two additional points. The first is that the analytical categories we frequently utilize in investigating religious traditions must also adapt if we are truly to do justice to tradition's paradoxical character.

The second point, a theme woven throughout this book, is that the ending of one iteration of a religious tradition is often tantamount to the beginning of another. Specifically, the common wisdom that today's American Catholics are less religious than their predecessors is in reality neither common nor particularly wise. This presumption lacks wisdom in that it almost unfailingly highlights one way the faith has been lived in the past, determines this to be normative, and then dismisses what might depart from it as being somehow less religious. But seeing things in this manner actually reveals a blindness to the constitutively changing nature of religious traditions, as well as their variability from one cultural context to the next. Moreover, this perspective may seem commonplace if one is in the habit of privileging the viewpoints of those religious elites and scholarly observers who are overly invested in or enamored with the Catholicism of the past. If, however, one takes the less frequently traveled route of speaking to everyday Catholics who take their tradition seriously and whose lives are thus sacralized by it, one gets an entirely different perspective. Far more common, one discovers, is the reality that these people may be different from their parents or grandparents in how they practice their faith, but they are hardly less religious. They sound different from Catholics a century or even a few decades ago, and they tend to be more insistent about living their faith as they see fit. Yet I see little evidence to support slapdash assumptions concerning the waning of religious sentiments among Catholics.

Of course, this book is less an argument about this particular matter than a conversation about matters of faith in general. It is ultimately up to readers to decide whether an end of one manifestation of American Catholicism is also the beginning of another. Thus, I invite all to lend an ear—and then perhaps even to contribute—to the conversation that follows.

Acknowledgments

IN MY OPINION, THE BEST THING ABOUT WRITING A BOOK IS NOT FINISHING IT. It is being nearly finished, with only the "Acknowledgments" section left to go. This is because, even though writing often seems like a lonely task, thinking about whom to acknowledge is a great reminder of what a cooperative venture it really is. I am reminded of this right now, and all I feel is tremendous gratitude.

Those who come to mind first, not surprisingly, are the people I have been talking to and thinking about for quite some time now. These are the Bay Area parishioners who so kindly agreed to be observed, surveyed, and, of course, rather extensively interviewed for this book. To "bare one's soul" is a cliché. In this case, though, it is a precise description. With nothing much to gain for themselves, these parishioners revealed their most private longings and fears. They talked about how they understand God and how they pray, what they doubt and who they admire, where they have experienced holiness, and when they have failed to be the persons they wish to be. Sometimes they wept or, if addressing an especially sensitive topic, asked that I turn the tape recorder off. They showed both great anger and side-splitting humor. They told stories they claimed to never have told before and others I strongly suspect they had repeated on numerous occasions. In nearly every case, though, they willingly disclosed the deepest parts of themselves. This, I have come to see in ways I did not know before embarking upon this research, is an act of profound generosity, for which I am extremely grateful.

This project would not have been feasible without the funding assistance supplied by three institutions. The first, the Louisville Institute, supported the data-gathering phase of this study. I am particularly thankful to executive director James Lewis for graciously encouraging me to move ahead with this project at precisely the time when I most needed spurring on. The other two institutions—the Henry Luce Foundation and the Association of Theological Schools—together awarded me a Henry Luce III Fellows in Theology grant, which enabled me to take a year-long sabbatical from teaching during which this book was written. Aside from providing funds, the executive staff at these institutions simply could not have been more supportive of my work. I especially want to thank Michael Gilligan and Lynn Szwaja at the Luce Foundation and Daniel Aleshire, William Myers, and Fran Pacienza at the Association of Theological Schools. I am grateful also to the other members of my Luce Fellows cohort, who, while coming from different academic disciplines and engaged in projects that were entirely different from my own, all proved to be extremely solicitous interlocutors. They are Bruce Hindmarsh, Kevin Madigan, Otto Maduro, Gene Outka, Gabriel Said Reynolds, and Elisabeth Schüssler Fiorenza.

A fourth institution deserving of my appreciation is, of course, Oxford University Press. I have learned much from the books this press has produced in the past, and now I have learned about the countless ways its staff members make these books better by dint of their professionalism. I am especially thankful to my editor, Theo Calderara, with whom working, even when doing difficult things, has been only a pleasure.

For someone who takes a certain measure of pride in competently serving students, I am truly humbled by the amount and quality of help I have received from my students during every stage of this project. My research assistants did not always have extensive experience and training in some of the tasks I assigned them. Nonetheless, they all dived into this work with enthusiasm and verve that, in their contagiousness, kept me going on more occasions than I could ever recount. I am thankful to research assistants Maureen Day, Katie Hennessey, Damon Mayrl, Chris Morrissey, Brad Nabors, and Aaron Welch. I am also indebted to the people (most of whom either are or were students) who so ably transcribed and often translated the many tape-recorded interviews for this project. They are Wendy Arce, Sara Bauermeister, Dana Bell, Sharon Fennema, Claire Foley, Corinna Guerrero, Craig Harris, Jennifer Hughes, Kristen Hurley, Kyle Lierk, Quang Luu, Carrie Rehak, Lu Tunmore, and Elaine Yastishock.

In addition, I am fortunate to have a number of colleagues who are without doubt greatly responsible for making this book better than it would have been without their thoughtful criticisms and recommendations. For taking the time to read some or all of the manuscript and presenting me with much-needed feedback, I am grateful to Gary Adler, John Coleman, Stephen Ellingson, Dean Hoge, William McKinney, Wade Clark Roof, Hal Sanks, Barry Stenger, Patricia Wittberg, Richard Wood, and David Yamane.

Finally, I would like to express my very deepest appreciation to two more people. The first is my wife, Sheri Hostetler, who cared for me during this project in more ways than I could have ever thought to ask. As if that were not enough, she also read and commented on each chapter as it was written, helped me hash out my ideas, and listened patiently as I talked (or complained) about the ins and outs of the writing process. The other person, our son, Patrick, did little by way of commenting on chapters, hashing out ideas, or listening to a writer's tribulations. Instead, he simply assisted his mother in continually reminding me that, despite occasional temptations to think otherwise, the world is indeed beautiful, each breath is precious, and with every ending and in every moment there also lurks a new beginning.

PART I

Getting Situated:
The View from Afar

1

Context

Past Changes and the Present Conversation

Ending and Beginning

"The thing about American Catholicism is that it both exists and doesn't exist!" Bill McNamara blurts out these words but then seems surprised by them, as if he had happened unexpectedly upon someone from his past. He tarries a bit, reflecting. "What do I mean by that?" he asks, now seemingly reacquainted and rightly confident that he has anticipated my next question. "I mean it exists in the sense that it's an *it*, something you and I can talk about, and we can identify elements of it and so forth. But it doesn't exist as some monolithic, unchanging thing. It's not as if any one person understands it and lives it out the same way all the time or in quite the same way as anyone else."

Even though Bill was among the very first people I interviewed for this book, I permitted myself an early conclusion: He knows what he is talking about. After many cups of tea and through constant interruptions by Rusty, his seal-point Siamese—whose name, like those of all of the respondents in this book, is a pseudonym—Bill's account of his life and faith demolished the idea that American Catholicism could be "some monolithic, unchanging thing."

Born into a working-class family in the early 1930s, Bill grew up in an almost entirely Irish section of Philadelphia. His upbringing was typical of the "urban villagers" about whom sociologist Herbert Gans once wrote so compellingly.[1] The ethnically defined neighborhood, the modest economic means, the large family that included Bill and five younger siblings, the clearly prescribed gender roles to which his contractor father and stay-at-home mother purportedly strictly conformed, the traditional—and, in this case, traditionally Catholic—mores: Bill can recall it all in vivid, if not wistful, detail. The particulars of his religious upbringing are especially memorable to him. He attended nearby parochial schools until he was swayed by an unexpectedly generous financial aid package to enroll in a large public university, where he majored in accounting. He went to church each week without fail, and, unless serving as an altar boy for an unpopular (read: inordinately early) Mass, he was typically accompanied by his entire immediate family. This instilled in him an enduring love for the beauty of the Mass and especially its music, which he still compares favorably to the "cacophonous crap" one hears at other, mercifully unnamed parishes. One of the younger parish priests served as a "friend and kind of mentor" for Bill who could talk to him about nearly anything, including at one point his own—admittedly short-lived—thoughts of entering the seminary. And, of course, there are the stories that seem to be standard fare among Catholics of Bill's generation. From the accounts of his mentor's many kindnesses to the somewhat overwrought "ruler-wielding nun" tales, from now-humorous accounts of first confession trepidation ("Hell, it was scary in that little booth!") to feelings of intense piety while accompanying Jesus along the Stations of the Cross each Friday afternoon during Lent, Bill's world was Catholic through and through.

However, once he entered his twenties, that world came to an end. "I never had any animosity like a lot of gay Catholics who had bad experiences in school or things like that," he confides. "I wasn't *against* it, but I didn't feel that comfortable with it anymore." Always attracted to men, Bill first became sexually active at the age of twenty-six. Then, rather than concealing from others what he considers his "honest, true self," he moved to San Francisco, where he got a well-paying job with an insurance company and eventually began his new life as an openly gay man. He closed the door on his Catholicism slowly at first, then finally slammed it shut. This age-old tradition seemed incongruous with his new city and job, new friends, and, after ten years or so, a relationship and then a newfound level of intimacy with Daniel, his partner for eighteen years. Daniel attended weekly Mass at Most Holy Redeemer church in the city's burgeoning gay enclave, the Castro District. But he went a bit less often when he and Bill bought a house together across the bay in the Oakland Hills. Bill, on the other hand, preferred to sleep late most Sundays.

Everything changed when Daniel contracted AIDS, and Bill became his primary care provider. This tragedy brought Bill agonizing stress and heartache, but it also introduced him to a face of Catholicism that he had not previously known. The AIDS Support Group at Most Holy Redeemer sent volunteers to help tend to Daniel's health and personal needs, which, toward the end of his life, required daily visits. Even in his grief, Bill was impressed by these people's witness to their—and once his—faith. This was not the intolerably dogmatic "Churchianity" that had come to seem ossified and irrelevant to him. Nor, of course, was this the vicious "God hates fags" message he had heard while doing some church shopping before moving from Philadelphia. He found this open-hearted and open-minded incarnation of the faith to be very alluring. So much so, in fact, that Bill began attending Mass at Most Holy Redeemer not long after Daniel's death and soon became an active member of first the AIDS Support Group and then the parish itself.

Bill's story might appear to fit the familiar "lapsed Catholic returns to Mother Church" mold, but Bill has not returned to anything; he has begun something new. On the one hand, he is quite the unabashed Catholic: "I love the traditions, and I love the mystery; I think it's a very, very, very rich religion." On the other hand, though, he is adamant about his freedom, even obligation, to mine those riches on his own terms and in accordance with his own needs. He has chosen to be a member of Most Holy Redeemer across the San Francisco Bay rather than of his own neighborhood parish, which he considers less "open and affirming" to gay Catholics. He respects priests enormously (although he is less generous in his assessment of bishops), but he is also a strong advocate for the laity's role in both pastoral ministry and parish governance. He is a "greeter" at the main (10 AM) Mass on Sundays and has sponsored several Rite of Christian Initiation for Adults (RCIA) candidates. At the same time, he bristles at the thought of being presumptuous enough to even talk to others about faith in a way that might be perceived as inappropriately pushy. He calls himself a "very strong Catholic" but, without hint of apology, eagerly embraces the pejoratively intended moniker "cafeteria Catholic" as a testament to his own religious agency and capacity for discernment. In short, Bill has begun something new as a Catholic in response to developments in his personal life and because he has lived through a period in which the American church itself has witnessed important social and cultural changes. As a result, it has also begun something quite innovative.

A New American Catholicism for a New Century

The Catholic Ghetto: In but not Necessarily of American Society

Any assessment of American Catholicism at the outset of the twenty-first century requires at least a broad sense of its overall trajectory throughout the twentieth. It began with the theological tumult caused by the 1899 encyclical *Testem benevolentiae (A Testament of Esteem)*, which Pope Leo XIII addressed to Cardinal James Gibbons. This papal letter condemned various "new opinions" that constituted what has been dubbed the "Americanist heresy" or simply "Americanism." "The underlying principle of these new opinions," Leo summarized, "is that, in order to more easily attract those who differ from her, the church should shape her teachings more in accord with the spirit of the age and relax some of her ancient severity and make some concessions to new opinions."[2] No one articulated these opinions more fervently than the American Catholic convert and founder of the Paulist fathers,

Isaac Thomas Hecker, whom the pope specifically mentioned in his letter. Growing in popularity with religious liberals throughout both the United States and in France, especially after the translation of his biography,[3] Hecker lauded his nation's experience of democracy and religious liberty, the genesis of which he attributed to the workings of the Holy Spirit.

To the Vatican, this seemed more than simply a harmless celebration of "certain endowments of mind which belong to the American people."[4] It posed an ecclesiological challenge. Hecker's contention that the laity's honing of democratic habits would better enable them to develop "active" Christian virtues, grow spiritually, and appreciate religious diversity appeared to undermine the church's own doctrinal authority and its preeminent role in the economy of salvation. This was considered anathema despite the fact that the religious liberty codified in the First Amendment to the Constitution actually helped facilitate the American church's remarkable growth. In 1789, the inaugural year of both the Constitution and the first Catholic diocese in the United States (Baltimore), Catholics numbered a scant thirty-five thousand of an overall population of four million.[5] Partly abetted by the religious liberty enjoyed by waves of Catholic immigrants, by the time *Testem benevolentiae* was written, Catholics were the nation's single largest denomination (12 million) and represented nearly one-sixth of its total population.[6] This hardly mattered to the pope, however. The Vatican continued to insist on religious monopoly as expressed in Leo XIII's earlier encyclical (*Immortale Dei*, 1885), which deemed the unification of church and state—and thus legal restrictions on religious liberty—the church's preferred political arrangement.

Because members of the American hierarchy were not known for doctrinal dissent or for their inclination to challenge Rome and because *Testem benevolentiae* itself did not single out specific prelates for censure, Americanism has come to be viewed as a "phantom" heresy.[7] Yet, for reasons having to do with the novelty and perceived grandeur of the American experiment, as well as efforts to gain acceptance within a largely Protestant country, some church leaders embraced the national culture a bit too uncritically by Vatican standards. Representative of this tendency was Archbishop John Ireland, who, at the Third Plenary Council of Baltimore in 1884, intoned the following: "There is no conflict between the Catholic Church and America. I could not utter one syllable that would belie, however remotely, either the Church or the Republic, and when I assert, as I now solemnly do, that the principles of the Church are in thorough harmony with the interests of the Republic, I know in the depths of my soul that I speak the truth."[8]

In stark contrast to such nationalist sentiment, the Vatican understood its religious dominion as distinctly transnational. Moreover, especially in the wake of the teaching on papal infallibility promulgated at the First Vatican Council (1870), it was confident that it—not the laity, not democratic culture, and not any given bishop—spoke the truth. "One in unity of doctrine as in the unity of government, such is the Catholic Church," insisted Leo XIII in closing his encyclical, "and since God has established its center and foundation in the Chair of St. Peter, one which is rightly called Rome, 'for where Peter is, there is the Church.'"[9] This settled the matter. The church would remain closed to the democratic trends that increasingly defined the modern age. Intellectual trends, incidentally, fared no better. A few years later and in the same spirit of resistance to modernity, Leo XIII's successor, Pope Pius X, issued an encyclical repudiating modern scholarly methods, especially the historical-critical study of the Bible.[10]

With these two pronouncements and the generally orthodox tenor of the American hierarchy, the ensuing decades were a rare period when the triumphalist and typically exaggerative expression *Roma locuta est; causa finita est* [Rome has spoken; the case is closed] actually rang true. "As if repentant for the theological deviations denounced in the encyclical," writes sociologist Michael Cuneo of *Testem benevolentiae*'s aftermath, "the American church retreated in the years following its release into a cultural ghetto, effectively shutting itself off from the ideological enticements of the broader society."[11]

No worldview was more impervious to such enticements than neoscholasticism, the revival of the medieval philosophy of Thomas Aquinas, which, during the first half of the twentieth century, became the officially sanctioned Catholic system of thought.[12] It posited a divinely established moral order that was accessible to human reason through natural law, and, above all, it defied the relativism and subjectivism purportedly rampant within contemporary society. Self-confident in its perception of an underlying design amid the chaotic fray of modern life, neoscholasticism functioned as a kind of countercultural epistemology wielded by intellectual luminaries such as French philosopher Jacques Maritain and English historian Christopher Dawson, as well as by notable Catholic activists intent on establishing a rationally ordered and more just society. And it shaped the religious sensibilities of rank-and-file Catholics themselves. With religious truth attainable through the use of right reason, as the church taught, rote memorization became the necessary and, in the eyes of most, near-sufficient means of attaining salvation. "Q. Who made the world?" reads the first lesson of the famed *Baltimore Catechism* (1891); "A. God made the world." Further, as generations of Catholics can still recite from their schooldays, it continued: "Q. Who is God? A. God is the Creator of Heaven and earth and of all things. Q. What is man? A. Man is a creature composed of body and soul and made in the image and likeness of God." When mastered, the battery of one hundred questions and swaggeringly unambiguous answers—a whopping 515 in the final 1949 edition—had a gratifying completeness about them.

This type of catechesis helped in settling Catholics into a distinctive mental landscape uninhabited by their fellow citizens. That this remained true well into the twentieth century (in at least some locations) is reflected in Gerhard Lenski's classic study of religious attitudes in 1950s' Detroit.[13] Lenski discovered that not only did nearly three-quarters of all Catholics attend weekly Mass, but, compared to Protestants, they also exhibited far more "doctrinal orthodoxy." Lenski asked whether they believed that (1) God exists; (2) God "is like a Heavenly Father who watches over you"; (3) God answers prayers; (4) there is life after death; (5) "in the next life some people will be punished and others rewarded"; (6) God expects people to attend church every week; and (7) Jesus was the Son of God sent into the world to save people from sin. A full 62 percent of all Catholic respondents agreed with each and every one of these items, whereas only 38 percent of black Protestants and 32 percent of white Protestants did.[14] These theological beliefs translated into traditionalist moral convictions as well. About three in five Catholics considered birth control, divorce, and conducting business on Sundays to be "always or usually wrong," which was substantially higher than for either group of Protestants.[15]

Helpful for understanding this high-water mark of doctrinal orthodoxy is the oft-quoted dictum attributed to the fifth-century theologian and papal secretary Prosper of Aquitaine: *lex orandi lex credendi* [the law of praying founds the law of believing].[16] People's doctrinal beliefs, in other words, are less a function of their acceptance of theological propositions than a reflection of what they claim to know about the sacred through their everyday piety and personal experience. Another way of putting this is to say that the regnant Catholic worldview expressed via the categories of neoscholasticism seemed plausible and emotionally appealing to the faithful because Catholics shared a distinctive religious ethos.[17] Predominant until the years following the Second World War, this ethos or collective sensibility is best captured in historian Jay Dolan's depiction of a "devotional Catholicism" characterized by four central traits.[18]

The first is an emphasis on ecclesial authority. With its loss of the Papal States to the Italian government (1859) and with them any claims to temporal authority, the Vatican began to focus more intently upon wielding spiritual and moral power.[19] The First Vatican Council's declaration of papal infallibility, the promulgation of a revised Code of Canon Law (1917), an emphasis on the submissiveness of Jesus, the Suffering Savior, and incessant reminders to the laity of the countless church regulations concerning everything from holy "days of obligation" to the latest papal pronouncement—these were all instantiations of clerical control. Indeed, the very distinction between a putatively sacred clergy and worldly laity, as well as numerous theological legitimations of the church's hierarchical authority structure, meant that the duty of most Catholics was basically, to use a hackneyed though not entirely inaccurate phrase, to "pray, pay, and obey."

Well-known references to "Catholic guilt" are a vestige of a second devotionalist trait, a widespread preoccupation with sin. Catholic moral theology was undoubtedly, for lack of a better word, guilty of this preoccupation. "The miasma of sin which emanates from the penitential literature and from the vast majority of manuals of moral theology," notes one expert on the subject, "is not only distasteful, but profoundly disquieting."[20] It was, if not distasteful, equally disquieting for the people in the pews, as is evidenced by the fact that they flocked to church confessionals in unprecedented numbers. And, if regular reception of the Sacrament of Penance did not exacerbate feelings of personal sinfulness, there were other reminders. Prayer books and devotional guides stressed moral purity and the need to resist society's unremitting barrage of temptations. Devotions to the Sacred Heart of Jesus emphasized the need for repentance, while those directed toward Mary told people that, as immaculate, she alone was free from sin's stain. Parish missions, with their de rigueur sermons on hell, chastised Catholics for being caught up in sin, while the Communion of Saints, as moral exemplars, ceaselessly prodded them to overcome its grip.

Just as their role in the expiation of sin shored up the clergy's authority, the same is true of Catholics' emphasis on ritual, the third trait of their devotionalism. Without priests to administer them, there simply were no sacraments and thus no sense of religious identity among Catholics for whom baptism, first communion, confirmation, and marriage were generally considered the most important points along the arc of their earthly lives. Furthermore, rituals were equally important for sacralizing time. The year was marked by the anticipation of Advent, the fasting of Lent, and feast days such as those commemorating Saint Patrick for the Irish, Saint Boniface for Germans, Saint Stanislaus for Poles, and Our Lady of Guadalupe for Mexicans. Even each week was marked by meatless Fridays and, of course, the sacrifice of the Mass, whose solemnity and mysteriousness were enhanced by liturgical accoutrements such as candles, incense, bells, elaborate robes, ornate statuary and architecture, and the holy—and, for most, wholly unintelligible—language, Latin.

Widespread belief in the Real Presence of Jesus in the Mass is indicative of the final devotionalist trait, which Dolan labels an "openness to the miraculous." In addition to the Eucharist and other sacraments, most Catholics believed that sacramentals also provided them with an everyday access to God's grace. These ranged from making the sign of the cross with holy water to praying the Rosary and from saying grace before meals to having the parish priest bless a new house. It was not uncommon for Catholics to discern supernatural power within relics, scapulars, and other holy objects. Shrines such as Our Lady of Lourdes in France, Our Lady of Fatima in Portugal, and Our Lady of Mount Carmel in Italian Harlem saw waves of pilgrims seeking messages for loved ones, inspiration for the soul, and wondrous cures for the body. Rare, too, were the Catholics who did not know they could turn to Saint Christopher for safe journey, Saint Anthony for a lost object, or, if especially unfortunate, Saint Jude for whatever hopeless cause they happened to face.[21]

Not simply doctrinally orthodox, as Lenski discovered, the Catholic world during the first part of the past century was also distinctive in being a uniquely hierarchical, sin-conscious, ritualized, and enchanted one as well.

The endurance of this Catholic subculture is attributable partly to its separateness from the wider American society. Renowned convert and activist Dorothy Day sums this up in her 1952 autobiography, noting that "Catholics were a nation apart, a people within a people, making little impression on the tremendous non-Catholic population of the country."[22] A number of factors account for this social marginalization. One was Catholics' relatively low social and economic standing. Of the more than sixteen thousand prominent citizens who listed their religious affiliations in the 1930–1931 volume of *Who's Who in America*, only 740 (4.5 percent of the total) were Catholic.[23] By midcentury things had changed very little. Surveys indicated that a full two-thirds of all Catholics were "lower class," and slightly more than two in five of them had graduated from high school.[24]

Another reason was that many Catholics were new to the country. In 1930, for example, nearly two-thirds of Chicago's Catholics were first- and second-generation immigrants, more than half of whom belonged to the "national parishes" founded by and composed of various ethnic groups.[25] With their perceived cultural distance from the WASP-dominated mainstream came geographic distance as well. In the years immediately preceding the Second World War, half of all American Catholics claimed to reside in neighborhoods where Catholics constituted the majority of all inhabitants.[26] Finally, both the marginalization of Catholics and the in-group solidarity among them were fueled by out-group hostility. Catholics faced vitriol from the Ku Klux Klan, discrimination within public institutions, attempts at slowing their growth through xenophobic immigration legislation, and a latent popular antipathy that—as the outpouring of anti-Catholic rhetoric during the unsuccessful 1928 presidential bid by Irish Catholic Al Smith demonstrated—could surface at any time.[27]

Such animosity, along with Catholics' prevailing sense that American culture was enmeshed in cultural relativism and the commercial glorification of sin, convinced them to turn inward. They created what historian Charles Morris calls a "separate universe" marked by an "aggressive self-ghettoizing" that was facilitated by the creation of an entire constellation of Catholic institutions.[28] Notably, by 1950, in excess of fifteen thousand parishes had been established in the United States. More than half of these (8,128) built elementary schools, which, in addition to the 1,581 parish or diocesan high schools and the 1,318 privately established schools, meant that more than 3.5 million children were receiving Catholic educations in any given year. At the same time, nearly a quarter-million students (mostly Catholic) were enrolled in the nation's 234 Catholic colleges and universities. Also included in this Catholic universe were 867 hospitals, 353 orphanages, and 261 homes for elderly people.[29]

Other lesser-known "parallel" organizations proliferated wildly as well. Catholics could read separate newspapers, join the Catholic Book Club, listen to the weekly "Catholic Hour" on the radio, and subscribe to the general-interest periodical *Catholic Digest*. They could enroll their children in parochial schools, encourage them to join the Catholic Boy Scouts or Catholic Girl Scouts, and send them to summer camps run by the Catholic Youth Organization (CYO). If they were professionals, they could become members of a Catholic bar association, the Catholic Press Association, the Catholic Physicians' Guild, the National Council of Catholic Nurses, or the Association of Catholic Trade Unionists. If artists or academics, perhaps the Catholic Writers' Guild of America, the Catholic Poetry Society of America, the Catholic Economic Association, or even the American Catholic Sociological Society would make for a good fit.[30]

The point is that, until midcentury or so, Catholics went about their everyday lives within a kind of cultural fortress that defended them from the encroachments of an at times hostile society. "We grew up different," recalls writer Garry Wills of his 1950s' boyhood. In the opening pages of his book on American Catholic culture, he states that, in retrospect, the difference was visceral and enduring:

> We "born Catholics," even when we leave or lose our own church, rarely feel at home in any other. The habits of childhood are tenacious, and Catholicism was first experienced by us as a vast set of intermeshed childhood habits—prayers offered, heads ducked in unison, crossings, chants, nuns in the classroom alternately too sweet and too severe, priests garbed black on the street and brilliant at the altar; churches lit and darkened, clothed and stripped to the rhythm of liturgical recurrences; the crib in winter, purple Februaries, and lilies in the spring; confession as intimidation and comfort (comfort, if nothing else, that the intimidation was survived), communion as revery and discomfort; faith as a creed, and the creed as catechism, Latin responses, salvation by rote, all things going to a rhythm, memorized, old things always returning, eternal in that sense, no matter how transitory.[31]

Growing up at about the same time, historian Doris Kearns Goodwin also remembers the feeling of being different—different rituals and aesthetic, different religious heroes and idioms, different education, recitations, stories, and fears. But, for her, it was the sense of separateness, of being set apart from other New Yorkers, that was paramount:

> So rich were the traditions and the liturgy of my church that I could not imagine being anything other than Catholic. Though there were Jews and Protestants on our block—the Lubars and the Barthas were Jewish, the

Friedles and the Greenes Protestant—I knew almost nothing about these other religions. . . . Although I observed the fellowship that other religions provided, I had no inkling of what beliefs they inculcated in their followers. We were taught only that these people were non-Catholics and that we should not read their literature or inquire about their beliefs. Furthermore, it was, we thought, a grievous sin for us to set foot in one of their churches or synagogues.[32]

As with other writers who reminisce about this period, Wills and Goodwin can be forgiven for intermittent lapses into nostalgia. This, in many ways, was a heyday for the nation's then 40 million Catholics. By the close of the 1950s their number was double what it had been only two decades earlier, and across the country four to five new churches opened each week.[33] Seminaries and convents were forced to expand as the numbers of vowed religious swelled to all-time highs. And, even for people like Bill McNamara, who eventually experienced it as unduly confining, this cultural fortress provided Catholics with a strong sense of security and identity.

Discerning the Signs of the Times at Midcentury

This sense was also quite fleeting. Among observers astute enough to notice cracks in its subcultural ramparts and walls is Alan Ehrenhalt, whose study of 1950s' Chicago is an evocative reminder that this was also a transitional time for the American church. Saint Nicholas of Tolentine parish, he recounts, was truly a "world unto itself," replete with its own devotional societies, voluntary associations, ever-present clergy, and a parochial school that educated generations of parishioners from their respective Irish, Polish, German, Italian, and Lithuanian enclaves. Despite feelings of difference and separateness engendered from within it, this world was actually very much in flux. The 1950s, Ehrenhalt cautions, "were not a period of stasis but of rapid and bewildering change," which was ultimately reflected in parishes like Saint Nicholas.[34] A consequence of the immigration restriction laws was that, absent successive waves of new arrivals, the American church began to lose its immigrant character, thereby accelerating the cultural assimilation of its membership.[35] An overwhelmingly urban church, it was profoundly affected by postwar suburbanization, which facilitated the social integration of Catholics, many of whom found themselves living in religiously plural neighborhoods for the first time.[36] Finally, Catholics' "unalloyed" support for the war effort meant that they composed a significant portion of the nation's armed forces and were thus able to take full advantage of the G. I. Bill, which, by the early 1960s, enabled them to catch up to Protestants in terms of educational attainment, occupational status, and household income.[37]

These assimilationist trends also created new rifts among Catholics. "Unknown to most of these parishioners," Ehrenhalt reveals in his discussion of Saint Nicholas's, "they were practicing a brand of Catholicism that was being called into question during those years by the rising generation of better-educated and more sophisticated clergy and laymen."[38] As Ehrenhalt suggests, Catholic and other intellectuals began to look askance at this religious subculture and deride it for being out of step with the times.[39] What is more, this growing fissure between the Catholic faithful and its intellectual elite was not the only one. As early as the 1950s sociologists began detecting divisions among the laity, as well as increasingly obvious discrepancies between their manner of being Catholic and church leaders' expectations.

Witness, for example, sociologist Joseph Fichter's groundbreaking study of Catholics in early 1950s New Orleans. While noting some people's conformity to traditional norms, "the interesting fact of American urban life," his research revealed, "is that there is also a conformity to change, and this social change seems to be proceeding in the direction away from religious patterns toward secular patterns of behavior."[40] Reasons he gives for this vary from Catholics' increased consumption of the mass media to their "extraparochial activities" with people (often non-Catholics) on the basis of shared interests. As a result, their connections to the church showed signs of weakening. Fichter found that only 7 percent of the Catholics in his study were of the "nuclear" type, fulfilling virtually all of the normative requirements and practices of the church, and that 41 percent were of the "modal" type, who fulfilled most of these. Most surprising to him was that 13 percent were "marginal" Catholics who were "partially accepting of the values of the religious institution" and that a full 39 percent were "dormant" Catholics who were no longer practicing their faith.[41] Like Bill McNamara's recollections, Wills's and Goodwin's memoirs indicate that this was a time when the ties that bound Catholics together tended to be a good deal tighter than at present. Fichter, though, reminds us that the halcyon notion that this was a time of lock-step uniformity of belief and commitment is, in fact, more imagined than real.

Another writer who detected some shaking—if not outright crumbling—of Catholicism's cultural fortress was Will Herberg, whose insightful *Protestant, Catholic, Jew* was likely the most widely read sociological study of American religion in the 1950s. Contrary to Fichter, he identified the situation of American Catholicism not as one in which its distinctive values were only partially accepted by the rank and file. In reality, he contended, its values were scarcely distinguishable from those institutionalized throughout American society as a whole. Softening its prior sectarianism, the watchwords for the American church could no longer be *extra ecclesium nulla salus* [outside the church, no salvation]. Rather, Herberg noted, the broad-based and growing tendency to construe the faith in more culturally affirming terms meant the average Catholic "could not help but regard American society as intrinsically pluralistic, and his own church as one among several."[42] No longer comparable to a fortress, Herberg instead depicted American Catholicism, as well as the other two mainstream faiths, as part of a "triple melting pot" of cultural assimilation. Like them, Catholicism inculcated countercultural values far less than it functioned "to provide the sanctification and dynamic for goals and values otherwise established."[43] Nor did it focus on authority and sin nearly as much as it secured for the faithful a self-assured "peace of mind," the comfort of "a spiritual anodyne designed to allay the pains and vexations of existence."[44] As fully assimilated and in full embrace of the dominant culture, "American Catholicism has successfully negotiated the transition from a foreign church to an American religious community," Herberg concluded—and then famously added, "it is now part of the American Way of Life."[45]

Had Herberg looked at 1950s' America more closely, he would have noticed that the so-called American way of life was actually more culturally disparate and politically contested than he portrayed it. Moreover, had he been able to look into the future, he would have realized that, in light of the 1960s' cultural revolution and its aftermath, this was also a precarious and ultimately short-lived social formation. Yet, looking more deeply than most, he rightly highlighted the ways each of these three religious traditions had adapted to a religiously pluralistic context. Like Ehrenhalt and Fichter, he was able to see that, instead of the decade of conformism and stasis these years are typically claimed to have been, the 1950s actually constituted an important transitional period for the American church. Even for those who could not perceive this at the time, John Kennedy's election to the presidency in 1960 left little doubt that Catholics had indeed come of age and taken their place within the American mainstream.

The Ideological Impact of Vatican II

If this youthful and urbane Catholic president demonstrated to Catholics (and other Americans) that they no longer huddled behind the walls of a cultural fortress, the Second Vatican Council (1962–1965) told them this in explicitly theological language. Convened by seventy-seven-year-old and thus unlikely ecclesial reformer Pope John XXIII, Vatican II was intended to be, as he put it, an *aggiornamento,* an "updating" of the church. It was to be akin to opening the church's windows in order to allow the fresh air of contemporary thinking to breeze through its premodern edifice. This was precisely what happened. Truly an ecumenical council, it was attended by more than twenty-six hundred bishops and four hundred expert advisors from around the world, and news of its ongoing deliberations was broadcast to Catholics everywhere. What they discovered from hearing these reports, reading or simply learning about the sixteen documents the bishops produced, as well as from the eventual implementation of changes those deliberations and documents proposed, was a new way of understanding their religion within a modern context. The council provided Catholics with a new set of theological categories, a valuable set of new idioms for better connecting their centuries-old faith with their fast-changing lives and mounting awareness of just how quickly the world itself was changing.[46]

The central theological category the council reexamined was the church itself. The council came to envision the church not institutionally as a clergy-run, hierarchical bureaucracy but far more communally, equating it with the entire "people of God." Although the council never denied the importance of an ordained leadership, this shift in emphasis carried with it a number of implications for the church's self-understanding. For one, it became clear that a monarchical model of ecclesial governance, whereby the pope ruled the church and local bishops functioned as his vicars, was no longer tenable. The council instead endorsed a more decentralized, collegial model that took the integrity of local churches far more seriously than in times past. "In and from such individual churches there comes into being the one and only Catholic Church," reads the "Dogmatic Constitution on the Church" (*Lumen gentium*), which continues: "For this reason each individual bishop represents his own church, but all of them together in union with the pope represent the entire church joined in the bond of peace, love, and unity."[47]

Another implication of this communal model of the church is the greater respect it has accorded cultural diversity. More appreciative of its global character, the "Pastoral Constitution on the Church in the Modern World" (*Gaudium et spes*) insists that the church "is not bound exclusively and indissolubly to any race or nation, nor to any particular way of life or any customary pattern of living, ancient or recent."[48] In fact, assert the bishops, if the church is not to be allied with any one culture, then it is most faithful to its universal calling when open to the wisdom embedded within all cultures. "Faithful to her own tradition and at the same time conscious of her universal mission," they write, "she can enter into communion with various cultural modes, to her own enrichment and theirs too."[49]

Finally, especially since decentralization and an endorsement of cultural diversity have historically not been the church's strong suits, the bishops depicted it in distinctly fluid terms, always struggling to better approximate its own ideals. Basically unseating sixteenth-century theologian Robert Bellarmine's notion of the church as an immutably flawless, "perfect society," they much preferred the more changeable, historically conscious notion of a ceaselessly journeying "pilgrim church." This notion, a retrieval of the age-old principle of *ecclesia semper reformanda* [the church is always in the need of reform], reflects a self-critical awareness that the church often falls short of its own goals.[50] "In the present age, too," the bishops candidly admit in *Gaudium et spes*, "it does not escape the church how great a distance lies between the message she offers and the human failings of those to whom the gospel is entrusted."[51]

Recognizing the church's various imperfections, of course, also legitimated the very sort of reform-minded self-examination Vatican II set out to accomplish. Indeed, along with reassessing the overall meaning of the church, the council continued in this "updating" vein by looking outside it. One of the council's more thorough-going changes had to do with how it instructed Catholics to view the wider world. Abandoning its longstanding defensive stance toward a purportedly sin-ridden world from which the faithful needed to be protected, conciliar documents are marked by a then unprecedented openness with respect to how the church ought best to know about, relate to, and act within the surrounding world.

First, it *knows about* the world, the bishops maintain, when Catholics take up their "duty of scrutinizing the signs of the times and of interpreting them in the light of the gospel."[52] They do this when they respect and seek to learn from different cultures. They also do this when they integrate developments in the human and social sciences with what they have come to know through faith. While never denouncing neoscholasticism, by highlighting cultural diversity and giving a nod to secular academic disciplines, the bishops nevertheless divested it of its erstwhile monopoly status in uncovering and articulating religious wisdom. The church, the council insisted, both teaches and, importantly, learns about the world from the world.

Second, by addressing themselves to "not only the sons of the Church and to all who invoke the name of Christ, but to the whole of humanity" the bishops signaled their intent for the church to *relate to* the world in a more conciliatory fashion.[53] Nothing demonstrates this better than the council's discussions of other religions. It would be difficult to imagine a more dramatic change in attitude than the one that occurred between Pope Pius IX's "Syllabus of Errors" (1864), which declared that "error has no rights," and Vatican II's "Declaration on Religious Freedom," which claimed that religious freedom was an inviolable right founded upon the dignity of the human person. The council's "Decree on Ecumenism" reflects this attitudinal change by describing the ecumenical movement as seeking the restoration of Christian unity rather than facilitating the return of non-Catholics to the one, true faith. It also appears in the "Declaration on the Relationship of the Church to Non-Christian Religions." In it the bishops maintain that "the Catholic Church rejects nothing which is true and holy in these religions" and continue: "She looks with sincere respect upon those ways of conduct and of life, those rules and teachings which, though differing in many particulars from what she holds and sets forth, nevertheless often reflect a ray of that Truth which enlightens all men."[54] Equally respectful is their discussion of atheism. Instead of condemnation, *Gaudium et spes* offers an invitation for "atheists to examine the gospel of Christ with an open mind."[55]

Third, with respect to how it *acts within* the world, the council redirected the church from its seeming preoccupation with wariness, judgment, and withdrawal to a sense of worldly mission characterized by amity, witness, and, most of all, service. "Inspired by no earthly ambition," the bishops write, "the church seeks but a solitary goal: to carry forward the work of Christ Himself under the lead of the befriending Spirit. And Christ entered this world to give witness to the truth, to rescue and not to sit in judgment, to serve and not to be served."[56]

The council complemented its looking outward with a critical gaze directed inward. This resulted in thoughtful and often innovative documents on priestly training and ministry, the episcopacy, vowed religious life, church communications, missionary activity, and Christian education. But perhaps the most important development to emerge from Vatican II was a revaluation of the laity. Not merely members of the church, the council's communal vision and ubiquitous use of the phrase "people of God" denote that laypeople *are* the church.

As such and as equal participants with ordained clergy in "the one priesthood of Christ," their action in the world is the church's action.[57] The council, in effect, did away with anachronistic, though tenacious, notions of the laity as the "worldly" and passive flock and replaced them with innumerable reminders that they, too, share a call to holiness and service within the context of their everyday lives. "Incorporated into Christ's Mystical Body through baptism and strengthened by the power of the Holy Spirit through confirmation," the bishops write of the laity, "they are assigned to the apostolate by the Lord himself."[58] The bishops warn against perpetuating the "false opposition between professional and social activities on the one part, and the religious life on the other." In fact, they continue, "the Christian who neglects his temporal duties neglects his duties toward his neighbor and even God, and jeopardizes his eternal salvation."[59]

This call to holiness and service within daily life also extends, the bishops emphasized, to the governance and sacramental life of the church itself. Consequently, the council promoted both lay parish leadership and the liturgical reforms that, when put into practice, were at first quite jarring to many Catholics. These included the restructuring and simplifying of various Catholic rites, encouraging the laity to participate in the church's communal worship, turning the altars around so that priests face the worshipping community, and conducting the Mass in the vernacular rather than in Latin. If the church is truly the "people of God," the bishops essentially reason, its sacraments need to be accessible and understandable to all in order to be the efficacious signs of divine grace they are considered to be.

By recasting the faithful's activity within both the world and the church in more vocational terms, the council also stressed the religious worth of personal experience and reflection. It upheld the authority of individual reasoning that had long been a key theme (though a largely neglected one) of Catholic theology.

Maintaining that "conscience is the most sacred core and sanctuary" of each individual, the bishops urged that it be exercised freely and afforded respect by others in order to reflect the person's inherent worth as a creature of God.[60] Fundamentally, this means that the magisterium's longstanding proclivity for a "because I told you so" style of religious instruction is not simply unrealistic but also contrary to church teaching on human dignity. This renewed appreciation of individual conscience, argues sociologist Michele Dillon, represents nothing less than a crucial "redrawing of interpretive authority" whereby the laity's communal discernment on matters pertaining to faith and morals has become as central to religious understanding as are pronouncements from the hierarchy.[61] "Vatican II accordingly legitimated the creation of a deliberative church," she writes, "wherein participants' interpretations of Catholicism would be compelled by communal, practical reason, rather than the power of magisterial office alone."[62]

Moreover, in a spirit diametrically different from the allergy to "new opinions" expressed in *Testem benevolentiae*, the bishops point out that God's revelation develops historically partly through the experience and ongoing reflection of ordinary believers: "This tradition which comes from the apostles develops in the Church with the help of the Holy Spirit. For there is a growth in the understanding of the realities and the world which have been handed down. This happens through the contemplation and the study made by believers, who treasure these things in their hearts, through the intimate understanding of spiritual things they experience, and through the preaching of those who have received through Episcopal succession the sure gift of truth."[63]

A more elevated assessment of the laity's role in the church would be difficult to imagine. Growth in understanding the Catholic tradition, the bishops suggest, occurs not only through the instruction of church leaders but also as a result of the contemplation, study, and personal experience of all of the faithful. Such statements certainly have not fallen on deaf ears. They have given American Catholics a sense (or simply reaffirmed their already emerging sense) of their own agency when it comes to thinking through and taking responsibility for their religious lives.

From Catholic Ghetto to Living along an Eight-Lane Superhighway

As critical as Vatican II's reforms were, they did not simply *cause* the transformation of American Catholicism that became so glaringly apparent in their aftermath. After all, the church's cultural fortress had been under assault by various assimilation trends well before the council was even convened. A better way to put it would be to say that the council provided American Catholics with an officially sanctioned language for comprehending and discussing the changes so many of them were already experiencing. These new theological categories, in effect, made religious change thinkable both for and as Catholics. They provided them with the tools to conceptualize their faith in light of their new sociocultural position within the American mainstream.

Bear in mind that these tools were not always sufficiently sharpened and that this conceptualization process has seldom been free of theological controversy.[64] Alongside various theological innovations, plenty of traditionalist concepts and doctrines were also retained within conciliar documents. Taking stock of this reality, theologian T. Howland Sanks rightly notes that the council's "juxtaposition of diverse ecclesiologies, its internal incoherence and ambiguity, resulted in a lack of clarity of vision, a lack of certainty, and a massive identity crisis."[65] This, too, is one of the council's important legacies since it is precisely this ambiguity that has goaded Catholics to think for themselves and rely on what Dillon calls their own "interpretive authority" as they live out their faith.

Vatican II also had a destabilizing effect for many people. The church had once seemed so intractable and firm amid the shifting sands of the contemporary. But, by changing in such a public way, the scales of immutability fell from many Catholics' eyes, and they came to see the church as a changeable institution. This effect was exacerbated in 1968, when Pope Paul VI ignored the advice of a commission he had established to study the moral implications of birth control and issued the encyclical *Humanae vitae (Of Human Life)*, which reiterates the church's prohibition of artificial contraception. Because this position was so contrary to that of the majority of the American faithful (as well as to many publicly dissenting theologians) and created such an uproar, it revealed to the laity the intrinsically contested nature of the church as an institution, and, consequently, it further validated their own ability to dissent.[66]

Vatican II, then, did not so much transform the American church as it opened it to a broader culture that was itself being transformed in certain monumental ways. Using an apt metaphor, sociologist Peter Berger states the matter effectively: "The Catholic church in America had successfully maintained a robust subculture whose inhabitants were kept relatively safe from the surrounding cognitive turbulence. Vatican II *intended,* in the words of John XIII, to 'open windows in the wall'; the unintended consequence of this so-called *aggiornamento* was to open an eight-lane superhighway through the center of the Catholic ghetto—*everything* came roaring in."[67]

What roared in during the 1960s were some fast-moving vehicles for religious change. For example, whatever the destabilizing effect of Vatican II might have been, it was certainly enhanced by the civil rights movement and the sexual revolution, which, by challenging deeply ingrained social structures and mores, altered the seemingly unalterable and gave Catholics a sense that change was, somewhat ironically, a constant of modern life. Discoveries of elected officials' duplicity in the midst of influential events such as the Vietnam War and Watergate helped breed a generalized distrust of public institutions that did not spare churches. A wildly expanding mass media helped create a youth culture and, for young and old, diminished the relative importance of the family and the church in the transmission of cultural values and beliefs. Americans' frequently noted individualism—"doing your own thing"—meant that generalized expectations of religious "preference" began to replace loyalty to the faith of one's birth as the new coin of the religious realm.

This list could certainly go on. Most important to note is that these and other important vehicles for religious change did not bypass the American church because Catholics had become so thoroughly assimilated by the early 1960s. The same, of course, is true today. Numbering nearly 70 million, Catholics now make up nearly one-quarter of the U.S. population, still the nation's largest denomination. With mainstream status has come a loss of distinctiveness. Now far from marginalized, Catholics are currently at or just above national averages with respect to educational attainment, occupational status, and family income.[68] Generally speaking, they live in the same neighborhoods as other Americans, not necessarily in Catholic ones. They read the same books and see the same movies, not just those given the hierarchy's imprimatur. They belong to the same associations and do not restrict themselves to various Catholic equivalents. Despite *Humanae vitae,* Catholics overwhelmingly disagree with their church's denunciation of birth control, as evidenced by the fact that their families are no longer significantly larger than those of other Americans. Their divorce rate is approaching that of the nation as a whole, and this is likely to increase since nearly two-thirds of them say one can be a good Catholic "without obeying the church hierarchy's teaching on divorce and remarriage."[69] Their rate of interfaith marriage is also rising rapidly.

And what has come of the four traits that, in Dolan's estimation, once defined Catholic devotionalism? The most obvious change in the first of these, authority, is that there seems to be less of it. In 1965, at the close of the Second Vatican Council, there were 58,132 priests in the United States, about one per eight hundred Catholics. By 2002 that number had dropped to 45,713, or one considerably older and more overworked priest for approximately every fourteen hundred Catholics. During that same period the number of sisters in religious orders fell from 179,954 to about 75,000.[70] This should not be surprising given that Vatican II's more egalitarian conception of church had the unintended consequence of reducing the benefits of entering the religious life (e.g., high status, power) while maintaining its relatively high costs (e.g., celibacy, relative poverty). This combination, once described as a "worst of both worlds" scenario, likely goes a long way toward accounting for the increased defections from religious life after Vatican II and for the lower rates of recruitment among American Catholics since then.[71] In conjunction with the smaller numbers of these "authorities," there also seems to be less awareness of what they are actually saying. Catholics have long been known for their comparative unfamiliarity with the Bible.[72] Their lack of knowledge concerning the church's teachings is a more recent development. That it seems to be worsening is evidenced by a recent study of young adult Catholics. Only about half of them have ever even heard of Vatican II, only one-fourth have heard about John Paul II's 1995 statement criticizing what he called a contemporary "culture of death," and fewer than one-sixth have ever heard of the U.S. bishops' much-publicized 1986 pastoral letter on economic justice.[73]

Even when they are aware of what is being said, American Catholics are seldom loath to talk back to official teachings. More than four in five of them agree that "being a Catholic is a very important part of who I am," whereas a little more than half believe "Catholicism contains a greater share of the truth than other religions do." Similarly, more than three-quarters say that both the sacraments and "spiritual and personal growth" are very important to them, whereas less than half of all Catholics say this about "the teaching authority claimed by the Vatican." What this indicates is that many continue to identify strongly as Catholics but that the locus of religious authority has for them shifted away from the institution and, consonant with the growing sense of their "interpretive authority," toward the individual. This is reflected in the majority of American Catholics, who agree that there should be more democratic decision making in church affairs. It also becomes evident when they agree that one can be a "good Catholic" without doing things such as obeying church teaching on abortion (58 percent), donating time or money to their parish (58 percent), and having their marriages approved by the church (67 percent).[74] Furthermore, it is reflected in the dissenting views of the nearly two-thirds of American Catholics who say that women should be allowed to be priests, three-quarters who favor married men as priests, and the approximately nine in ten who disagree with the church's prohibition of artificial contraception.[75] Importantly, this disagreement does not necessarily result in Catholics "voting with their feet" and leaving. Often most drawn to the church's sacramental tradition and community, many have become accustomed to "defecting in place" when it comes to whatever doctrines they disagree with.[76]

Also shifting is Catholics' overall conception of God and thus devotionalism's focus on sin. Gone, it seems, is the God of judgment, who, in keeping scrupulous tally of the faithful's venial and mortal sins, was ultimately punitive as well. Enter, for many present-day Catholics, a more personal God who understands rather than judges human frailties, who loves unconditionally rather than punishes unflinchingly, and who, in short, is "there for you." This general shift in images of God has come with such a remarkable de-emphasis on sin that, the data suggest, people may soon fail to "get" the long-told collection of jokes that end with punch-line allusions to "Catholic guilt." For instance, one study has found that, while two-thirds of American Catholics claim that God loves them "a great deal," only half report feeling guilty of sin within the past year, which is a significantly lower proportion than for Protestant respondents.[77] With this dimming sense of sin is a diminishing Sacrament of Penance. Only one in five Catholics goes to private confession at least "several times a year," and, even with the growing popularity of communal confessions, only 14 percent claim to have received the sacrament within the previous thirty days.[78]

These data are no doubt partly a function of American Catholics' overall waning attachment to a third hallmark of devotionalism, ritual. Probably the best available evidence for this is eroding church attendance. In the 1950s, about three-quarters of the faithful attended Mass each week. Now roughly one-third attend weekly, another third attend occasionally, and the final third never attend. Even though Catholicism is known as a liturgically orientated faith, this trend shows no signs of reversing. Three-quarters of the American faithful maintain that one can be a "good Catholic" without going to church each week.[79] That this change is more the result of Catholic assimilation than of broader cultural changes within American society is supported by the reality that Protestant weekly churchgoing fell less precipitously during this same time period, from approximately 44 percent to 26 percent. One way in which Catholic ritual resembles that of Protestants, however, is in the shedding of its most distinctive elements. The *Novus ordo* Mass instituted by Vatican II to replace the four-centuries-old Tridentine Latin Mass largely divested Catholic worship of its mysterious tenor—its "smells and bells," as some call it. Even the more quotidian ritual of eating fish on Fridays, done away with by the American bishops in the years after the council, no longer functions as a subtle way for Catholics to distinguish themselves from other people.

The solemnity of the Tridentine Mass and even meatless Fridays were also a part of the fourth trait of devotional Catholicism, its "openness to the miraculous." This trait is extremely difficult to measure since, if extant, it is likely to take different forms for different people and in different contexts. Nonetheless, ways of manifesting this openness that were popular during the first half of the past century are significantly less so today. Whereas two-thirds of American Catholics say they start and/or end each day with private prayer, only three in ten of them say devotions to Mary or to other saints, and only two in ten pray the Rosary.[80]

One study of particularly committed "core" Catholics has found that three-quarters of them never participate in novenas (nine consecutive evenings of prayer), more than half never attend Benediction of the Blessed Sacrament (a devotional service featuring Eucharistic adoration), and 44 percent never participate in the Stations of the Cross.[81] Such practices—along with angels and saints, praying for souls in purgatory, votive candles, religious medals and scapulars, pilgrimages and relics, and May crownings—which once reminded the faithful that their world was thoroughly and accessibly enchanted, are now (although not explicitly prohibited) seldom promoted by the church. This is partly because they seem to many to be hopelessly old-fashioned and reminiscent of the marginalized status that Catholics worked so hard to surmount. It is also an unintended result of the council's encouraging Catholics to seek holiness through more worldly pursuits and by participating more in the Mass, which have thus become more central to their religious lives, thereby pushing other practices to the periphery.

In the midst of these changes, one thing seems obvious and more than a little ironic. That is, the Americanist heresy that to Pope Leo XIII appeared poised ominously outside the church's walls has, like a Trojan horse, been pulled unsuspectingly within. His abiding concern, voiced in *Testem benevolentiae,* that the church would "shape her teachings more in accord with the spirit of the age and relax some of her ancient severity and make some concessions to new opinions" is precisely what American Catholics have done.

What is more, they have embraced not only Americanism but also the very notion of heresy itself. Derived from the Greek verb *hairein,* meaning "to choose," heresy is in this sense a defining characteristic of American Catholics, who, since Vatican II, have been asked to discern the "signs of the times," think critically, and indeed choose whatever beliefs and courses of action are in accord with their own consciences.[82] Caught up in what sociologists Wade Clark Roof and William McKinney call the "new voluntarism" in American religion, Catholics are about as likely as other citizens to describe their faith as a "religious preference" and are apt to make choices about their religious convictions and practices for—if not always by—themselves.[83] Gaining some insight into how they do this is indispensable for understanding American Catholics in this new century. In fact, the primary goal of this book is to investigate the manner in which American Catholics remain faithful while at the same time making their own choices about which features of "the spirit of the age" to celebrate or castigate and which "new opinions" to accept or reject.

"The Thing about American Catholicism": Having the Conversation

Why This Conversation Is Necessary—Rationale

When Bill McNamara explains that the thing about American Catholicism is that it exists as an institutional entity but not as "some monolithic, unchanging thing," he is clearly on to something. About the church not being unchanging he says, "It's not as if any one person understands it and lives it out the same way all the time" or, he continues with respect to its not being monolithic, "in quite the same way as anyone else." Bill has come to these insights largely by dint of his own experience. The changes in the church are particularly obvious to him. Now in his early seventies, his own lifetime has coincided with the extraordinary transformation of American

Catholicism described earlier. It is also difficult to imagine him thinking of the church as a monolith. If, however, he ever needed a reminder that his way of being Catholic is not precisely the same as anyone else's, he has only to start up a conversation with one of his fellow parishioners to recall that this is indeed the case.

Like many of them, Bill would have no trouble recognizing himself in at least some of the survey data I have just cited. The only problem is that such quantitative data, while very informative, cannot truly capture the complexities of people's religious agency and moral discernment. Often substituting for these are mere slogans that, even when initially grounded in sound research, can conceal as much as they reveal. The phrase "cafeteria Catholic" is one of them. Typically used as a shorthand denunciation of liberal Catholics' supposed proclivity for blithely picking and choosing from among church teachings, it is not a particularly useful label, given that such religious choices are not always casually made, nor are they made solely by religious liberals. On the contrary, people commonly exercise their religious agency with great seriousness. And religious conservatives are hardly exempt from the need to make choices even though they typically place different items on their theological lunch trays. The more sympathetic phrase "good enough Catholic" has obvious shortcomings as well.[84] It suggests (and implicitly advocates) that in a complicated society such as ours in which clear-cut truths are hard to come by and the imperative to choose is unavoidable, Catholics can and do take comfort in living out their faith as they see fit and as well as they can. The problem here is that, in reality, Catholics often feel anything but good enough. Their one-time responses to sociologists' closed-ended surveys may create the appearance of certainty regarding the issues they are queried about. Yet, within the flow of their actual lives, they tend to be far less definitive and self-assured. It is not at all uncommon for them to harbor serious doubts about whether their convictions about issues, understanding of church teachings, or even their own religious selves are in fact good enough. Finally, even the more useful term "communal Catholics," while applicable to many, may lead us to neglect important nuances.[85] Referring to contemporary Catholics who are drawn to the worldview and community engendered by their faith but are relatively indifferent to the institutional church, it misses many people's willingness to participate within and engage the institution at the local, parish level.

The purpose of this book is to investigate some of these and other subtle distinctions that are often missed in discussions—scholarly and otherwise—of American Catholics. The people introduced in the chapters ahead are not unwilling to make choices, are not always unwaveringly confident that their decisions are good enough in terms of helping them realize their higher selves, and, as distinctly active parishioners all, are hardly indifferent to the institutional component of their faith. Such nuances come to the fore because this book is based on a strategy not always undertaken in other investigations—engaging Catholics in thoughtful, honest conversation. Doing this is the best way to let insights emerge *from* people's accounts of their religious lives and to avoid the simplistic labels often used *about* their religious lives. With this in mind, I selected six very different parishes located throughout the San Francisco Bay Area and spoke with forty to fifty self-described "active" parishioners at each. Essentially, we discussed how they understand and practice their faith and, in short, how a two-millennia-old religious tradition gives meaning to their decidedly modern lives. Conversations such as these are critical because they excavate deeper levels of cultural complexity than even the best national surveys can reach. They also make it abundantly clear that, despite the widespread presumption that American Catholics are becoming inexorably less religious, it is more accurate to say that, compared to their forbearers, they are simply religious in a different way. Interestingly, in this simple distinction is where much of the complexity lies and where extended conversations become the sharpest, best-suited tool for inquiry.

How This Conversation Proceeds—Methodology

Unlike various and often excellent books on American Catholics that advocate a position, promote an agenda, or have an ideological axe to grind, this one steps back a bit in order to be less prescriptive and more descriptive. In other words, rather than focusing on American Catholicism as codified within theological texts and magisterial pronouncements that prescribe how people *ought* to live their faith, I delve into what is often called "lived religion." [86] In other words, I attempt to do justice to the ways laypeople actually do negotiate with religious tradition and try to connect to what they hold most sacred amid the busyness and ambiguities of everyday life. Put another way, while recognizing that these two dimensions of religiosity depend upon and flow into one another, this book privileges nonofficial religion over the more official versions articulated by religious elites.[87]

Thus, not content to be an "armchair quarterback," I got out of my office and went into the parishes to speak with Catholic laypeople. Before doing so I first consulted with several Catholic leaders in the Bay Area, as well as various staff people at the main offices of the Diocese of Oakland, the diocese in which I both work and reside. After asking many questions and poring over the demographic data for all eighty-five parishes in the diocese, I selected a purposive sample of five that I felt would give me as disparate and inclusive a snapshot of American Catholics as possible. Because I was concerned about underrepresenting gay and lesbian Catholics, I also added Bill McNamara's Most Holy Redeemer parish from the Archdiocese of San Francisco. The parishes I selected are the following:

1. Saint Mary–Saint Francis de Sales Parish: Located in a poor neighborhood adjacent to Oakland's downtown area, it comprises Anglo, Filipino,

and Vietnamese (the largest of these three) populations, with some African Americans; most are working and middle class.

2. Saint Louis Bertrand Parish: Formerly made up of mostly Catholics of German descent, this predominantly working-class parish in a poor East Oakland neighborhood is now composed primarily of an African American community and a large and fast-growing Latino community.

3. Saint Monica Parish: Located on the eastern side of the Oakland Hills in the relatively affluent suburb of Moraga, this parish is made up of mostly middle- and upper-middle-class Anglos.

4. Saint Augustine Parish: This parish is located fifteen miles east of Oakland in the "exurban" bedroom community of Pleasanton; it is made up of mostly middle-class Anglos and lesser numbers of Asians and Latinos.

5. Saint Margaret Mary Parish: Comprising mostly middle-class Anglos and some Asians and Latinos, this parish is located in a busy East Oakland neighborhood adjacent to an expressway and, insofar as it still conducts some of its main masses in Latin, has become a magnet parish for Catholic conservatives.

6. Most Holy Redeemer Parish: The only parish selected for this study located outside of the East Bay (within San Francisco's Castro District), this parish is composed of primarily middle-class Anglos, the majority of whom are gay or lesbian.

Note that some parishes in this sample are made up largely of white members, while others serve various minority groups; some lean toward racial homogeneity, and others are more heterogeneous. Some of the parishes are relatively affluent, and others quite poor. Most have a majority of heterosexuals, while one is predominantly homosexual. They are situated in urban, suburban, and exurban locales. They vary in size. Some attract parishioners from significant distances, and others are more neighborhood-based parishes. Reputably liberal and conservative parishes are included. In brief, I chose my six-parish sample with an eye toward gaining as broad a cross-section of lived Catholicism as possible while holding geographic region as a constant. That this effort was largely successful is illustrated by the demographic sketch of this study's participants provided in Appendix A.

As important as analytical breadth is for a study such as this, my main goal has been to go into greater depth than is typically possible with broad-based surveys. To achieve this, I undertook a "triangulation" approach, whereby I (actually "we" is more accurate since I hired and trained a few graduate students as research assistants) employed multiple methods.[88] First, we became acquainted with the culture of each parish by getting to know people and hanging out at various events. More formally known as conducting "participant observation," this entailed activities such as attending masses and other rituals, going to meetings and social gatherings, participating in classes and informal conversations, and, in sum, trying to understand American Catholicism in situ as "lived religion" within each parish culture.

Second, we conducted nearly three hundred tape-recorded, semistructured interviews that lasted approximately two hours each; I conducted about half of these myself.[89] After getting permission to conduct this research from the pastor and, in some cases, the parish council, we requested the names of and contact information for about thirty active parishioners. In each case, a number of laypeople knowledgeable about which parishioners were involved in the various parish ministries assembled these listings. We supplemented these lists by asking people we interviewed for the names of other active church members, and, if they were mentioned with some regularity, we then included them to ensure that we interviewed at least forty active parishioners at each parish. These are the people who participate in worship as acolytes or lectors, teach religious education to children or adults, serve on the parish council or some other standing committee, and volunteer for everything from cleaning the church to chairing a capital campaign. In short, they are among those who are the most invested in their parishes and enable them to function on a day-to-day basis. Once we contacted them and scheduled a time and place (usually in the interviewees' homes or in rooms specially designated for us at the parishes), we engaged them in conversation about their faith; for non-English speakers, some of these conversations were with research assistants who were fluent in either Spanish or Vietnamese.

As delineated in the interview schedule we used (see Appendix B)—which I devised after conducting fourteen pilot interviews to help determine which issues to focus on—we asked them about their identity as Catholics. Specifically, we asked whether they believed they were good Catholics and, in any case, exactly what that might mean to them. We also asked whether they ever disagreed with church teachings and why, if they had ever considered leaving the church and why, and what they thought of other Christian and non-Christian faiths. We inquired about why they are so active within their parishes and the extent to which that involvement spills over into other community efforts. Noting that they give much to their parishes, we also asked what they get in return, what type and degree of community exists within them, and what their parishes do particularly well (or, alternatively, not so well). We queried them about their views on all manner of topics ranging from abortion to homosexuality, women's ordination to the recent pedophilia scandal, and from disparate social justice issues to the U.S. war with Iraq. We also presented them with various Bible passages and then asked them to interpret these and comment on whatever salience they may (or may not) have for their own lives. In short, we engaged them in conversation, and we definitely did the lion's share of the listening. That they had plenty to say is perhaps best indicated by the thousands of pages of single-spaced, typed interview transcripts produced to capture their reflections. That what they said was important and likely seldom articulated was less quantifiably represented by the not so few occasions when they sobbed during interview sessions, told us some of the most personal, tragic, or baffling aspects of their lives, cathartically hugged us when our conversations came to an end, or contacted us days later with whatever corrections or additional information had occurred to them.

Finally, we also asked each of the interviewees to fill out a four-page, closed-ended survey inquiring about demographic information and their views on various theological and ecclesiological issues. Probably due to their positive experiences with the interview process as well as our not-so-subtle telephone reminders, all but ten of the 267 interviewees (not including the fourteen in the pilot study) filled out and returned these forms. An additional forty-four African American, Asian, and Latino parishioners—fourteen at Saint Augustine's and thirty at Saint Louis Bertrand's—were not interviewed but agreed to fill out surveys during various meetings and gatherings. We requested this because, while these racial groups are well represented among our interviewees, we wanted to overrepresent them in the surveys in order to make better comparisons. In total, then, we received completed surveys from 301 parishioners.

Many of the questions in this survey were taken (with permission) from a nationwide survey designed by William V. D'Antonio and his colleagues and administered in 1999 and again (with some revisions) in 2005 through the Gallup organization. Their most recent data, which I reference throughout this work, are presented in their important book, *American Catholics Today: New Realities of Their Faith and Their Church* (2007).[90] I chose this strategy in order to illustrate that, even though the active parishioners introduced in this book reside in the liberal Bay Area, they are not so different from American Catholics as a whole with respect to their exercise of religious agency. Some readers might be tempted to think that these parishioners' proclivity for negotiating with the tenets and practices of their faith is unique to the "California scene," but this is demonstrably not the case. Consider, for instance, the percentages of people in first the D'Antonio study and then in the present Bay Area study who agree that one can be a "good Catholic" without practicing or believing the items listed in table 1.1.

At least two things are obvious from these numbers. The first is that both groups are apt to allow significant latitude when it comes to thinking through church rules and what are often taken to be the more institutional aspects of the faith, whereas they allow far less when the issues are more theologically central subjects such as the resurrection of Jesus and the Eucharist. The other thing is that, despite the fact that the Bay Area is generally more liberal than the nation as a whole, the specifically active members of these six parishes are actually *less* likely than Catholics nationally to say that people who do not practice or believe in the items mentioned can be "good Catholics." The only exception is the papal infallibility question, but, because this was included only in an earlier (1993) survey, responses to this item may now also follow this general pattern.

This pattern serves as a reminder that some differences exist between these two groupings. The Bay Area sample comprises people who tend to be older, better educated, and better off economically than Catholics nationally. Moreover, as distinctly active members of their parishes, they are also significantly more committed to the church. D'Antonio and his colleagues measured this commitment by posing the three questions delineated in table 1.2. For both their survey and my own, this table lists the percentage of respondents who (1) say the Catholic Church is either the most important aspect of their lives or among the most important; (2) respond with a 1 or a 2 on a seven-point scale, where 1 signifies "I would never leave the Catholic Church" and 7 means "Yes, I might leave the Catholic Church"; and (3) say they attend Mass at least once a week.

Obviously, by these measurements, the active Catholics in the Bay Area study are far more committed, a finding that becomes particularly evident when these measures are combined into a scale (table 1.3). In other words, D'Antonio and his colleagues label as highly committed those people who respond to *all three* of these questions in the ways designated above. On the other hand, scoring low on commitment are those who meet *at least two* of the following three conditions: (1) say the Catholic Church is not important at all; (2) score 5, 6, or 7 on the seven-point scale with regard to leaving the church; and (3) attend Mass seldom or never.

TABLE 1.1. "Please tell me if you think a person can be a good Catholic without performing these actions or affirming these beliefs." Numbers represent percentages of those who responded "yes."

	D'Antonio study	Bay Area study
1. Without going to church every Sunday	76	61
2. Without their marriage being approved by the Catholic Church	67	61
3. Without obeying the church hierarchy's teaching on divorce and remarriage	66	60
4. Without believing in the infallibility of the pope	50	59
5. Without donating time or money to help the parish	58	42
6. Without believing that Jesus physically rose from the dead	23	16
7. Without believing that, in the Mass, the bread and wine actually become the body and blood of Jesus	36	22

Note: The national datum for Item 4 was taken from a 1993 survey that appears in D'Antonio et al. (1996); all other percentages appear in D'Antonio et al. (2007).

TABLE 1.2. Three indicators of commitment (in %)

	D'Antonio study	Bay Area study
1. How important is the Catholic Church to you personally? (those who answered "the most important" or "among the most important parts of my life")	44	80
2. On a scale from 1 to 7, with 1 being "I would never leave the Catholic Church" and 7 being "Yes, I might leave the Catholic Church," where would you place yourself on this scale? (those who answered "1" or "2")	56	78
3. How often do you attend Mass? (those who answered "at least once a week")	34	81

Everyone else they categorize as having a "medium" level of commitment. Using this scale for both studies illustrates just how committed these active Bay Area parishioners are.

One reason it is important to mention this is to point out that, while table 1.1 indicates that these parishioners' attitudes track quite closely with those of Catholics elsewhere, this book does not claim to provide a strictly representative study of the American church. My goal is instead to better understand the complex and innumerable ways in which contemporary Catholics make sense of their faith. This is not simply a view from afar. Rather, it is an effort to enter the religious "sausage factory" and unblinkingly examine, primarily through conversation, the internal processes at work. Another reason it is important to note that the focus is on especially committed and active Catholics is to accentuate the reality that the religious uncertainty, grappling, and negotiation recorded in these pages are evident even among the most active "pillars" of local parish communities. These people and their fluid relationship with their religious tradition cannot simply be reduced (or trivialized) to "cafeteria," "good enough," or "communal" Catholics. They are actually what many—including members of the church hierarchy—would very likely consider to be among the most exemplary of Catholics. As such, they do much to influence the culture of their respective parishes. They also confront us with the rather bracing fact that Catholics' tendency to negotiate with their faith tradition, experience real uncertainties about it, and look askance at many of its more institutionalized features is evident even among those generally considered the most committed and serious of the faithful.

To what extent church leaders (both clergy and lay) take their religious insights and concerns seriously is ultimately an open question. As a sociologist most concerned with presenting my findings as clearly and even-handedly as possible, I claim a certain distance from such matters. Yet, religious leaders and others among the faithful who are concerned about the future of their church must come to some

TABLE 1.3. Commitment to the Catholic Church (in %)

	Low	Medium	High
D'Antonio study	15	64	21
Bay Area study	0	43	57

kind of evaluative decision about the validity of this relatively new sensibility among American Catholics. Is Bill McNamara's return to the church and newfound understanding of his faith truly an authentic manifestation of Catholicism? How much tension between the reality of "lived religion" and the theology expressed in official religious teachings is appropriate? Are the experiences and opinions of the people presented in this book a problem for this two-thousand-year-old religious tradition, or do they have something worthwhile to offer it as it unfolds through history? These and other issues raised here are matters for Catholics to discuss and decide.

There are reasons to think that church leaders could and, on the basis of the church's own teaching, even should listen attentively to the Catholics who appear in the pages that follow. In other words, as this book's title denotes, I provide readers a sense of how the American faithful understand themselves as Catholics. However, this title also evokes a normative theological category as well. Endorsed by Vatican II, the notion of *sensus fidelium* [sense of the faithful] essentially means that the lived faith of the rank-and-file "people of God" should indeed be valued as a source of theological insight that, in turn, should be mined as such to ensure the vitality of the tradition.[91] Whether or not this will occur is both unknown and, as suggested, a topic beyond the scope of this study. What is known, however, is that if this does occur, it will likely come as a result of more listening, more awareness, and more of the very sort of open conversations with Catholics upon which this book is based.

2

Framework

A "Cultured" Look at American Catholicism

An Analytical Caveat: You Could Use Some Culture!

Making sense of American Catholic life entails a good deal of analytical complexity. People do not simply absorb the ideas declared from pulpits and elaborated upon in theological texts. They actively negotiate with them. Knowing the contents of *The Catechism of the Catholic Church,* for example, tells one very little about what various Catholics know or think about their faith. Recognizing, as Michele Dillon does, that Catholics exercise considerable "interpretive authority" when engaging their tradition requires that we pay attention to the reality that they do so as full-blooded, complicated individuals who change over time and differ from one another in many ways. We must also remember that, as the term "lived religion" connotes, this process is never divorced from the flow of people's everyday lives. People are usually more aware of some religious meanings than others. Certain values may seem more or less relevant to their lives. They may find particular practices to be evocative and discard others they deem less so. And they may feel personally competent to draw upon or articulate some religious ideas while assuming that others are better left for Catholics of a different stripe. Like other people, then, Catholics actively negotiate with the religious meanings accessible to them in much the same way as they do other cultural meanings.

Thus, one cannot truly understand contemporary American Catholicism without, as I do in this chapter, offering some assessment of the meaning of culture and its place in shaping people's sense of what is sacred to them. Even though this became clearer for me with each interview I conducted, probably the best illustration of what I mean came as a result of my having missed one of these sessions. A few months after interviewing Bill McNamara in his Oakland Hills home, I (almost literally) bumped into him outside the fellowship hall at Most Holy Redeemer as I was grouchily pacing the sidewalk wondering when my next interviewee would arrive. Bill was there to help feed the neighborhood's homeless population, many of whom come to the fellowship hall every Wednesday evening for a hot meal served by parish volunteers. Early for this dinner and indefatigably polite, he helped me pass the time by chatting about everything from parish gossip to the current exhibit at San Francisco's Museum of Modern Art (MOMA). In fact, by the time I acknowledged the frustrating reality—alas, an occupational hazard among sociologists—that I had been stood up by my prospective interviewee, Bill had planted a seed in my mind.

"I could use some culture!" I thought self-accusingly while driving home and recalling how cheap MOMA tickets were on Wednesday nights. So, determined to make the most of my trip to San Francisco, I was soon at the museum and, per Bill's recommendation, taking in an exhibit featuring the work of Belgian surrealist René Magritte. Men in bowler hats; billowy, cumulus-cartoonesque clouds; cows and fruit and boulders airily suspended like and with crescent moons: It was all, true to its billing, quite surreal. I had to laugh and then muse a bit when looking at what immediately became my favorite painting in the collection, a replica of which now adorns my office. It was of a curvy pipe, the kind that middle-class men of the artist's generation might have smoked in the evening; beneath the pipe were the cursively painted words "Ceci n'est pas une pipe" (This is not a pipe). "Now, that's culture," I thought at that moment and, to this day, declare to unsuspecting students on the rare occasions when they inquire about that print in my office.

That my students usually respond with looks of confusion is hardly surprising. Most are not familiar with René Magritte, they may be nervously unsure about what is typically smoked in the sort of pipe depicted (I do work in Berkeley, after all), and, like most of us, they are not entirely certain what is meant by "culture." Often the word is simply conflated with "high culture." This elitist, Philistinism-eschewing construal of culture is perhaps best captured in nineteenth-century essayist Matthew Arnold's famous definition of it as "the best that has been thought and known."[1] Commensurately, when I say "Now, that's culture," I could be saying that, because Magritte's oeuvre has been elevated to such high stature within the art world, this representative painting instantiates the very finest of artistic achievement. Another more common option equates culture with a specific society or with some identifiable subgroup within a larger society. Here the implied distinction is not between presumably "high" culture and "mass" or "folk" culture, which are actually quite fluid and contested demarcations. Rather, it is between particular ways of life. In this case, saying "Now, that's culture" suggests something to the effect that the painting is somehow representative of "Belgian culture" (not, for instance, "American culture") or "surrealist culture" (not "academic culture") or "middle-class culture" (not "ghetto culture").

Neither of these two understandings of culture—what we may call the elitist and societal construals respectively—captures the particular understanding I wish to highlight. Instead of categories deployed *within* everyday life in order to make evaluative distinctions (elitist) or maintain collective identities (societal), culture is also a semiotic dimension *of* everyday life.[2] Culture, in this signifying or representational sense, refers to the historically transmitted repertoires of symbols that shape people's perceptions of reality and, at the same time, render that reality meaningful to them.[3] This sense, of course, is not disconnected from the other two. The recognition of high culture as such is certainly a symbolic accomplishment. After all, the purported superiority of a pinot noir over a Bud Light, a Shakespearian tragedy over a horror flick, and a Magritte painting over a black-velvet rendition of dogs playing poker is less inherent in these cultural objects than conferred upon them in order to signify distinctions in social status among their consumers.[4] The same is true of collective identities. To suggest, for example, that racial groups are defined solely by physiology or that social classes are defined exclusively by bank accounts would blind us to the myriad of symbolic ways in which language, role expectations, and images disseminated through the mass media all function to perpetuate these and other group identities.[5]

Thus, after gazing at Magritte's pipe and reading his tongue-in-cheek caveat, "Ceci n'est pas une pipe," my thinking "Now, that's culture" is really nothing more than registering my agreement with him. It is not a pipe; it is a representation of one. This distinction is evocative of culture in the representational sense because the painted pipe is a symbolic means of presenting a reality that is often mistakenly taken to be completely encapsulated by the representation itself. But, Magritte reminds us, the painting of the pipe is not the pipe any more than my finger pointing at a painting is the painting, a map of Berkeley is Berkeley, a sonnet is love for an absent suitor, or a religious doctrine is, as theologian H. Richard Niebuhr once put it, the God behind the "little faiths in little gods" of presumed theological certainty.[6]

Nonetheless, by pointing to what is alleged to be more important than something else, by mapping acceptable courses of action within specific contexts, by making present to consciousness that which is either material (a pipe) or nonmaterial (a pining love), and by delineating that which is ultimately true and sacred, culture exists as a symbolic world for us. From what philosopher William James once called the "big blooming buzzing confusion" of our otherwise unbearably chaotic experience, culture confers order and presents us with a meaningful world in which our own lives make sense.[7]

This is what makes culture a kind of religious phenomenon. It coordinates thought and action to the extent that people adhere to it together. It functions as a symbolic world that impinges upon us because we have faith in it, faith that others have faith in it, faith that others have faith that we have faith in it, and so on. Everything from classrooms to rock concerts, occupational statuses to gender roles, elevator riding to sexual activity—all would be well-nigh impossible absent our collective devotion to behavioral codes, categorizations, and shared definitions of these situations. Moreover, cultural missteps are generally treated as a kind of apostasy. To test this, simply behave in a classroom as you would at a rock concert (with respect to overall comportment), treat your female boss like your mother (with respect to expectations of nurturance), and confuse the social codes of elevator ridership and sex (with respect to interpersonal spacing, as well as type and volume of locutions) to get a sense of just how vociferously transgressing cultural norms is typically cast as taboo.[8]

Not only does culture have a religious quality to it, but religion is also inextricably cultural in the representational sense we are considering here. Religions, in other words, are repertoires of symbols that specifically represent what is taken to be sacred. Importantly, this semiotic approach should not be understood as necessarily exhausting the totality of religion or, as sociologists are often accused, somehow debunking it. While sociologists pay attention to the symbols that believers draw upon when expressing what is sacred to them, they must stop short of speculating about whatever realities might or might not lie beyond those cultural expressions. Indeed, to have the disclaimer "Ceci n'est pas Dieu" printed somewhere in the opening pages of theology texts, hymnals, and magisterial pronouncements to differentiate these symbolic expressions from that which is called God would neither necessarily detract from these symbols' importance nor deny the reality of what they endeavor to represent.

If this semiotic approach does not necessarily cast religious symbols as disconnected from reality, it surely sensitizes us to the fact that how we access and deploy them is inevitably connected to broader social dynamics.[9] The ways that social classes, gender roles, and ethnic identities are reproduced often shape believers' affinities for distinctive kinds of religious expression. Shifts in the patterns of educational attainment affect the ways in which religious messages are both conveyed and interpreted. Changes in family and work life often alter how people participate in religious institutions. There is much to consider. Yet, likely the most useful manner in which to begin thinking about American Catholics' understanding of what it means to be religious is to bracket such analytically focused considerations and, for the moment at least, to think as macroscopically as possible.[10] At this macro- or societal level of analysis, the situation of religious culture is best encapsulated by a single term: secularization.

At the Societal Level: Religious Culture as Available

Secularization has become something of a social scientific shibboleth, continually referenced but seldom carefully examined. Often the term is used simply to denote religion's precipitous or even inexorable decline. This usage tends to rely on a kind of seesaw model: Whereas things once tilted oppositely, now the rise of modernity entails an accompanying fall in religious belief and practice.

The problems with this model are legion. Among the most serious is an unduly simplistic notion of what precisely is rising and falling. There is no one thing called "modernity."[11] Some modern contexts allow people to tap into alternative sources of power (for example, academic credentials, political connections) from which they can challenge religious authority.[12] Other versions of modernity encourage greater religious conviction and mobilization, as in the modern Middle East.[13] Similarly, there is no single version of "religiosity." When particular forms of devotion decline, many people think this entails the decline of religion in general. However, to equate trends such as a drop in church attendance, for example, with an ebbing of religiosity per se would be to arbitrarily ignore the simultaneous rise in less church-centered religious practices.

Another problem is this model's ahistorical, more-religion-back-then-less-religion-now character. This, too, is untenable. The doe-eyed notion that societies were once populated entirely by deeply knowledgeable, orthodox, and pious citizens is perhaps best captured by the title of a thoughtful book on the nuclear family, "the way we never were."[14] The actual historical record is clear. When nations—or, more likely, political leaders for political purposes—converted to Christianity, for example, the masses were not necessarily Christianized as a result.[15] Assuming otherwise is often a function of making generalizations about the past based on the writings of familiar thinkers. Even though we can learn much from reading the works of Martin Luther, Thomas Aquinas, and Moses Maimonides, assuming they were representative of their contemporaries makes as much sense as claiming that today's rank-and-file Protestants, Catholics, and Jews understand and live out their faiths as do their coreligionists who happen to be professional theologians.

Nor are modern people especially irreligious. A full 95 percent of American adults claim to believe in God. Almost two-thirds say they believe "without doubt," about one-fifth say they believe with "some doubts" (this response category, incidentally, might well have been chosen by Luther, Aquinas, and Maimonides if such surveys had existed centuries ago), and about one-tenth say they believe in a "higher power."[16] Nearly three in five adults say they pray daily and more than four in five describe religion as "very" or "somewhat" important to them.[17] Whereas a half century ago theologian Paul Tillich could confidently describe Americans' attention to matters of the spirit as "lost beyond hope," now the language of spirituality has become remarkably pervasive, perhaps to a historically unprecedented degree.[18] The four in five adults who currently say they feel the need to grow spiritually marks a 50 percent increase in the proportion who said this only two decades ago.[19] And while there may be a "yea-saying" bias for such questions—a tendency to portray oneself as more religious than might actually be the case—even this suggests just how strong cultural expectations of religiosity truly are within American society.

If the empirical evidence indicates that religious belief and practice, albeit always changing, remain stubbornly resilient in the United States, then what does it mean to describe our society as "secularized"? It means that, similar to other nations, American society is marked by a distinctive structure in which religious norms and authority have been largely removed from public institutions.[20] Untethered from religious control, these institutions operate according to their own internal logics. No longer subject to religious ideals such as "just war" criteria and the Christianization of society, the state agencies responsible for collective governance are themselves governed by the logic of power accrual and exertion. No longer shaped by religious teachings such as equating usury (charging interest for loans) with sinfulness and practices such as enforcing business contracts through church courts, economic enterprises are largely driven by the pursuit of profit. No longer subject to ecclesial oversight, science is judged according to its own empirical standards.

In short, by differentiating themselves from religion, such institutions have dethroned religion somewhat. It has become one institution among others, eminently separable in many people's minds from various spheres of public life. This is why one can speak of "religious culture."[21] Far less influential in steering the workings of other societal institutions, religion is largely divested of such functions and, like culture as a whole, becomes for people more a locus of self-expression and meaning making. Religious traditions are now most operative in making sacred symbols and meanings accessible to people who, with the demonopolization of Christianity in Western societies like the United States, are now freer than ever to draw upon these as their needs require.[22]

When we understand secularization in this manner, certain commonly held presumptions about contemporary religion seem far less tenable. For example, much has been made of the presumed effects of religious pluralism for diminishing the taken-for-granted validity of one's particular faith.[23] As a result, many contend, people will be less likely to believe earnestly in any specific religious "preference," and the level of aggregate religiosity will fall accordingly. Such assertions do not reflect reality, however. Regarding *individual* conviction, there is no persuasive evidence that the need to select from among available religious options necessarily compromises people's capacity to believe fervently. In fact, given the importance Americans confer upon individual choice, treating religious identity as a preference is likely to bind them to their convictions more tightly than might otherwise be the case.[24]

This, moreover, leads us to question religious pluralism's supposed role in the *aggregate* decline of religion as well. In much the same way as producing multiple flavors of ice cream enhances the likelihood of increasing the total number of ice cream consumers, the plurality of religious offerings in the United States has actually contributed to the nation's high level of religiosity.[25] The deregulated nature of its "religious economy" ensures that there will be sufficient variety to satisfy most tastes. Conservative and liberal teachings; "high church" and "low church" liturgies; "this-worldly" and "other-worldly" spiritual paths; meditative and ecstatic practices; established religious communities and "new immigrant" churches: This dizzying array of religious offerings appeals to a much wider swath of the American public, who, despite predictions to the contrary, are much more religiously involved as a consequence.

Secularism, then, is the context within which Americans tap into the symbolic repertoires that give their lives a sense of coherence and direction. Religious meanings are certainly distinctive in signifying something about the sacred. At the same time, they are not so distinctive from other cultural meanings with respect to people's access to them. They have largely ceased to be imposed by the state, and they are no longer reaffirmed in everyday consciousnesses by being privileged within other institutional settings. They are simply available for people to draw upon and deploy amid their individual lives in much the same way as are the other components of culture to which they have access. Clergy and other "experts" no longer monopolize what are taken to be valid interpretations of faith traditions, and, concomitantly, laypeople are no longer reticent to interpret religious symbols and meanings as they see fit.

At the Individual Level: Religious Culture as Appropriated

The question of how Catholics access the religious culture available to them is best addressed from the micro- or individual level of analysis. Put simply, individual Catholics actively appropriate the religious symbols and meanings with which they are familiar. Both the remarkable variety among American Catholics and the religious changes that individual believers experience over the course of their lives give testimony to the fact that they are not "cultural dopes."[26] They are not passive recipients of a religious culture that is simply planted in their brains and then directs their actions in essentially predictable ways. Rather, as sociologist Ann Swidler helpfully conceives it, culture is a symbolic repertoire or "tool kit," and individuals actively select and make use of its symbolic tools on the basis of what they are doing, who they consider themselves to be, and which components they feel competent to utilize.[27]

Most Catholics have access to such symbolic tools as stories and beliefs about Jesus, church teachings, the pope's latest comments, themes within religious hymnody, and so forth. They are offered parables—depicting everything from prodigal sons to unexpectedly good Samaritans—that provide them with recipes for action when faced with roughly similar situations. They are presented with values such as faithfulness and respect for the intrinsic dignity of each person and with exemplars such as Saint Paul perceiving the holy as if through a glass darkly and Mother Teresa tending to the poorest of the poor. Objects from crèche to crucifix; images from Cana to Calvary; phrases that denote "doubting Thomases" and "dark nights of the soul"—all these and more texture the Catholic imagination. And it is not uncommon for Catholics to wed these specifically religious meanings to ones that are *extra*religious. In other words, they supplement what they know about the sacred through their faith tradition with ideas gleaned from books and newspapers, images portrayed in television programs and movies, and cultural narratives derived from multiple sources such as capitalism (the "American Dream"), Enlightenment rationalism (knowledge equals progress), and the Romantic tradition ("do your own thing").

Complicating matters further, Catholics share their fellow citizens' propensity for *inter*religious appropriation in place of strict "brand loyalty" to any one faith. Americans tend to no longer treat religion as an "ascribed" status, an aspect of identity like sex or race, which is determined by circumstances of birth and largely resistant to change. Instead, they are now more apt to see it as an "achieved" status, something every bit as determined by choice as one's profession or political party. Whereas a 1955 Gallup poll found that only one person in twenty-five no longer adhered to the faith of their childhood, now one-third of all Americans switch denominations (or religions) in their lifetimes, and one in ten do so three or more times.[28] American Catholics are less likely to switch than, for example, their Protestant counterparts. Yet, they are just as likely to engage in interreligious appropriation in light of their growing recognition of what historian Martin Marty once called the "merits of borrowing." That one-fifth of all American Catholics consider themselves to be "born again" and more than one-quarter of them believe in reincarnation should disabuse anyone of the notion that religious traditions, including Catholicism, are hermetically sealed and thus impervious to the constant flow of beliefs and practices occurring around them.[29]

Finally, if interreligious appropriation is a reflection of Catholics' access to the concepts and practices of other faith traditions, *intra*religious appropriation is a function of their having access to a wealth of interpretations of their own tradition. People tend to think of Catholicism as a kind of unified "cultural system" or a preassembled constellation of symbols appropriated completely or not at all.[30] In practice, though, the watchwords for people's use of religious culture are "some assembly required." Thus, it makes better sense to follow sociologist James Beckford's lead in seeing religions, for better or worse, as cultural "resources" that people tap as their needs dictate.[31] As such, their symbols and meanings are appropriated more heterogeneously than is frequently acknowledged.[32] Some people are far less knowledgeable than others when it comes to specific Catholic (and other) symbols and are not as likely to draw upon them as meaning-making tools. Likewise, some people may find that certain symbols resonate with their experience, while others, who may have had different life experiences or have different religious tastes and affinities, might think otherwise. Some social contexts and issues seem to lend themselves to being addressed in religious terms, and others might not. Sometimes religious meanings are highly elaborated and thought through; at other times or by other people, they simply serve a kind of decorative function, making little impact on how individual actors think and behave.

In sum, Catholics always appropriate the religious culture available to them in disparate ways. As important as this is for understanding twenty-first-century American Catholicism, it is just as important, once again, to avoid getting caught up in much of the contemporary rhetoric about it. Like other Americans, Catholics negotiate with religious culture, but they do not do this in a pell-mell fashion. This is because their religious tradition is marked, like all traditions, with a certain "givenness" by which some avenues for individual appropriation are imaginable and thus open to them, whereas others are not.[33] Their faiths, in other words, are not "religion à la carte," as if the menu of cultural options were unlimited. Nor do they practice an anything-goes, "pastiche style" of spirituality unencumbered by the imaginative parameters of their tradition.[34] Contrary to such popular conceits, Catholics are actually constrained by their religious tradition in the sense that it equips them to understand, expect, and even want certain insights about and connections to the sacred—and not others. Moreover, their appropriation of religious culture is also frequently constrained by the specific versions of it presented to them within their local parishes.

At the Organizational Level: Religious Culture as Allocated

When attending to religious culture at the meso- or organizational level, one must first note that congregations (including Catholic parishes) are not the only places where religion gets institutionalized in contemporary society. Schools, service agencies, publishing houses, advocacy groups, communities of vowed religious—each of these are important institutional forms of religion.[35] Still, congregations are the primary means by which religion is socially organized for Americans today. Currently there are more than three hundred thousand congregations in the United States. This, as sociologist Michael Emerson reminds us, is even more than "all the McDonald's, Wendy's, Subways, Burger Kings, and Pizza Huts, combined."[36] The more than nineteen thousand Catholic parishes compose about 6 percent of this total, but, since on average they are considerably larger than other congregations, they are where a full 29 percent of churchgoers in the United States actually worship.[37]

Of course, parishes offer far more than a place for collective worship. They assist in the transmission of values and contribute to the identity formation of both the young and, less obviously, the not so young. They perform a status-granting function by providing people with social roles in service to and recognizable by their peers. They promote social solidarity by offering fellowship opportunities and reinforcing notions of community obligation. By addressing the needs of the poor and marginalized, they function as social service providers while, by critiquing society on the basis of their publicly proclaimed values, they (at least potentially) serve as seedbeds for social reform.[38]

Another, less frequently acknowledged function of parishes is their role in allocating religious culture to the faithful.[39] They are institutional carriers of the religious meanings embedded in the symbolic repertoire that is the Catholic tradition, but not every parish does this the same way. Each one customizes this repertoire to better reflect the lived reality of its members. Over time they engender what sociologist Gary Alan Fine calls "idiocultures," which are localized versions of a broader meaning system that, in turn, becomes the source for new, collectively shared meanings, customs, and beliefs.[40] This is not to suggest that each parish is entirely idiosyncratic. As with the Little League teams Fine studied, different parishes each coalesce around a relatively uniform set of goals (connectedness to the sacred rather than winning games), practices (celebrating the Mass rather than peer teasing), language (theological terminology rather than "preadolescent slang"), and normative expectations (piety rather than sportsmanship) operative from one to the next. Within those parameters, though, parishes engender their own religious style—their own ways of construing and enacting the Catholic faith. They inevitably valorize some components of Catholic culture as more central than others and, in doing so, make these components more readily available to their members and thus more likely to be appropriated by them.[41]

An interesting feedback loop is operative in parishes' allocation of Catholic culture to their members. Within a single metropolitan area like the Bay Area, parishes are distinct from one another due to patterns of human geography. There are more middle-class white people in suburban parishes, there are more working-class Latinos in inner-city parishes, and so on. This localized variability is exacerbated by a feature of what one sociologist calls "de facto congregationalism," the propensity of Catholics (and others) to seek out and become involved in whichever local churches seem most suited to their religious sensibilities.[42] When many people do this over time, this ultimately affects which aspects of Catholic culture particular churches are likely to highlight in catering to the needs of specific populations. Coming full circle, this then influences which symbolic tools actually get allocated to parishioners, become familiar to them, and then come to make sense to them by virtue of their participation in a given parish. The six parishes that I studied, by presenting the faith in their own distinctive ways, have performed this culturally allocative role for the parishioners we will meet in subsequent chapters.

Saint Mary–Saint Francis de Sales

This church, the very first built in what is now the Diocese of Oakland, was initially a small adobe chapel (called the Church of San Antonio) erected in 1850, the year California became a state. Shortly thereafter, Vincente Peralta, whose father the Spanish Crown had granted 44,800 acres of what is now several East Bay cities three decades earlier, sold his land to American investors. In 1854 they incorporated the city of Oakland. In 1868, the adobe chapel was replaced by the much larger cruciform church building called Saint Mary, Immaculate Conception. Before it was divided up into many smaller parishes, Saint Mary functioned as a mission serving a vast area that stretched from the city of Pinole to the north all the way to Mission San José more than fifty miles south.

From the very beginning, an acceptance and even a celebration of cultural diversity have been the parish's leitmotifs. First were the Spanish and Mexican *Californios*. Then, on the heels of the gold rush, came the mostly white Americans, including large numbers of Irish and Italian immigrants. African Americans came during World War II to work in the Kaiser Shipyards, and soon afterward Mexicans arrived in larger numbers. Most relevant with respect to the parish's present membership was the arrival of Filipinos in the late 1960s and, beginning in the 1970s, the emergence of an increasingly vibrant Vietnamese community. These were the dominant groups until the 1989 Loma Prieta earthquake severely damaged the diocese's beautiful Saint Francis de Sales Cathedral, eventually requiring it to be torn down. Since Saint Mary's was located nearby, the church generously agreed to open its doors to the cathedral's mostly white parishioners, creating, with their 1993 merger, one of the diocese's most ethnically diverse parishes, situated near the downtown area in what had become a poor section of the city.[43]

With fewer than nine hundred parishioners, Saint Mary–Saint Francis de Sales now comprises three distinct worship communities, each with its own Sunday Mass. About two hundred families attend the 8:45 AM Mass, at which the entire liturgy is conducted in Vietnamese. A slight majority of the one hundred or so families regularly attending the 10:30 AM Mass are Anglo; most of the rest are Latino, Chinese, and African American. Finally, the 12:30 PM service is dominated by the approximately fifty Filipino families that attend regularly. This Mass is conducted in English (with some Tagalog), and, as with the Vietnamese service, there are numerous musical, costume, and narrative elements that serve as reminders of these parishioners' homeland and ethnic culture.

Highlighting cultural diversity—as a reminder of the church's worldwide scope and the need to defy ethnocentric versions of it—is central to the culture of this parish. Numerous examples illustrate this characteristic. The pastor, a white American Jesuit, learned to speak Vietnamese, and the parish usually houses at least a couple of Vietnamese priests who help out at the parish while on sabbatical or pursuing graduate degrees at local schools. The parish council is made up of an equal number of members from each of the three worship communities. On each side of the church's main altar is enshrined a large and colorful pictorial. One is a bas-relief depiction of the 117 Vietnamese Catholics martyred between 1820 and 1862, all standing in the company of Jesus. The other, encased in bamboo, shows various aspects of Philippine topography and culture and, most notably, features an image of the *Santo Niño* [Holy Child], a key figure in traditional Filipino devotionalism. For several hours each Saturday, the church's four classrooms are converted into the Vietnamese Language and Cultural School for youngsters who, in many parents' estimation, are assimilating into American culture at an alarming rate. Saint Mary–Saint Francis has also become a "magnet parish" for Filipinos who travel considerable distances for worship and participate in the parish-sponsored *cursillo* [short course] program. In addition, in order to properly ritualize this appreciation of diversity, the parish has about ten "union liturgies" each year, in which the three communities worship together to celebrate feast days such as Christmas, Easter, and Pentecost, and to commemorate important cultural icons such as the 117 Vietnamese martyrs and San Lorenzo Ruiz (b. 1610), the first Filipino saint.

Relatedly, the parish is marked by a sense of itself (especially among regulars of the 10:30 AM Mass) as socially progressive. With respect to liturgy, they have removed the kneelers deemed synonymous with pre–Vatican II piety, they use gender-inclusive language, the Bible is carried between the pews for all—not just the clergy—to touch before the reading of the gospel, laypeople are frequently invited to give reflections in lieu of priests' homilies before Communion, and the pastor uses phrases such as the "Kin[g]dom of God" in order to flout triumphalist images of divinity. Manifestations of the parish's outreach include the 1970s' creation of Saint Mary's Center, which provides assistance to poor people, and Saint Mary's Garden Elderly Housing for low-income seniors, both of which are now independent organizations. The use of parish facilities by various Catholic Charities programs, as well as for a winter shelter at which parishioners volunteer to help house and feed thirty homeless people for four months each year, are other manifestations of this. Nearly every week a second collection is taken to help support a social service agency, and the church's social justice teachings are standard fare for adult education sessions, as well as the most frequent topics for guest speakers at the parish.

Saint Louis Bertrand

Saint Mary–Saint Francis de Sales and this next parish have some interesting similarities. First, it, too, has a long history. The parish was founded in 1908, and, after celebrating Mass in a parishioner's home for more than a year, Saint Louis Bertrand Church was built and formally dedicated in 1910. Five decades later, this traditional stone church was torn down and replaced with a larger, more modern structure, in which the pews are arranged as a vast semicircle centered on the altar. Second, it is made up of parishioners with relatively modest incomes. Located in an East Oakland neighborhood about eight miles from downtown on a stretch of International Boulevard known for its high incidence of drug dealing, prostitution, and violence, the church is in the midst of one of the city's most economically depressed sections. Third and closely related, this parish's outreach is shaped by the needs with which it is most familiar. It offers a "Golden Friends" activity program for seniors and a mentoring program for youth. It runs a food pantry at the church for struggling families, and the parish also participates in Oakland Community Organizations, a local group established to hold political leaders accountable for rectifying neighborhood problems.

Perhaps the most obvious similarity is the way this parish has also experienced and responded to rather dramatic demographic shifts. Initially a largely Italian and Portuguese parish, it also witnessed an influx of African Americans who, beginning during World War II, came from the South in search of jobs in the city's shipyards. This trend, along with an accompanying white flight to outlying cities and towns, meant that, by the late 1960s, Saint Louis Bertrand was a predominantly black parish, whose vibrancy and reputation were enhanced by having its own parochial elementary and middle school. (It has since become a privately run charter school that pays much-needed rent to the parish.) Before long, this also changed. With so many African Americans either leaving the neighborhood or, particularly among the young, disaffiliating from the church, they have now become a minority relative to the Latino population, which has expanded in the past two decades. Whereas about six hundred (mostly African American) adults and children regularly worshipped at the church in the early 1980s, now more than twenty-five hundred people do. About 80 percent of them are Latino, and another 5 percent are Pacific Islander (especially Tongan).

The culture of the parish reflects this racial composition. Harkening back to many black parishioners' Louisiana roots, the parish holds an annual "crab feed," which is its biggest fundraiser and the best-attended social function for the African American community. The Knights of Saint Peter Claver and its auxiliary, the Ladies of Saint Peter Claver, service organizations for black Catholics founded in the 1940s in response to the racially segregated Knights of Columbus, are important and highly visible groups composed of many of the parish notables. Especially at the 9 AM Sunday Mass, which is attended primarily by African Americans, Black History Month is an important time for celebrating racial pride and achievement within the liturgy, and black religious leaders are frequent guests at this Mass throughout the year. A Saturday evening Mass and two on Sundays (11 AM and 6 PM), on the other hand, are conducted in Spanish, and, unlike the Mass in English held at 9 AM, they are celebrated in a fully packed church.

As one of thirty parishes in the diocese now offering Mass in Spanish, Saint Louis Bertrand has accommodated its Latino parishioners by spawning a set of parallel programs for them. Along with an English-speaking Leadership Council, there is a Hispanic Leadership Council. The parish also holds separate baptismal and catechism classes, youth groups, Bible study groups, and choirs. Other services and ministries offered specifically to Latinos include the more than twenty small communities that meet in people's homes for prayer and mutual support, the adoration of the Blessed Sacrament each Saturday morning, the scores of *quinceañeras* held at the church each year for young Latinas, and, of course, the annual celebration of Our Lady of Guadalupe.

At the same time, significant differences exist between these first two parishes. Saint Louis Bertrand is both larger and faster growing than Saint Mary–Saint Francis. Despite this and largely because its parishioners tend to be poorer than those at the other parish, Saint Louis Bertrand is without doubt the church in this study with the fewest resources at its disposal. Finally, likely due to this second point and to the size and language differences between the two communities, it is clear that Saint Louis Bertrand is actually, as one parishioner candidly admitted, "two communities under one roof." Nowhere is this fact more obvious than when parishioners from both Saint Mary–Saint Francis and Saint Louis Bertrand describe their respective churches. Whereas the former typically laud their parish as a locus of cultural diversity, the latter—among both African Americans and Latinos—are quite consistent in describing their parish as a place where they have simply learned to respect the other group.

Saint Monica

The differences between Saint Mary–Saint Francis and Saint Louis Bertrand, while very real, pale in comparison to the more glaring differences between both of them and Saint Monica. Nestled within the rolling pastures and wooded glens on the eastern side of the Oakland Hills, the relatively affluent town of Moraga is only about twelve miles from downtown Oakland, but it seems to be as far as one could imagine from the urban cacophony and bustle within which these other parishes function. Also unlike the other churches, Saint Monica is a newcomer to the diocese. It was established in 1965, and, after worshipping at nearby Saint Mary's College for several years, its parishioners finally began construction in a newly purchased pear orchard near Moraga's central square and celebrated the first Mass in their completed building in 1974. Doubling its original membership, now about fifteen hundred adults and children regularly attend Mass at Saint Monica. This membership, incidentally, is very different from that of the other two parishes. Its families are overwhelmingly Anglo (with some Latinos and Asians), middle- to upper-middle-class, and headed by well-educated professionals, including many stay-at-home mothers. As a result, the parish's initiatives are very well supported. Ten years after completing its beautiful church, the congregation added a parish center, administrative offices, and meeting rooms. It has also just finished building its $4.7 million Parish Education and Activities Center (PEACe) next to the church, which, by adding about ten thousand square feet of usable space, should go a long way toward meeting the needs of this active community.

At the core of the parish's self-understanding is its support and promotion of various activities. The menu is impressive. Adults can become active in everything from a cancer support group to a Rosary prayer group for the healing of body and soul; they can attend weekly adult education lectures and a monthly book review group to open their minds; they can do advocacy work with a parish-based Pax Christi group focused on peacemaking or a Respect for Life group that concentrates on pro-life issues. The women's guild and the men's club are mostly for fellowship and service, while women and men have their own groups for scripture reading and discussion as well. The pastoral council and the personnel and finance committees are for people interested in parish governance, whereas the groups devoted to Eucharistic ministry, hospitality, liturgy planning, and serving as lectors or ushers at Mass are for those drawn to more sacramental activities.

In addition to being a hub of activity, parishioners think of—and, for the most part, approve of—their parish as more progressive than most. This is evident in a number of aspects. The church itself has an in-the-round layout that, in ensuring that no worshipper is seated far from the central altar, seems to reflect Vatican II's notion of the church as the entire "people of God." Until her recent retirement, the parish was led by a female pastoral administrator for nearly a decade. For about that same period, her widely acknowledged organizational prowess was complemented by the homiletic skills of a priest who served as associate pastor and was equally well known, occasionally derided, and widely respected for his theologically liberal homilies on social justice, peacemaking, consumerism, and so on.

The parish has become a center (though this is not mentioned in its parish hand-book) for the Voice of the Faithful, a national organization of reform-minded Cath-olics that formed at the outset of the latest sex scandal in the Catholic Church.

Finally, parishioners generally frame their outreach in progressive terms. Indeed, for the past five years, 7–8 percent ($50,000–$65,000) of the parish's total expendi-tures have been directed to community outreach. Here "community" is sometimes understood as the parish community, as with the Helping Hands committee, which provides meals and other assistance to Saint Monica families in crisis. Sometimes it means being connected to other Bay Area organizations, as with the volunteers who work with Catholic Charities or with the Saint Vincent de Paul Society. And, more often than not, this means addressing needs within Oakland by allocating funds to local organizations or distributing items such as day-old food to various pantries (the Muffin People program) and shoes and school uniforms to children enrolled in an East Oakland parochial school (the Shoes-That-Fit program).

Perhaps more than anything, though, Saint Monica is about enhancing family life. Knowing that family schedules are extremely tight during the week, the parish sponsors many activities and events on Sundays, when people are most able to set aside time for them. These are generally focused on children. The Advent fair; pump-kin painting on the Sunday before Halloween; the annual blessing of the animals (mostly pets); the Children's Liturgy of the Word, when children gather around the altar for a blessing during Mass and then go to various classrooms for activities and instruction: These activities and programs are most plentiful. The parish currently has about forty volunteers teaching twenty-five religious education classes to more than four hundred children of all ages. It sponsors youth groups and choirs, a vaca-tion Bible camp, summer work camps in Mexico and elsewhere, a drop-in crafts pro-gram, and Catholic Youth Organization (CYO) basketball teams. Moreover, in light of their concern that a local Presbyterian church is attracting too many of their high school-age youth, they have recently made kids in their late teens a top priority.

Saint Augustine

Located at the intersection of two major expressways about twenty miles southeast of Oakland, the exurban city of Pleasanton was the size Moraga is now—about six-teen thousand residents—in the mid-1960s. Because these new expressways put it within commuting distance of Oakland, San Francisco, the Lawrence Livermore National Laboratory, and the high-tech industries strewn throughout Silicon Valley, Pleasanton's population has exploded to nearly seventy thousand. Not surprisingly, the history of Saint Augustine Church is also one of impressive growth. Even though Saint Augustine did not become an official parish until 1901, the church, modeled after a Swiss village chapel and decorated in the Gothic style, was constructed in the center of town in 1882, not many years after Pleasanton was incorporated (1869). This sufficed until the onset of the city's population boom, when, in 1968, a larger, saucer-shaped church (with pews arranged in a half-circle) was built atop a hill on what was then the edge of town. While able to accommodate further growth for a time, it, too, eventually met the limits of its capacity. Hence, the parish embarked on yet another building project, which culminated in 2000 with the dedication of Saint Elizabeth Seton Church. In order to maximize staff (especially clergy) and financial resources, the church leadership made the innovative decision to maintain a single parish—dubbed the Catholic Community of Pleasanton—consisting of two churches rather than become two separate parishes.

If Saint Monica is well resourced, the Catholic Community of Pleasanton is abundantly so. Attendance at its combined nine weekend masses at the two churches regularly exceeds thirty-five hundred worshippers. Its parishioners, who are approximately 90 percent Anglo, while the remainder is split into about equal numbers of Latinos and Asians (especially Filipinos), are generally middle class. This accounts for the parish's $1.6 million budget, which maintains, in addition to four priests and three deacons, a seventeen-member pastoral staff.

Also, if the activities and ministries at Saint Monica's are plentiful, here they are actually overwhelming in their variety and number. In brief, the parish's sixty-four ministries fall mostly within four distinct categories. Under "liturgical and prayerful ministries" come altar servers and greeters, Eucharistic ministers (at Mass, as well as to those who are home or hospital bound), lectors, choir members, the liturgy committee, the art and environment committee, and so on. "Community outreach and social ministries" include traditional initiatives such as the Blue Army of Mary (promoting a devotion to Our Lady of Fatima), a weekly bingo night, the Knights of Columbus, Pax Christi, the Saint Vincent de Paul Society, and the CYO, for which the parish is planning to build a $5 million activity center in order to accommodate, among other activities, its fifty-two basketball teams. Other, more novel, ministries are a Catholic counseling service, a marriage encounter group, committees that welcome parish newcomers with gift baskets brought to their homes and with bimonthly wine-and-cheese socials, and parish council committees devoted to endeavors such as social justice (to which 4 percent of the operating budget is allocated), evangelization, and spiritual life.

Along with the approximately one hundred catechism classes instructing about sixteen hundred children each year, the parish offers other innovative programs that fall within its "faith formation and youth ministries" category. For instance, it sponsors a children's choir and a faith-formation program for adults with developmental disabilities. Also, in lieu of enrolling individual children in the faith-formation program, entire families are given the option to participate (along with other families) in the program. Finally, under the category "adult formation and family life ministries" are numerous small groups that focus on scripture study, young adults, returning Catholics, and various support groups (e.g., AIDS, bereavement, single mothers). Among the more notable ventures are the many guest speakers and adult education series the parish sponsors, as well as the more than thirty small Christian communities (with nearly five hundred participants) that meet regularly for prayer and fellowship.

In many ways, of course, the culture of Saint Augustine Church—the Catholic Community of Pleasanton church upon which I focused—is similar to that of Saint Monica. The parishioners' demographics are roughly similar. Like Saint Monica, Saint Augustine is clearly a very active parish. Many (though not all) of the parishioners would be comfortable labeling themselves as progressive, and supporting families is one of the church's central concerns. However, these two cultures are quite different in one respect. Even though members of both Saint Monica and Saint Augustine say that their parish gives them a kind of hometown feel, the explicit use of community language is unique at Saint Augustine, which parishioners often describe as a "community of communities." Perhaps this is a function of having a strong pastor who is particularly outspoken on matters (or, in his view, the serious societal and spiritual problems) associated with American individualism. Or perhaps it reflects a particularly acute sense of rootlessness engendered by living in a fast-paced and fast-growing exurban locale like Pleasanton. Whatever the case, fostering a sense of community is a primary feature of this church's identity.

Saint Margaret Mary

About three miles southeast of downtown Oakland, travelers driving along a stretch of Interstate 580 can look upward and see a venerable stone-gray, Gothic-style church with slate roof, adjoining rectory, and a steel fence surrounding neatly manicured grounds. Looming amid a neighborhood that consists of equal numbers of apartment buildings and bungalows, this is Saint Margaret Mary Church. Founded in 1922, Mass was celebrated in a tiny wooden chapel until 1931, when the present structure—described that year in the *Oakland Tribune* as "one of the finest examples of Gothic art in the state"—was erected in its place.

Whether aesthetically knowledgeable or not, passersby who choose to park their cars and enter the church would likely agree with this assessment. All of the statuary, the ornate altar, stained-glass windows, the pristine white walls that contrast starkly with the dark wooden pews, doors, and arched ceiling—the visual effect is striking. Entering the church, one also gets the sense of coming into an entirely different world. Even with the Interstate 580 traffic whizzing by interminably, within the church's thick walls one finds silence and, quite often, the lingering hint of incense. Unlike in the other churches discussed so far, in Saint Margaret

Mary one finds missals largely in Latin, kneelers in the pews, and a wood railing separating these from the main altar. Confessionals are used three times each week for the Sacrament of Penance (and not for storage as at Saint Mary–Saint Francis de Sales). During Mass, people are exceptionally well attired, and many women, young and old, wear lace head coverings. Scattered in the back of the other churches, one might find brochures that describe various parish-based groups, community events, or the U.S. Bishops' *Faithful Citizenship* pamphlet, which delineates the church's social justice teachings and their relevance for contemporary public issues. Here the brochures are for specifically Catholic relief organizations not affiliated with the parish, and the titles of pamphlets announce things such as "Heaven Opened by the Practice of the Three Hail Marys" and "Hell Exists and We Might Go There."

This is not a parish that—as Saint Mary–Saint Francis and Saint Louis Bertrand do—accentuates ethnic differences. Its parishioners are mostly white (about 5 percent are Latino, another 5 percent Asian, and a few are African American). Never are these racial differences publicly celebrated or even noted as a feature of the worshiping community. Nor, like Saint Monica and Saint Augustine, is this parish a locus of various activities. For one thing, it is quite small. Slightly more than four hundred people worship here each week, which is about two hundred fewer than was the case only fifteen years ago. The parish is staffed with just two part-time priests (one also works for the diocese; the other is actually retired) and one part-time lay office manager. Thus, the parish sponsors little nonliturgical activity. Four volunteers teach four elementary-level children and seven high school–level youths in its religious education program, and four adults are enrolled in the Rite of Christian Initiation for Adults (RCIA) program. The parish has an adult choir (composed mostly of paid singers), two children's choirs, and ad hoc groups of people who pray the Rosary after the 8 AM weekday Mass and to Our Mother of Perpetual Help on Tuesday mornings. Every week the members of Saint Anne's Guild meticulously clean the church and raise funds for the purchase of flowers, vestments, and sacred vessels. This group also sponsors, as fundraisers, the parish's two social events of the year, the fall Oktoberfest and the Saint Patrick's Day dinner in the spring.

As enjoyable as such community-building events are, they are simply not as central to the culture of Saint Margaret Mary. Without doubt, this parish is focused not only on liturgy but also on what parishioners consider to be a more reverent, solemn, and, according to most, a more authentic liturgy. Two weekend masses (Saturday at 5 PM and Sunday at 8:30 AM), in accordance with Vatican II's transition to the use of the vernacular, are celebrated in English. Better attended, though, are the two later Sunday masses, which tend to attract more traditionalist—often, interestingly, younger couples with numerous (typically home-schooled) children—from both near and frequently quite far away. The first of these is the 10:30 AM *Novus ordo* Mass, the seldom-used Mass, revised at the council, that is sung in Latin by both priest and laity. The second, established by special permission of Bishop John Cummins in 1989, is the preconciliar Latin Mass (using the Roman Missal of 1962) celebrated at 12:30 PM. It is now the parish's best-attended weekly liturgy.

At none of these masses will one hear opening jokes or pop culture references from homilists. There is no hand-holding during the Lord's Prayer or handshakes when the priest offers a sign of peace. One looks in vain for a tantrumy child, someone in overly casual or revealing dress, or a subtle wave from one parishioner to another after receiving the Eucharist (while kneeling, not standing). Almost without exception, however, parishioners have stories about witnessing such putative transgressions at other churches where they have worshipped. Not here, though. Here worship—especially at the two Latin masses—is especially solemn, and it is central to the parish's overall identity as the place where liturgy is still done "correctly."

This, of course, relates to another element of this collective identity: its countercultural tenor. Parishioners generally eschew claims of progressiveness, and much of their identity is actually forged in contradistinction to what they see as the therapeutic and relativist nature of progressivism, as well as the amoral and alarmingly secular character of contemporary American society as a whole. They are not about attracting new parishioners by making the faith more appealing to them. They are not about meeting people's emotional, social or, in short, nonsacramental needs. They have collections for various Catholic charitable and religious institutions. However, as the $300 (of a nearly $200,000 annual budget) allotted for "parish charity" attests, they are not about social ministries. They are, however, about the miracle of the Mass and a traditional version of Catholicism that, in their eyes, others trivialize, which in turn engenders among Saint Margaret Mary parishioners a sense of cultural resistance.

Most Holy Redeemer

At first glance, one might assume that Saint Margaret Mary and Most Holy Redeemer would have absolutely nothing in common. Even something as simple as stepping into these two churches is to experience a startling contrast. When entering the first, one leaves the quiet neighborhood overlooking the Interstate and is immediately confronted by a life-size statue of Our Lady of Fatima, and, in the darkening distance, one can see the elaborate altar set apart from the pews facing it. At Most Holy Redeemer, though, one steps inside and leaves behind the exuberant din of the restaurants, bars, and the lively street scene that makes the predominantly gay and lesbian Castro District one of the most electric and distinctive neighborhoods in San Francisco. Upon entering this church, one is struck by the high ceilings and clean, stately look of its Edwardian architecture; one is also a bit dazzled by its lemon-yellow interior highlighted everywhere by bright white moldings. The first thing one encounters here is a huge granite bowl (with baptismal font) filled with holy water. On the alcove wall directly across from this is a long scroll on which is written the many names of parishioners who have died of AIDS. Peering in further, one notices that the low podium on which the altar sits extends into the very center of the church, surrounded by pews arranged in a horseshoe-shaped layout.

If first impressions are not enough, then learning that about three-quarters of this approximately one-thousand-member church identify themselves as gay or lesbian would be enough for most observers to conclude that this parish and Saint Margaret Mary are total opposites. But, by relying on first impressions, one would miss an important commonality. As at Saint Margaret Mary, the culture of Most Holy Redeemer has an oppositional tone. Here the parish culture is resistant to what is perceived (and, according to most parishioners, often experienced) as society's heteronormativity and, even in California, persistent homophobia. Moreover, while parishioners at Saint Margaret Mary often cast themselves in resistance to what they see as the post–Vatican II church's excessive embrace of contemporary trends, here the resistance is to a church hierarchy that, in the words of a recent church document, deems homosexuality to be "objectively disordered." This sense of opposition also extends to a wider gay community that, in the estimation of many at Most Holy Redeemer, has—albeit understandably, in their view—largely rejected religion and, in doing so, given short shrift to an essential component of human experience.

Of course, this parish was not always known, as it is now, as one where members can be both openly gay and resiliently Catholic. Established in 1900 to serve the Irish, Italian, and German families living in what was then known as Eureka Valley, the parish was located on what, for a while at least, were the quiet outskirts of a fast-growing city. Shortly after the Second World War, with the combined forces of expanding urbanization and the development of new roads enabling the white middle class to exchange this neighborhood for bedroom communities elsewhere, the parish lost many of its members, and, before long, it was unquestionably dying. At about the same time, attracted by the relatively cheap Queen Anne and Victorian homes, possibilities for opening new businesses, and the tolerant atmosphere of 1960s-era San Francisco, a burgeoning gay enclave established itself in the neighborhood. This initially did little to change Most Holy Redeemer's near-moribund condition. The parish became an occasional lightning rod for gay activists angry at the church, and the church, in turn, did not especially welcome its new neighbors. But this finally changed in the early 1980s with the arrival of new, more progressive parish leadership. In 1982 an energetic gay and lesbian outreach committee began efforts throughout the neighborhood, and, with the establishment in 1985 of the parish's widely respected AIDS support group, Most Holy Redeemer turned a corner, became better connected to gay and lesbian Catholics in the neighborhood (and eventually beyond), and began to grow significantly.

That it now functions as a magnet parish for a membership that is largely gay and lesbian is not the only unusual thing about Most Holy Redeemer. Although it resembles some other parishes in this study by being mostly white with a considerable minority of Asians and Latinos, a full three-quarters of the parishioners are male, about half are single, about one-third are in same-sex marriages or "domestic partnerships," and there are very few children in this parish. Talk of the church as being composed of "gays and grays" is also fairly accurate—about half of its members are older than fifty-five years of age, and many of these are elderly straight couples (or often widows) who have been in the parish for decades. Also noteworthy is the high educational attainment of the parishioners. Nearly three-quarters have a college degree, about one-third have at least some graduate-level education, and, accounting for their marked theological sophistication, just fewer than one in ten have at least some seminary education.

At Mass—especially the main 10 AM Sunday Mass, which is followed by a very lively and well-attended fellowship hour—people are just as likely to sing loudly and pray (often kneeling) fervently as they are to hold the hand of a same-sex partner or friend and, during the sign of peace, to kiss that person affectionately. The parish prides itself on its inclusiveness and its outreach through initiatives like the AIDS support group (which provides emotional comfort and in-house assistance to people with the disease), the Wednesday night suppers that feed the local homeless population, and the reconnecting program that focuses on Catholics who, like many current parishioners at some point in their lives, have disaffiliated from the church. For a parish with a small staff (two priests and three laypeople) and a tight budget (due largely to a recent renovation necessitated by earthquake damage), there are plenty of typically volunteer-initiated small groups and activities at Most Holy Redeemer. The ones people mention first, though, are those that focus on the needs of people they consider—akin to how they often consider themselves—to be somehow marginalized within the larger community.

Ce N'est Pas le Catholicisme Américain

We human beings are "cultured" in that we relentlessly order and evaluate our reality through symbols. To disregard this would be to lose sight of the meaning-making drama always unfolding before and enacted by us. It would also mean being blind to the reality that philosopher Ernst Cassirer's *animal symbolicum* is truly, in the end, *homo fides*.[44] The symbolic animal is the person of faith in the sense that culture—the symbolic world that we construct, in which we reside, and which, in more ways than we can ever fully know, resides in us—orders our existence largely to the extent that it is a matter of collective fidelity. This is also the case because what we endeavor to encapsulate within our symbolic world is, like the horizon spilling before us, ceaselessly widening. Beyond the culturally constructed norms of classroom etiquette, beyond gender role expectations, beyond the tacitly pre-scribed behavioral codes of elevator ridership—in short, beyond the routinizing of ordinary interactions we also, however gropingly, name, define, and narrate the extraordinary, that which we consider ultimately significant. What is worthwhile? What is just? Who is God? Such questions summon us beyond the hum of everyday life and toward attempts to symbolize that which we experience as transcending it.

What is true of human beings generally is surely no less true of American Catholics in particular. Nonetheless, we can forget this by giving in to the popular but hidebound assumption that the laity are less religious now than they were at some previous time. Often this conviction is derived from privileging one iteration of American Catholicism—a process eased somewhat by romanticization or selec-tive memory—perceiving it as normative, and dubbing whatever differs from it as perforce less religious. But more nuance is needed here. If, as rhetorician Kenneth Burke once observed, "every way of seeing is a way of not seeing," then investigating religiosity merely through the analytical lenses of "same," "more," and "less" is to leave far too much unseen.[45] Seeing more is possible if we replace these lenses with one that focuses on how Catholics continually negotiate cultural meanings. Seeing in this way, in other words, is to acknowledge that Catholics see the world through cultural categories that, insofar as they are always in flux, engender newfound ways of thinking through and enacting their religious identities. Not "same," not "more," and, despite the prevailing opinion, not "less"—American Catholics are actually differently religious because, like other human beings, their connectedness to the sacred is shaped by culture, and culture is constantly in motion.

Within American secular society, religious culture is significantly liberated from steering other public institutions and is now far more *available* as a symbolic cache through which expressivity and meaning making are largely facilitated. At the same time, individuals, Catholics included, are freer than ever to *appropriate* whatever religious and other symbols they consider most fitting to advance their own life plans and cobble together their own sense of the sacred. As they do this, they do not have access to the totality of religious culture, which is always unevenly distributed. The parishioners in this study, for instance, gain access to religious cul-ture through parishes that are more apt to *allocate* some aspects of the broader religious tradition to them than others.

In the course of tracking this these realities, I have seen my own seeing through a number of cultural frames. At first, I saw myself as a sociological Jane Goodall—"Catholics in the Mist"—until I realized that, rather than primarily observing, I was spending most of my time actually talking with my subjects. Then I likened myself to a sociological detective, a kind of Durkheimian Sherlock Holmes meticulously searching for clues to unlock the mystery of American Catholic culture and iden-tity. As dashing and, to be frank, self-aggrandizing as this analogy was, it was not particularly helpful given the fact that, unlike the master sleuth, who was always able to unravel a case once and for all, the manner in which people live out their faiths is not so "elementary." Rather, it is always changing, taking interpretive twists and turns, and thus never amenable to dramatically announced final verdicts.

This is why I now see my own seeing in terms of an art lover. Rather than the art critic, who proclaims one expression superior to another, I aim to be more globally appreciative. Moreover, like the art lover who earnestly tries to describe a beautiful painting to a friend, I know that this book on American Catholicism does not capture its totality. While based on laborious research, it is still a description, a recounting, an earnestly wrought representation derived from a "cultured" being and thus reflects a limited range of vision presented through a finite set of analyti-cal categories. Perhaps this is obvious to most readers. What may be less obvious is that the story I recount is itself based on the accounts Catholic parishioners give of themselves. What they say about God, the church, community, and their very selves are not those things, but their own fleeting representations of those things. Like the painting of some curvy pipe, they are expressions, and, like the art lover, I am nevertheless and quite appreciatively drawn to these expressions—to the color and texture, the never-straight lines, and even to the cursively painted words that must always caption the cultural tableau: *Ce n'est pas le catholicisme américain.* This is an appropriate reminder simply because there exists no one thing called American Catholicism. Rather than being something *to which* someone can point, it is actu-ally a confluence of symbols, practices, and narratives *with which* people point to their multiform sense of the sacred, which, in turn, always evades whatever frames are used to depict it. Still, I am drawn. I want to know this work as well as the expe-riences from which it originates. So, in the next four chapters—which focus on the broad cultural strokes of self, institution, community, and civil society—I lean in closer to investigate more carefully.

PART II

Leaning Closer: Examining the Brushstrokes

3

Self

Rooting and Uprooting

Sacralizing the Self: The Need for Roots

Vietnamese Martyrs

Even in the temperate East Bay, mornings in late November can be chilly, especially when the fog creeps in and nestles along the avenues and between the buildings in and around downtown Oakland. This particular Sunday morning was like that. Getting out of my car, I could see my breath mingle with the vaporous gray that shrouded the entire neighborhood. The whole scene came alive unexpectedly when, turning onto Jefferson Street, I noticed first not Saint Mary–Saint Francis de Sales's imposing church building but its rear parking lot ablaze in color. I saw priests in blood-red vestments; twenty or so women in red-and-gold traditional Vietnamese dress bearing similarly colored banners; men in bright purple traditional dress carrying the crucifix, the Bible, musical instruments, and decorative umbrellas and holding aloft a large pagoda-like shrine loaded with flowers of all kinds; young girls in traditional dress of various colors; boys wearing white shirts with red ties; and scores of other parishioners in their usual Sunday attire. Although quite a sight, when they began to move, it was really the sound that was most striking. As everyone walked around the church, the booming drums and clash-clanking cymbals announced to all (who could not help but listen) that, although it might appear otherwise, this neighborhood—even the weed-riven, crumbling sidewalks they walked upon, even the newspaper pages and other litter gusting past them, and even the vandalized and partly stripped car and the bail bonds office they marched by—was truly holy ground.

Inside, the church was completely filled with people, mostly Vietnamese families, as well as members of the other two (one mostly Anglo, the other mostly Filipino) worship communities. Usually the twelve large, stained-glass windows and the beautiful plaques representing the various Stations of the Cross are the first to catch one's eye. But, amid the vibrant costumes, banners, and flowers, today these were scarcely noticeable and, in any case, now seemed somewhat drab by comparison. Usually the choir—this one singing in Vietnamese—encourages a reverential mood. But as the procession continued up the center aisle, the entire building was shaken by a thunderous bass drum. Usually the wooden scent emanating from the pews and floorboards dominates. This morning, though, it was the smell of incense, which was solemnly carried around the main altar and then to the pagoda-like shrine, which had been placed in front of the bas-relief representation of the 117 Vietnamese Catholic martyrs canonized together in 1988. Customarily, too, the Mass begins promptly and often rather abruptly. However, on this day, as the traditional dancers still themselves and as the choir sings more softly, the three concelebrating priests linger by this shrine. They bow and pray and offer incense until the martyrs, who are depicted standing together in the alcove, come to look as though they, like the parishioners in the parking lot moments earlier, are enveloped in a wispy morning fog.

The parish calls masses like this one "union liturgies" because they unite the three worship communities. Yet, this particular one also unites those in attendance with the Vietnamese martyrs themselves. This connection became more evident as the Mass continued. The first reading from the prophet Ezekiel, read in Tagalog, likened God to a shepherd. "As a shepherd tends his flock when he finds himself among his scattered sheep, so will I tend my sheep," the passage begins and, a few verses later, concludes with the reminder that "As for you, my sheep, says the Lord, I will judge between one sheep and another, between rams and goats." Proclaimed in English, the second reading (from Saint Paul's first epistle to the Corinthians) similarly dealt with themes of hardship, as well as God's care and ultimate justice. "For just as in Adam all die," the lector announced, "so too in Christ shall all be brought to life, but each one in proper order: Christ the first fruits; then, at his coming, those who belong to Christ; then comes the end, when he hands over the kingdom to his God and Father, when he has destroyed every sovereignty and every authority and power." Finally, one of the priests read the gospel aloud in Vietnamese. This was the portion of Matthew's crucifixion account of how Jesus was flanked by two criminals, one reviling him and the other asking that he be remembered "when you come into your kingdom."

In each of these cases, the hardship borne by only some of the sheep, only "those who belong to Christ," and by only one criminal and not the other—by those, in other words, who remain or become faithful in the face of suffering—is ultimately rewarded. The faithful at Saint Mary–Saint Francis de Sales are encouraged to embrace this same understanding of the world and to identify with the 117 martyrs, who exemplified fidelity in the face of death. This does not mean, of course, that these parishioners must literally seek martyrdom. Rather, as the church bulletin illustrates, martyrdom is reframed in a manner that makes it more relevant and manageable. "Their [the 117 martyrs'] martyrdom teaches us Christians that our lives are precious, but if we will live the Gospel we must be courageous enough to escape from our passion for materialism and desire for luxury a little every day," it instructs them. "Also, we must get ourselves involved in the struggle of protecting faith, justice, and human rights in our country and in the whole world."

Just as those gathered are united with the Vietnamese martyrs through this more achievable sense of martyrdom, most are also united with them as Vietnamese. The music, dancing, clothing, language, shrines (one with a metallic cutout in the shape of Vietnam), and banners all conjured up a sensibility that was distinctly Vietnamese. The Mass carved out a space in which that ethnic identity could be manifested and even sacralized. If this were not enough, then surely the celebration in the parking lot after the Mass made this even more apparent. Complete with music and dancing performed mostly by children, as well as lots of Vietnamese food prepared by the parents, it enabled the parishioners to be Catholic together and, for some, to enact their ethnic identity in an unabashed manner not always available to them within mainstream American society.

Celebrating Black History

Stepping into Saint Louis Bertrand church at 9 AM on a Sunday morning is like being transported to another place. Away from the boarded-up shops and garish fast-food restaurants; away from the men already gathering in front of liquor stores and the prostitutes strolling their routes along International Avenue; away from the trucks, buses, and blaring car stereos—to enter this cavernously rounded church is to be suddenly whisked into the company of familiar, welcoming faces and to be drenched in yellow light slanting in from the tinted windows looming high above. People meander and then quickstep from pew to pew, dispensing hugs and waves and sharing laughter. Nothing new there. In fact, this will be repeated later in the Mass when, in lieu of a simple handshake and in keeping with the informal tenor of the parish, the sign of peace becomes a prolonged and garrulous meet-and-greet session. Still, indications were that this first Sunday in February was special. Draped in the front of the church was a hundred-foot-long kente cloth. Prominently seated in the front two center pews were several members of Saint Peter Claver Ladies Auxiliary and a few teenaged Daughters of Saint Peter Claver, all dressed entirely in white with either white fez-style caps adorned with tassels or white lace head coverings. Then, as the twenty-member children's choir sang "Kum Ba Yah, My Lord," four altar servers, all girls, proceeded down the center aisle carrying a crucifix, an American flag, and another banner bearing colors that typically appear on African national flags (green, black, yellow, and red). They were followed by the presiding priest, dressed in vestments of those same colors.

Special indeed. It was the first Sunday of Black History Month. As the missal explained, this week focused on "celebrating youth leaders and educators." Subsequent weeks would be dedicated to black business leaders, family traditions, and, during the last week in February, a celebration of black worship traditions. Each week the Mass would be followed by a brunch in the charter school's cafeteria (next to the church), during which local vendors would sell figurines, cosmetics, and, most prominently, African crafts and prints depicting events and heroes from African American history. Like the annual crab feed the weekend before, Black History Month has been celebrated at the parish as long as anyone can remember, and most black parishioners enthusiastically regard it as one of the highlights of the year.

This enthusiasm was certainly evident at that first week's Mass, as were a couple of ironies. The first was that, scattered throughout the only side of the largely empty church that was actually open, fewer than half of the approximately 150 people in attendance at this black history celebration were black. Three of the four altar servers, about half of the children's choir, and many of those seated in the pews were Latinos. And, especially in light of the week's youth emphasis, the fact that only a few African American children were present made the frequently heard complaint that the church was failing to attract the younger generation all the more credible.

Another irony was that there was precious little black history recollected during the Mass. On the walls and bulletin boards in the church foyer and elsewhere were numerous copies of a poster that depicted "100 Great African Americans." There were pamphlets that recounted the lives of Martin Luther King Jr. and the recently deceased Coretta Scott King. Everyone seemed to have a copy of a one-page handout that listed items—the traffic light, the guitar, the pencil sharpener, the air conditioner, and so forth—invented by African Americans, all of which fall under the rubric of "facts you weren't taught in school." Interestingly, though, there was no effort to look to the past during the liturgy. Contrary to the Vietnamese martyrs Mass, the hardships that blacks had once endured were not mentioned. Nor were these sufferings or their present-day equivalents connected to the wisdom of the past as expressed in the three scripture passages for the day, two of which were read too softly to be audible and none of which were alluded to later.

Instead of looking to the community's past, the morning's theme was a call to surmount one's personal shortcomings and defeatist attitudes, which were presumed to be in abundance, and then take responsibility for creating a brighter future. "Freedom is never given; it is won," read the quote by A. Philip Randolph on the commemorative bookmark distributed to those in attendance. Also distributed was a poem written by Edgar A. Guest, purported to be George Washington Carver's favorite, extolling the capacity of all who earnestly apply themselves to succeed in the world. It concludes with the following stanza: "Courage must come from the soul within, the man must furnish the will to win. So figure it out for yourself, my lad, you were born with all that the great have had. With your equipment they all began, get ahold of yourself and say: 'I can.'" This same "I can" trope appeared in yet another handout, this one an excerpt from Nelson Mandela's 1994 inaugural speech. "Our deepest fear is not that we are inadequate," it begins. "Our deepest fear is that we are powerful beyond measure. It is our light, not our darkness, that most frightens us. We ask ourselves, 'Who am I to be brilliant, gorgeous, talented and fabulous?' Actually, who are you *not* to be? You are a child of God. Your playing small doesn't serve the world."

This theme was reiterated throughout the Mass. For example, instead of the typical "Lord, hear our prayer" response to the Prayers of the Faithful, the lectors spoke of young parishioners' "failure to obey parents," which was followed by the unusual collective response, "We beg for your mercy." They also spoke of "giving in to the temptations of the body and of weak wills," followed by "We beg for your mercy." They delineated numerous examples of "failing to do the right thing," once again followed by "We beg for your mercy." Similarly, the homily delivered by the young, Nigerian-born priest, Father Mulemi, revolved around a thoroughgoing presumption of strife and disempowerment within the African American community. "Dreams don't come true unless you empower yourself," "black history means never giving up," "freedom is a task that doesn't end until you defeat your biggest enemy, sin," he told them, assuming that such reminders were necessary and applicable to those who listened. Not inclined to delve into these matters in much detail, Father Mulemi echoed Martin Luther King Jr. by looking beyond the hardships of the present. "I have a dream that as a community we can one day free East Oakland from the grip of drugs," he announced. "I have a dream that East Oakland can overcome the violence it sees daily. I have a dream that we will take the time to make sure our kids stay on the right path. I have a dream that we can learn to face life's difficulties and succeed, knowing that we ourselves are black history."

Father Mulemi went on like this for some time. He did not particularly focus on who his African Americans parishioners, beyond certain presumptions about them, really are. Nor, even at the outset of Black History Month, did he overly concern himself with who they had been. Rather, his emphasis was on who they should be. The effect was to acknowledge the strains evident in the African American experience and embed them within a broader narrative that gives them meaning. In one way, this is quite different from what occurred at the Vietnamese martyrs Mass. There the uprootedness of the immigrant and the outsider status of the ethnic minority were situated within a broader narrative that reached into the distant past. The difficulties of their everyday lives were connected to scripture, to a communion of seventeenth-to-nineteenth-century martyrs, and, in short, to a meaning-conferring past that served as a prism for understanding the present reality of Vietnamese Catholics in West Oakland. In East Oakland, however, Father Mulemi drew his parishioners' attention to a meaning-conferring future that, although presently accessible only as a dream, situates their African American identity within an unfolding story that tells of far better times ahead. Of course, the one thing these two narratives have in common is that, regardless of whether they are told in the past or the future tense, they are truly sacred stories. They root the Vietnamese and African American self within the cosmic drama and within a collective understanding of what God is doing in the world.

Modern Rootlessness and the Cultivation of the Catholic Self

These churches attempt to root the self within the broader context of divine purpose. Significant theologically, their efforts reflect a frequently overlooked "this-worldly" quality of the Catholic tradition, whereby individuals and communities have the capacity to discern God's purposes and even to assist in bringing them to fruition.[1] They are also important for more immediate reasons. Attempts to root the self within a meaningful past or future have become especially critical in light of the seeming rootlessness of modern life. Reflecting the felt precariousness of the contemporary self, the "vocabulary of human deficit" has come to proliferate virtually unabated.[2] Anorexic, antisocial, anxious, authoritarian, bulimic, burned out, compulsive, depressed, externally controlled—on and on goes the alphabetized lexicon through which we have learned to experience ourselves as deficient. Sensitive to such deficiencies and in light of the fact that the "identity crisis" has become a normative facet of individual development within only the last few decades, we have now become anything but deficient in our yen for inner investigation.[3] This is why, since only the 1960s, there has been a similarly robust growth in the number of hyphenated words that reveal our fixation on scrutinizing ourselves: self-fulfillment, self-acceptance, self-esteem, self-actualization, self-expression, self-image, self-awareness, and self-identity.[4]

The social sources of this rootlessness are various. For example, no longer steered by an overarching religious worldview, society's different social institutions often engender a sense of fragmentation because, on any given day, we interact within a number of them, which call forth equally different iterations of our own identities.[5] Serially citizen, customer, parent, religious adherent, and so forth, we find that the experience of a unified sense of self can be hard to come by.[6] Another source is the personal destabilization that comes from what philosopher Jean-Paul Sartre called the sheer "vertigo" of seemingly infinite possibilities for selfhood.[7] The greater occupational and lifestyle choices available to us, as well as the mass media's role in populating our consciousnesses with both real and fictional others, remind us of the arbitrariness and partiality of our own identities. In addition, with the waning of communally reinforced social roles and norms, even our ability to confidently choose from among the possibilities for selfhood is frequently undermined by an accompanying "dissipation of objectivity."[8] As a result, one experiences less certainty about things, tends to have a "perspective" on this or that, and makes life choices with a more provisional ("until further notice") quality about them.

While provocative, insights such as these miss another, far more generative side of the self's rootlessness. In other words, the very same challenges to identity construction also lead to quests for meaning that owe much of their form and content to the fragmented, destabilized, and uncertain experience of self that is now pervasive. Though we may have lost the strongly prescribed identities that largely characterized tightly bounded societies of the past, in their place has emerged a generalized concern for individual authenticity. This language of authenticity reflects people's still unextinguished desire to do the often difficult work of discovering a sense of meaningfulness that is now not so readily attainable.[9]

This is why sociologist Anthony Giddens is correct in his assessment that "in the context of the post-traditional order, the self becomes a reflexive project."[10] By "reflexive," Giddens means that, increasingly aware of the relative rootlessness of individual identity, people are inclined to carve out their sense of self in a very intentional, continuously revisable, and self-conscious manner. Sensing themselves as "cultured" in the representational sense described in chapter 2, they frequently take it upon themselves to appropriate whichever symbolic meanings resonate most with who they want to be in the world. Moreover, as the word "project" suggests, this cultural work—or this process of negotiating with the cultural meanings available to us—requires considerable effort over time. The irony is that, even in the posttraditional order Giddens describes, this project of identity construction often involves people's attempts to reflexively engage the age-old religious traditions that are most familiar to them.[11]

This is because these traditions bear overarching stories, and being "storied" is fundamental to having a particular identity.[12] It is to situate oneself within a coherent cultural narrative that makes sense of one's world, defines one's place within it, and provides information about what things we should accomplish, avoid, and even hope for during (and perhaps beyond) the course of a lifetime. "In order to have a sense of who we are," notes philosopher Charles Taylor in his important book on the modern self, "we have to have a notion of how we have become, and of where we are going."[13] This, of course, is no less true of the Catholic self, which is situated within a story about how the faithful have come from God and, as announced and manifested in the person of Jesus Christ, how they are also heading toward a fuller realization of the divine purpose, which is best expressed by the symbol of the "kingdom of God."

This story is not simply told and heard, however; it is also lived. As such, it shapes the identities of individual communities that, since they have their own distinctive histories, come to reinterpret that broader story in their own unique ways. The local church cultures then retain the symbols, metaphors, and practices borne of these "little stories." As illustrated by the commemoration of the Vietnamese martyrs (which, as Taylor would have it, puts the emphasis on "how we have become") and Black History Month (which chiefly emphasizes "where we are going"), these meanings are offered to parish-based Catholics, who then appropriate whichever elements of these stories resonate with their own experiences and particular sensibilities.

An important aspect of this ongoing appropriation of Catholic culture is that it never occurs in a vacuum. Among active parishioners like the ones interviewed for this book, it is largely done within their churches. More than that, though, it is also done quite relationally. People learn how to be Catholic by being told the story of how they are connected to the sacred, by putting that story into practice in their daily lives, and, crucially, by interacting with and comparing themselves to other Catholics. Through their relationships with others they acquire what social theorist Pierre Bourdieu calls "a feel for the game," a sense of how culture—in this case, Catholic culture—can be accessed, deployed, and improvised amid changing circumstances.[14] Like the basketball player who intuitively knows how to drive toward the basket even when faced with a configuration of players on the court he has never exactly seen before, having a feel for the symbols of the larger Christian story is to have an intuitive sense of how to use them in innovative ways in novel situations. It is to undertake the project of self-consciously rooting the self within a modern world marked by a novel sense of rootlessness.

In short, when people have a feel for this particular game, it means they have attained the requisite cultural competence to negotiate with their religious tradition. Parishioners acquire this by paying attention to how others live out their faiths. They also do it by taking stock of the things they hear others say, even when they might not agree with what has been said. They hear certain scripts again and again, and these help them to better consolidate and express their own identities as Catholics. Sometimes these can be as elaborated as accounts of what the Eucharist means to them or why it was (or was not) important for them to be married in the church. At other times, these can be seemingly simple phrases that, upon closer scrutiny, actually reveal key areas of identity negotiation. Like archeologists sifting through large bins of dirt to discover shards of pottery left by some ancient civilization, the careful sifter of discourse finds what I call conversational shards, which continually appear in parishioners' interactions with one another and represent important loci of cultural improvisation. Dusting off a few of these and examining them more closely should enable us to appreciate the subtle means by which Catholics attempt to root themselves within a sacred and ultimately sacralizing narrative.

Some Conversational Shards Unearthed

"My Faith"

When parishioners describe themselves as Catholic, it is interesting to discover what they do not say. Rarely does one detect references to "Catholicism" (much less "Roman Catholicism" or "American Catholicism") or to "the Catholic faith" or, as one would more likely hear in a religious studies classroom, to a "Catholic worldview." Rather, they say things like "my faith is very important to me." Or they might confide that "I don't know where I'd be without my faith." After a bit of reflection, they might also say something akin to "my faith has really grown over the years" and, as one woman added wryly, "whether I've wanted it to or not!" This, they and so many others suggest, is not about systematic theology or magisterial teachings or reciting the prayers correctly. It is about faith in things unseen and the worth of a sacred narrative that has yet to unfold completely. As the essential modifier "my" attests, it is also deeply personal and, as such, quite fluid.

One might conclude that this simply reflects a shift to what sociologist Robert Wuthnow calls a "seeker-orientated spirituality." Contrasted with a previously dominant "dwelling-orientated" style focused on firm commitments to churches and traditional beliefs, this spiritual style privileges journeying over steadfastness, questioning over obedience, and a commitment to personal growth at the expense of one's obligations to the gathered community.[15] This cultural shift is real. Yet, even though it seems to be in full bloom across the American religious landscape, it does not fully capture the complexity of the situation. These parishioners are actually hybrids of sorts. They are what might be labeled "indwelt seekers"—quite active within and loyal to their institution but with the caveat that the faith they hold dear must resonate with their own experience and make sense to them on their own terms.[16]

For instance, one might be tempted to read the first two items in table 3.1 and conclude that Bay Area Catholics, as well as Catholics nationally (whose response rates are shown in parentheses), simply mirror the cultural shift that Wuthnow describes. After all, if the Vatican's teaching authority (Item 1) can serve as a credible proxy for his dwelling type and spirituality and personal growth (Item 2) can do so

TABLE 3.1. "As a Catholic, how important is each of the following to you?" (in %).

	Very important	Somewhat important	Not important at all
1. The teaching authority claimed by the Vatican	38 (42)	44 (47)	18 (10)
2. Spirituality and personal growth	89 (78)	11 (20)	0 (2)
3. The sacraments, such as the Eucharist and marriage	87 (76)	11 (20)	1 (4)
4. The spirit of community among Catholics	82 (65)	17 (30)	1 (4)
5. Church involvement in activities directed towards social justice and helping the poor	79 (72)	21 (25)	0 (3)
6. Getting involved in parish groups and activities	59	38	3

Note: When available, national percentages (in parentheses) may not add up to 100 since "Don't know" and "Refused to answer" categories are not recorded here. National percentages for items 1 and 3 are from D'Antonio et al. (2007), while items 2, 4, and 5 are taken from D'Antonio et al. (2001). Parish data may also not add up to 100 percent due to rounding off.

for the seeking type, then the fact that a modest 38 percent and a full 89 percent of parishioners consider these to be "very important," respectively, could easily lead one to surmise that Catholics are making a wholesale trade of one spiritual style for another.

Nevertheless, this would be an oversimplification. As table 3.1 also reveals, large percentages of Catholics report that other credible indicators of the dwelling style—sacraments (Item 3), community (Item 4), and involvement in activities within and beyond the parish (Items 5 and 6)—are also "very important" to them. As distinctly active parishioners, the Bay Area respondents report that this is even more the case for themselves than it is for American Catholics as a whole.

Sarah Henslin is a good example of someone who has long found a spiritual home within the church. A thirty-five-year-old religious studies teacher at a Catholic high school in San Francisco and active in the children's faith-formation and liturgy programs at Saint Mary–Saint Francis de Sales parish, she is deeply committed to Catholic institutions and to many traditional Catholic ideas and practices. "In my view," she says, "a good Catholic is someone who prays, who commits himself or herself to a faith community, who participates in the sacraments, and I think there has to be some level of commitment to justice, to the most vulnerable in our society." Getting more personal, she continues: "I was never a twenty-something who kind of went away from going to church. I've always gone to church on a regular basis—every Sunday. But, as I've gotten older, I think more about the meaning of baptism and of the Eucharist, and I think they're about looking at the world with a sense of awe and wonder, at the beauty of God's creation and God's presence in everything. I mean, my faith is really so tied up in this sacramental sense of God being present with us." It would be difficult to imagine someone whose sense of the sacred resides more comfortably within a Catholic framework. Nonetheless, tied up in this sense of sacramentalism is what she tellingly labels "my faith." When asked to expand upon this, she adds:

> I don't think I'm a relativist or a cafeteria Catholic by any means. For me, trying to decide what church teachings to agree with is a product of measuring people's experiences and measuring my own experience. When I do that I bring to it a sense of prayer and faith in a God who becomes human and reminds us that, if there's a complex human condition, then there's a complex God. So, when we talk about human behavior and sin and grace, we need to remember that it's all so murky and mucky, that things are not so clear-cut but that there's also a richness in that. Also, I feel like there's a space to engage all this at this parish and, therefore, to grow in faith. I think there's a strong, shared sense that being a good Catholic also means to practice discernment and judgment and to make decisions based on a well-informed conscience.

Although dwelling firmly within the institutional church, Henslin exhibits an equally serious commitment to her own seeking. She is the one who decides which church teachings are valid, based on the extent to which they square with her and others' life experiences. Her faith is described in the most active of terms—she wants to engage others in her parish, she needs to deploy her own powers of discernment and judgment, and she expects to grow in faith. Finally, her religious self simply cannot be passive because she knows that the world's complexities are not effectively accessed through lethargy. Obscured in murkiness and muckiness, deeper insights about the world and about God can be reached only by actively making her own careful decisions about how best to be a religious person.

Critically, this approach—detailed by Henslin and many others within these six Bay Area churches—should not be confused with the one perhaps best captured in the increasingly pervasive American mantra: "I'm not religious, I'm more spiritual." There are similarities, of course. Equipped and encouraged to do so by a religious culture informed by Americans' well-known distrust of institutions and vaunted individualism, many parishioners distinguish what they consider to be "religious" from what they typically commend as more "spiritual." They generally do so to differentiate whatever dogmatisms, hypocrisies, and ecclesial irrelevancies they detect in the former from the sense of deep, personal meaning evoked by the latter. Whereas the "religious," they often explain, smacks of the institution and its ongoing maintenance, spirituality has an "experientialist" quality.[17] It feels more relevant to them, more individually expressive, and hence more real. But these parishioners, perhaps unlike their less active counterparts, do not simply throw the Bible out with the bathwater. When they differentiate between religion and spirituality, it is not to reject religious institutions. By identifying themselves as more spiritual than religious, they mean to describe their personal faith as a connection to the sacred that both dwells within a single religious tradition and, at the same time, continues in its seeking. It is fluid, with a yet-to-be-realized goal. To have faith is to aspire, as Henslin puts it, "to grow in faith."

Spiritual growth is typically framed in one of three ways. For some, it means acquiring greater knowledge. Take, for instance, Kelly Schutt, who is active in the women's Bible study group at Saint Augustine's parish. "This could be very immature spiritually, and maybe that's where I am," she confesses when asked about how Catholicism relates to other world religions, "but this is what fills me, and I don't think I need to worry too much about how other people find their faith." After describing herself as a strong Catholic, she comes back to this theme: "I don't agree with everything the church teaches, but this is where I found my faith. So, for me, a strong Catholic is somebody who's continuously trying to gain knowledge in their faith. I read, and I try to understand as many customs and traditions as I can. And I've got books next to my bed. I'm constantly looking things up because I strive to understand what it is to be a Catholic. I think it's important, but I really haven't figured it all out yet."

Others are just as forthcoming as Schutt about not having figured it all out yet. However, for them, growing as a Catholic is more about action than knowledge. Jeramy Faris, one of the main organizers of Most Holy Redeemer's Wednesday night suppers for local homeless people, evaluates his actions with an eye toward his own spiritual growth. "I consider myself a Catholic who tries hard," he says, "but I'm aware of just how short of the mark I usually fall." Describing why this does not give him a low opinion of himself, he says:

> Somehow I dust myself off and get sent on my way again. I feel immensely loved by God. I feel encouraged by God. And I feel forgiven by God when I need forgiveness, which is about once an hour. I can see in the way we're created that even our best efforts can lead to something undesirable, whereas I also see how faults, how vanity, how covetousness can be used to lead us to very good things. So I don't think anyone ever attains absolute goodness. I think we learn about what this is by doing. We try to gear ourselves toward it while realizing how unobtainable it is and forgive ourselves for not being "it."

Third, there are people like Diane Huff, who regularly meets with other Saint Monica parishioners to provide them with spiritual direction. She equates growing in faith with experiencing and more fully entering into a loving relationship with God. "People are hungry," she insists. "They want more of God." And, if this is true of people generally, it is especially true of church leaders:

> They need to have strong prayer lives. They need to have pastoral care for themselves. They need to be on a faith journey. They need to be struggling with their own faith because then they are going to grow, and they're going to understand the needs of other people who are also struggling. The leadership needs to be on this journey because, in my experience, when people realize how much they're loved by God, they are so grateful and so joyous that the automatic response is to love. And, so, if the leadership is doing its spiritual work, they will meet God, and, when they meet God, they will love, and they will be creative, and they'll know what to offer to their congregations.

The Bible study leader, the social activist, and the spiritual director each want to grow in faith because they know they have not yet arrived at their final destinations as Catholics. Moreover, in the absence of clear road signs that mark their journeys, they, like Sarah Henslin, know they need to practice careful discernment. Far more wary than previous generations of religious authority located outside of themselves, they know they need to look within. They realize they must continue to hone a special sensitivity to what "fills" them (Schutt), when they "feel encouraged by God" (Faris), and just how much "they're loved by God" (Huff) if they are to grow and become better persons.

The utter seriousness with which they monitor and evaluate their own growth should keep anyone from dismissively branding them "cafeteria Catholics." The problem with this term is that it both reveals and conceals certain aspects of Catholics' identity construction. What it reveals, of course, is that they indeed exercise their own agency by observing certain components of their tradition and discarding others. A good indicator of this is whether they agree with the statement "It's important to obey church teachings even if I don't understand them" (table 3.2).

With nearly two-thirds expressing some level of disagreement with this statement, it is clear that these parishioners, like the majority (52 percent) of American Catholics, are avowedly selective in their appropriation of church teachings. Table 3.2 also reveals that parish cultures vary greatly in the degree to which they facilitate and even normalize the doctrinal selectivity among parishioners. For example, at Most Holy Redeemer, the politically progressive magnet parish for gays and lesbians, respondents almost universally reject the statement. Similarly, liberal Saint Monica's percentages on this item are nearly the reverse of those one finds among the traditionalist parishioners at Saint Margaret Mary.

TABLE 3.2. "It's important to obey church teachings even if I don't understand them" (in %).

	Strongly agree	Somewhat agree	Somewhat disagree	Strongly disagree
Most Holy Redeemer	0	5	58	38
St. Monica	0	13	67	20
St. Mary–St. Francis de Sales	2	30	51	16
St. Augustine	5	29	45	21
St. Louis Bertrand	14	28	44	14
St. Margaret Mary	37	47	11	5
Total	9 (19)	26 (26)	46 (27)	19 (25)

Note: Percentages listed in parentheses are from the 1995 national survey discussed in Davidson et al. (1997) and available in the Association of Religion Data Archive (http://www.thearda.com/Archive/Files/Descriptions/NATCATH.asp). They are rounded off and do not include the authors' "Not sure" category (2.4%). Parish data may also not add up to 100 percent due to rounding off.

What table 3.2 and the term "cafeteria Catholicism" conceal, however, are the various meanings people assign to this doctrinal selectivity. Often they describe it in a very pejorative way. Many people, for instance, mention cafeteria Catholicism as an indicator of what they are not and of a type of superficial faith that is contrary to their own. Evident to some extent within all of the parishes, this tendency is understandably prevalent at Saint Margaret Mary. There, people are more apt to presume an ideological uniformity among committed Catholics, whom they see as resisting a seeping "do your own thing" mentality within American culture by remaining steadfast in their allegiance to church teaching. In reality, though, even this parish demonstrates plenty of ideological diversity. Of the Saint Margaret Mary parishioners surveyed, the proportion of those who claim that one can be a good Catholic without believing that Jesus physically rose from the dead or that the bread and wine become the actual body and blood of Jesus during the Mass is only 7 percent for each question. In contrast, the proportions who agree that one can be a good Catholic without obeying church teaching on birth control (35 percent), without attending church every Sunday (40 percent), and without getting married in the church (40 percent) are much larger.

Moreover, even when some of Saint Margaret Mary's parishioners castigate what one called the "wishy-washiness of cafeteria Catholicism," they often find it difficult to make good on their own claims of unwavering acceptance of the church's teachings. Sandra Badillo seems to exemplify this difficulty. She is a middle-aged accountant who drives from her bedroom community thirty miles away to attend the Latin Tridentine Mass every Sunday and, as a member of Saint Anne's Guild, spends one Saturday each month decorating and cleaning the church. Like most people at Saint Margaret Mary, she says the Latin Mass seems "more reverential" to her even though, as a Latina, her first language is actually Spanish. She also likes its uniformity. Unlike what she derides as "ethnic masses," in which language and customs are variable, and unlike the homilies at many other parishes where she claims the message differs depending on which priest delivers it, at this parish "it's the same message and same religion for everyone." This is partly due to the use of Latin and the fact that homilies there, which are typically delivered by the same one or two priests, tend to be too general and too brief to display much ideological variation at all.

This is also due, she claims, to the fact that doctrinal selectivity is categorically discouraged in both her family and her parish. "There's the term 'cafeteria Catholicism,' where you can go and pick and choose what you want to believe in," she explains, "but that's not something we feel you have an option to do. It's clear that part of our religion is our faith, and this is about church teachings and, frankly, about following what the church teaches." As clear as this is, things become, to use an earlier expression, increasingly "murky and mucky" when this clear-cut ideal crosses paths with real-life issues. At such points, the phrase "my faith" might actually be the better descriptor of what Badillo vehemently insists is "our faith."

When, for example, she justifies her disagreement with the church's prohibition on the use of contraception, she differentiates between this issue and those that are "core" to the faith, and she also explains that "you can disagree, but you can't go against the church" in any way that converts private dissent into public discord. When Badillo explains her disagreement with the pope's denunciation of the then portending U.S. war with Iraq, she clarifies that he was not speaking ex cathedra and that, if she "researched the issue in more detail," she might one day change her view. When she explains her disagreement with the church's position against capital punishment, she concedes that, "I'll be honest with you: I don't think I'm wrong, but that doesn't mean I'm not wrong." Elaborating somewhat, she says, "I think this is where I'm at on this issue at this point in my life. So I feel like I might have to develop or grow in order to understand this teaching. Something could bring me around to another way of thinking, but I'm just not there right now." Finally, when candidly expressing her fears that her appreciation of "nice things" and her comfortable lifestyle may be making her overly materialistic, she simply exclaims, "That's why I go to confession; you'd be surprised what kind of things I do penance for!"

Since Badillo is hardly a maverick outlier at her church, it seems that the appropriation of Catholic culture among Saint Margaret Mary's parishioners is not so uniform after all. If one scratches the surface of her self-described "conservative religious stance," one discovers plenty of selectivity and desire for personal growth. She is selective in her approach to church teachings (albeit privately so), and, as her reference to confession conveys, she is inconsistent in her capacity to live out even those teachings she considers to be very important. Meanwhile, she envisions a future version of her self that, through such things as researching various social issues and experiencing further religious growth, might one day be in fuller accord with the church's teachings. That is her goal, but, she demurs, "I'm just not there right now."

Wherever she in fact is, it is really not so far from Sarah Henslin, a self-described "liberal with a capital L." Henslin, too, resists the cafeteria Catholic label. Not surprisingly, she is less wedded to a vision of ideological uniformity within the church than is Badillo, much more forthcoming about her doctrinal selectivity, and certainly more convinced that this selectivity is necessitated by the lack of insight that church leaders exhibit rather than a result of her own shortcomings. That notwithstanding, it is interesting that she and Badillo, self-described liberal and conservative, are really quite similar in framing their religious agency in terms of discernment. Only Henslin talks about discernment explicitly. But they both embrace the notion by differentiating the kinds of religious choices they make from those made willy-nilly or for the sake of convenience. For both, the stereotypical cafeteria Catholic serves as a foil for reminding them that their faiths, while challenged by real-life issues and growing in often unexpected directions, are by comparison still clearly rooted within a religious tradition and enlivened by a serious commitment to discernment.

This same commitment, ironically, is evident in parishioners who actually embrace the cafeteria Catholic symbol. For some, it represents a perfectly legitimate stage of religious growth. "I don't mind when people treat the religion like some kind of buffet," says Saint Monica parish council member Elaine Gaskill. "I'd rather that people take just some things than not take anything at all." "Besides," she continues, "my experience is that this often whets people's appetites for more; they get comfortable at the buffet table, and then they can take their time and explore what's really appealing *to them!*" Instead of being construed as a means to a more satisfying end, others treat cafeteria Catholicism as an end in itself. This is true of Paul Min, a long-time Eucharistic minister at Most Holy Redeemer: "I'm definitely a cafeteria Catholic. I get to choose. I don't have to eat string beans if I don't like them, and, if I want more dessert, then that's fine, too. It's fine as long as I know what the main staples are: They're the Eucharist, the parish, our lives together, and a strong sense of spirituality. Really, I get to choose because every spirituality is different. When God calls to us, he calls us to be a better person than who we are. He doesn't call us to be a different person."

No longer cast pejoratively, both Gaskill and Min still use the notion of a cafeteria Catholic to accentuate the importance of discernment for the spiritual self. Gaskill presumes that it represents a stage at which people take time to discerningly "explore," and Min qualifies acceptable religious choices on the basis of people's ability to distinguish theological side dishes from the main courses. Another thing they have in common is their underlying agreement that this discernment should be done in a manner that is attentive to the individual's needs and particularities. "What's really appealing *to them*" as individuals is what warrants exploration in Gaskill's view. Similarly, Min advocates religious choice making as a way to tailor one's faith in light of what he sees as the uniqueness of every person and thus of every spirituality. In each case and similar to the majority of parishioners in this study, living out one's faith is discussed in terms of a reflexive or self-conscious project. It means to grow, to be discerning, and to be attentive to what seems most authentic to the individual.

"For Me"

The flipside of respecting "what's really appealing *to them*" is parishioners' reticence to universalize what is appealing, sensible, or true "for me." Because people typically perceive their faith as being so individualized, they tend to be reluctant to present their beliefs and commitments as presumptively applicable to others. "The Catholic religion is what's valid for me," "this is where, for me at least, God is present," "it's the best religion for me"—one hears this conversational shard with great frequency at these churches. "For me" seems to signify a widespread unwillingness to either judgmentally underestimate the validity of other people's truths or hubristically overestimate the validity of one's own. This reticence has also been well documented by sociologists as a prominent characteristic of contemporary American religion. Among Presbyterian baby boomers, for instance, Dean Hoge and his colleagues have noted the prevalence of "lay liberalism," an attitude defined by the rejection of the notion that Christianity is the only true religion.[18] Alan Wolfe has described middle-class Americans' religiosity as an increasingly nondogmatic "quiet faith" that has seemingly added an eleventh commandment: "Thou shalt not judge."[19] And, most famously, a young nurse named Sheila Larson came to epitomize Americans' growing preference for a highly personalized ilk of religiosity for Robert Bellah and his colleagues. "My faith has carried me a long way," she told them during an interview. "It's Sheilaism. Just my own little voice."[20]

How this broader tendency plays itself out among Catholics is worth considering in some detail. The first thing to note is that, even for the smattering of females actually named Sheila within these parishes, their faith is certainly not Sheilaism. That there is a considerable degree of personal identification with the Catholic tradition is evident in their responses to the statement "I could be just as happy in some other church; it wouldn't have to be Catholic." As table 3.3 points out, only about one-quarter (27 percent) of Bay Area parishioners expressed any level of agreement with this statement. As specifically active parishioners, they are

TABLE 3.3. "I could be just as happy in some other church; it wouldn't have to be Catholic" (in %).

	Strongly agree	Somewhat agree	Somewhat disagree	Strongly disagree
Most Holy Redeemer	7	18	48	27
St. Monica	9	11	47	33
St. Mary–St. Francis de Sales	7	21	52	19
St. Augustine	3	25	46	25
St. Louis Bertrand	15	25	35	25
St. Margaret Mary	2	3	30	65
Total	8 (22)	19 (20)	42 (14)	31 (39)

Note: Percentages listed in parentheses are from the 1995 national survey discussed in Davidson et al. (1997) and available in the Association of Religion Data Archive (http://www.thearda.com/Archive/Files/Descriptions/NATCATH.asp). They are rounded off and do not include the authors' "Not sure" category (5.4%). Parish data may also not add up to 100 percent due to rounding off.

significantly less likely to say they would be happy elsewhere than Catholics nationally (42 percent). Nevertheless, at the same time, these parishioners are remarkably similar to other Catholics with respect to their assessment of whether "Catholicism contains a greater share of truth than other religions do."

American Catholics are not as adamant about this as are church leaders in Rome, who, with the recent publication of *Dominus Jesus* (2000), seem to have a more conservative, if not triumphalist, viewpoint concerning the value of other faiths. "If it is true that the followers of other religions can receive divine grace," the text reads, "it is also certain that *objectively speaking* they are in a gravely deficient situation in comparison with those who, in the church, have the fullness of the means of salvation."[21] Table 3.4 tells us neither just how "gravely deficient" these respondents consider the situation of non-Catholics to be nor whether they consider themselves to have access to the means of salvation in its "fullness." Yet, it does suggest that a sizeable majority of both Bay Area parishioners and Catholics nationally (57 percent and 55 percent, respectively) believe that their faith's share of divinely revealed truth is greater than that of other religions. Predictably, the proportion of people who make this claim varies by parish. Only about one-quarter of parishioners at Most Holy Redeemer do so, whereas more than nine in ten of those at Saint Margaret Mary do.

However, below the surface, things are more complicated. Possessing a greater share of religious truth, parishioners generally say in interviews, does not mean Catholicism has anything like a monopoly on it. In other words, even though in surveys they can seem very much in accord with *Dominus Jesus*'s theological certainty, when engaged in more considered conversation, they demonstrate ambivalence.

TABLE 3.4. "Catholicism contains a greater share of truth than other religions do" (in %).

	Strongly agree	Somewhat agree	Somewhat disagree	Strongly disagree
Most Holy Redeemer	0	26	42	32
St. Monica	14	45	30	11
St. Mary–St. Francis de Sales	18	39	39	4
St. Augustine	12	27	50	10
St. Louis Bertrand	33	36	23	9
St. Margaret Mary	65	27	5	3
Total	23 (18)	34 (37)	32 (22)	11 (20)

Note: National percentages are taken from D'Antonio et al. (2007). Shown in parentheses, these may not add up to 100 percent due to rounding off and because "Don't know" and "Refused to answer" categories (2%) are not recorded in this table. Parish data may also not add up to 100 percent due to rounding off.

They generally resist relying on black-and-white verities and offer reflections that, as the great G. F. W. Hegel once noted of philosophy, are painted "grey in grey."[22] This ambivalence, evident within all of the churches in this study, is surprisingly rife within Saint Margaret Mary as well.

To demonstrate this, let us return to Sandra Badillo. When asked whether she thinks the Catholic faith is truer than other faiths, she responds without any hint of uncertainty whatsoever. "Yes, I do," she declares and immediately amplifies this with, "If I didn't, I wouldn't be in this religion!" Then, when asked to elaborate, she begins to paint in considerably grayer hues:

First of all, I was brought up in this religion, and part of the faith is that this is the way Jesus wanted us to get to heaven—to go through him. Many of the other religions are a break-off of our religion; we know that. Do I think they're wrong? Not necessarily. Do I think they're not going to heaven? No, not necessarily. I just happen to believe, and my faith tells me, that this is the religion that was meant for me and for many to go through to go to heaven. I have a lot of friends that are in other religions. But do I try to convert them? Not probably to the extent that I should. But, you know, I can't make that judgment for them.

You said that Catholicism was meant for you to get to heaven. Do you think that means that other religions are meant for other people and are best for them?

In my opinion, no. But, like I said, I can't judge them. I can't make that call for them. Do I . . . umm. I believe that the Catholic Church is the true religion. I believe that.

Okay, but what is your view of non-Christian religions then? If your access to heaven is through Jesus, what's your understanding of religions that don't focus on Jesus?

Well, I know that Jesus gave us the Catholic religion and that [it] did break off of the Jewish religion. So, do I think that Judaism is wrong in what it believes? To a certain extent, I have to say "yes" if I'm honest and if I follow my religion. But do I think they're bad or they . . . or, say, Buddhists don't possess religious truth or have any chance of going to heaven? No, I can't make that judgment. I don't know, so I can't make that judgment.

Unlike the "official" view articulated in *Dominus Jesus,* notice the prevarication of religion in its "nonofficial," "lived" mode. Consistent with Badillo's responding "strongly agree" to the survey question about Catholicism containing a greater share of religious truth, she insists that she would not be Catholic if it were not the truest religion. But then she softens this. She was simply "brought up" in the faith, she says, and she "just happen[s] to believe" what she does about Catholicism. She then trades "our religion" for "my faith." And, as though alleviating her qualms that she "should" try to convert others, she explains that Catholicism was meant, if not for them, then certainly "for me." Eventually, after rallying somewhat and re-asserting that Catholicism is "the true religion," she can bring herself to claim only that Judaism is wrong "to a certain extent." But, even this claim is largely muffled because judging other religions seems to feel too much like judging other people, whom she is loath to write off as "bad" or as being unable to possess religious truth or make their way into heaven.

Some may want to chide Badillo for what they perceive as an intolerable level of "wishy-washiness" in her responses. In light of her own difficulty and ambivalence, she herself may wonder whether they would be justified in doing so. Three times, she might recall, she used the phrase "I can't make that judgment" and seemed exasperated at finally having to admit "I don't know" in order to curtail this line of questioning. Still, such an accusation seems unduly harsh. Her ambivalence is hardly unique among parishioners, even the more conservative ones at Saint Margaret Mary. While not completely universal, a sense that one's perspective on religious truth is just one among legitimate others is pervasive in each parish. As suggested earlier, it is also a widespread feature of American religion more broadly. When anthropologists Robert Lynd and Helen Lynd visited Muncie, Indiana (or "Middletown," as they pseudonymously called it), in the 1920s, they found that 94 percent of their respondents agreed that "Christianity is the one true religion, and all people should be converted to it."[23] However, when researchers returned to Muncie a little more than a half century later, they were surprised to discover that, even though religious conviction and practice remained alive and well, only 41 per-cent of the city's inhabitants continued to agree with this statement.[24]

Further, to look upon this reality in an accusatory manner seems not only harsh but also shortsighted. The prevailing tendency, of course, is to see it as a "going-to-hell-in-a-handbasket" evisceration of religious seriousness and commit-ment. The problem is that that tendency is based on the arbitrary presumption that painting theologically in black and white is somehow preferable to painting in gray. On the contrary, the conversational shard "for me" actually reflects and helps to engender a religious sensibility that is grayer, more self-monitoring, and more provisional but, in the end, no less religious. Even if it is not always appreciated or recognized as such by those who exhibit it, this sensibility is marked by a capac-ity to step back from one's religious convictions and see them as existing within a wider world of possible convictions one might hold. "This capacity of understand-ing one's own view as just that—*a view*—forces attention to biography, history, and experience and creates consciousness about the positioned nature of all our perspectives," writes sociologist Wade Clark Roof of this more reflexive approach to one's faith. "Such awareness is basis for understanding not just oneself in a deeply personal sense, but encourages a profound sociological imagination, or recognition of one's own views, values, and identity in relation to others."[25]

This very sort of recognition has become commonplace among parishioners. Prominent among those "others" in relation to whom parishioners position their own religious perspectives are non-Catholics. All of them say they have acquain-tances, coworkers, and close friends who adhere to different faiths or no faith. Nearly all of them also have non-Catholic siblings, spouses, or children with whom they report having many meaningful conversations about all manner of religious topics. This daily exposure to religious pluralism generally does not make them "hetero-glossic," whereby they are knowledgeably conversant in other religious traditions.[26] Rather, to coin a phrase, they are more "heterognostic" in the sense that they sim-ply know about other denominations and religions; they have these faiths on their "radar screens," as it were. In fact, this recognition of religious diversity—combined with their frequent and freely admitted ignorance about the theological and his-torical particularities of other faiths—generates a religious sensibility that is quite at ease with its own unknowing. Badillo's "I don't know" echoes throughout the parishes and, compared to her admission, usually does so with a far less apologetic timbre. This is because such avowals generally signify parishioners' acute awareness of just how complex religious understanding is, as well as their own limited capaci-ties for attaining it.

Some focus on the inscrutability of God when expressing this sensibility. This is what Saint Mary–Saint Francis de Sales Eucharistic minister Paula Kraus empha-sizes when, after describing her earlier "Buddhist phase," she reflects on religious pluralism. "I think it's because God is so great and so unfathomable that there are going to be different ways for each of us to draw near to God," she says and then explains:

> I think there are a lot of different truths, and, in the end, doesn't the world benefit from the contemplative who is praying for the world in the monastery? And from the person who is feeding people at Saint Anthony's? And the person trying to put some truth into politics? And the people who are digging ditches to make money to feed their families and who are nice to the guy digging next to them? And isn't the world better when different kinds of people take different approaches to God—whether it be in temples or churches or in Zen meditation centers or in nature or wherever it is that they try to find and worship this God, who can't be contained in any of these places and is beyond all our imaginations?

Rather than focusing upon the God who is "beyond all our imaginations," parishioners are just as likely to illustrate their awareness of religious complexity by focusing on other people, especially on the non-Catholics they know and respect. "There are lots of ways to find God, and I don't think Catholics have a lock on *the* way," explains David Somers, one of the long-time pillars of Saint Monica parish. "I know of a lot of terrific, terrific Protestant people, Jewish people, Buddhists. Heck, I went to UC–Berkeley, so I met all kinds of people with different takes on everything, including God."

Like Kraus and many other parishioners, Somers basically contends that diverse religious paths are entirely appropriate because no single one of them could possibly encapsulate the impenetrable mystery of God. Others take a different approach by suggesting that religious differences are in fact relatively superficial and are much less important than what believers of all stripes hold in common. This is Peter Gaudet's view. A lector and leader of a weekly Bible-study group at Saint Augustine parish, he has held this view since college and it has only been confirmed in the years since his daughter married a Muslim. He likes to tell the story of the first time he accompanied her to the local mosque. "The sermon was the usual stuff," he recollects. "You know, support the children, support widows, take care of one another. I thought, 'Gee, that sounds familiar!' And so it just reinforced what I see as the fact that, beneath it all, the rules and behaviors promulgated by all the religions are pretty much the same."

People like Gaudet demonstrate that the widespread nonjudgmentalism among Catholic laity, although often deprecated as "wishy-washiness," actually engenders in them an appreciation for other faiths, as well as for the uncontainable mysteriousness of God. Though they do not agree with the majority (54 percent) of their fellow citizens who agree that "all major religions, such as Christianity, Hinduism,

Buddhism, and Islam, are *equally good* ways of knowing about God," they certainly sound very much like the three-quarters of all American adults who say these religions all "contain *some truth* about God."[27]

One indication of just how common this religiously inclusive attitude is can be gleaned from the reality that no vice is as routinely disparaged within the parishes as judgmentalism. Other groups that have come to represent this vice vary in accordance with parishioners' own experiences. At Saint Louis Bertrand, where African Americans have Jehovah's Witnesses within their circle of family and friends, many people often mention this denomination as signifying what they are not. "They think they have all the answers," asserted one parishioner; "They just turn me off because they act so righteous," said another; "I'm not judgmental enough to see things their way," offered a third. Meanwhile, especially in light of their fears that a nearby community church might be luring many of their young people away, it is the "dogmatic," "know-it-all," "holier-than-thou" evangelicals who play this role for parishioners at Saint Monica. Whereas at Most Holy Redeemer it is the propensity of conservatives within the church hierarchy to make sweeping judgments about gays and lesbians that parishioners single out for particular censure and to highlight what their more "accepting" version of the faith is not.

But what, then, is this faith? If people have a strong appreciation for other religions and at the same time distinguish between their own religious selves and those of purportedly judgmental others to indicate what they are not, then why are they Catholic? This is essentially the question I posed to Peter Gaudet after hearing his mosque story. "Because I was born into it," he says. "It's what I'm comfortable with. It's easy, it's familiar. So why should I go to the trouble of finding something else when this is getting me in touch with God?" This same "comfort" language is used not only by "cradle Catholics" like Gaudet but by converts as well. While Kelly Schutt is enthusiastic about growing in her knowledge of the Catholic faith, she also says, "I truly believe everyone's path to God is valid." Asked then to clarify why she is Catholic, she continues, "My way to God is through Jesus Christ. If it were through Mohammed, I could be a devout Muslim. But my faith in Jesus is so strong. Really, I'm not that boxed in to being a Catholic because of the rules and so forth. It's more because this is where I feel comfortable."

Both show strong "brand loyalty" to their faith. Yet, like so many others, they have blunted its doctrinal edges with their own embrace of religious unknowing and resistance to religious judgment. This, in turn, has made their fit with Catholicism feel more comfortable to them. They are self-conscious about this fit. Gaudet knows that it is largely due to an accident of birth that he is most comfortable within the symbolic world of Catholicism. Similarly, Schutt is most comfortable resting in her devotion to Jesus. Nonetheless, she can readily imagine that, if the particularities of her biography or temperament were different, this could easily be otherwise. The truth of what is true for them, they each suggest, is less a reflection of what they discern to be true in some ultimate sense and more a function of its fit with who they are or have become as individuals.

"A Good Person"

The subtle caveat "for me" reflects parishioners' negotiation with the Catholic tradition by blunting its doctrinal edges. Another species of negotiation takes the focus off of doctrines altogether and places it upon the moral commitments derived from the church's doctrinal teachings. This subtle exchange of religious "orthodoxy" (correct belief) for what some liberation theologians have called "orthopraxy" (correct action) as a way of defining oneself as Catholic is commonplace within these six churches.[28] Of course, the sacraments, the parish community, and their comfort with the culture of Catholicism are important to people, and they cite them as key elements of their faith. Still, when queried about what best defines a good Catholic, parishioners almost unfailingly equate this with simply trying to be "a good person." Like the nonideological "Golden Rule Christians," whom sociologist Nancy Ammerman has found to increasingly populate American churches, parishioners are typically short on systematic theology and biblical scholarship and instead shift the weight of their religious identities more to the practice of everyday virtues.[29] It is as though they have carefully (or, often, not so carefully) filtered their religious tradition, cast aside the dregs of dogma and judgment, and are now satisfied with the refreshingly pure elixir of living a good life to the best of their abilities. Consider their responses to the statement "How a person lives is more important than whether or not he or she is a Catholic" (see table 3.5). More than four in five Catholics in the United States, as well as in Bay Area parishes, express some level of agreement with this statement. Only at traditionalist Saint Margaret Mary and

TABLE 3.5. "How a person lives is more important than whether or not he or she is a Catholic" (in %).

	Strongly agree	Somewhat agree	Somewhat disagree	Strongly disagree
Most Holy Redeemer	78	20	2	0
St. Monica	80	20	0	0
St. Mary–St. Francis de Sales	55	29	11	5
St. Augustine	52	38	9	2
St. Louis Bertrand	44	32	14	10
St. Margaret Mary	29	31	29	11
Total	55 (68)	29 (20)	11 (6)	5 (6)

Note: National percentages are taken from D'Antonio et al. (2007). Parish data may not add up to 100 percent due to rounding off.

those parishes with sizeable numbers of Latinos and Asians (about three in ten of each group disagrees) does one find significant dissent.

Since pragmatism is America's most notable contribution to Western philosophy, it is not surprising that American Catholics would be religious pragmatists and prefer highlighting the practical fruits of religious conviction over the particular ideological form that conviction takes.[30] Moreover, references to being "a good person" dovetail with other trends mentioned in this chapter. Consonant with the invocation of "my faith," these references presume an image of a morally serious self toward which one strives to grow. Being "a good person" also has a common-denominator flair to it since, true to the nondogmatic openness denoted by the repeated phrase "for me," being a good person is generally seen as a possibility open to people of all faiths, as well as those who profess no faith. As with these other conversational shards, this one, perhaps especially so, requires Catholics to be reflexive. A desire to be good does not come with a prefabricated template. When the project of being a distinctively Catholic self shifts its focus toward the ethical and the practice of everyday virtues, it thereby moves in a less clearly defined direction. The markers along this way are not as obvious as, say, simply believing a given doctrine or reciting a given prayer. They must be carefully sought through self-assessment and an ongoing monitoring of one's progress. Precisely because this way of carving out one's Catholic identity is less explicitly articulated by the tradition, people need to do considerable cultural work in order to understand both what it truly means to be a good person and the extent to which this ideal ought to impinge upon their very real lives.

One way to see this negotiation process in action is to direct people toward an ethically instructive part of their faith tradition and observe how they interpret and build upon it. Since stories are integral to identity and since most parishioners are not particularly well versed in Catholic moral theology or the church's social teachings, I chose to do this by reading well-known stories from scripture to them. One of these stories is the Last Judgment passage in the Gospel of Matthew (Mt. 25:31–46). The scene is a memorable one. Jesus, referred to as "the Son of Man," "the King," and, by the people themselves, as "Lord," is seated upon his heavenly throne before "all the nations." He judges these people and separates them "as a shepherd separates the sheep from the goats." The former, he proclaims, fed him when he was hungry, gave a drink to him when he thirsted, welcomed him when he was a stranger, clothed him when he was naked, cared for him when he was sick, and visited him when imprisoned. They are then welcomed to "inherit the Kingdom prepared for you from the foundation of the world." When they, and subsequently the goats, inquire about this, Jesus tells them that how they acted toward "one of the least of my brothers and sisters" was how they also acted toward him. Then the sheep are welcomed into heaven, whereas the goats "go away into eternal punishment." This is a passage of singular importance for Catholics. Without exception, all of the parishioners I interviewed said they had heard or read it many times, knew it well, and considered it to be especially meaningful to them.

This passage has long fascinated and perplexed professional theologians. However, what has been interesting to them is not what makes the story meaningful to parishioners. They did not mention the fact that Jesus was finding both sheep and goats among "all the nations" to explain (or explain away) the possibility for non-Christians to be saved. That the Kingdom was prepared for the elect "from the foundation of the world" led no one to cite this passage as support for a belief in predestination. Moreover, for a story that concludes with some people going into "eternal punishment" and others into "eternal life," there was little evidence of reflection on what this might mean beyond most parishioners stating without much elaboration that they believe in heaven but are not so convinced about hell.[31]

On the contrary, it represents for them the obligation to be a good person. This might sound simple—and many parishioners laud its simplicity—but, for it to actually apply to their busy and complex lives, they have to self-consciously negotiate with the text. For many, this is centered on coming to some conclusion regarding the goodness of the good person. Saint Monica choir member Dale Perrow contended that this passage truly epitomizes what it means to be a good Catholic. When pushed on this point a bit, he responded:

> I would say that being a good Catholic in the traditional sense is going to Mass regularly, giving your time and money to the church, praying regularly, and embodying the beliefs of the Catholic religion in how you treat other people. I try to do that stuff. Overall, though, being a good Catholic is a goal that I'm trying to attain. And, since I don't know many of the fundamental doctrines of the religion, I mostly do this by trying to be a good person.

> *How does that relate to the Last Judgment passage I just read to you?*

> When I hear that passage, I'm reminded that we're called to do things for other people. I try to do that stuff, but it's a pretty daunting task. I wonder sometimes how good I have to be to be good.

> *How good do you have to be to be good?*

> Ahh, Jeez! I knew you'd ask that question! I don't think you have to be Mother Teresa good or anything. I think we're called to do those things in the story, but I don't think I have to do all of them now. I think the story is

showing us the ideal, and then we're supposed to grow toward that. I'm in process, and that's the direction I'm hoping to grow spiritually.

Like many people I interviewed, Perrow felt some uneasiness in hearing this text not because of its reference to hell but because, even though he wants to be a good person, this role is loosely defined in American culture. He is left to wonder about this. One gets the impression that his definition, which presents him with a "pretty daunting task," still raises the moral bar quite high, even if not Mother Teresa high. Yet, he claims, he does not have to reach it now because he shares his fellow Catholics' presumption of personal growth. Being a good person is a "goal" or an "ideal" that does not stand in judgment upon his present self because he is "in process." He expects that whatever ethical shortcomings he might display at the moment are sufficiently overshadowed by his anticipation of a future, inevitably better, iteration of this self.

Other people's definitions of goodness lower the moral bar somewhat. Rather than being exasperated by the overwhelming prospect of doing all of the things mentioned in the gospel story, they stress the relative ease of doing any one of those things. For them, being a good person is more like practicing, as the once-popular bumper stickers would have it, "random acts of kindness." These, they typically insist, do not require a heroic level of virtue. They require a mere openness to attending to whatever needs happen to come their way. The couples who regularly volunteer at the local soup kitchen or are in the habit of mowing an elderly neighbor's lawn; the boss who treats his employees with respect; the woman who cannot walk down hippie-and-homeless-haven Telegraph Avenue without divesting herself of all of her loose change; the friend who does errands for a homebound neighbor—parishioners who construe goodness in this way are brimming with stories of people they know who have modeled this kind of everyday virtue. In contrast to Perrow's understanding, this is not a species of goodness realizable only in the aspirational future. Because anyone can do these small, manageable acts, they are thus seen as things people *should* do in their present lives. No growth is necessary. Nor, ironically for a passage that depicts the Last Judgment, is there much judgment language used because, parishioners generally explain, such small acts are not so easily detected by peering outsiders. People who might look like goats because they do not feed the hungry might actually be sheep because they clothe the naked; those who are not ministering to the sick, they suggest, might actually be doing some good at the local prison or elsewhere. The implied message is that doing good assumes so many doable forms that is it unthinkable to assume that everyone is not doing at least something.

While this passage makes some people ponder what being good is really all about, for others it pushes the question of personhood to the forefront. Here, too, one finds two clearly demarcated interpretive strands. The first, which casts the self in more communitarian terms, interprets the Last Judgment story as one that envisions the self as interdependent with other selves. References to the traditional Catholic notion of the community as the "body of Christ" are rare among parishioners, but it captures the crux of their thinking. "Everyone's capacity is different," explains Saint Mary–Saint Francis de Sales altar server Mariam Weldon. "Some things should be done by some people, and other things by other people. I think the gospel is telling us that the Kingdom is about people using their talents to the best of their ability while trusting that others will do the same." Sandy Reimers, long active in youth ministry at Saint Augustine, seems to share this trust. Like Dale Perrow, she admits to feeling overwhelmed at all of the things the passage seems to mandate. Still, she says, just as most of society's problems are created by many people acting in concert, the same is true of efforts to alleviate those problems. "That's why I do ministry with young people," she confides. "You know, I can't hammer a nail straight. I'm just not good at that. But I can use my talents to inspire one hundred teenagers to go down to Mexico to build houses for the poor. And I can help to open their eyes to see that every person on earth is Jesus; that every person in the world is their brother or sister and is a precious child of God. So, in a way, what they end up doing for the 'least of these' is partly what I've done."

Instead of looking outward and defining personhood communally, the second interpretive strand looks within. People who take this approach, like the others, insist that the passage is about being a good person. But then they proceed to demythologize it, explaining that the sheep and the goats are symbols for the duality inherent within human nature. The representative voice here belongs to Lisa Dodson, one of the most active parishioners at Saint Mary–Saint Francis de Sales:

> I think that God knows that we are very complex people and that there are days, moments, times when we act like sheep, and we do the right thing, and we see a hungry person, and we give them food, we work toward affordable housing, whatever. And then there's times when we wake up, and we're goats, and we're like, "Screw you, buy your own hamburger!" or "Get a job!" or whatever to people on the street. I think the separation of the sheep from the goats is where this part of us gets thrown into the fire; that God takes those parts of us that aren't inclined to help, that aren't inclined to share ourselves, that aren't inclined to be generous, and gets rid of them. And you know what? In the end, I want those parts of me thrown out, and I want what is most life giving and closest to the divine nature in me to be saved. I want that.

Dodson is extremely thoughtful and sincere, and in that sense, too, she is representative of other parishioners in this study. Still, in commencing and concluding her comments with "I think that" and "I want that," she also reminds us of a key characteristic of this conversational shard. Despite its ubiquity in conversations among Catholics, it is every bit as individuated as are "my faith" and "for me." What one parishioner thinks about goodness or most wants to be as a person is very likely to differ from what the next parishioner says. Thus, understandings of goodness and personhood are variable enough to keep even this shard from helping to create a thicker consensus on what it means to be Catholic.

Who would expect otherwise? With the shift of religious authority from what the renowned philosopher Immanuel Kant called "heteronomous" authority—instantiated, for example, in religious leaders and theologians—to the individual self, one discovers an unprecedented level of freedom, as well as a heretofore underappreciated burden.[32] This is because to situate religious authority within the self is to fuse it with the lingering sense of rootlessness described earlier. Signs of this are easy to detect. Parishioners are unceasingly forthcoming about their feelings of fragmentation. It is not at all uncommon for them to admit being weighed down by the challenges they face in bringing their religious selves to the office, to the voting booth, to their lifestyle choices, to their relationships, and so forth. In feeling the multidirectional pull wrought by their awareness of other ways of being Catholic (or non-Catholic), they also admit to feeling destabilized. Should they be "Mother Teresa good" or simply practice "random acts of kindness"? Should they connect to the sacred the way their parish priest does or like their Catholic and non-Catholic siblings do or like their Buddhist roommate does or like their Muslim husband does? They are aware of all of these and countless other ways of being religious and are not always sure how to adjudicate among them. Thus, they are also uncertain. They want to grow spiritually, and they practice discernment, but they are also quick to admit to their own vast unknowing when it comes to the fuzziness of the moral life, the intricacies of other faith traditions, and the inextricable mystery of God.

Even as it is marked by this real sense of fragmentation, instability, and uncertainty, parishioners' negotiation with their religious tradition is both a rooting and an uprooting. For instance, at first glance it might seem that the masses that commemorate the Vietnamese martyrs and Black History Month are simply and firmly rooted in tradition. Yet closer inspection reveals that these are in fact extremely innovative rituals. The symbols; the interpretations of scripture; the incorporation of certain nonliturgical practices into the Mass; the explicit deployment of Vietnamese and African American culture as foci of sacralization: There is much that would be entirely unfamiliar to people raised within the "devotional Catholicism" of a century ago.

Conversely, many people envision the shift toward the acceptance of Catholics' religious agency as reflected in omnipresent phrases such as "my faith," "for me," and "a good person" as tantamount to an uprooting of the tradition, a diminishing of Catholic identity. However, coming to this equally one-sided conclusion would require casting a blind eye to the reality that one stumbles upon these conversational shards on distinctly religious terrain. One hears these phrases from parishioners who are extremely earnest about their faith and obviously deeply rooted within Catholic tradition. As they take its symbols and meanings seriously while also negotiating with them, they engender a different kind of Catholic self that is confronted by and attuned to the problems of the modern self more generally. But this raises the issue of religious authority. How can Catholics exercise their own religious authority and, at the same time, take seriously a religious tradition that vests authority in a vast hierarchy?

4

✠

Institution

Dilemmas of Authenticity and Authority

Returning to Dust, Flying over the Rainbow

Ash Wednesday

The sound of bells pealing overhead made me look up and notice the tower and adjacent walls that, topped with ramparts, give Saint Margaret Mary's church building the imposing feel of a medieval fortress. This seems appropriate since its parishioners share a sense that much about contemporary society—individualism, relativism, impiety—demands stalwart resistance. The ringing also told me I was not late for the 5 PM Ash Wednesday service. As I sat in a rearward pew, one of about 120 in attendance, the bells suddenly stopped, and all was quiet. Many were kneeling with hands clasped in prayer, most of the women wore black lace head coverings, and a few people on both sides of the church were standing in line outside of confessional booths. No one spoke. Not a whisper, not an infant crying, not a glad-handing greeter. Then the softer chime of still more bells sounded out from the sacristy, and all those assembled rose to their feet in voiceless unison.

The priest, Father Koenig, wore incredibly ornate purple vestments with a matching tasseled biretta, whereas the two acolytes—both twenty-something males and, like Father Koenig, both absolutely meticulous in grooming and comportment—were dressed in plain black cassocks and intricately laced white surplices. Each stood one step below and to either side of Father Koenig, reverently held the hem of his vestments, and then, with him, moved and bowed and genuflected in near-perfect synchronization. Their backs to the pews, the acolytes stood motionless while Father Koenig, speaking in Latin (with an Eastern European accent), commenced with the antiphon and followed with the responsory, interspersed with "amens" coming from the pews behind him. Together they moved so reverentially, almost mechanically, that the three seemed like figurines in an heirloom timepiece as they carried out the ritual blessing of the ashes and then incensed them, along with the entire altar. "Moménto, homo, quia pulvis es, et in púlverem revertéris," Father Koenig reminded the acolytes as he made the sign of the cross with dark ashes on their pale foreheads: "Remember, man, that you are dust, and unto dust you shall return" (Gen. 3:19).

Without any obvious cue, people then stood and made their way up the center aisle to receive their ashes. "Moménto, homo, quia pulvis es, et in púlverem revertéris," I heard as I knelt at the farthest end of the altar rail. Heads were bowed; some people's lips moved in silent prayer. "Moménto, homo, quia pulvis es, et in púlverem revertéris." Making his way toward my end of the altar rail, Father Koenig kept one impeccably manicured hand over his heart, while the other made the exact same robotic motion as it reached into the vessel carefully held by one of the acolytes and applied ashes onto one forehead after another. Off to the side, the second acolyte stood completely still with hands held symmetrically together directly below his chin. "Moménto, homo, quia pulvis es, et in púlverem revertéris." "Amen," I said (and meant it) and returned to my seat.

When everyone had done the same, the acolytes painstakingly disrobed Father Koenig down to his cassock and, with all solemnity, rerobed him in another, equally stunning set of purple vestments. Then he began the Mass. Again in Latin and with their backs to the people, Father Koenig and the acolytes performed the liturgy in a fastidiously choreographed manner. After reciting the first reading in Latin, Father Koenig repeated it in English: "'Thus, says the Lord,' the prophet Joel declares, 'Return to me with your whole heart, with fasting, and weeping, and mourning; rend your hearts, not your garments, and return to the Lord, your God'" (Jl. 2:12). The same was done with the gospel. "'When you fast, don't go around looking dismal like hypocrites,' Jesus says to his disciples, and then explains, 'As for you, when you fast, groom your hair and wash your face. In that way, no one can see you are fasting but your Father who is invisible; and your Father who sees what is invisible will repay you'" (Mt. 6:16, 18–19).

Ashes reminding them of their mortality and scripture readings reminding them of the need for fasting and repentance underscore the seriousness with which the faithful are to renew their Christian commitment during the Lenten season. In his homily, which was delivered slowly in English and lasted no more than a couple of minutes, Father Koenig touched on these themes: "We were sentenced to death. In Genesis we discover that the consequence of sin for humanity is death. That is why penance is so very important. Penance is a way for us to come closer to God. As we see in today's readings, it has long been required and practiced by man. Ashes, therefore, are an exterior sign of what is at the heart of the human condition. Thou art dust, and unto dust you shall return; that sums it up in a profound way."

This is the way the need for repentance is commonly summed up in other parishes as well. Usually in Ash Wednesday homilies, particularly since Vatican II, this theme is also connected to baptismal imagery since the day marks the beginning of a time when Catholics are asked to rededicate themselves to the faith into which they were once initiated through baptism. But this was not the connection Father Koenig made. Instead, he focused on the notion (far more prevalent during the Middle Ages) that individuals' penance mystically unites with Christ's redemptive work and thus is "efficient" (i.e., brings about the intended effect) in assisting others in gaining salvation. In this vein he continued:

> But, with Christ, our penance is truly efficient because our penance is, in reality, to do the penance of Christ. Fasting and other sacrifices taken up during the Lenten season are truly efficient because we do it in union with Christ's sacrifice. Only because we are members of the mystical body of Christ are we truly assured that our penance is not simply moral effort. Rather, we know in faith that the penance that we do is efficient for the whole of the body of Christ and not just for ourselves as individuals. Fasting and abstinence, especially during the holy season of Lent, bring us closer to Christ, and they have the power to purify us, and they are efficient in that they contribute to purifying the whole body of Christ. This is what we desire. These ashes we place on our heads are a visible sign of this inner desire. And so I pray that we all have a blessed and, in this sense, a truly fruitful season of Lent. That, in coming closer to Christ, we will be prepared for the miracle of Easter, for Christ's victory over death. For it is his victory and *only this* that enables us, too, to have the ultimate victory over sin and victory over death.

No clever turns of phrase. No homespun anecdote artfully told. Not one for homiletic flourish, Father Koenig simply told his listeners that their lives are sacramental and that their action is inseparable from divine action. As the Mass continued, he told them this in other ways as well. The exaggeratedly slow, reverential manner in which he consecrated and handled the bread and wine told them that Jesus was truly in their midst and being sacrificed before their eyes. At the conclusion of the Mass, the incredibly long litany of saints from whom he requested favor told the worshippers that they were truly in mystical communion with both the living and the holy departed. After leading the kneeling parishioners in numerous traditional prayers (e.g., "Hail, Holy Queen"), Father Koenig called upon the members of Christ's mystical body one after another, and each time the assembly responded with "Pray for us." "God, the Son," he said, and they called back, "Pray for us."

"God, the Holy Ghost." "Pray for us." "Saint Michael, Archangel." "Pray for us." "Saint Francis of Assisi." "Pray for us." "Saint Stephen, first martyr." "Pray for us." On and on this went until the bells sounded once more.

Gay Pride Sunday

While Ash Wednesday is not officially a "holy day of obligation" for Catholics, Pride Sunday is treated that way by many at Most Holy Redeemer. In anticipation of marching in the enormous parade later that day, lots of people wore electric blue T-shirts with "Most Holy Redeemer: An Inclusive Catholic Community" scrolled in white lettering across the front. Always beautiful, the church interior looked even more so courtesy of the splashes of color provided by two large rainbow-colored banners on the altar. Aside from the banners and T-shirts, though, hints that this was a special day for this mostly gay church were relatively subtle.

The church prides itself on its inclusiveness. Moreover, it emphasizes the need for the broader Catholic Church to be more accepting of people who do not identify as heterosexual. The gathering song, titled "Lover of Us All," conveyed God's inclusiveness. So, too, did the lector, an openly transgendered woman, who accentuated a verse in the second reading, "And he died *for all* that those who live might live no longer for themselves but for him who for their sake died and was raised" (2 Cor. 5:15). Father Jeffries added his own subtle emphasis during his homily on the gospel passage that depicts Jesus, much to the gratitude of his frightened disciples, miraculously quelling a storm and thus saving themselves and their boat from certain catastrophe (Mk. 4:35–41). "This is a story about the need to have faith in the face of adversity," he said, knowing full well the anguish many of the assembled have seen in the face of the AIDS epidemic and their myriad experiences of homophobic exclusion. "Jesus loves everyone, and he will never abandon you," he assured them.

Given the parish's consistently "open and affirming" ethos and the fact that it was Pride Sunday, Father Jeffries did not have to explicitly focus on the issues of homosexuality and discrimination, yet this was the subtext of his remarks on adversity. Some parishioners have suggested that, with the recent arrival of a new archbishop, it might be best not to overplay their identity as the Bay Area's "gay parish" anyway. Thus they were relieved by the decision to march in the parade but not sponsor a booth at the all-day celebration. After all, photographs taken a few years earlier of the Most Holy Redeemer booth situated next to the one sponsored by the drag nuns, Sisters of Perpetual Indulgence, did not further their cause of being seen by outsiders as serious Catholics. Nor, alas, did the situation the following year, when they were surrounded by a bevy of anti-Bush-Cheney activists wielding "Lick Bush, Beat Dick" signs. "Oh, well," said one parishioner, intentionally misquoting Saint Augustine, "I guess you just have to hate the sign and love the signer."

Although references to this special day were indeed subtle during the Mass, Father Jeffries made sure to conclude on an appropriate note. "In recognition of Gay Pride Sunday," he said, "Let us remember that everyone is precious in the eyes of the Lord." Then, somewhat apologetically, he informed them that "I'm going to the parade staging area to bless the parish float, but I won't be riding in it this year because I don't want to look forward to another midweek meeting with the archbishop!" With that, everyone burst into laughter. Father Jeffries, making the sign of the cross with his outstretched hand, blessed the congregation, and, as a concluding "hymn," everyone lent their voices to a rousing rendition of "Somewhere over the Rainbow." The lyrics were printed in that week's order of service, but no one had to look at them. The people in the pews filled the church with music, and the organist, with muscular tattooed arms and Mohawk haircut, did the same by opening all of the stops. Tears filled many parishioners' eyes, and many reached out to hold a hand or place an arm around a loved one. As the song ended, people made a beeline to the exit in order to get on the "float"—an old-fashioned, though motorized, trolley car—that waited outside.

The next time I saw it, I was one among thousands of others packed along the parade route on San Francisco's Market Street. A short distance from me were two fundamentalist preachers and several supporters bearing signs that said such things as "Adam and Steve Will Burn in Hell" and "Homosexuality Is Satan's Work." As one gay-identified or gay-friendly organization and performing group after another passed, they yelled out threats of damnation and commanded all who listened (neither a large nor an appreciative audience) to "Stop slapping the hand of mercy away! Stop slapping the face of Jesus!" I thought for certain that these denunciations were at their vociferous peak when the Gays for Atheism, some scantily clad, marched by.

But then came that freshly blessed trolley car festooned with balloons and filled with people wearing electric blue T-shirts and waving rainbow flags of all sizes. Surrounding them were similarly attired fellow parishioners eagerly distributing Mardi Gras–style beaded necklaces on which were attached the words "Jesus Never Hated." Others carried a large "Most Holy Redeemer Catholic Church" banner, as well as additional signs that said "God Is Love" and "Jesus Loves All." The two preachers clearly disagreed. They got as close as the sidewalk barriers would allow in order to damn and denounce even more aggressively. With fingers pointing at one of the marchers—a man I immediately recognized as a longtime greeter at the 10 AM Sunday Mass—they came within a few feet of him and declared, "You'll spend eternity in Hell!" "I'm counting on better accommodations," he responded, smiling. "Pervert!" one yelled. "Jesus never hated," replied the greeter as he walked to keep up with the others. "Fornicators and queers have no place in the Kingdom." "God loves everybody," he replied, marching past. "Blasphemer!" "God bless you." On and on went this litany.

"Official" Religion from a "Nonofficial" Perspective

The simplest way to understand these two events would be to place them at either end of an imagined spectrum of American Catholicism. One might even offer them as ritualized manifestations of the much-ballyhooed "culture wars," with religious conservatives and liberals in separate, mutually antagonistic camps vying for cultural dominance.[1] The simplest way of conceptualizing things is seldom the best way, though. In fact, study after study has shown that Americans' sociopolitical views are not becoming increasingly polarized and that most contemporary issues do not engender a Manichean struggle between people who adhere to diametrically opposed moral worldviews.[2]

The initial appearance of diametrical opposition notwithstanding, there is actually much that this "traditionalist" church and this "progressive" one have in common. A touch of irony is one thing. Though Jesus explicitly told his followers not to display their fasting to observers, people at Saint Margaret Mary, like Catholics worldwide, mark themselves with ashen crosses. Conversely, while the Vatican insists on marking homosexuals as separate, as people with an inclination tantamount to an "objective disorder," members at Most Holy Redeemer (and elsewhere) are determined to remove that stigma by emphasizing inclusiveness and pointing out, as Father Jeffries put it, that "everyone is precious in the eyes of the Lord."[3]

A second commonality is each parish's negotiation with tradition. Saint Margaret Mary's parishioners like to think of themselves as following, not negotiating with, the tradition. But this neglects the fact that the exaggeratedly reverential manner in which the Ash Wednesday service was conducted is not "old-time religion" in a Catholic vein. Instead, it is a self-conscious, liturgical riposte to the purportedly irreverent fashion in which masses are conducted in other churches. At the same time, even though Most Holy Redeemer is often criticized as too radical, one would be hard pressed to think of messages more central to church tradition than "God is love" and "Jesus never hated." One had only to visit the week prior to Pride Sunday to see the parish's celebration of the Solemnity of the Body and Blood of Christ to be convinced of its commitment to tradition. This featured an outdoor Eucharistic procession with the Blessed Sacrament displayed in a golden monstrance for all to see and revere.

Third, people within neither parish practice their faith in a manner entirely disconnected from institutional authority. Most Holy Redeemer has created a parish culture in which inclusiveness is paramount. Still, Father Jeffries wanted nothing more than to avoid another midweek meeting at which, he suspected, the archbishop would have presented him with a different version of what is most authoritative within the church. Not dissimilarly, traditional values and the faithful's participation in Christ's mystical body are authoritative for Saint Margaret Mary parishioners.

Yet, this can run them afoul of church leaders who consider them out of step with the direction that Vatican II outlined for the church.

This third point about parishes' connection to the broader institution is particularly significant. One of the reasons their parishioners can abide being in some tension with religious authorities is that they have a shared understanding of the church as an institutional reality. In other words, as much as they are reflexive about their own faith, they are also institutionally reflexive.[4] They know that institutionalization is absolutely necessary for objectifying, consolidating, and thus passing on their religious tradition to subsequent generations. Yet, at the same time, they are generally well aware that the processes of institutionalization inevitably distort that tradition. To re-use the three above-mentioned points, this *irony* obliges people to *negotiate* with religious tradition in the hopes of determining what is most *authoritative* to them.

No one has captured this irony better than sociologist Thomas O'Dea in his landmark 1961 article "Five Dilemmas in the Institutionalization of Religion." "Religion both needs most and suffers most from institutionalization," he wrote. "The subtle, the unusual, the charismatic, the supra-empirical must be given expression in tangible, ordinary, and empirical social forms."[5] A numinous and extraordinary experience of the sacred "needs most" to be institutionalized but, in the process, it "suffers most" from becoming routinized.[6] Probably very few, if any, parishioners have read O'Dea's work. Nonetheless, their often intuitive grasp of the dilemmas he presents enables them to perceive their church in a relatively objectified manner as an institution that is at once both necessary to and potentially distorting of Christ's message.

To demonstrate this, I address O'Dea's five dilemmas. As we will see, with the exception of the final one concerning power, parishioners are quite reflexive about these dilemmas. They understand that their church needs to (1) use symbols that can lose their resonance over time (symbolic dilemma); (2) formulate doctrines that can devolve into mere legalisms (dilemma of delimitation); (3) generate a bureaucratic structure that can lose touch with the laity (dilemma of administrative order); and (4) appeal to people's (especially potential leaders') various personal interests, which can come to loom larger than those of the church itself (dilemma of mixed motivation); whereas they seem less aware that (5) their accommodating to dominant sociocultural norms can eventually undermine the laity's capacity to create the kind of church institution they seem to want (dilemma of power).

I present each of these dilemmas of "official" religion from the distinctly "non-official" perspective of laypeople. This is because they are not simply the church hierarchy's "business." Rather, they profoundly affect the laity as well. Laypeople's awareness of these quandaries affords them a certain objectifying distance that enables them to see their church as, among other things, a strategizing and flawed institutional actor. This, in turn, seems to free (or obligate) them to negotiate with certain dimensions of their tradition in much the same way as they do, as the previous chapter demonstrates, when focusing more explicitly on their own identities as Catholics.

The Symbolic Dilemma

As discussed, humans are "cultured" beings who order their realities by actively appropriating the symbols available to them. Catholics have no dearth of symbols upon which to draw. As sociologist Andrew Greeley argues, it is their access to a wondrously lush "rain forest of metaphors" for representing the sacred that largely explains why they like being Catholic and why, despite their frequent disagreements with church leadership, they remain within the fold.[7] The sacraments and various outdoor processions; practices like having one's throat blessed on the feast of Saint Blaise or kissing the wood of the Cross on Good Friday; "material culture" such as religious medals, holy water, incense, and votive candles: The symbols flourish. Of course, this does not mean they are always effective in engendering in individual believers the sense of holiness they are intended to represent. Symbols, as one theologian put it, can "die" as life situations change, thus losing their resonance among the faithful and failing to elicit from them the same emotions and attitudes they once did.[8] "To retain the original experience, with its supraempirical relation to the ultimate and the sacred," writes O'Dea, summarizing this symbolic dilemma, "it must be given expression in symbolic forms which are themselves empirical and profane, and which with repetition become prosaic and everyday in character."[9] If usually not breeding contempt for them, in other words, familiarity can certainly make religious symbols seem less resonant over time.

As illuminating as this is, such insights are not the sole province of scholars like O'Dea. Parishioners display their understanding of this symbolic dilemma with remarkable frequency. Most, perhaps all, of them would be extremely reticent to describe themselves as "deconstructionists." Yet one way they exhibit both their awareness of this dilemma and their self-conscious intent to resolve it for themselves is by subtly deconstructing their tradition—in other words, by understanding and appropriating Catholic symbols as symbols. Oftentimes this occurs when they discuss the changes in the church wrought by Vatican II. These accounts invariably include stories about their (or others') shift from *accepting* symbols as immutable realities to now *interpreting* symbols as representative of realities that transcend the "empirical and profane" forms through which they are expressed. These "then, but now" stories can be exaggerated via the haze of retrospection. Still, they indicate Catholics' willingness to select whichever religious symbols work for them, as well as their capacity to rework the ones they believe have become somewhat stale.

One Saint Monica parishioner, for example, tells a story from her college days about the time she sat down to have lunch with her roommate. Very hungry and very interested in the hamburger she was raising to her mouth, she was interrupted by the roommate, who, also a Catholic, had just realized and then informed her that it was Friday. "I was so mad at her," she recalled, still sounding quite angry. "I just put the hamburger down and had a very inadequate coleslaw lunch." Asked whether her reaction was the appropriate one, she shakes her head and laughs, seemingly at herself. "Oh, no. I should have eaten the dumb hamburger. It's a perfectly good symbol [meatless Fridays] to remind people of the need to make sacrifices. But it seems silly now; it's so outdated. I don't think eating salmon is more sacrificial or somehow morally superior to eating at Burger King." Many people provide similar examples of how religious practices associated with the devotional Catholicism of the past have come to seem hollow.

After this set of examples, the next largest category of "then, but now" stories focuses on hell. Even the minority of parishioners who claim to believe in hell do so with a strong tendency toward what one scholar calls "religious metaphorization."[10] "Hell used to scare the hell out of me," reminisces a member of Saint Augustine parish. "I still believe in it, but I imagine it differently now." He continues:

> It's not about fire and brimstone and all that anymore, I can tell you that. I read Dante's *The Divine Comedy* a few years back. He had lots of fire and brimstone, too. But what I most appreciated about his vision was that each person's hell conformed to what kind of person they were. So, I guess, my vision is kind of similar in that I think we create our own hells. God's love is raining down on us all the time. All we have to do is be open to it. But if you're cutting yourself off from other people and you're focused inward—closed in on yourself—then you're cutting yourself off from God's love. That's hell as far as I'm concerned. I don't know how long it lasts or who experiences it, but I do think it represents something we do to ourselves.

These two Catholics are similar in the sense that they have not only come to see a traditional practice and image as symbols. They have also discerned them to be less effective symbols than they once were, and thus they feel entitled to reject or rework them as they see fit.

Especially worrisome to many church leaders are indications that more central aspects of the faith are no longer immune to this kind of symbolic negotiation. For instance, a much discussed and debated 1994 *New York Times* poll posed the following question to a national sample of Catholics: "Which of the following comes closest to what you believe takes place at Mass: 1. the bread and wine are changed into the body and blood of Christ, or 2. the bread and wine are symbolic reminders of Christ?"[11] Only about one-third of those surveyed selected the first response (the Real Presence of Christ), which is what the church actually teaches. Among Catholics who attend Mass every or almost every week, that percentage rose to 44 percent, with a slight majority (51 percent) still choosing the "symbolic reminders" response. Whether these data suggest a creeping metaphorization of the Real Presence in the Eucharist is an open question.[12] However, it is evident that Catholics are not shy about reworking even the most important of symbols if they do not make sense to them.

Deborah Ragin is another good example. A Eucharistic minister at Most Holy Redeemer, she ardently believes in the Real Presence because of her sacramental view of the world, whereby God is understood as present within every aspect of creation.[13] Yet, the very same sacramental imagination that leads her to believe in one Catholic doctrine causes her to see another as a religious symbol that has outlived its usefulness. She says she used to believe that Jesus was "born of the Virgin Mary," but that was when she was younger and, she admits, before she had done much "real, honest thinking" about her faith. Now she sees this as an outdated and patriarchal symbol that once represented the holiness of the Holy Family but is actually contrary to a deeper sense of sacramentalism. "Sex, like everything in the entire cosmos, is so natural and yet so close to God," she says. "I can't see our wonderful God doing anything so unnatural and so violent in becoming one with us. To keep pushing that doctrine is just another example of the shattered vision many of our church leaders seem to have."

Like Ragin, many parishioners are intent on employing their own religious imaginations to arrive at a clearer, more individually compelling version of the faith and vision of the sacred. This, too, reflects their awareness of O'Dea's symbolic dilemma. They deconstruct those symbols that no longer or insufficiently express a sense of ultimacy for them while recognizing the inevitability of symbolization. This recognition seems to goad them into becoming theological "constructivists" as well.[14] We have already seen instances of this. Incorporating Vietnamese and African American identity into the Mass are good examples. So, too, are the highly stylized liturgies at Saint Margaret Mary and expressions of gay pride at Most Holy Redeemer. These are all attempts to resymbolize the sacred and thus revivify people's experience of it. Doing this kind of improvisational work on the symbols of their age-old faith—pouring the old wine of tradition into new symbolic wineskins—is how more and more Catholics attempt to rectify the symbolic dilemma.

Among parishioners' numerous "construction areas," perhaps the most interesting to observe is, as the title of a widely read book on American spirituality puts it, their symbolic "working on God."[15] Table 4.1 tells us some basic things about what parishioners say about God's existence, as well as their views about the Bible, a major source of their knowledge about God.

The first and most obvious thing to notice in table 4.1 is that these active parishioners believe in God. The proportion (81 percent) who say they believe with "no doubts" well exceeds the three in five American adults who say this. Whereas the

TABLE 4.1. Opinions about God's existence and the Bible (in %).

	Most Holy Redeemer	St. Monica	St. Mary–St. Francis	St. Augustine	St. Louis Bertrand	St. Margaret Mary	Total
Opinions about God's existence [a]							
I don't believe in a personal God but I do believe in a higher power of some kind.	2	2	0	3	4	0	2 (7)
While I have doubts, I feel that I do believe in God.	17	31	26	19	7	5	17 (15)
I know God really exists, and I have no doubts about it.	81	67	74	78	88	95	81 (60)
Opinions about the Bible [b]							
It is the actual word of God and is to be taken literally, word for word.	2	2	9	12	38	10	15 (34)
It is the inspired word of God, but not everything in it should be taken literally, word for word.	81	89	84	86	53	89	78 (47)
It is an ancient book of fables, legends, history, and moral precepts recorded by men.	17	9	7	2	8	0	7 (16)

[a] National data (listed in parentheses), which are taken from the 2000 General Social Survey, do not include "Don't know" (3.6%) and "No answer" (5.2%) categories. They also do not include the following categories also offered to Bay Area parishioners but selected by none of them: "I don't believe in God" (2.6%); "I don't know whether there is a God, and I don't believe there is any way to find out" (3.8%); and "I find myself believing in God some of the time but not at others" (3.2%). Parish data may not add up to 100 percent due to rounding off.

[b] National data (listed in parentheses), which are taken from the 2004 General Social Survey, do not include "Other" (1.7%), "Don't know" (1.0%), and "No answer" (0.5%) categories. Parish data may not add up to 100 percent due to rounding off.

proportion who believe with some doubts—hardly uncommon among even the most saintly past and present—is about the same as that for Americans as a whole. Second, consonant with church teaching, they understand biblical narratives and discourse about God as largely symbolic, a fact that gives them further license to exercise their own religious imaginations when conceptualizing divinity. The 78 percent who say the Bible is inspired by God but should not be taken literally is significantly higher than the 47 percent of Americans who say this. Furthermore, their rate of biblical literalism is less than half that of the 34 percent of Americans who say scripture should be taken "word for word." Third, as usual, these data reveal interesting variations among parishes. For instance, conservative Saint Louis Bertrand and Saint Margaret Mary parishes seem to harbor less religious doubt within them, Saint Louis Bertrand (the parish with the lowest average level of educational attainment) evinces more literalism, people at Most Holy Redeemer are the most willing to think of the Bible as an ancient book of fables, and so on.

Conversations with Catholics also reveal their desire to reconceptualize God in ways that better resonate with their experiences. They clearly see themselves as constructing new symbolic images, which becomes obvious when they discuss the inadequacies of their previous, now seemingly unsophisticated, understandings of God. Referencing these, they offer caveats incessantly. "God isn't up there with a scorecard deciding who wins and who loses." "I don't think God's an accountant keeping track of every little thing people do." "God's not some kind of puppeteer pulling all the strings and making everything happen just the way He wants." "God doesn't follow some stupid job description, especially not the one we devise ourselves." And so it goes. Occasionally parishioners will talk in ways that reflect these kinds of judgmental, controlling, and largely domesticated images of God, but overwhelmingly they do not. "This is a theological 'hard-hat area'!," these caveats seem to declare. Moreover, when parishioners talk about God, three very noticeable themes emerge from the images they construct: theological reflexivity, divine inscrutability, and the subjective confirmation of their beliefs.

Consider the first theme. In much the same way as Catholics often recognize symbols of God as symbols when they want to deconstruct them, the same is true when they attempt to fashion more meaningful images. Let us return to Deborah Ragin as someone who exemplifies the self-conscious approach to symbols, which the term *reflexivity* denotes. "Sometimes I can fall back into the wrong God," she admits, explaining how she still feels the pull of dogmatism's "shattered vision" that "too often mistakes words about God for the reality of God." Encouraged to say more about this, she adds:

> I believe the real God is so beyond us, beyond me, that we only get fleeting
> glimpses when we're especially open. It can happen when I feel the rain or see

a little kitten or, you know, when I reflect on all the millions of good things that are happening everyday. Or, even now as I'm having this great conversation with you, Jerome. But I have to admit that I'm not always aware and open. I think that some of the bad projections or bad images of God I was raised with still make this kind of openness difficult sometimes. So I focus on more life-giving, beautiful images. It's also what I love about centering prayer: You can just let go and be in God's presence without any words.

Second, if parishioners like her increasingly assume responsibility for their own symbols for God, they certainly do not feel any responsibility for understanding God. As we saw in the previous chapter, many focus on their sense of divine inscrutability to legitimate their embrace of religious pluralism. But there is more to it than this. They also tend to embrace God's mysteriousness as a way of highlighting the vast chasm between humanity and the sacred Other. "I was raised in the era of the *Baltimore Catechism*," explained Delores Cimino, a member of Saint Augustine's church for more than four decades. "Back then, they seemed to put God in a box. But after a divorce, a lot of heartache, and a lot of living, I think I've learned, among a few other things, that God doesn't even come close to fitting in that box." Reflecting further on this, she referred to a television program she had recently seen about a boy in India who was being blinded by particularly invasive bacteria. Asked what this tells her about God, she replied:

> It is the very same God who made that bacteria on the bank of the Ganges that eats at the boy's eye who created your wife and son, who you love so much. I believe God is loving even if He also makes that bacteria. My youngest daughter just turned forty-eight on Sunday, and she tells me she has a heart murmur, a little tear in one of her valves. I went to church that day. It was the day for the Veneration of the Cross. And I was sitting next to this woman who lost her child when he was twelve, and not a day goes by when she doesn't think about that little boy. So I thought there are all sorts of crosses and that maybe my daughter will die. But you can't blame God.

Why not?

> It is life. The Cross isn't an interruption of life; it's a part of what life really is. God doesn't have His finger on you or me or my daughter, saying, "I'm going to make this and this happen." That's too simple. Creation is unexplainable, and God is, too. But my belief as a Christian is that God is loving, and love is the proper response to that, and it's the proper response to my daughter's situation, to that damn bacteria, to everything.

Like Ragin, Cimino knows perhaps all too well that procrustean images that seem to contain God in a rigid box are "too simple." Less simple symbols, they both agree, must not faint-heartedly diminish the absolute otherness of a God who can be experienced in both life and death, in the rain and amid conversations, and in bacteria and heart murmurs. Not surprisingly, when asked to provide Bible passages that are especially meaningful to them, both of these women (like many people) mention the story in Mark's gospel when the disciples try to shoo children away from Jesus. Instead, Jesus tells them, "Let the children come to me, do not hinder them; for to such belongs the kingdom of God" (Mk. 10:14). They know this is one biblical symbol among many, but they also suggest that, by comparing themselves to unsophisticated children relative to the mysterious sacred, this symbol remains meaningful to them.

These two themes relate to the shift in religious authority described in the previous chapter. Not content with a "Father knows best" approach to their faith, Catholics often assume for themselves the burden of distinguishing the symbols they find meaningful from those they do not. Also, given their sense of God's inscrutability, they know there is no guarantee that religious leaders are better equipped to fathom the unfathomable than they themselves are. Without a literalist reliance on scripture and without ceding their religious authority to magisterial pronouncements, the only way for them to know that what they know about God is actually true is through their own subjective experience. Over and over, people confirm the validity of their symbolic constructions by pointing within. Such symbols, as religious studies scholar Adam Seligman contends, are today most apt to be "innerly justified" in light of whether they coincide with significant, especially emotionally charged, personal experiences.[16]

Consider the story Diane Mencken tells of the time her three-year-old son went into severe anaphylactic shock outside a local restaurant. This long-time volunteer with Saint Augustine's religious education program recalls that her previous image of God was that of a judge who "basically decided who was naughty or nice" and a kind of "white knight who's there to protect people from harm." However, true to the "then, but now" pattern, this all changed as she got older. Like Ragin and Cimino, she began to see God as a loving presence permeating everything in ways too complex to entirely understand. "Kneeling next to my son in that parking lot really affirmed what I had come to believe about God," she says with tears filling her eyes:

> His voice had already started to go up a pitch, and so, with my medical background, I knew his airway was closing. There was nothing I could do but stand and wait and connect with who we are. At that moment I felt a deeper love than I've ever felt. It wasn't like God saved my son. It was

"Here we are," you know? I knelt there, and I felt a very concrete presence right here, behind my right shoulder. I felt it more clearly than how I'm seeing you sitting in that chair right now. And it was filled with peace and love and understanding. And I knew at that moment that it really didn't matter what happened to my son, as weird as that might sound. I knew in my head he might die or, if the oxygen was cut off from his brain for too long, he might be brain damaged. But I also knew it didn't matter, and, at the same time, it was like I could feel the whole world's suffering. And that didn't matter either except I felt the same love for the world as I did for my son. It was all crammed into that moment.

At this point, there was a break in the interview in order to find some Kleenex for Mencken, who had begun to sob. Returning, she summed up the experience: "I think I will mine that experience for the rest of my life. I mean it didn't change my spirituality or anything, but it confirmed and deepened what I've come to believe. The experience was as beautiful as it was painful. I guess it did help me to appreciate that better: that it's sometimes essential for pain and joy to come together."

Mencken is no stranger to O'Dea's symbolic dilemma. She understands that her access to God is mediated by the symbols available to her and that they can lose their impact over time, especially as she herself changes. She also knows that their worth is best discerned by looking within and authenticating what she believes about God through the most reliable means at her disposal: her own subjective experience of sacredness.

The Dilemma of Delimitation

In order to make the message of a religion comprehensible to its followers and to protect it from the corrosive effects of idiosyncratic interpretation, some definition and concretization of that message is necessary. Yet, reminiscent of Saint Paul's warning that "the letter killeth, but the spirit giveth life" (2 Cor. 3:6), O'Dea argues that delimiting the religion's sense of the holy Inscrutable through the use of wholly scrutable theological doctrines and ethical rules can drain the faith of its vitality. "While the dangers of distortion of the faith of the church require these definitions of dogma and morals," he writes, "once established, the definitions themselves pose the possibility of another kind of distortion. They become a vast intellectual structure which serves not to guide the faith of untrained specialists but rather to burden it."[17] Closely related to the previous dilemma, this one shifts the focus from the effectiveness of symbols to the potentially burdensome effect that propositional expressions of the faith will have on believers' embrace of its fundamental message.

Once again, Catholics actually appear to be aware of both this dilemma and its accompanying burdens. Generally conceding the need for official definitions and teachings, they nevertheless tend to rely on their own holistic understanding of the faith to discern which of these are binding on them and which are not. Table 4.2 provides a good illustration of this. It records percentages of active parishioners who say that one can be a "good Catholic" without doing or believing the things listed.

A few things are worth noting. One is that, similar to what the previous tables have shown, each parish has its own culture, one that is somewhat or extremely different from the others. Also, as usual, the "total" response rates among them track very consistently with those of American Catholics as a whole (shown in parentheses). No doubt because they are parish based and generally more committed as Catholics, with the exception of Item 4 on papal infallibility (for which I had to use 1993 data, so this may no longer be an exception), the distinctly active parishioners in this study are dependably *less* likely than Catholics nationally to provide the more theologically liberal response. Finally, taken in the aggregate, these respondents do not at all appear to be overly burdened by O'Dea's dilemma of delimitation. The rules and regulations that define a Catholic in good standing may indeed have evolved (or devolved, as some might have it) into a "vast intellectual structure," but the rank and file seem to possess their own internalized sense of which among these are most central to the faith. Doctrines concerning the Real Presence (Item 7) and Jesus's Resurrection (Item 8) are far more likely to be cited by parishioners as theological sine qua nons for marking the boundaries of Catholic identity than, for example, obeying church teaching that prohibits the use of contraception (Item 1).

This tendency to push certain components of the tradition to the periphery largely reflects what psychologist Eugene Kennedy sees as the gradual supplanting of one culture of American Catholicism for another. "Culture One" Catholics, he calls them, strongly identify with the church as a hierarchical institution to which they look for authoritative teachings, with which they then attempt to comply. "Culture Two" Catholics, who often still consider themselves serious Catholics, emphasize personal autonomy and accordingly are less willing to obey or even remain attuned to institutional directives. "Culture One gave birth to Culture Two," Kennedy observes, "taught it powerful ideals, including the moral obligation of its members to believe and think for themselves. And so they have. They form their own consciences as they confront multiple daily choices; they exhibit a readiness to do this without necessarily perceiving themselves as rebels against the institutional order of the first culture. To act independently and responsibly cannot always be accurately depicted as a revolt against authority. Most people," he concludes, "regard it as growing up."[18]

Most of the people interviewed for this book would say the same. Although both types of Catholics can be found within each of the six parishes in this study,

TABLE 4.2. "Please tell me if you think a person can be a good Catholic without performing these actions or affirming these beliefs." Numbers represent percentages of people who responded "yes."

	Most Holy Redeemer	St. Monica	St. Mary–St. Francis	St. Augustine	St. Louis Bertrand	St. Margaret Mary	Total
1. Without obeying the church hierarchy's teaching on birth control	95	93	61	81	47	35	68 (75)
2. Without going to church every Sunday	83	80	56	70	46	40	61 (76)
3. Without their marriage being approved by the Catholic Church	90	78	50	66	46	40	61 (67)
4. Without believing in the infallibility of the pope	95	78	64	66	41	18	59 (50)
5. Without obeying the church's teaching against engaging in homosexual relations	93	71	49	71	27	15	53 (NA)
6. Without obeying the church hierarchy's teaching regarding abortion	78	27	33	47	23	13	36 (58)
7. Without believing that, in the Mass, the bread and wine actually become the body and blood of Jesus	34	20	25	27	17	8	22 (36)
8. Without believing that Jesus physically rose from the dead	28	22	16	14	14	8	16 (23)

Note: National percentages (listed in parentheses) are taken from D'Antonio et al. (2007), except for Item 4, which is taken from D'Antonio et al. (1996).

the active parishioners I interviewed are much more likely to fit the "Culture Two" mold, and they also tend to present this in a very positive light. In doing so, no one mentioned the great nineteenth-century theologian and cardinal John Henry Newman, but they almost always made implicit use of his famous distinction between notional and real assent to religious truth.[19] They are able to surmount the dilemma of delimitation, they consistently suggest, because rather than simply accepting various concepts and doctrines about God intellectually (notional assent), they have experienced the power of the Christian faith in their lives and assimilated its overall logic within their own imaginations. This felt sense of real assent functions as a kind of theological filter that greatly reduces those components of Catholicism's "vast intellectual structure" they consider germane to them.

About three-quarters of American adults tell pollsters that, rather than indicating weakened piety, questioning can actually strengthen one's religious faith. In accordance with this general trend toward decreasing institutional control over individuals' beliefs, the proportion of American Catholics (79 percent) who say they would follow their own consciences when faced with moral questions dwarfs the relatively scant 16 percent who say they would adhere to papal teachings.[20] As noted earlier, this exercise of religious agency, along with attendant expectations of discernment and personal growth, is reflected in parishioners' incessant references to "my faith."

They find notional assent alone to be inadequate and, in myriad ways, express their desire to move beyond it. Saint Monica choir member Dale Perrow epitomizes this. For him, it is actually intellectual suspicion, not assent, that is most precipitous of spiritual maturity. "I think you should always doubt because that gives you the drive to mature religiously," he says. "Questioning things keeps you from becoming passive, becoming like some kind of sheep. 'Baa, baaaa!' That's not the sound of a spiritually alive person. We have to question in order to grow, and we have to grow if we want to be fully human." Asked how this squares with his identity as a Catholic, he explains:

Being a good Catholic is about choosing to follow Jesus through the church but not letting the church corrupt your faith. By that I mean that being very faithful to your conscience is extremely important. And, by that I mean that, when confronted with issues in life, you have to take the time to inform yourself. You might end up being in opposition to what the church teaches, but you need to follow the higher road of being true to yourself and having a clean conscience before God. So I think someone can be a fantastic Catholic and be in opposition to set guidelines and rules if they've done their homework—if they've considered church teaching but, most of all, let the example of Jesus inform their conscience.

Perrow sees notional assent as passive, sheeplike, and linked to an institutional apparatus that is potentially corrupting of something deeper and more fully alive. That something is the Holy Spirit, many are quick to specify. Real assent to Catholicism is widely taken to mean being moved to see the world in a new way and respond to it with love. "The Spirit of God enables you to see how holy the world really is and how precious every single person is," says Denise Jarry, a founding member of the women's spirituality group at Saint Monica. Moreover, the subjective confirmation of her convictions, provided by her experience of the Spirit, also enables her to see the institution in a more critical manner. "The church focuses too much on doctrinal trappings and maintaining itself as an institution and not enough on the Gospel," she says. "It's going to have to change, and it has a perfect example in how to do this in Christ. He was a devout Jew but didn't knuckle under the system. He said, 'You're missing the basic point; you're missing God.' You see, he was growing in his sense of the Spirit. But church leaders tend to be too rigid. It saddens me to see them missing God."

Spanning high above "set guidelines and rules," posits Perrow, is the higher road of the informed conscience. Furthermore, in Jarry's view, trumping the institution's interest in maintaining itself and its rigid adherence to "doctrinal trappings" is that "sense of the Spirit," toward which Jesus grew and toward which his followers must also aspire if they are not to miss God. Both, in other words, subtly point to their real assent to religious truth, which leaves them relatively unencumbered by the "definitions of doctrine and morals" O'Dea describes as necessary for religious institutions.

They both also point to the example of Jesus as the model for doing the theological filtering required of mature Catholics. This pointing is likewise done in a subtle way. About 70 percent of Americans identify Jesus as God, and about two-thirds claim he was "without sin." Nearly nine in ten Catholics describe the belief that he was both fully human and fully God as either "very" or "fairly" important to them.[21] Bay Area parishioners share this "high Christology" and overwhelmingly believe in the divinity of Jesus. Yet, when they go beyond saying what they believe and, in a more constructivist mode, actually *use* their understanding of Jesus to help them differentiate the notional from the real—the institutionally controlled expressions of faith from their own experience of faith—they just as overwhelmingly base this on what they claim to know about the humanity of Jesus. It is then that they tap into the deep-seated strand in American culture that distinguishes between what historian Stephen Prothero labels the "religion *of* Jesus" and the "religion *about* Jesus," whereby the former is typically used to criticize the latter.[22]

Perrow relies on the religion *of* Jesus—his exemplary life, his way of seeing the world—to inform his conscience and, when necessary, to be in opposition to the institutional pronouncements about Jesus. So, too, does Jarry criticize the church hierarchy based on her image of Jesus, who, growing in his sense of the sacred, refused to knuckle under to the dominant religious institutions of his day. As a "regular guy," a "roughly hewn man," "someone who got enlightened," a "person filled with love"—people inevitably use labels that connote Jesus's humanity when accounting for how he relates to their faith as Catholics. This is especially true when they criticize the "vast intellectual structure" *about* Jesus. "Nobody ever says this," explains Most Holy Redeemer homeless activist Jeramy Faris, "but isn't it obvious why Jesus hung out with prostitutes and tax collectors and, you know, common laborers, fishermen? It's because they were his spiritual guides; they kept him on track. I think he liked people on the fringes of acceptability. And I think they kept him from falling into all the normative categories and from seeing the world from the center." Faris is correct: Most parishioners do not say these people on the fringes actually kept Jesus on the right track. Yet they are extremely likely to say that Jesus does this for them. "Jesus was like the ultimate shit disturber!" asserts Natalie Poston, a volunteer with Saint Augustine's RCIA and family faith-formation programs. "He was the one who wasn't afraid to say, 'I think you all got it backward.' He turned people's view of the world upside down. You know, he told people that what seems weak is actually strong, the last shall be first, stuff like that." To the question of how this influences her today, she responds:

> It influences me greatly because it means I don't have to be tied down by a tradition that doesn't feel true to me. I can still participate but, at the same time, not be afraid to say, "What does this mean?" "Where does this doctrine come from?" "How can we change that teaching?" Jesus doesn't talk much about saving your sorry self from hell. He never tells us how many points to rack up in order to get into heaven. He says to not be afraid to ask questions and shake things up; he says to focus on the big picture of loving your neighbor rather than focusing on a bunch of commandments; he says to get in touch with your divinity. To me, Jesus' life says, "Go hit the home run; go out there and be big-hearted and make a difference." I don't get all caught up in the minutiae—in the "I believe this doctrine, or I didn't steal today, so I'm a good Catholic" stuff—because life is bigger than that, and our challenge is bigger than that.

Similar to sociologist Michele Dillon's depiction of pro-change Catholics "using doctrine to critique doctrine," people like Poston deploy a "low Christology" and use the example of the less acceptable and big-hearted Jesus to critique the church as a definition-obsessed institution.[23] Rather than hitting a home run by staying close to the religion *of* Jesus, they contend, the church too often takes its eye off the ball by making endless pronouncements *about* the sacred and, in the process, ends up striking out with many parishioners.

The Dilemma of Administrative Order

If Catholics negotiate with theological elaborations *about* Jesus, they do the same with an ecclesial bureaucracy that has grown *beyond* anything Jesus could ever have imagined. This brings us to O'Dea's third dilemma, "the necessity of developing a system of administrative order versus the danger of its over-elaboration."[24] Such a system, which he always recognizes as indispensable to maintaining the church's place in the social world, inevitably becomes unwieldy and resistant to change and, as such, also comes with certain dangers he spells out. "Not only can the structure become overelaborated and alienated from contemporary problems," O'Dea writes, "but it can contribute to the alienation of office holders from the rank-and-file members of the group."[25]

This dilemma and its accompanying dangers are hardly news to most parishioners. They understand that formal organizations, as one scholar puts it, "are a prominent, if not the dominant, characteristic of modern societies."[26] In addition, they know that their church is, among other things, a religious organization replete with the same kinds of shortcomings they have come to know through their daily interactions with organizations of other kinds. "Do you know another church where everybody is a saint?" asks one Saint Augustine member who seems to sum up most parishioners' basic attitude. "That church doesn't exist. If you're waiting to find the perfect church, the perfect environment, the perfect message, and the perfect people, you're going to spend the rest of your life in vain because you're not going to find it. Of course, there are problems in the church, but that doesn't have to prevent you from living a Christian life."

Even though aspirations about perfecting the institution usually take a back seat to parishioners simply trying to live out their faiths to the best of their abilities, this does not mean that they are blind to ways they think it could and should be improved. Like Catholics nationally, they are wary of what famed political sociologist Robert Michels once called "the iron law of oligarchy," the strong tendency of unmonitored organizational leaders to amass increasing power, pursue their own interests and, in the process, subvert the organization's foundational ideals.[27] This is one of the reasons they want more democratic decision making at all levels within the church.[28] One nationwide study has found that, not including "matters of faith," majorities of Catholics favored "more democratic decision making in church affairs" at each of the parish (66 percent), diocesan (61 percent), and even Vatican (55 percent) levels.[29] Table 4.3 demonstrates that a desire for greater lay participation is about as evident in the Bay Area as it is nationally (data in parentheses).

As the first two items indicate, the closer decisions get to the life of the parish, the more people want to assist in making them. Once again the local and national samples of Catholics track fairly closely. However, since my respondents

TABLE 4.3. "For each of the following areas of church life, please tell me if you think the Catholic laity should have the right to participate or should not have the right to participate." Numbers represent percentages of people who responded "should."

	Most Holy Redeemer	St. Monica	St. Mary– St. Francis	St. Augustine	St. Louis Bertrand	St. Margaret Mary	Total
1. Deciding how parish income should be spent	95	98	86	92	78	75	87 (89)
2. Selecting the priests for their parish	98	89	64	53	78	35	69 (71)
3. Deciding whether women should be ordained to the priesthood	90	87	57	66	49	23	61 (64)
4. Making church policy about birth control	88	78	52	54	51	20	57 (62)
5. Making church policy about divorce	88	76	52	54	45	15	54 (61)

Note: National percentages (listed in parentheses) are taken from D'Antonio et al. (2007), except for Items 4 and 5, which are taken from D'Antonio et al. (1996).

are especially active within their parishes, it is not surprising that they would want more voice in managing parish finances (Item 1) and that they would be somewhat more cautious about delving into matters of church policy (Items 2–5) than those within the national sample.

Greater lay participation is one way Catholics seem to want to resolve the dilemma of administrative order. Furthermore, along with this resistance to potentially oligarchical *administering,* they also tend to resist the excessive *orderliness* of administrative order. In other words, parishioners truly appreciate and respect the catholicity of their church; as one reflected, "It's amazing that it's the same church in Oakland as it is in Ireland and Kenya and in the Philippines." Still, many are equally insistent about differentiating catholicity as a kind of unity-in-difference worthy of their amazement from a meticulously ordered, prepackaged, and overly standardized version of the faith they claim is often bequeathed to them by church leaders. In this excessive orderliness they appear to detect a religious equivalent of the creeping "McDonaldization" that sociologist George Ritzer sees as an increasingly defining feature of contemporary institutions and culture.[30] A Big Mac prepared at one McDonalds restaurant is essentially the same as one prepared at another franchise across town, but, as one parishioner muses, "the religious life is supposed to be a lot messier than I think some people realize."

People illustrate this broad appreciation for religious messiness in many ways. Some mention the ways in which the church has changed over the centuries or, as previously discussed, how their own religious understanding has altered over the years. Some highlight disagreements among theologians or the fact that divergent gospel accounts of Jesus's life and ministry have quite intentionally been included together in the biblical canon. Most often, though, people who talk about the messiness of the religious life point to the messiness of their parish communities. Many of them see this resistance to excessive orderliness as a kind of spiritual gift. Being receptive to other perspectives is generally construed as a way for people to escape their "comfort zones" and to further open themselves to God's grace. "I think there's room under the tent for everybody," says Saint Mary–Saint Francis parishioner Joyce Wallace. "Diversity and dissent are necessary because they shake things up a bit and keep people from being complacent. After all, we're all after the same thing: finding God in one another." Others see it as an obligation. Frank DeLong, another Saint Mary–Saint Francis parishioner, attributes the decreasingly ordered and increasingly messy—albeit strengthened, he insists—nature of his own faith to his interactions with the Vietnamese and Filipino parishioners who serve with him on the parish council. "I now have much more of a sense that things do move, things are revealed, and our knowledge of truth grows over time," he says. "It's not rigid or fixed. Some people want it to be that way. You know, 'God said it, I believe it, conversation over!' But it's really much more complex than that. They [the Vietnamese and Filipino parishioners] have had different experiences, and they often have different priorities and different ways of seeing things. We can't walk away from all that. We're responsible to struggle with this stuff together."

These Catholics prefer lay participation to oligarchy. And, in place of McDonaldization, they prefer minimal standardization. They view their parish less as a local Vatican franchise and more as a site where the disorderliness of lived religion opens them to God's grace and obliges them to grapple with their own biases. Without doubt, these are their often strongly articulated preferences, and these two organizational tendencies are frequently described as being highly problematic. It is also clear that parishioners typically see the dilemma of administrative order as simply that—a dilemma. They know that some organization is necessary, even as they likewise know that it is far from perfect and, in the end, far less important to them than their own efforts to connect with the sacred. Nowhere is this ability to hold both horns of the dilemma more obvious than in their discussions of the church's sex abuse scandal. In 2004 a national survey listed twelve pressing church issues and asked Catholics which of these they considered to be "a serious problem." The top two (and the only two that more than three-quarters of Catholics deemed serious) were "that some priests have sexually abused young people" (85 percent) and "that some bishops have not done enough to stop priests from sexually abusing young people" (77 percent).[31] Bay Area parishioners also see this scandal as a serious problem. When discussing it, they offer three additional points that demonstrate, to a degree that surveys cannot, their capacity for reflexivity about the church as an organization.

First, they use distinctly organizational language to depict the church hierarchy and thus this scandal. "I think the magisterium of the church is a corporation," explains Saint Augustine's Delores Cimino. "And I feel no more allegiance to it than I would feel to the Bank of America. I really don't think of myself as Catholic in that sense. Actually, I think the pope and the whole hierarchy don't constitute the church and are more about institutional self-preservation than anything else." Many people echo these sentiments. Joyce Wallace certainly does, and, when queried about whether the scandal has affected either her faith or her attitude toward the church, she responded:

> No. It makes me outraged; it makes me angry, but I have for a very, very long time seen the church as a multinational corporation that has every motive to behave in a certain way. When I read articles in the paper about the scandal, I always think that this is how any corporation would behave in a lawsuit. It's upsetting to me because, in Boston, the cardinal was much more interested in protecting the church financially and protecting— maybe not individual priests—but certainly the reputation of the church

than he was in protecting children. And, to me, this is antithetical to Christ's teaching and to what the church's teaching should be, so that was upsetting. But in terms of affecting my faith, no.

Second, as Wallace mentions and as we saw with respect to the previous dilemma, people use the example of Jesus as a means of criticizing the institution for its emphasis on self-preservation. They do not stop there, though. In the interest of comparing the faith's foundational message with what they see as the church's present-day succumbing to O'Dea's "danger of its over-elaboration," people offer all kinds of biblical allusions. For instance, one very liberal parishioner from Saint Monica compares the institution to King David, who, while chosen by God, still fell into sin with Bathsheba and, rather than trusting in God, turned toward military might and treaties with other nations. A very conservative parishioner at Saint Margaret Mary, on the other hand, compares both offending priests and irresponsible bishops to Judas Iscariot. "There was a bad seed among the original Twelve," he notes, "and just because Judas betrayed Jesus doesn't mean I shouldn't be a Christian." Finally, several people of various ideological stripes use Saint Peter as an interpretive key when coming to grips with the scandal. "I went to Rome and to Saint Peter's Basilica a few years back and thought, 'This is the closest thing to a corporate headquarters I've ever seen in my life,'" reflected one of them. After mentioning the gospels' accounts of Peter's at times weak faith and his threefold denial of Christ, this parishioner concluded, "But it was really appropriate for Jesus to found his church on Peter because he's weak and he abandons Jesus and, basically, because he reminds us of who the church has been ever since."

Finally, this scandal may have adversely affected some Catholics' faith and even tempted (or caused) some to leave the church. Without exception, though, these parishioners say this has not been the case with them. Time and again, they repeat Wallace's refrain distinguishing the organizational logic of the institutional church from their own faith or, as the more traditionalist would have it, from the true church, as Christ intended it to be. Some are quite forthcoming about their hopes that something positive will ultimately come from the scandal. These range from bringing more Catholics to the realization that church leaders are "just human," to eliminating celibacy requirements or homosexuals from the priesthood, to opening new avenues for lay participation in church governance. No one knows for sure whether or to what extent any of these things will occur. According to these accounts, what most people do understand is that, just as there is a difference between notional and real assent, differences also exist between commitment to the church as an institution and commitment to the faith. As with the previous dilemma, they negotiate this one by privileging the second of these categories over the first.

The Dilemma of Mixed Motivation

According to O'Dea, a key trait of any fledgling religious group at its initial, pre-institutionalized stage is that, unable to provide members with many extrinsic benefits, it tends to attract only those who are single-mindedly devoted to the values and lifestyle embodied by the group's founder. This stage, however, does not last long. In order to survive, groups must be able to create a stable structure (complete with defined statuses and roles) capable of steering a variety of motivations toward its goals and, in doing so, appeal to a broader swath of people. Yet, by bringing into its fold people with mixed motivations, the group may strengthen itself as a social institution while reducing the level of commitment to its founding values.

O'Dea's primary example of this is the creation of a professional clergy. "There comes into existence a body of men for whom the clerical life offers not simply the 'religious' satisfactions of the earlier charismatic period," he writes, "but also prestige and respectability, power and influence, in both church and society, and satisfactions derived from the use of personal talents in teaching, leadership, etc. Moreover, the *maintenance* of the situation in which these rewards are forthcoming tends to become an element in the motivation of the group."[32] Because clergy have an interest in maintaining their status within both the church and the broader society, O'Dea argues, these mixed motivations also make it more difficult to resolve some of the problems associated with the dilemma of administrative order. "Genuine organizational reform becomes threatening to the status, security and self-validation of the incumbents of office," he observes.[33]

Such issues—as well as laypeople's overall awareness of this fourth dilemma—are most clearly reflected in conversations about the church's restricting its priesthood to men. Of course, not everyone sees this as a by-product of institutionalization. Throughout the parishes, especially at Saint Margaret Mary, people echo the three basic reasons the Vatican gives to explain its ban on women's ordination.[34] Some, for instance, agree with the Vatican's position that its teaching respects the intention of Christ, whose apostles were all men. "Women helped Jesus in his ministry, but not as priests," explained one Saint Margaret Mary parishioner. "If Jesus wanted women to be priests, he could have made his mother or some of these other women priestesses or one of the twelve apostles."

Others rely upon the argument that a clear delineation of gender roles is integral to the church's unchanging tradition. "It has a long tradition that goes back hundreds or thousands of years," says another from this same parish. "Biologically, men and women are different, and that doesn't mean one is better or worse than the other; it's just that we're different, and we do different things better. Just because I can't be a priest doesn't mean I'm not valuable. I get to stay at home and raise the children, without whom there'd be no church. No matter how many priests or popes there are, they'll never be a mom, and that role is really very special."

Finally, heard almost solely at Saint Margaret Mary, some people rely on the Vatican's position that, because the priest acts *in persona Christi* [in the person of Christ] during the consecration of the Eucharist, he must resemble Christ physically. By physically, they are quick to add, they do not mean with respect to race or height, for example. They claim that sex differences are symbolically important because they reveal something profound about humanity's relationship with God. "Marriage is a sign that points us toward some ultimate realities," one parishioner explained:

> It is there to help us understand the union Christ has with his church. In God's becoming man, he demonstrates a relationship with us where, in essence, we're the bride and he's the bridegroom. He's the man, and we— all of humanity—are in the position of the woman, where he initiates the love; we receive his love into us, and then we give our love back to him. So, to have a priest who's acting in the person of Christ during the Mass to be anything other than a man, to have a woman on the altar, would be a bride and a woman uniting. It's more a symbol of lesbianism than anything else. It's an incomplete sign. We're sexual beings. By nature, the male is the active half, and the woman receives. And that's how we're in relationship with God. We don't initiate it; we give of ourselves by receiving. And so it's important for men to symbolize that on the altar.

Most American Catholics do not consider these three reasons to be reasonable at all. Despite John Paul II's 1994 pronouncement that his restricting the priesthood to men is a judgment that "is to be definitively held by all the church's faithful" and that further discussion of the issue is prohibited, they generally neither hold this view nor feel particularly obliged to hold their tongues when the issue arises in conversation.[35] With respect to their opinions on the matter, table 4.4 shows that a majority of both the Bay Area Catholics interviewed for this study and Catholics nationally (data in parentheses) either "strongly" or "somewhat" agree that it would be a good thing if, in descending order of acceptability, married men (Item 1), celibate women (Item 2), and married women (Item 3) were admitted into the priesthood.

It is clear that, papal pronouncements notwithstanding, many parishioners have thought, read, and talked about this issue quite a bit. For the most part, they are both opinionated and knowledgeable. They mention that some of the original apostles were married and that some of Jesus's most faithful supporters were women. They speak approvingly of the Eastern Rite churches (in union with Rome), which have had married priests since their beginnings, and of Protestant

TABLE 4.4. "Please indicate the extent to which you agree or disagree with the following statements." Numbers represent percentages of people who responded "Strongly agree" or "Somewhat agree."

	Most Holy Redeemer	St. Monica	St. Mary–St. Francis	St. Augustine	St. Louis Bertrand	St. Margaret Mary	Total
1. It would be a good thing if married men were allowed to be ordained as priests.	95	98	59	86	69	25	73 (75)
2. It would be a good thing if celibate women were allowed to be ordained as priests.	90	82	66	85	46	15	64 (61)
3. It would be a good thing if married women were allowed to be ordained as priests	90	84	51	78	43	15	60 (54)

Note: National percentages (listed in parentheses) are taken from D'Antonio et al. (2007).

churches with both married and women clergy. These observations are typically conjoined with assertions to the effect that including women and married persons among their ranks enables clergy to better relate to the everyday challenges lay-people face. They also talk about the fact that the early church had no ordained leadership and that, in some of his epistles, Saint Paul mentions women (Phoebe, Priscilla, and Prisca) celebrating Eucharist in household churches. They speak historically and point out that many Roman Rite priests were married until the eleventh century, when Pope Gregory VII appropriated the monastic discipline of celibacy largely in order to keep priests' families from inheriting church property. They look to the present and wonder why the Vatican seems to be condoning priests with common-law wives throughout Latin America and Africa, whether Rome is fearful that women will dominate the priesthood (in light of the fact that they are more numerous than men in most parishes), and, if the Eucharist is central to the faith, why church leaders are willing to abide an increasing shortage of priests, which effectively limits people's access to the sacrament. They also wonder about the three reasons the Vatican gives for an exclusively male priesthood. The apostles were all male only because Jesus lived in a patriarchal society, some people note. Others talk about both church tradition and gender roles as constantly changing, not fixed. And people bristle especially at the notion that resembling Christ should be limited to his maleness. "*In persona Christi* is basically Latin for 'has a penis,'" one parishioner, a former priest, mocked.

This mocking tone should not be overlooked. Frequently harrumphing with exasperation, people sum up the church's policy against women's ordination in es-pecially uncomplimentary terms: "just plain stupid," "a complete disgrace," "made-up bullshit," "horse pucky," and so on. "Priests are supposed to *be* like Jesus, not *pee* like Jesus," chuckled one person. "It's like Colonel Sanders refusing to hire people who don't look like chickens," mused another. Like American Catholics' widespread frustration with the Vatican's prohibition of contraception and their indignation at the recent sex-abuse scandal, this policy may in time engender what social theorist Jürgen Habermas calls a "legitimation crisis," a widespread weakening of institu-tional loyalty.[36] It might not shake the foundations of people's faith. Yet, especially for younger generations of Catholics, who seem increasingly disconnected from the institutional church, it could prove very damaging to their trust in the institution that has historically claimed to be the societal embodiment of that faith.

For many people this policy threatens to undermine the church's legitimacy as an institution because it seems to them to be more about maintaining the privileges of a clerical caste than bringing people closer to God. Colleen Barry, a Eucharistic minister at Most Holy Redeemer, is particularly eloquent on this point. A cradle Catholic who left the church for several years in her twenties and then attended an Episcopalian church for several more before moving to San Francisco with her husband, she loves her parish but looks askance at church leadership. "The way I look at it, there's the corporate church, and there's the spiritual church," she says. Invited to expand upon this, she is more than happy to do so:

> I think the spiritual church is the Body of Christ, the community celebrat-
> ing Mass and helping each other to attain spiritual growth in our lives.
> I see the corporate church as being everything above the parish, the whole
> Catholic hierarchy. I look at that like I look at any other corporation, and
> they could probably teach Enron a few tricks, if you asked me. The idea
> that only men can be priests is a good example. If the priest is supposed to
> symbolize Christ, then this role should include everyone because everyone
> makes up the Body of Christ on earth. The church is the whole People of
> God, so I think that should be reflected in the leadership, too. And I don't
> see that restriction coming from Christ. I see it coming from people, par-
> ticularly men, particularly white men, and now third-world men have
> really bought into it. The priesthood is a means to status within the church
> and within society. It's been that way in this country, and now it's happen-
> ing in the third world. So it's really not a vital manifestation of anybody's
> faith. It's kind of like the Pharisees during the time of Christ, you know,
> only more powerful and trickier.

Not everyone is as eloquent as Barry, and she is one of only a few of my interviewees who claim membership in the Voice of the Faithful, the thirty-thousand-member-strong organization intent on making church leaders more accountable to lay oversight. Nevertheless, much of what she says would resonate with the majority of the parishioners I interviewed. Like them, she does not question the need for professionally trained clergy. Like them, she is aware that people have mixed motivations for seeking leadership roles. Also like other parishioners, she assumes a mocking tone when discussing the church's all-male clergy, and she essentially interprets the Vatican's intransigence as just another instance of what one sociologist calls the "strategies of exclusion," which limit access to personally rewarding professions of all kinds.[37]

Parishioners get particularly exercised about women's ordination not only because it is, as often described, a "rights" issue but also because this issue intersects with the other institutional dilemmas described in this chapter. The symbolic dilemma is certainly not far from Barry's mind. Even if the symbol of a presumably celibate male representing Christ made some sense long ago in the context of a more hierarchical ecclesiology, she suggests, that symbol is now outdated. Moreover, in failing to represent the full diversity of "the whole People of God," it is religiously detrimental as well. She also seems to have no trouble with some theological delimitation. It is simply that the church's teaching about an exclusively male priesthood does not seem to her at all central to Catholicism. It strikes her as peripheral ("it's really not a vital manifestation of anybody's faith"), especially as viewed through the prism of Jesus's example ("I don't see that restriction coming from Christ"). Finally, her distinction between the spiritual and the corporate church (the latter depicted as a trickier Enron) is as clear a delineation of the dilemma of administrative order as one could imagine. For Barry, insight about God does not come in standardized packaging delivered from on high. It is messier and localized, and, when actually attained, it is inevitably the result of ordinary people, including clergy, "helping each other" to grow in faith.

Of course, creating the kind of spiritual church Barry envisions is a tall order. O'Dea gives us a clue as to why. Even though nearly all of his analysis of this fourth dilemma focuses on clergy, he suggests that the establishment of a viable religious institution requires that it appeal to the mixed motivations among its rank and file as well. By welcoming people motivated by things such as the force of religious habit, individualized religious goals, or their own desire for respectability, the institution gains adherents and thus stability. Nonetheless, observes O'Dea, this can also bring about a "lukewarmness" in religious conviction.[38] What this suggests is that, unlike the sample of active parishioners in this study, not everyone in the pews is especially enthusiastic or participatory. Despite most American Catholics' contention that the priesthood should not be restricted to celibate males, not everyone is as zealous about this issue as Barry. Nor would many be as willing as she is to invest a supererogatory amount of time and effort into "helping each other" to grow in faith. In other words, Catholics like her are reflexive about the institutional dilemmas discussed in this chapter, but, critically, this does not always mean that much can be done to build consensus and resolve these quandaries. The reason can be found in O'Dea's final dilemma.

The Dilemma of Power

A religious worldview must coincide at least somewhat with other social institutions and dominant cultural values if it is to gain widespread acceptance. When this occurs, however, adherence to the faith may come to be based more on conformity to societal expectations than upon the seriously considered and freely chosen commitment that O'Dea contends is indispensable for maintaining a strong faith. "Religion cannot but relate itself to the other institutions of society and to the cultural values," he says. "Yet such accommodation tends toward a coalescing of religion and power. The alliance of religion and secular power creates a situation in which apparent religiosity often conceals a deeper cynicism and a growing unbelief."[39] Power corrupts, in this instance, because state sponsorship of a particular religion or simply cultural expectations of piety come to replace deeply held commitment as the wellspring of members' affiliation. As O'Dea puts it, this "weakens the bonds of the religious community by weakening voluntary adherence and thereby diluting the religious ethos and substituting external pressures for interior conviction."[40]

There is good reason to expect Catholics to be as aware of this dilemma as they are of the others. Some certainly are. They often take a measure of pride when, instead of accommodating to influential social institutions, the church criticizes them. They highlight, for example, its resistance to the state in areas such as immigration policy, capital punishment, and the war with Iraq. They also point to the long tradition of Catholic social teachings as evidence of their church's principled, at times prophetic, lack of conformity to the profit-maximizing logic of the capitalist market and its corporate actors. In short, parishioners who talk this way approve of their church's propensity to "talk back" to other institutions and thus actually resist the kind of power O'Dea thinks could undermine the church.

Only a minority of parishioners talk this way, though. Many others discuss such matters with an entirely different accent. Apparently turning a deaf ear to the church's social teachings, nearly two-thirds of American Catholics agree that "the church should stick to religion and not be involved with economic or political issues."[41] When queried about whether "Catholics have a duty to try to close the gap between the rich and the poor," more than four in ten actually disagree.[42] Even when they do agree with church teaching, they typically, often with great alacrity, attribute this to their own private deliberations. Seldom does one hear parishioners admit—and, when they do, it usually sounds like the admission of a personal failing—to having their ethical views altered by some magisterial teaching. Most sound very much like Larry McMichael, a religious education teacher at Saint Monica. "I don't think the church could get me to think or do anything I didn't already think or didn't want to do," he offers with a certain exuberance. "I know the pope and bishops came out against the war [with Iraq], but that really didn't influence me. My mind was already made up. It's the same with other people. There are people who are for the war and who are incredibly conservative on other issues, too, and then there are people who are on the completely opposite side of the political spectrum. But, in order to be in community together, we have to let that stuff go." Trumping ethical discussion within the parish, he concludes, is the desire to be in a presumably disagreement-free version of community. And both preceding and trumping church teaching is his own moral compass, a mind that "was already made up."

People like McMichael remind us that the church is not always as successful in getting the faithful to take stands on various issues as many would like. They also illustrate the wisdom of sociologist Mark Chaves's contention that, instead of declining religious belief, affiliation, or practice, a secular society is marked by the declining authority of religious professionals.[43] Because of this, church leaders face unprecedented difficulties in regulating adherents' beliefs and actions. They may want to replace what many personalize as "my faith" with, as the church's official profession puts it, the "one, holy, Catholic, and apostolic" faith. They may look to the day when that bellowing cacophony of the faithful—each tending to express what is true "for me"—becomes muted and then together sing out revealed truth from the same song sheet. They may also prefer the laity to see themselves as good people because they are good Catholics, rather than the other way around. Nonetheless, because church leaders' diminished authority and the increased interpretive authority of the individual self have occurred in tandem, such hopes are not likely to be realized any time soon.

Exercising religious agency is not the same as exorcizing the dilemma of power, however. Parishioners may feel that they are free agents, but certain dimensions of power are operative in ways that they usually fail to perceive.[44] For instance, seldom do they demonstrate a strong sense that their religious lives are influenced by other social institutions, which are powerful because they present them with additional obligations as citizens, consumers, workers, parents, and so forth. How much free time they possess; where they live and who they know; what they feel they can accomplish and hope for in the world: Such things are not simply given to people de novo. They are largely internalized through the course of living within specific institutional arrangements that, in turn, affect people's understandings of where religious identity and practice might fit into their lives.

There is an additional dimension of power to consider as well. Although he gives it short analytical shrift, O'Dea hints at it when he speaks of power as wielded by social institutions and, importantly, manifested through certain "cultural values." If parishioners have a hard time seeing how competing demands from other institutions influence their religious lives, they are relatively blind to the power of cultural expectations even when they think in explicitly religious terms. People like McMichael, who claim to be free from the power of religious authorities, are hardly free from this additional, more subtle dimension of power. To use a distinction from social theorist Michel Foucault, power is not merely, as McMichael construes it, a repressive force. It is also a productive one. Understanding power in this way, Foucault argues, is to acknowledge "that it doesn't only weigh on us as a force that says no, but that it traverses and produces things, it induces pleasure, forms knowledge, produces discourse."[45]

What this implies is that, even though Catholics are active appropriators of the cultural symbols available to them, how they go about doing this is largely prescribed to them by what one sociologist calls the "deep meanings" encoded within American culture.[46] These are at once the most taken-for-granted assumptions about how the world works, as well as the least reflected-upon interpretive schemas for discerning meaning within it. While consistently posing as a thwarting of power, then, the deeply ingrained expectation that Catholics make up their own minds when it comes to matters of faith is actually an example of the identity-constituting power that permeates the dominant culture. Rather than simply a cultural "value," as O'Dea would have it, it is a pervasive and largely unnoticed "deep meaning" carried within the culture itself that tells Catholics not only that they *can* exercise their own religious agency but also that they *should*. This normalization of religious agency is enormously influential precisely because it is rarely perceived as a type of power. As Foucault suggests, it is seen as something people find pleasurable, have learned how to exercise competently, and about which they have devised an elaborate discourse. Moreover, like deep meanings generally, it produces the very kind of self that has a fundamental disposition toward this manner of thinking and acting.[47] To use a phrase made famous by eighteenth-century philosopher Jean-Jacques Rousseau, the deep cultural expectation that Catholics should make up their own minds when it comes to living out their faiths is a species of misrecognized power because they, in effect, are "forced to be free."[48] They cannot easily escape their religious agency because remaining true to this fundamental disposition—this culturally shaped inclination to make up their own minds about the sacred—is an important component of what being religious actually means to them.

This has significant consequences. One is that parishioners usually have a hard time making sense of religious authority as being in any way authoritative. When asked their opinion about the proper exercise of church authority, they are nearly univocal in framing this in deliberative terms.[49] Church leaders, they say, should be "a source of information," "provide spiritual guidance," "teach while also drawing upon the insights and experience of the people," "be in dialogue with laypeople and, at the same time, respect their intelligence," and so on. This seems clear enough. Yet, they typically run into difficulty when trying to express the theological and ethical worth of the proposed deliberations these views imply. In other words, they want things such as information, guidance, teaching, and dialogue from church leaders, but these are equally available to them elsewhere. Catholics, of course, draw upon elements of their religious tradition when thinking through matters of faith. They also draw upon books they have read, movies they have seen, classes they have taken, and the people they know, love, and speak with amid the daily round of their lives. Very often in conversations with parishioners, insights from all of these sources appear together as what one philosopher describes as a mélange of conceptual "fragments" that defy assembly into a consistent and communally shared approach to life.[50] Therefore, even if the church were more deliberative, parishioners would likely remain unclear about how this might inform their own highly personalized projects of constructing—from a variety of sources—an understanding of the faith that feels authentic to them.

Another consequence of Catholics' religious agency is the difficulty of bringing about the deliberative church that so many seem to desire. To see this, consider that members of institutions typically respond to problematic situations (such as those derived from various dilemmas) in one of three ways.[51] Sometimes people "exit" when they are disgruntled. It has often been said that, if taken as a whole, the ex- or "recovering" Catholics in the United States would amount to the nation's second largest religious category (after "Catholic"). Anecdotal evidence suggests that, for many ex-Catholics, their all-too-familiar acquaintance with some of O'Dea's dilemmas likely played a part in their leaving the church.

Rather than voting with their feet, others—like Voice of the Faithful member Colleen Barry—make their disgruntlement known by selecting the "voice" option, whereby they openly criticize the institution in the hope of transforming it from within. As important as this and other pro-change groups are, however, their combined memberships claim only a small minority of the American Catholic population, and only a handful of respondents in this study belong to any of them.

Most of these parishioners have made a de facto selection of the third possible response, "loyalty." Whereas many of them have exited during at least one point in their lives, they are now connected to the institution and, while often critical, their active involvement actually helps to maintain it. When the focus is on individuals' own religious selves, the institution can be blithely written off as relatively unimportant, as we saw with Cimino's comparing the church with the Bank of America. It may also be castigated as immoral, which was the point of Barry's reference to Enron. This does very little to resolve institutional dilemmas, though. Regardless of any misgivings people may have, when they participate within their local parishes mostly as a way of meeting their personal religious needs, they tend to come with little incentive to engage in the difficult work of bringing about institutional change. When this choice is made in the aggregate, it essentially performs the "latent function" of helping to perpetuate the institution as it is, warts and all.[52]

This state of affairs is unlikely to change soon. After all, like other Americans, increasing numbers of Catholics have undergone a shift in how they come to affiliate with religious institutions at the local level. According to sociologist Phillip Hammond, the "communal-expressive" form once dominated, whereby religious affiliation was largely an extension of "primary" groups such as families, neighborhoods, and work-based networks. Today, rather than relying on these overlapping social ties, people tend to attach themselves to religious institutions in an "individual-expressive" mode based on making voluntary connections with people outside of one's primary groups and, as discussed, in the pursuit of personally tailored religious goals.[53] This means that, even if individual parishioners did have strong opinions about how authority outside of the self might operate or how various institutional dilemmas might be resolved, their capacity to build consensus on such matters would be extremely limited. As "loyalists," most parishioners are simply not institutional reformers. If pressed to be, "exiting"—especially since people are less constrained by overlapping social ties within their churches from selecting this option—could easily become more appealing to them. If not from the church itself, Catholics are certainly freer than ever to exit from one parish and join another that better meets their needs.

Looking ahead, this also implies that people's understandings of what it means to be in community with one another as Catholics is frequently shaped by the "individual-expressive" manner in which they come together as church communities. This actually marks yet another commonality between the traditionalists at Saint Margaret Mary and the gays and lesbians at Most Holy Redeemer. These communities are generally not extensions of family, neighborhood, and work-based ties but are more apt to be based upon the self-selection of individuals whose goals—in establishing a closer or more distant relationship with the church as an authoritative institution, in accentuating their traditionalism or their homosexuality, and so forth—are quite personalized. This balance—that of creating parish communities but in a prevailingly "individual-expressive" mode—is the subject of the next chapter.

5

Community

Narratives for Belonging

Wherever Two or More Are Gathered

It has become something of a truism among observers of "lived religion" that faith provides people with both a framework for construing the world as meaningful and a sense of communal belonging. Unusual for a truism, this observation remains true despite the various cultural and social changes that are often mistakenly interpreted as spelling the demise of religion's "belonging function."[1] Culturally, for instance, the current explosion of popular spirituality does not necessarily signal a widespread turning away from institutional affiliations toward an atomized "do-it-yourself" style of meaning making. New institutional forms of religion—from the burgeoning small-group movement to evangelical "seeker churches" to community-serving parachurch organizations—have recently emerged as important carriers for people's spiritual quests while offering the added benefit of a sense of belonging.[2] And, as we have seen, rare are the Catholics who feel obliged to choose between their commitment to the parish community on the one hand and their own spiritual growth and sense of authenticity on the other. They choose both and, accordingly, bring their questing and often highly idiosyncratic spiritual selves to their parishes.

As with this overarching cultural trend, the social changes that have thoroughly transformed parishes have also not nullified their importance for community building. Before the Second World War, notes sociologist Michael Hornsby-Smith, "the parish frequently provided an all-embracing or total environment for the religious socialization of its members, with religious, educational, social welfare and entertainment functions for all circumstances and needs."[3] Things are entirely different now. Far more Catholic children get their educations in public schools than in the diminishing number of parochial schools.[4] Catholics' upward mobility and the government's involvement in social service provision have reduced the role of parishes in meeting members' material needs. The automobile, the television, and the creation of leisure industries have meant that parishes are no longer the centers of most Catholics' social lives. Even though parishes are officially understood as territorial units,[5] people are now much more likely to affiliate with the one or ones they want, with whom they want, to the extent they want, and for whatever set of reasons they want to privilege.

Despite these changes, a communal sensibility remains central to Catholic identity. It is officially emphasized in Vatican II ecclesiology, which envisions the church as the community of the faithful, the entire "People of God." More than that, though, it is also part of nonofficial Catholic culture. About two-thirds of American Catholics say that "the spirit of community among Catholics" is "very important" to them.[6] This proportion jumps to more than four-fifths among the active parishioners in this study. Liturgically centered Saint Margaret Mary is the only church at which the vast majority (only 48 percent) did not say this. Perhaps most interesting is that people's emphasis on the communal dimension of their faith is regularly connected to their frequent wariness of the larger institution. "I associate Catholicism with my parish, not the bigger church in Rome," explains a person from Saint Mary–Saint Francis de Sales. "The Catholic Church isn't a big part of my life, but I'd say that Saint Monica's is a very significant part of my life," says a second parishioner. "As far as I'm concerned, the Catholic Church is located in a queer little San Francisco neighborhood on 100 Diamond Street," asserts a third. Such statements echo resoundingly within these parishes and, along with expressing some tension with the church hierarchy, also seem to signify that what the late U.S. Congressman Thomas ("Tip") O'Neill claimed about politics is equally true of Catholics' connection to their church: It is all local.

Elizabeth Weiland, a "Hometown" Parish Member

When Elizabeth Weiland talks about her local parish, she is characteristically straightforward: "Saint Augustine's has changed my life." Far more circuitous has been the route she has taken to get to this place, geographically and personally. Born in the Midwest to unchurched and eventually divorced parents, she says that, even though she sometimes went to various church-based social functions in her town, "I basically had no religion growing up." She never considered this a problem, even after marrying a man whom she describes as a "mixed-message Catholic"— one whose parents did not attend church but was himself expected to do so at least through high school. Nor did she consider it particularly problematic when, in order to be married in the church, she had to promise to raise her children in the faith, which, she recalls, "I had no intention of doing."

All of this changed in the early 1990s, when she, right around her thirtieth birthday, moved with her husband to Southern California and experienced some unsettling feelings. "I guess I just felt a kind of spiritual emptiness," she says. "On the outside my life looked pretty good. But when I looked within, I could see that my attitudes were pretty ugly. I wasn't open to people; I felt cold." Around that time, a friend recommended that she attend a Pentecostal church. She tried it and immediately responded to the exuberance of its services, as well as the openness and warmth of its congregation. In fact, during most of their eight years in Southern California, Weiland spent Sunday mornings at a Pentecostal church, her husband did the same at a Catholic church, and soon their two children were going back and forth on alternate weekends. As the kids got older, the Weilands determined they should begin worshipping as a family, but "Where?" they asked. "Neither one of us wanted to give in," she admits. "But eventually I said, 'Fine, I'll be the bigger woman. We'll go to your rigid, stuffy Catholic Church!'"

While that particular church was indeed rigid and stuffy, after moving to Pleasanton for her husband's job, she soon discovered this description to be far from generalizable. She was amazed by all of the activity at Saint Augustine, and, after a couple of years of "just sitting on my hands in the back pew" because she was not Catholic, she signed up for Inquiry, a small group that met each Sunday to address questions about the faith. Intrigued by what she heard, Weiland eventually enrolled in the parish's RCIA program and soon became not just a Catholic but an especially active one. A college-educated, stay-at-home mom, she has devoted many of her skills and much of her free time to the parish despite her insistence that, before coming to Saint Augustine, she "never volunteered for anything." Nonetheless, she is currently an RCIA sponsor, offering personal support to a friend who is in the process of becoming Catholic. She is also a Eucharistic minister, a long-time member of a women's Bible-study group, and a regular attender of parish-based scripture classes. She and her husband have been active in the parish's marriage care ministry, in which they lead small group discussions with mostly younger couples. She has taught one of her sons' catechism classes for four straight years (at a different grade level each year) and now participates in the family faith-formation program, for which the Weilands meet with several other families one Friday evening each month to explore their faith.

"Explore" is precisely the right word for Weiland. Not interested in what she alliteratively disparages as "memorizing man-made minutiae," her faith is a "deeply personal thing." Accordingly, even as a Eucharistic minister, she claims to "have a problem" with the doctrine of the Real Presence. ("I realize it's more than bread and wine, but I can't get to the place where I accept that it turns into Christ's body and blood.") The same goes for the Sacrament of Penance. ("I confess my sins directly to God, and I know I'm forgiven because that's what the Bible says.") In addition, like many Catholics, she is quite candid about disagreeing with the church's teaching on contraception. ("I used to go against this, but, since my husband got a vasectomy, I guess I'm back in good standing!") These and other disagreements notwithstanding, she cherishes her involvement in the parish because she is convinced that even her deeply personal faith requires "the support of a faith community": "I'd say about half of my closest friends attend Saint Augustine's. Maybe less. Still, though, it makes me feel connected. I can be at the Safeway [supermarket] or at my gym and see people I know. That's a really good feeling. I also know they'd be there for me in a minute if there was ever something I needed."

Asked how she knows this, Weiland talks about the time when, overwhelmed with her two children (and feeling somewhat depressed), she missed an Ash Wednesday service, which prompted a fellow parishioner to drop by for conversation and to transfer ashes from her forehead to theirs. Then there was the time when, in the midst of making out their wills, she and her husband took another couple out to dinner in order to ask them (in lieu of the Weilands' own siblings) whether they would consider adopting their children (one of whom has a mental disability) in the event of their untimely deaths. "They both immediately said 'Yeah' without even looking at each other; we were all in tears," she said, with her own eyes beginning to moisten. Turning to her Bible-study group, she goes on and on about how the women there have made her more open about her own inner struggles; "we pray for each other all the time," she beams. Being held in prayer has truly been transformative for her. "About a year and a half ago, I was having this huge argument with my mother, and I was really open about it with my group." When asked how that was a source of support, she explains:

> Well, I knew she was coming over one day. And I prayed and prayed. You know, I was just saying, "Please, God, let me handle this! Please give me some peace with her!" And I remember being in the shower that morning, in the shower and just praying. And all of a sudden it was like an awakening. All that anger, that frustration went out of me. I had been praying for days, and I know for a fact that the other women were praying with me. It was at that moment, when I was alone in the shower, that I felt that I was really talking to God. It was like "wooosshh!" It was incredible, and it was a place I never would have arrived at without the support of that community of women. They've really helped me to be vulnerable and much more open to God's grace. Anyway, my mother came over, and it was great; everything worked out fine. Amazing. I think about that time a lot.

Natalia Acuña, a "Multicultural" Parish Member

Although they come from different worlds, Natalia Acuña and Elizabeth Weiland have some things in common. They are about the same age, they each have two children, and, although Acuña describes herself as a traditional Catholic in many respects, she is just as quick to speak her mind about how her religious views have changed over time. She has practiced birth control and chides the church for being out of touch with reality on the subject. ("My second child was conceived while we were using that rhythm method they always talk about!") She loves her faith but is loath to describe it as somehow better or truer than other religious traditions. ("Because I was born and raised Catholic, I want to give as much as I can to that, but I now have much more openness to other religions.") She sees absolutely no reason why women should not be allowed into the priesthood. ("If Maria could raise our Lord, then a woman could certainly run a church.") And she too is forthcoming about the support her parish has given her.

The most important time, she explains, was almost thirty years ago, when her mother, who took her to church nearly every day, died of a respiratory infection. Eighteen-year-old Acuña and her four younger brothers had to move from their small, rural town in central Mexico to Oakland, where her father had been employed for several years as a construction worker. This was an especially trying time for her. Everything she had come to love—her friends and extended family, the hilly countryside, the sense of knowing a place and being known within it—all this was seemingly gone for good. Gone, too, it seemed, was her adolescence since she now had to assume the role of surrogate mother to her brothers. Furthermore, the household was a tense one because her father no longer seemed to embody the same moral values her mother had always instilled in her (she preferred not to elaborate on this). Most of all, though, adjusting to life in the United States was difficult, and this made her turn to the church and eventually understand it in an entirely new way. "We didn't know the language, we had no friends, nobody to count on," she explains emphatically, "so we started coming here [Saint Louis Bertrand] for support." Continuing, she says that "Arriving here as an immigrant was a tremendous change, but experiencing discrimination, the rejection that I have experienced, this has helped me to grow. It helped me to become closer to the church and more part of the church than I was even in Mexico, where I went to Mass much more often. Basically, it helped me to experience God as being close to me. This helped me to grow as a Catholic—the knowledge that God was actually helping and supporting me rather than just punishing me, which is what I was taught before."

Examples of this kind of support are easy to come by. At that time, the Latino community at Saint Louis Bertrand was so small that a large curtain was installed to divide the church in half so that it did not seem so empty during the Spanish-language Mass. But Acuña recalls that it was more than sufficient for connecting her with a new network of friends. The previous long-time pastor helped her to find a job at a cannery when she was a teenager and, two decades later, encouraged her to matriculate at a local community college to attain an associate's degree in child development to assist her in teaching catechism classes more effectively. The new pastor has counseled her on a number of occasions with respect to her husband's alcoholism and has referred them both to the appropriate twelve-step groups.

Perhaps most of all, Acuña describes herself as becoming empowered at the parish. At first she was reluctant. "He [the former pastor] just pushed me into helping at the church!" she recalls with a feigned trepidation for the sake of verisimilitude. "He told me he wanted me to be a lector, and I said, 'I can read okay, but there's no way I can read in front of people!' But, even though my husband didn't want me to do it, he [the pastor] really pushed me to be a leader in the community." Since receiving that initial push, Acuña has indeed become a leader. She has taught catechism and served as a Eucharistic minister (despite some parishioners' disgruntlement about women doing so), and, of course, she has been a lector. She has also been involved in a number of church-based meetings with police and government officials focusing on ways to limit crime in the neighborhood, and she is a faithful participant in the group that picks up trash around the church on the first Saturday morning of each month. "You may think you don't have any talents," she reflects, "or you might say 'I can't do this' or 'What can I do to help?' That's what I said at first. I had so little education. But I've learned that everybody can make a difference. Honestly, it feels good. Doing something without expecting anything for it: It feels to me what we should be doing as Catholics."

Acuña strongly identifies as a Mexican Catholic. This is why she is also one of the coordinators of the annual festival celebrating the Virgin of Guadalupe. Hiring mariachi groups, organizing the traditional dance troupes, scheduling the various choirs to sing the mañanitas to the Virgin, decorating the church (especially placing flowers around the huge picture of the Virgin on the altar), making arrangements with the bishop, who presides at the festival's main Mass—one gets the impression that this is a very stressful time for her and the others who volunteer. Yet, "it's all worth it," she insists, "because maintaining these devotions is so important to Mexicans, so important for making them feel like they're part of a community that accepts them." Expanding on this point, Acuña speaks less of Mexicans and more about herself. "Especially when I was younger, this church was the only place where I could hear Spanish in a public way," she says. "It's always kept me in touch with my Spanish roots and my community as being Hispanic." Fast-forwarding to the present, she stresses that this is still important to her:

> When I go to work: English only. If you go anyplace, it's English only. We're always supposed to fit in with American traditions, the American way of thinking, American behavior. You know, I've always known what Christmas was, I knew what Thanksgiving was, and I knew what the Fourth of July was. But, it would have been so easy to forget about the Day of the Dead or the feast of Our Lady. Not here, though. Here I can experience Hispanic culture publicly the same way I experience it at home. That's one of the reasons I love coming to church. When I'm sitting in Mass, I feel like I'm still connected to my culture in some way.

Kevin Murray, an "Oppositional" Parish Member

Connecting to his culture definitely does not top Kevin Murray's list of priorities. In fact, he generally thinks of the parish community at Saint Margaret Mary as resisting the wider culture. "We go against the grain here," he reflects. "Because our values are similar, we're supported in living by them. . . . So it's supportive in the sense that we know we're not alone in this fight. And sometimes it feels like a fight to live Catholic lives, especially if you look at the news." Murray looks to his own upbringing as a reminder of what it means to be Catholic. Raised with his six siblings in a middle-class, Irish Catholic household in the outlying town of Lafayette (just a few miles from Saint Monica's Church), he describes his religious foundation as solid. He has always attended Mass and, through college, Catholic schools. He has a long history of involvement with pro-life activism in the Bay Area and actually met his wife during an Operation Rescue rally at which they were both arrested. While attending graduate school in architecture at the University of California at Berkeley, he participated in a weekly study group with other theologically conservative Catholics. Ever since getting married and eventually taking over his father's architecture firm, he, his wife, and their six children have attended the 6:30 AM Mass at a nearby church each weekday morning.

Though this church is only a few minutes from their house, after "a bit of bouncing around from parish to parish," the Murrays finally selected Saint Margaret Mary as their "main" church. They drive twenty miles to it each Sunday. There they hear the Mass in Latin. Incense and bells are used. The acolytes, all males, are typically older than usual and are very carefully trained. The Murrays find the music to be particularly beautiful and, to use a key word at this parish, extremely reverential. Most of all, says Murray, these sensory experiences are precisely the kinds to which he was exposed as a youngster and through which he first came to love the church. He says of his own children, "I want for them what's going to feed their little eyes and ears in the way that'll develop their faith the best."

Because there are fewer activities available to parishioners at Saint Margaret Mary, with the exception of his study group on the theology of the body, he is actually most active elsewhere. He and his wife offer a premarital seminar to engaged couples, and they have also been instrumental in establishing a Gregorian chant choir at the local church they attend daily. But he is adamant that Saint Margaret Mary is central to his spiritual life because, unlike most other parishes, it has not lost sight of what the Mass truly is. "Most parishes see the Mass as some kind of a social get-together, a communal meal, or a banquet," he says, referencing Vatican II imagery, "so their understanding of the Real Presence of Christ and the sacrificial nature of the Mass has been lost." Like many at Saint Margaret Mary, he suffers from no dearth of examples of what he sees as the widespread irreverence that accompanies this misunderstanding. People wearing shorts or miniskirts ("It's like being at the beach sometimes"); applause after musical interludes ("The music is supposed to draw our attention to God, not to the musicians"); receiving Communion in one's hands ("It's really not a cookie"); drops of wine left in communion vessels ("The Eucharistic ministers don't understand that it's Christ's sacred blood")—such examples are important identity markers for him, as well as for his fellow parishioners.

So, too, are references to religious relativism. Many parishes have a "live and let live" attitude toward other faiths, he complains, whereas they should be making it very clear to people that only the Catholic Church possesses the fullness of religious truth. "I tell my Protestant friends," he says about their purported misunderstanding of the Eucharist, "'You know, you have this great long-distance relationship with the Lord through the Bible. But, at some point, you have to be closer to the one you love; you have to touch.' That's because Christ intended to make our relationship both spiritual and physical through the sacraments." He contends that off-the-cuff paeans about needing to respect other religions reflect a troubling lack of respect for Catholicism. "It's like seeing people eating garbage when you have this wonderful food. Do you say, 'Oh, well, why don't we just let them live and be respectful to them?' No! We've got to share what we have instead of having this inferiority thing where we forget how wonderful it is. Did Christ say to his apostles, 'Oh, I have to respect your Jewish faith'?" he asks. "No, he taught them the truth!"

The desire to teach their own children "the truth" has brought a major change to the Murrays' lives. Several years ago, when their oldest was about to enter kindergarten, they decided to homeschool all of their children through high school. Most of this responsibility now falls to his wife, who is not employed outside their home. However, Murray attends meetings with other homeschooling parents, works with various religious nonprofits that facilitate curriculum development, and comes home early to assist his wife with instruction or other household tasks. Home-schooling is a commitment for the entire family, and they consider it well worth the sacrifices it entails because they are particularly wary of exposing their children to what they see as the many detrimental messages coming from the larger society. One problem Murray highlights is a wrong-headed attitude toward sexuality. "In our sinful world, it's been twisted," he asserts. "The sex craving is the strongest thing we've got. And it's ultimately a craving to get back to God, where our marriage in heaven is going to be the ultimate nuptial union. Now we're kind of tricked into thinking that we're going to find fulfillment in aiming our sexual desires toward just simple pleasure, where we won't find any ultimate fulfillment." Public schools are mandated to teach about things such as masturbation and tolerance for alternative lifestyles, he rues, and even teachers in Catholic schools "don't take their faith all that seriously." So, in Murray's view, that leaves the proper instruction of children to individual families supported by their parishes.

Another problem he sees is an attitude that puts a premium on feeling good and avoiding—through drugs, apathy, or a pervasive hedonism—any suffering whatsoever. Nevertheless, the Cross and "dying to oneself" are central to Catholicism, he explains:

> There are a million different ways we deny ourselves. I'd rather eat lunch alone with a newspaper. But a kid or two wants me to read a book or talk about something, and I just go, "Okay, you've got me." That's a dying to myself. Or I come home at the end of the day, and my wife says, "So, how was your day?" I might want to say, "Aaahh, fine," and then shut it all out, but instead I say, "Oh, here's what happened during my day." That's a dying. All the little ways we kind of deny ourselves for the good of somebody else are ways of picking up your Cross. This is why the Mass done appropriately like it's done at Saint Margaret Mary's is so important. It reminds us that we can unite our sufferings with Christ's suffering. And, regardless of what society says, we know that's redemptive and it reenergizes us to keep going.

Community Persistence and Variability

Some Conceptual Complexities

These stories show that Catholics' personally tailored projects of identity construction are both highly localized and communal in nature. They also complicate one of the most broadly accepted master narratives of contemporary social analysis: the inexorable decline of community that presumably accompanies the transformation from traditional to individualistic, modern societies.[7] Although they rarely provide the "all-encompassing or total environment" that Hornsby-Smith found normative before midcentury, parishes still help to create the ties that bind Catholics to one another. These ties look different from those of the past. Yet, if we take people like Weiland, Acuña, and Murray at their word, the choice between individualism and community does not appear to be such an either/or proposition after all. They are active members of their respective parish communities precisely *as* individuals. They chose their current parishes and would conceivably choose other ones if their individual needs should ever change. They are also involved in these communities on the basis of their own, self-styled determinations of what and how fervently they believe, whom they want to closely associate with, and which groups and ministries they have decided to devote their energies to. In short, they are very much what sociologist Stephen Warner calls "elective parochials," modern people who feel entitled to realize their highly individualized religious goals but do so by investing themselves within particular local communities.[8]

Such nuances notwithstanding, the fact that many Americans—Catholics included—still cling to the master narrative of decline is largely due to a collective vagueness about the very concept of community.[9] For instance, it is important to distinguish community from people's *feelings* of community, which, in fact, seem to be in a rather precarious state. National surveys have discovered that three-quarters of the public consider the "breakdown of communities" to be a serious problem, and more than four in five polled agree that "people don't seem to care about each other as much as they used to."[10] Along with plain nostalgia, such feelings likely derive from an ache for community that has long complemented American individualism as the two sides of a single coin. No respecters of local traditions and folkways, the government regulations, chain stores, and mass media, which now thoroughly penetrate local communities and corrode their distinctive luster, almost certainly contribute to this uneasy feeling.

Our vagueness about community is no doubt compounded by its remarkable variability. One can be part of the national community, the Asian community, the gay community, the Jewish community, and the Goth community all at once or one at a time, as a longstanding or a recently affiliated member, as fully integrated or intermittently associated. The concept truly has an all-purpose quality to it. In fact, in a review of researchers' operational definitions of community written more than a half century ago, one scholar exasperatedly discovered no less than ninety-four distinctive uses of the term.[11] Perhaps this is where we should drop the matter. Perhaps we should simply say about community what one Supreme Court Justice famously said about pornography—we know it when we see it.[12] Yet, since community is so caught up in people's personal experience of it, it would be preferable to simply concede that community is in the eye of the "belonger." Rather than making judgments on the basis of what we think we see, we are better off taking into account what people actually claim to experience. This is exactly what sociologist Kai Erikson did in his classic book on community. "It is the community that cushions pain," he writes, summarizing people's actual experience, "the community that provides a context for intimacy, the community that represents morality and serves as the repository of old traditions."[13]

Three Types of Church Community

It is instructive to also think about Erikson's dimensions of community in conjunction with parishioners' experiences of church membership. Each of the parishes I studied "serves as a repository of old traditions," as he puts it. They are all communities of memory in the sense that—through proclamation, ritual, and interaction—they preserve and enact the meanings associated with the Christian story.[14] Beyond denoting this commonality, what is most helpful about Erikson's definition is that it assists us in recognizing that parishes are distinguishable with respect to the other dimensions of community he mentions. A consequence of Catholics' increasingly "individual-expressive" mode of church affiliation is that they tend to select religious communities with which they have some affinity. As mentioned, when such choices are made in the aggregate, the result is the creation of distinctive parish cultures that emphasize certain meanings within the broader Catholic tradition and de-emphasize others. To illustrate this, let us consider one set of meanings that falls under the general rubric of what I call communal narratives, which are people's depictions of how they perceive their parish communities, as well as their experience within them.[15] These are collectively shared images of how people feel related to their fellow parishioners and, just as importantly, how their parish relates to the wider church and society.[16] By distinguishing among communal narratives, we see that the manner in which people come to imagine themselves as being in religious community varies from one parish to the next.

Some parishes, to use Erikson's phrasing, see the primary values of their community in terms of creating a "context for intimacy" by providing the kind of caring and emotional support that Elizabeth Weiland describes as so important to her. I call these "hometown" parishes and include both Saint Augustine and Saint Monica in this category. Next is a category of parishes that essentially "cushions pain" by helping to alleviate members' outsider status vis-à-vis the wider American culture. I label these "multicultural." Epitomized by Natalia Acuña's account of how her parish keeps her in touch with her Spanish roots and facilitates her empowerment, this category includes both Saint Louis Bertrand and Saint Mary–Saint Francis de Sales. Finally, while at first glance they seem to have little in common, Saint Margaret Mary and Most Holy Redeemer each fit comfortably within a category I call the "oppositional" parish. Each "represents morality," as Erikson would have it, by engendering a sense of collective resistance to a set of perceived wrongs within both church and society. Illustrative here, of course, is Kevin Murray's distinction between the values articulated in his parish and the unthinking tolerance toward irreverence, relativism, sexual permissiveness, and hedonism purportedly evidenced elsewhere.

These are not the only communal narratives available at these parishes; they are simply the most dominant ones, and thus they help to shape what people expect from their churches. As we have seen, they typically count on—and say they get— "support." But how people imagine this support and how they anticipate it helping them to pursue their religious goals vary according to parish type. Weiland says she needs "the support of a faith community" to live out her deeply personal faith, feel upheld in prayer, and feel less anonymous than she otherwise would. She concludes by saying that the women in her Bible-study groups have "really helped me to be vulnerable and much more open to God's grace." Acuña initially began attending Saint Louis Bertrand "for support," which she received in the form of a social network, a fuller sense of her leadership ability, and the reclamation of her identity as a Latina. She ends her account with the assertion that participating in her church community makes her "feel like I'm still connected in some way to my culture." Finally, Murray claims that his parish is "supportive in the sense that we know we're not alone in this fight," by which he refers to his and his fellow parishioners' agonistic relationship with the surrounding culture. It is difficult to take up one's cross, he acknowledges when concluding his thoughts on the matter. But the community at Saint Margaret Mary is continually reminded of its connection to Christ's redemptive suffering, and this, he is convinced, "reenergizes us to keep going."

These various types of parish communities provide different kinds of support as expressed through their dominant communal narratives. Before describing these more fully, I would like to make two points of clarification. First, communal narratives are collectively constructed and seem most coherent within specified social contexts. They make sense within parishes largely composed of people who, because of their roughly similar social locations and often shared ideological convictions, wrestle with the very kinds of problems and aspirations that, consequently, their parishes have become culturally tooled to support. For instance, as table 5.1 shows, respondents from the two hometown parishes are similar in the sense that—in addition to consisting almost entirely of people who live in and around Moraga and Pleasanton—they are predominantly white, middle- to upper-middle class, and generally very well educated. This is true even though the data for Saint Augustine overrepresents Latinos, who are considerably less affluent and less educated than their white counterparts in this particular parish. The multicultural parishes, the only ones in which white people are in the minority (among both members generally and, as the table shows, the active parishioners interviewed), truly are contexts in which issues of racial identity and cultural

TABLE 5.1. Selected Demographic Data on Three Parish Types (in %).

	Hometown parishes		Multicultural parishes		Oppositional parishes	
	St. Monica	St. Augustine	St. Louis Bertrand	St. Mary–St. Francis	Most Holy Redeemer	St. Margaret Mary
Socioeconomic status						
Under $50,000	9	31	74	29	29	34
$50,000–$99,999	33	22	23	52	26	40
$100,000–$149,999	20	29	2	12	18	20
$150,000 and over	38	17	2	7	26	6
Education						
College graduate or higher	90	68	31	82	83	68
Race/ethnicity						
White	93	75	8	34	81	70
Hispanic	2	24	56	5	5	8
African American	0	0	36	14	0	8
Asian/Pacific Islander	4	0	0	46	15	13
Ideological indicators						
Good Catholic without obeying church teaching on homosexual relations ("yes")	71	71	27	49	93	15
Teaching authority of the Vatican ("very important")	7	32	71	26	5	68
I would never leave the Catholic Church (Point 1 on a 7-point scale; Point 7 means Yes, I might leave the Catholic Church)	39	49	76	61	24	90

Note: Parish data may not add up to 100 percent due to rounding off.

differences regularly arise for parishioners. Finally, as the table's "ideological indicators" suggest, the members of oppositional parishes are those who see themselves and their parish as indeed having something to oppose on religious grounds. People at Most Holy Redeemer overwhelmingly disagree with what they perceive as homophobic attitudes within both the wider society and the Catholic Church, which only a quarter of them say they would never leave. At Saint Margaret Mary, on the other hand, people's oppositional sensibilities are directed more to what they see as problematic social mores (witness their responses to the homosexuality question), as well as to weakened devotion to the church and Vatican authority.

The second point is that these communal narratives owe much of their coherence to the fact that they are derived from longstanding and deeply resonant conceptualizations of community embedded within American culture. One of the reasons the themes investigated in the following sections are so salient among parishioners is that they represent important cultural veins that have long been mined by Americans intent on grappling with and ultimately imagining together what it means to be part of a community within modern society.

Hometown Parishes: Communal Narratives of Connection

The Place Where Everybody (or at Least Somebody) Knows Your Name

One such vein, broadly accessed by Americans when conceptualizing community, is best articulated within some of the more influential works of urban sociology. These have paid particular attention to the purported social and especially psychological impacts of city life, which they have depicted as problematic for sustaining intimate personal connections. The scholarly progenitor of this vein is social theorist Georg Simmel, author of the landmark 1905 essay "The Metropolis and Mental Life." In it he claimed the defining feature of urban living to be "the intensification of nervous stimulation," which required people to filter out most of the stimuli around them to avoid being overwhelmed. The result, he complained, was the development of a "blasé attitude" through which the individual comes to react "with his head instead of his heart" and learns to treat the swarming multitude of city dwellers with indifference, if not aversion.[17]

Especially significant for perpetuating this view of urbanism was the so-called Chicago school of sociology, which, from the 1910s to the Second World War, investigated the fast-changing character of that growing city. Its founder, Robert Park, was greatly influenced by Simmel and saw in urban life an impersonal, emotionally unsatisfying "mosaic of little worlds that touch but do not interpenetrate."[18] Much postwar scholarship carried this depersonalization trope further. In the 1950s and

1960s "mass society" theorists focused much of their attention on the potentially totalitarian effects of a socially atomized and thus politically manipulable public.[19] Turning in the 1970s to the presumed emotional toll of urban living, many observers bemoaned that, as the title of a popular book at the time announced, the United States was becoming "a nation of strangers."[20] One scholar stated the matter quite baldly: "The necessity to cope with large numbers of personally unknown others," she observed, "the emotionally painful, wrenching shift from tribalist to cosmopolitan, is part of the texture of modern life."[21]

As important as some of these studies truly were, by the 1980s this line of thinking had largely been exhausted. Studies that went beyond the apparent impersonality and anonymity of urban public life to investigate city dwellers' actual *personal* lives discovered that they were not so surrounded by an enveloping mass of strangers after all. In fact, we now know they have significantly more kinds of personal networks available to them (e.g., kinship, occupational, lifestyle) and have bonds of association that stretch far more widely than do their rural counterparts.[22]

This new scholarly consensus seems to matter little to members of the two hometown parishes, however. When talking about what being part of their parish means to them, they inevitably draw upon the cultural vein of urban depersonalization as a means of amplifying their own communal narratives of connection. While always individually tailored, these narratives reflect a common style. Parishioners basically characterize their church community as providing them with the feelings of social embeddedness many claim to have lost during their lifetimes. "It's like being back in your hometown," one parishioner, representative of many others, revealed, "It's that feeling of being connected, being known." They depict their churches as places where they find opportunities and learn to relate to others on a deeper, more intimate level than they can within the other social contexts they inhabit. At church, they say, they can bring up the things they consider most important in life, not the hurriedly mumbled "Hi, how's it going?" offerings of most public interactions or the conversational superficialities about sports teams or the weather. Instead of the anonymity of the relentlessly expanding crowd, they see church as a place, as the theme song for the sitcom *Cheers* once wistfully intoned, "where everybody knows your name"—or at least somebody does.

Surprisingly, these narratives of connection permeate the only two parishes in this study not located in the urban core of the Bay Area. For the people who give voice to them, though, establishing interpersonal connections is a pressing concern. Most of the interviewees from Saint Monica and Saint Augustine are transplants from other parts of the state or the country. Their college and often graduate school educations, as well as their professional occupations, have not uncommonly required them to sunder their ties to the communities in which they were raised. Their family ties are often similarly strained by divorce (as with Weiland's parents) and by siblings who live far away. As mostly middle-class white people—frequently with spouses from different backgrounds—their ethnic identities have mostly melted away. In addition, because they reside in outlying bedroom communities, they often work and commute so many hours during the week that the prospects of sustaining friendships with coworkers rushing to do the same are severely limited.[23] In short, these are people who experience what sociologist Robert Wuthnow describes as the kind of "porous social conditions" that make identifying with a particular locale and forging strong relationships within it a significant challenge.[24]

The Intermittent Community

Hometown parishes enable people like Elizabeth Weiland to surmount this challenge by immersing themselves in their churches. She is a rarity even among very active parishioners, though. Most are neither married to high-earning spouses nor stay-at-home mothers of school-age children with discretionary time available during the day. Almost no one claims, as she does, that about half of their closest friends are fellow church members. Rather than surmounting this challenge, then, connecting to their churches assists far more parishioners merely in coping with the porousness of their everyday lives. People in these parishes are much less apt to talk about community in terms of close friendships or ideological consensus than they are in terms of a very basic sense of belonging. They seldom offer much explanation. Experienced here is an inchoate "we-feeling" that, like much of religious faith itself, seems to be beyond words.[25] "You feel like you're all part of one whole," says Saint Monica's Joanne Ruddy, expressing what community means to her. "It's knowing people, it's relating to people. And your own spirituality is so personal that it's fantastic when you can find a group of people you can share that with [pause] . . . because they feel the same way, and they know what you're talking about and what you feel."

Religious community is also not considered particularly pervasive. Just as the porousness of their lives has caused them to reevaluate and readjust their expectations of neighborhood, family, and work, the same is true of their church. Even the exceptionally involved Weiland, for example, says her parish "makes me feel connected"— but it does not do this for her all of the time. She expects and thus experiences feelings of community to take what one anthropologist has described as a more "intermittent" form.[26] Usually dormant and only occasionally emergent, such fleeting experiences of community are nonetheless sufficient to sustain this generalized communal feeling. People are appreciative of the seemingly mundane occasions when unexpectedly crossing paths with fellow parishioners made their environs seem less depersonalized and anonymous. "It's really hard to describe," prefaces Elaine Richmond when explaining why she values being part of the Saint Augustine community:

It's a group of people who are working toward a common goal. They may not always think alike, they may have very differing opinions, with different backgrounds, but they come together for perhaps nothing more than weekly worship or maybe through various ministries, various activities, and, you know, they feel like they belong to something. So it's feeling connected to people. Not just at church, though. I see people I know on the street. I can go to the bank or grocery store, and people I've met at Saint Augustine's will know who I am. And, you know, they're really there for you, and you'd be there for them if some need arose.

Because people have "differing opinions" and often come from "different backgrounds," this feeling of connection is not ostensibly founded upon ideological or social similarity. Nor does it require especially clear definitions of what the "common goal" is or what this "something" to which they experience a sense of belonging is exactly. Rather, these narratives construe community as the felt experience of a social world that is populated, at least intermittently, not only by strangers but also by people who actually know your name and may even care about you. Such narratives articulate a relatively modest version of community marked by the mere *possibility* that they will come across attitudes that are not entirely blasé and that their own and others' little worlds might actually interpenetrate on occasion.

Community is also about intermittent experiences of care. Not a gushing current of sociability and altruism that carries people along, community in this more modest sense is again more akin to something they simply have on tap should the need arise. Weiland's "they'd be there for me in a minute" if necessary is a version of the same "there for you"/"there for them" refrain one hears from Richmond and many others in these hometown parishes. Such people indicate absolutely no need to wile away the hours hobnobbing with their neighbors over a picket fence. Nor do they even hint at a desire for their churches to become the hub of their social lives. On the other hand, they need to know that, when necessary, they have ready access to other people's solicitude. They need to know, to summarize just a sampling of their nearly countless examples, that even under the most porous of social conditions, people will drive them to the hospital when they sprain their ankle or rupture a spleen, people will visit them when they are bereaved or depressed, people will counsel them about their alcoholism or troubled marriage, and people will pray for them when they are unemployed or in one's first, anxiety-filled trimester.

A Noninstrumentalizing Haven

Local religious congregations have a well-earned reputation for providing the very kind of informal "quiet care" these examples illustrate.[27] Just about everyone from these hometown parishes can recall at least one time when they were "there" for a fellow parishioner and, in turn, when someone else showed them a kindness. No doubt such experiences greatly increase their confidence that community's beneficent, albeit intermittent, tap will flow generously when needed. Another reason for this confidence is their general perception that community participation enables people to hone the very types of expressive values—kindness, caring, generosity, and so forth—that make them dependable in a pinch. This is an important dimension of their connection narratives. They know about the rat race, many parishioners say. They know how to be competitive, how to think ahead and get ahead, how to strategize about their careers and retirements, and how to balance their budgets and budget their time. In a word, they know how to think and act instrumentally.

Such thinking and acting are critical, of course, for surviving in a capitalist society. However, as many hometown parishioners are quick to add, actually thriving as whole persons requires that they at least occasionally think about and act upon a different, more expressive set of values. Churches provide a locus for this. These communities serve as noninstrumentalizing havens where the values they hold most dear can be taken seriously, acted upon, and incorporated into their sense of self.[28] When giving examples of this, they very often highlight the help they get in raising more community-minded children. This is certainly true of David Healey, who became much more active at Saint Monica's when he realized that he and his wife needed help inculcating certain values in their children. "I think the messages delivered to youth in today's environment are very permissive and very consumer oriented," he says. "It eventually became important to us to have a set of morals reinforced more fully than them just seeing Mom and Dad living them out. We wanted them to be in a church where they could see them demonstrated by other adults, too." Others agree, and, along with deepening their children's notions of community, they often emphasize the need to broaden it as well. "Probably the most significant way it [his involvement at Saint Monica] has been a benefit is that it's given me an ability to talk to my children about community and the world," explains Chuck Tepperman, who likes to take his children with him when he volunteers each week to bring day-old bread to an inner-city homeless shelter. "Those are good opportunities to explain to them the need to do for others and to realize that our comfortable life in Moraga is not the whole world. I think it helps to overcome that 'he or she who has the most toys wins' attitude and to open their eyes to other communities and other types of people."

The noninstrumentalizing tenor of these churches is not mentioned solely with reference to children, though. With great regularity, people describe how their parish communities sustain discussions weightier than those they can have elsewhere and thus enable them to think more profoundly about life than they probably would otherwise. "Here the conversation goes beyond mortgage rates or how much people are earning or what they're driving and the rest of it," notes one Saint Augustine member. "Really, where else can you use words like love, sacrifice, justice, holiness—I could go on—and then expect other people to take you seriously?" asks another. Furthermore, if Tepperman is hopeful that his children will look at the world differently because of their parish, this is because he is convinced that this has happened to him. "Because I work with a bunch of bankers who are in the business of making money," he admits, "it would have been terribly easy to become truly self-centered, focused on just making lots of money and just having lots of pleasure. But I think I've grown. I really do think it's essential to think about more than all that."

A Triumph of the Therapeutic?

Narratives of connection are also highly personalist in that they cast assisting people in their quest for self-realization and personal development as a key function of church community.[29] This is not surprising given the importance of individual growth and authenticity among American Catholics generally. It also makes sense in light of these two churches' emphasis on expressive values in rearing better children and, as Tepperman insists, in helping to keep busy adults as focused on God and the inner life as they are on Mammon and "all that." This is not without an element of contradiction. On the one hand, these narratives depict parish-based community as a noninstrumentalizing haven; on the other, parishioners also envision it quite instrumentally as existing largely as a means of enhancing the self.

This personalist presumption derives from the cultural changes that, beginning in the mid-twentieth century, became particularly evident in the aftermath of the cultural upheaval of the 1960s.[30] One major study describes this period as a "culture shift," whereby greater levels of economic security precipitated a broad-based turn to "postmaterialist" values that emphasize such lofty goals as the development of people's intellectual and spiritual lives.[31] Another study meticulously documents a clearly discernible and widespread increase in the "preoccupation with self."[32] One of the most influential critics of this shift was social theorist Philip Rieff, who, in his widely read The Triumph of the Therapeutic, indicted personalism for substituting one religious paradigm, which upheld individual restrictions and clearly defined communal obligations, for another marked by a self-indulgent, morally flaccid adherence to "the gospel of self-fulfillment."[33] "A sense of well-being has become an end," he laments, "rather than a by-product of striving after some superior communal end."[34]

No doubt narcissism's blinders prevent many people, including numerous Catholic parishioners, from seeing beyond their individual concerns. Yet, while Rieff casts personalism as the opposite of community, it is actually sustained by cultural expectations carried within church communities. "Personalism develops in a kind of community in fact," writes sociologist Paul Lichterman, "one in which people create and practice norms of highly individualized expression."[35] This is precisely what occurs in these hometown parishes. Their innumerable ministries and small groups that serve individualized needs are at once the products of a personalist community ethos and the vehicles through which it is most actively perpetuated.

For example, Kelley Hannan's women's spirituality group at Saint Monica would very likely not exist if it were not for the quest for greater meaning in which she and the other group members are seriously engaged. Instead of being separate from "some superior communal end," as Rieff posits, pursuing a "sense of well-being" actually constitutes a significant part of what it means to her to be in community as a Catholic. The duality Rieff describes disappears when church community is imagined as a means to come to grips with "my faith," discern what is true "for me," and become a "good person" on one's individualized terms. "Community for me is where I can have honest, real conversation and where people are free to ask challenging questions," she begins and then continues as follows:

> I'm looking for an authenticity from the other members who are there and people who are willing to share their real-life stories of faith at a deep level—people who are looking beyond the superficial. . . . It [her group] feels like home. I feel like I can be nurtured; I feel like I can be myself. There are people there who are just willing to put it all out there, and what they think can be very different from church doctrine. Everybody there is comfortable with that, so it allows for us to be who we are. So I'd have to say it's community because it feels like home, a place where I can have my own spirituality affirmed.

Community is what works for her. At certain times it is "challenging" and pushes her toward "a deep level," and, at other times, it makes her feel "nurtured" and spiritually "affirmed." In any case, it is instrumental in bringing her into contact with other people and thereby enabling her to negotiate with her faith tradition in ways that make sense to her as a growing, discerning individual. Such sentiments are commonplace at these parishes. In addition, people depict their church communities as instrumental not only in terms of living out their faith, but also in helping them to negotiate other aspects of their lives. "Support is the first word that comes to mind for me," offers Saint Augustine's Doug O'Connell:

> It's when we're aware of one another and of the different problems we face in life: losing parents, losing jobs, those types of things. That support and caring are important for feeling like you're part of something and that someone knows what's going on in your life. I mean, I remember when Janice

[his wife] and I were having some marital issues. So, we went to the priest and then got connected to a marriage encounter group. That was really important because, even though I was afraid it was going to be sort of fluffy, it really helped us to communicate better and look at things differently. That's what I mean about community—those things are out there for you.

O'Connell's comments nicely recapitulate key themes. Described as "feeling like you're part of something," his sense of community is deeply affective. He is not anonymous all of the time because his parish is where "someone knows what's going on in your life." Because social conditions can be quite porous, he knows people need support when parents die (his siblings, for instance, are scattered throughout the country) and when they lose jobs. While he does not need support all of the time, he was certainly relieved to have had it on tap when his marriage hit a rough patch. Now, despite his earlier fears that such a thing would be too "fluffy," he spends about as much time in small groups as does Kelley Hannan. As one of the coordinators of Saint Augustine's marriage care ministries, even this retired accountant finds plenty of opportunity for expressing himself in public and, in doing so, finding some personal meaning in "being there" for others in his community.

Multicultural Parishes: Communal Narratives of Difference

A Melting Pot No More

A century ago, English playwright Israel Zangwill's *The Melting Pot* opened in Washington, D.C., to a rousingly appreciative audience, the first of many across the country, which included a delighted President Theodore Roosevelt. It tells the story of David Quixano, a young Russian Jewish composer in New York, who harbors the twin ambition of writing a symphony extolling the country's capacity for overcoming racial and cultural divisions and, closely related but more personally, of marrying the beautiful Vera, a Christian. "America is God's crucible, the great Melting-Pot where all the races of Europe are melting and reforming!" David exclaims to Vera about his adopted nation and in the hopes of advancing his romantic interests. "Germans and Frenchmen, Irishmen and Englishmen, Jews and Russians—into the Crucible with you all! God is making the American."[36] With this popular play, Zangwill bequeathed to the United States, a nation of immigrants, a powerful metaphor for conceptualizing the national community.

As the century unfolded, this assimilationist metaphor proved to be less helpful in imagining an increasingly diverse public. It has now been supplanted by the image of a cultural mosaic, the reasons for which are well known. The Civil Rights Act of 1964 and the Voting Rights Act enacted in 1965 gave African Americans a more prominent place within the broader society. A white ethnic revival began in the late 1960s and early 1970s. The Immigration and Nationality Act of 1965 opened the nation's doors to immigrants from all over the world. This was especially significant because it dramatically increased the level of legal immigration. Whereas an average of 206,000 immigrants had come to the United States each year between 1920 and 1965, that number increased to about 500,000 per year during the next two decades and then to nearly one million annually from the mid-1980s throughout the 1990s.[37] Perhaps the most notable (and mostly unintended) consequence of this legislation is that the lion's share of these so-called "new immigrants" has come from what were once designated "third-world" nations scattered throughout Africa, the Caribbean, the Middle East, and especially Latin American and Asia.[38] Only 13 percent of the nearly five million people who immigrated to the United States between 1985 and 1990 came from all of Europe, Canada, Australia, and New Zealand combined.[39]

Together with what some have called a group-based "rights revolution," this novel immigration pattern has rendered the melting-pot metaphor hopelessly outdated. In contrast to David Quixano's view that America is "where all the races of Europe are melting," current immigration patterns have relatively little to do with either Europe or strong cultural expectations that new arrivals must melt away all of the traits and customs that mark them as culturally distinctive. These patterns are also affecting the Catholic Church in the United States. Composing about one-quarter of the general population, Catholics make up a full 42 percent of all legal immigrants (and the majority of illegal immigrants) coming into this country.[40] Just how accommodating the institutional church has been to its various cultural groups is a matter of considerable debate.[41] Beyond all debate, though, is the fact that increasing ethnic diversity among American Catholics accounts for some interesting variations with respect to how parishioners imagine what it means to be in community.

For a window into this reality, consider the two multicultural parishes in this study. As within their hometown counterparts, parishioners' connections to other people are frequently strained by the porousness of their local communities. It is, therefore, not unusual for them to employ connection language when talking about their churches. They, too, mention that people are "there" for them when needed, that they can bring to the fore a more expressive side of themselves at church, and that their church participation assists them in becoming the kinds of persons they hope to be. The difference, however, is their abiding sense of difference. They imagine church community as a locus for collectively acknowledging and respecting the experience of being culturally "other." Community, for these parishioners, is primarily where the reality of being part of a minority group within both the nation and the church can be highlighted rather than melted away or simply overlooked.

Constituting about 3 percent of both American Catholics and Americans generally, people of Asian descent are a relatively small minority.[42] But, at Saint

Mary–Saint Francis de Sales, Vietnamese and Filipino parishioners are the majority. Anti-Communist and closely associated with the South Vietnamese government, which fell in 1975, Catholics were disproportionately represented among Vietnamese refugees who fled to the United States. Catholics are only 8 percent of Vietnam's total population but about one-third of the approximately one million Vietnamese now living in the United States.[43] Principally because they tend to live in the ethnic enclave that surrounds the church, more than half of all Saint Mary–Saint Francis parishioners are Vietnamese.

The other group of Asian Catholics at the church is Filipino. A significantly smaller group within this particular church, Filipinos number about two million nationwide, and, unlike Vietnamese Americans, they are as likely to be Catholic within the United States (about 85 percent) as they are in the Philippines.[44] They are also much less likely than their Vietnamese coreligionists to be newcomers to the United States (Filipino immigration to this country began in the 1910s), residentially concentrated (many live in outlying areas and commute to downtown Oakland for worship), and, given their English language competency and higher educational attainment, they are also less likely to be economically insecure.

Conversely, economic insecurity is a fact of life for many within the second multicultural parish, Saint Louis Bertrand, which comprises mostly a large (and growing) group of Latinos and a small (and shrinking) group of African Americans. At about 12 percent of the general population, Latinos make up about three in ten of all American Catholics because most (about 57 percent) of the Latinos in the United States are Catholic.[45] Nearly all of the Latinos at Saint Louis Bertrand are of Mexican heritage. The vast majority of them are first- or second-generation immigrants, many of whom speak very little English and, according to parish leaders' best estimates, roughly half of whom are undocumented. African Americans account for approximately 10 percent of the general population. Since fewer are Catholic (about 7 percent), African Americans now make up only about 5 percent of all Catholics in the United States. This number seems to be creeping upward due to conversions among black families who are sending their children to inner-city parochial schools and to the fact that large proportions of African and Caribbean immigrants are Catholic. However, things are different at Saint Louis Bertrand. The size of the African American community is only about one-sixth that of the burgeoning Latino population. And, rather than being "new immigrants," the families of most of these parishioners arrived mostly from Louisiana during the Second World War or shortly thereafter.

The distinctions among these groups are real and well worth the rich scholarly exploration that, for numerous reasons, has commenced in earnest only within the past few decades.[46] For instance, the label "Confucianized Christianity" is sometimes used for Vietnamese Catholics to denote their retention of certain cultural expressions from their homeland. As indicated by their disproportionately high rate of vocations to the priesthood, they tend to hold religious leadership in especially high esteem. Filipinos' religious identity has been influenced by their homeland's strong "folk Catholicism," the blending of an age-old animistic belief system with the highly traditional Catholicism of its Spanish colonizers. Due largely to the wherewithal made possible by their high educational attainment and occupational status, combined with their religious traditionalism, they are also known for getting involved in extraparochial movements such as Cursillo and Couples for Christ. For their part, Mexican Catholics have retained a uniquely devotional faith. Compared to Anglo Catholics, for example, they are more likely to be faithful to practices such as going to private confessions, making the Stations of the Cross, praying the Rosary, and having priests bless their households. Finally, black Catholics are also quite distinctive. They are the group most likely to say that religion is important to their lives, and, compared to white Catholics, they are more likely to prefer traditional liturgy, to be in interfaith marriages, and to report having frequent spiritual experiences.[47] Each of these groups, furthermore, has its own forms of popular piety, religious feasts and celebrations, styles of worship, devotionally significant material culture, and so forth.

Of course, so much more could be said about the many differences among these groups. For the present purposes, though, it is equally important to pay attention to a noticeable similarity. Members of these multicultural parishes perceive community through the lens of their outsider status and, accordingly, employ narratives of difference in conceptualizing it. They tend to express the meaning of community by accessing another influential cultural vein: the American discourse on citizenship. This discourse, albeit interminably evolving and complex, gives pride of place to two central concepts indispensable to constructing communal narratives at multicultural parishes. The first, as political theorist Judith Shklar stresses in her book *American Citizenship,* is inclusion. "The struggle for citizenship in America has, therefore, been overwhelmingly a demand for inclusion in the polity," she writes, "an effort to break down excluding barriers to recognition."[48] In addition, Shklar hints at but does not delve into a second indispensable concept: recognition. Here the representative voice is that of philosopher Charles Taylor. "Our identity is partly shaped by recognition or its absence, often by the *mis*recognition of others," he notes in encapsulating his basic argument, "and so a person or group of people can suffer real damage, real distortion, if the people or society around them mirror back to them a confining or demeaning or contemptible picture of themselves."[49]

Defying Misrecognition

Narratives of difference emphasize the community's role in sustaining an alternative vision of oneself and one's place in the world. The church community is typically described by its members as the place where the often misrecognizing gaze of what famed social theorist George Herbert Mead called the "generalized other"—or the dominant viewpoint of the wider society—does not entirely hold sway. Instead, people are surrounded by the socioculturally similar "particular" others, those who mirror back to them a different, far less confining picture of themselves.[50] These are the people closest to them. They are the ones whose image of them is based on an intimate knowledge of the complicated details of their lives rather than of the distortive stereotypes all-too-confidently imposed upon them by outsiders.[51] In short, fellow parishioners recognize and uphold features of their reality that would otherwise go un- or misrecognized.

Take the reality of hardship. Given the ideological power of the American Dream, Americans are much more apt to focus on the prospects of ultimate success rather than recognize the adversity so many people face.[52] Not at these two parishes, though. The challenges, slights, and pains associated with personal hardship are frequently brought to light and interpreted in religious terms. "Because African Americans have been poor for a long time, we've had to rely on God a bit more and pray to Him a bit more, and so we've grown closer to Him," says one Saint Louis Bertrand parishioner of the economic challenges many in her community have faced. "Especially the older people. We all know what it's like to be looked down upon," said a Saint Mary–Saint Francis parishioner of the racism and condescension many in his Vietnamese community have experienced, "and that's really taught us how important it is to become more like Jesus and turn the other cheek."

Perhaps the most glaring example of this is parishioners' discussions of the violence they often know firsthand. Just as they resist being misrecognized as simply "poor" or racialized "other" by finding religious value within these categorizations, they also resist being cast merely as victims by upholding the religious meanings engendered through encounters with violence. One Saint Louis Bertrand parishioner, Armando Vasquez, offers a story he says he has told many times. Three young men assaulted him. "They were going to kill me, but before they did," he concludes, "I raised my hand, and I blessed them and said, 'I forgive you in the name of the Father, Son, and Holy Spirit.' They just looked at me and didn't know what to do, so they left without saying a word." Evelyn Garcia, one of Natalia Acuña's close friends, talks candidly about her own heart-wrenching acquaintance with violence. "When my son was killed, I was burning with pain," she explained. "I was thinking, 'Why, why, why?'" What has changed since then? Garcia answered as follows: "Right after this happened I was in my house, and people from the church kept coming to me to talk about forgiveness, how God forgives. So we spoke a lot about forgiveness, how God forgives, how Christ even forgave when on the cross. And eventually my soul took pleasure in being able to forgive. My family thought I was crazy, but this is better. Even today we can always tell when someone is suffering, and we say, 'Come here, let's talk about forgiveness.'" Not simply something done to them, people in these parishes do something to violence and the other hardships they confront. They uphold them for the purpose of finding religious meaning amid adversity.

Within these parishes, members also deal openly with their minority status. They do not blithely overlook this reality as just a way station along the cultural tracks leading to the presumably desirable and reachable destination of a color-blind society. Rather than envisioning cultural differences as something American society ought to travel beyond, multicultural parishes help people to see them as important destinations in themselves. At Saint Louis Bertrand the parish community helps Acuña stay in touch with her Spanish roots. The African American community emphasizes Black History Month, the annual crab feed, and the frequent incorporation of gospel music and other Afrocentric symbols in the liturgy. Saint Mary–Saint Francis has masses in Vietnamese and Tagalog, as well as culturally specific celebrations and activities. "The church is really the only part of my life where I get to really feel Filipino," confesses one parishioner, a member of both Cursillo and a weekly novena group.

One frequently hears similar statements at these parishes. Among its other important functions, the church community helps to pass on these cultures. Not succumbing to the prevailing tendency in the United States to describe cultural outsiders in panethnic terms—as "Asian," for example—Minh Nguyen is a good example of someone who is much more specific.[53] "Continuing to be Vietnamese is very important to us," he says of his community. This is why he and a group of volunteers began a Vietnamese language school at the church, which now instructs about one hundred children for several hours each Saturday. Asked what community means to him, he immediately talks about all of the work he has put into this now ten-year venture: "It's being able to be who you really are. This is why I love the church so much, and it's why our school is important. I feel very proud of my heritage and my culture. And there are quite a few things, I'm proud to say, that we feel are culturally better than what we have here in this society. So I think we should let the children know about their culture and know that we have those things—like a strong respect for elders, for example. Then they can choose to be what they think is best." Of course, the relationship between religious and cultural identity tends to be mutually sustaining. The church community assists people in maintaining their cultural difference, and this, as many people point out, enlivens their sense of being Catholic. This is what David Tran, another longtime volunteer with the language school, identifies as quite important. "My English is good enough that I could attend Mass at any parish, but it wouldn't be the same," he says. "Even though I've spent the second eighteen or so years of my life in the U.S., when I pray in Vietnamese it just hits me harder, and it sinks in deeper than in English. So that's a big part of what this community does for me."

Another thing church community is consistently said to do for people is provide them with an institutional space in which to exercise their talents and then hold
them up for collective recognition. Because they often lack the requisite education
or, as is common among immigrants, because the credentials and work experience
they acquired in their homelands do not easily translate into high-status occupations in the United States, many hold jobs that fail to provide them with meaningful opportunities for leadership. Such opportunities, they repeatedly mention, are
available within their churches. Their narratives of difference denote this situation
as being different from that experienced by other Americans and point to parish
involvement as a legitimate, alternative way to make use of one's skills in a public
setting. People are extremely forthcoming in crediting the parish with enhancing
their feelings of self-worth. Community is often characterized as providing people
with what Martin Luther King Jr. once called the "sense of somebodiness" that can
be a rare find among less well-heeled citizens.[54]

This is certainly what Harold Davis found at Saint Louis Bertrand. Almost
sixty years old, he talks candidly about the discrimination he and other African
Americans have experienced and especially about how his anger about this nearly
tore him apart. The church did not save him from the "various self-destructive
behaviors" in which he was engaged for some time. Still, he says, it gave him a place
to direct his energies once he became less angry and more committed to "getting on
with my life." Now a greeter at the 9 AM Mass and well known within the parish as
somebody to rely upon when things need to get done, he admits to being unable to
imagine his life apart from his church. "Well, for me, it's where you can stand and be
counted," he says. "This church is where I feel like I can do something that's good.
I'm not going to be a congressman, and installing fences [his current job] doesn't
make me feel like I'm having much of an impact on the world. But, here, people
know what I can do and what I stand for. People truly do depend on me here."
Others frame the sense of somebodiness they experience less in terms of how it
benefits themselves than how it benefits those around them. Huon Tan is one of
these. Once a civil engineer in Vietnam, he is now employed as a grounds manager
at a local community college. At Saint Mary–Saint Francis, though, he is without
doubt one of the more recognized community leaders: "I have the good feeling of
knowing that I'm useful and that I'm well liked and that I'm helping people." Here
he sounds much like Davis—until he elaborates:

Looking at the American lifestyle, the thing that worries me most are my
children. It is very hard to raise children. They go to American school
from morning to evening, year-round. So they could start to follow a different path unless I can be a good role model for them. I have told them
they should follow my example; they should do the things I do and don't

do what I don't. At church I'm able to avoid many bad habits and demonstrate to them my good ones. When I see my children look at me [pause;
voice cracks with emotion] . . . when they look up to me, I know that staying true to my church responsibilities is worth it. They see me the way
I want them to see me and how I want them to live when they get older.

Inclusion, Not Assimilation

Tan's telling phrase, "they see me the way I want them to see me," sums up a critical dimension of what it means to seek recognition. Narratives of difference not
only highlight what makes people distinctive, they also present those traits in ways
parishioners most want them to be regarded by others. Hardship, as we have seen,
is held up not simply for its own sake but also as a sign of religious commitment in
the face of adversity. Cultural identity is held up as well, but not as something either
merely clung to or carelessly set aside. People want to be perceived as undertaking
the more complicated and discerning process of incorporating some elements of
the dominant culture and rejecting others.[55] Furthermore, more than fence install-
ers or grounds managers, they also want to be recognized by their own children and
other parishioners as community leaders, competent people who reclaim some of
the status they consider their due.

This is not all of what community entails. Another facet of it is to be accorded
their proper place beyond their own group—to be included. Within multicultural
parishes, this theme is never simply equated with assimilation. Instead, narratives
of difference inevitably balance the desire for inclusion with the need to maintain
group identity.

Some people say their church community helps them to find this equilibrium
with respect to assuming their place as an American. Often this is expressed in an
assertive mode. For example, Esteban Soja, one of the parishioners at Saint Louis
Bertrand involved in Oakland Community Organizing, equates community with the
kind of group solidarity that enables people to collectively identify and then pursue
their interests. The social justice message of the Gospel, combined with his awareness that other parishioners share his desire for a better life, he insists, gives him the
strength to work to attain the same safe neighborhoods and good public schools that
other Americans so often take for granted. "One of the things that makes us a community," he says of his parish, "is that everybody's in the same boat because they've
got the same pain. As Christians, we're called to a more abundant life in heaven
but also here on earth. Especially Latinos and black people. Since we're poorer and
have less opportunity, we have to work together to make a good life here."

Less politically assertive than Soja, others identify their community's role as
simply helping them to cope with the unique struggles they face. Peter Khuat, a

member of the Vietnamese choir at Saint Mary–Saint Francis, was once literally in the same boat with some of his fellow parishioners who escaped Vietnam by sailing to Malaysia before coming to the United States in the early 1980s. He credits the help he received at church for his successful transition to life in his new country. "You know, when you come to a new country, you discover that you've lost your language, most of the people you ever knew. You've lost everything," he recalls. "This community was crucial to me because I could feel safe. I could feel strong again. I felt like I could fit in and that I could cope a little better."

Parishioners also seek inclusion, not assimilation, within the church itself. Over and over again they describe their identity as Catholics as being synonymous with and contingent upon their distinctive ways of being Catholic. No theme is articulated more frequently than the role their church communities play in enabling them to be part of the larger church in their own way and through their unique practices, beliefs, and celebrations. In this respect, narratives of difference are consistent in rejecting two commonly held misconceptions about what is often referred to as the "popular" religiosity evident within various Catholic subcultures. The first is the notion that these distinctive practices, beliefs, and celebrations are merely cultural remnants that, removed from the social contexts that previously sustained them, will inevitably wither away. The falsity of this presumption is nicely illustrated by Maria Lopez, who is also one of the organizers of Saint Louis Bertrand's annual Virgin of Guadalupe celebration. "We work much harder at these festivals and traditions here [in the United States] than we ever had to do back in Jalisco [Mexico], where it was like they just occurred more naturally, without much effort," she says. People work hard to reproduce these religious customs, she further explains, both to retain a sense of cultural difference and to counterbalance the effects of living in a different society:

> It seems like there's little time for God in this country. The alarm clock rings at four in the morning. Rushed, you have to make your lunch, prepare yourself to go to work. Right after work, you have to fight the traffic. You arrive home physically exhausted to prepare supper, to get your clothes ready for the next day, and so on. So you are not prepared to have a relationship with God. That worries me. And I'm especially worried about the children. Because they are in a different culture and their lives are so different, I'm worried that there will be a time when they won't be able to understand what it is to have a relationship with God. So I think we have to work at giving them the same kind of faith we, the older generation, were born into.

Lopez's mention of passing on "the same kind of faith" from one generation to the next hints at a second misconception about these customs: that they are merely cultural window dressing. Speaking with parishioners, one becomes disabused of this notion rather quickly. Absent such customs, they generally contend, the faith would no longer be the same. To no longer observe these customs is to no longer be Catholic at all. This, for example, is the view of Felix Tacata, a member of the parish council at Saint Mary–Saint Francis. Unlike other parishes to which he has belonged over the years, this one has earned his respect because it takes seriously his and other Filipinos' involvement in activities such as the Cursillo movement, group adoration of the Eucharist, extravagant All Soul's Day celebrations, and their practice of visiting others' homes for nine-evening novenas after the death of a loved one. "I'm not saying these traditions are better or worse than anyone else's," he clarifies. "But if I'm going to be Catholic, I'm going to have to be allowed to practice my faith this way because that's what defines being Catholic for me and for most of the other Filipinos I know. That's why I'm here. It's because this parish really gets it."

Internalizing or Respecting Diversity?

Rare at Saint Louis Bertrand, statements like Tacata's abound at Saint Mary–Saint Francis de Sales. When asked exactly what this particular parish "gets," no one has much difficulty in responding. "People here seem to understand that the word 'Catholic' comes from the word—the Greek word, I think—for 'universal,'" Tacata says. "Everyone is welcomed to bring something new to the church, something from their own cultural backgrounds that makes their faith more alive to them. That seems to make the church more alive, and I think it results in broadening the perspective of everyone else." Expressed here is a third concept that appears in much of the contemporary discourse on citizenship. This is the notion that, in addition to being inclusive and allowing for mutual recognition, authentic community acquaints people with a variety of perspectives and, in doing so, facilitates an enlargement of their thought and awareness.[56] Political philosopher Seyla Benhabib gets to the heart of it when she states that "the cultivation of one's moral imagination flourishes in such a culture in which the self-centered perspective of the individual is constantly challenged by the multiplicity and diversity of perspectives that constitute public life."[57]

Avowals of being afforded the opportunity to interact with and even internalize a "multiplicity and diversity of perspectives" is characteristic of the narratives of difference at Saint Mary–Saint Francis. Church community, one hears from parishioners there, is about "getting out of your comfort zone," "broadening your horizons," and realizing that "it's really not 'my way or the highway' after all." Ideally this realization goes both ways. This is certainly the opinion of Phong Luong, a Eucharistic minister and lector who, because his family had ties to the overthrown South

Vietnamese government, had spent nearly ten years in a Vietnamese internment camp before emigrating to the United States. "Many of the [white] people here are thinking about changes in the church and in society," he says, "but sometimes I have to remind them that they had Vatican II, but we had a civil war. And now we're in a whole new country. I remind them of that to let them know that faith is different for us, and we sometimes need it for different reasons. I think they're starting to think about some of these things now, too." When asked if this indeed goes both ways, he responds, "Oh, yes. Absolutely." When prodded, he clarifies: "Vietnamese people tend to sometimes have too much respect for leaders and make themselves too small, but now we have learned that it's okay to question things sometimes, that it can be done respectfully. And we've also learned that getting involved in the church is a way to make your faith stronger." Lisa Dodson, one of the true pillars of the parish, agrees with this assessment. She describes this church as creating the very sort of inclusive and diverse culture to which Benhabib refers:

> I think Saint Mary–Saint Francis has taught me to respect and celebrate diversity as an authentic expression of God's work. That sounds cheesy and cliché to say, but I really believe that. . . . When you celebrate liturgy as three communities in one, and you've got to listen to the gospel in Vietnamese, and you've got to listen to the intercessions in Tagalog, and you've got to learn to pray that way—not just with other languages but with new songs, new traditions, new rituals, stuff like that—it's very powerful and revelatory of new ways of experiencing God in the world. I mean, you have to go with it or get lost. Because that's the way it is here. And, if you stay, you learn to incorporate other people's experiences with your own. It's interesting. You listen to the intercessionary prayers on Sunday in Tagalog, and you don't understand a word of it, but then you hear the word "purgatorio," and you realize, "They're at it again. They're still on that thing about the souls in purgatory!" But that's their way, just like I—a white woman from the Midwest—have my way. That's the thing. We're both still here, and we're both open to each other.

Obviously, no one can truly step into the shoes of another. As with the themes of recognition and inclusivity, this notion of internalizing others' perspectives is a desideratum. If, as journalist Leon Wieseltier has claimed, "the American achievement is not the multicultural society, it is the multicultural individual," people at Saint Mary–Saint Francis are presented with the expectation that becoming such an individual should be, if short of an achievement, then surely a shared aspiration.[58]

At Saint Louis Bertrand, on the other hand, one seldom hears such sentiments. Here one comes across the more commonplace "respect diversity" stance. "I think this community teaches people about getting along with people who are different from them," muses one parishioner. "Respecting other ways of doing things," says another, "is key to being part of this church." Accounting for this difference in parish cultures is not a simple matter. Both are led by strong, Anglo pastors who, in addition to English, speak another language used at the church (Vietnamese in one case and Spanish in the other). However, even though both men and many active parishioners are deeply committed to creating a single parish community, most of them admit that Saint Louis Bertrand feels much more like separate worship communities sharing a single building. This could be due to the fact that Saint Mary–Saint Francis has more "union liturgies" each year that are energetically promoted and specifically intended to display and honor the parish's rich assortment of cultures. This church is also administered by a parish council on which an equal number of representatives from each of the three main worship communities serve. Finally, it was the Vietnamese and Filipino parishioners who very deliberately invited the third (largely white) community into their parish in the aftermath of the earthquake that closed Saint Francis de Sales Cathedral. This is very different from the scenario at Saint Louis Bertrand, where the combining of the two communities was an unintended consequence of demographic shifts.

Although some at Saint Louis Bertrand say they would like to see their parish move from a thinner respect for cultural pluralism to a heftier multicultural ethos, one model is not inherently superior to the other. Church-based scholars are often divided on this issue.[59] Some are hopeful that the well-integrated multicultural parish will become the norm of the future. Others, however, are fearful that this could water down the cultural distinctions on everything from theological styles, to ritual expressions, to efforts at redressing problems and injustices unique to each particular group. Most noteworthy here is that, unlike the connection narratives discovered in hometown parishes, the narratives of difference are themselves different from one parish to the other in this important respect.

Oppositional Parishes: Communal Narratives of Resistance

Oppositional Communities as Protective and Transformational

Members of the two oppositional parishes in this study have much in common. They both sometimes use the connection language that is prevalent within hometown parishes when talking about community and why it matters to them. As in multicultural parishes, they also rely on difference language when discussing what they see as their own (traditionalist or homosexual) "minority" status. Their most noticeable commonality is their collective use of a third language (far more pervasive than these others) that identifies their church communities as social spaces in which certain elements of the Catholic Church and American society can be both questioned and resisted. Like the other narratives, this narrative of resistance is not plucked out of thin air. It, once again, is a product of an important symbolic vein Americans have long tapped into when formulating the meaning of community. This is the discourse on civil society.

This cultural vein runs especially deep in the United States and other Western democracies. The birth of the modern nation-state itself gave birth to thoughtful reflection upon civil society as a social space, independent of governments, in which people could gather together, hone a sense of group solidarity, and cooperatively advance their common interests and deepest values. "To be attached to the sub-division, to love the little platoon we belong to in a society," the eighteenth-century political thinker Edmund Burke famously claimed, "is the first principle (the germ as it were) of public affections."[60] His contemporary, Scottish philosopher Adam Ferguson, found civil society to be indispensable in enabling people "to consult, to persuade, to oppose, to kindle in the society of his fellow-creatures, and to lose the sense of his personal interest or safety, in the ardor of his friendships and his oppositions."[61] Thus, groups within civil society serve to both generate interpersonal affections and, as the phrases "little platoon" and "the ardor of his friendships and his oppositions" suggest, to resist whatever aspects of society and culture such groups find intolerable.

Today, community-based resistance is typically thought of in one of two ways. The first, more defensively conceived, is resistance in the protective sense. Here a community acquires its most fundamental identity by shielding itself from forces believed to assail it. One important book that takes up this theme describes the communal "mediating structures" that exist between individuals and large public institutions as "the value-generating and value-maintaining agencies in society."[62] If these are not protected from becoming disempowered, the authors contend, then the humane and sublime values they bear may in time become lost as well. A second, more offensive-minded meaning depicts resistance as transformative. Rather than as precarious "subcultures" impinged upon by the surrounding society, in this version communities are cast as "movement cultures" that foment opposition to some aspect of the wider world that needs to be changed.[63] Labeling groups within civil society as "free spaces," one scholarly exemplar considers them imperative for bringing about social change because "communal groups that people own themselves allow them to rework ideas and themes from the dominant culture in ways which bring forth hidden and potentially subversive dimensions."[64]

Whether expressed with a protective or a transformational emphasis, narratives of resistance construe community in terms of its opposition to some set of grievances. The church community "represents morality," as Kai Erikson puts it, because the members of both oppositional parishes imagine it as taking a principled stance against what they deem injurious to themselves and to what they hold sacred.

Reverence within an Irreverent Church and Society

Saint Margaret Mary is unique among the parishes in this study in downplaying the importance of community. Most parishioners do not live near one another. Celebrations of Oktoberfest and Saint Patrick's Day, the two annual parish-based social gatherings, are relatively brief affairs. Parishioners themselves are quick to de-emphasize the importance of community as opposed to the primary reason for their church involvement: worship. "I'm not going for community; I can get that in a lot of other places," says one churchgoer. "I don't go to church to commune with other people," informs another, "I go to commune with God." Infrequent expressions of appreciation for community are uniformly minimalist—"It's nice when people stand around and talk after Mass." Compared to worship, these are typically viewed as, in the words of one parishioner, "just an added bonus."

Considering the regularity with which one hears such disclaimers, it is tempting to write off community as a salient category at this parish. Giving in to this temptation, though, would mean equating community solely with sociability and not with ideological compatibility. Sharon Sager, a longtime choir member who commutes more than twenty miles to the parish every Sunday, is one of many people who makes this distinction:

I see the same people on Sundays or at parish functions—Oktoberfest and Saint Patrick's Day. If you notice, you'll see that, when people get out of Mass, they don't disperse. They stand around in little groups talking to one another. You know, people will say, "Hello, how are you? Haven't see you in a while. How's your mother?" Things like that.

Are people doing and saying those kinds of things how you'd define what community means at your church?

Not really. Here it means that people are joined in the same cause, the same ideas, the same thoughts, the same vision of what the future should look like. That's community here: that people are on the same page with the same goals. What keeps this all together—and keeps us from splintering into all different directions—is the Mass. That's where we all get the vision I'm talking about.

How would you describe this vision?

Oh, that's easy. It's having a sense of reverence. It's a deep understanding of holiness and a respect for God.

Answering this final question is just as easy for her fellow parishioners as it is for Sager. As described in chapter 3, there is actually far less ideological uniformity among them with respect to their theological and ethical views than they either realize or are willing to admit. But this is not the case with this sense of reverence. Other people clearly read from the same song sheet as does Sager and sing the praises of reverence as a virtue that is widely shared within the parish.

This is most obvious on those occasions when they turn their attention to what they typically perceive as a prevailing tendency toward irreverence in contemporary life. Since, like Sager, everyone describes the Mass as paramount to parish life, it is also where they first turn to illustrate this trend and, in the process, describe their community. Nearly without exception, people's narratives of resistance come with a sizeable helping of "previous parish" tales. At other churches, they have tried to pray as children scurried about, ate food in the pews, and sniped at one another—"it was like an English reformatory," said one. They have been aghast as the Eucharistic rite was prefaced by liturgical dancers, conga drums, and hand clapping—"I thought the circus was in town!" exclaimed another. They have been embarrassed and outraged when, at the "sign of peace," the liturgy degenerated into handshakes, backslapping, and across-the-aisle hugs and kisses—"I came for the sacrifice of the Mass, and I got a ten-minute love fest," shrugged a third. Such tales, which are often told with much derision and sarcasm, flow from them as a constant stream of reminders of what their parish is against. These also put the reverence of their own church into sharper relief. "A liturgical prayer is fine," says Saint Margaret Mary lector Donald Straits, "but it's not the Mass; that's special." Asked why exactly, he is at no loss for words:

> Because, once that host is changed, the body of Christ is there. Well, if Christ is abiding in our midst, then I think the proper response is "My God!" I always think back to when God came to Moses in the burning bush, and Moses couldn't even look. I mean, it was so tremendous to have God come to him that he had to hide himself because it was so overwhelming and such a reverent moment. It seems that that kind of reverence has been lost in the Catholic Church over the years. I've seen people come to Mass [at his previous parish] in curlers and jogging suits, and you could see them chewing gum. It's like Christ needs to return to the temple and say, "Excuse me, this is my father's house. What are you doing?" You know, there's a time for playing and joking with friends and being casual, but there's also a time for reverence. But I think that, sadly, over the last twenty-five years or so, maybe longer, the church has changed greatly.

When Strait mentions that the church has changed during the course of his lifetime, he is referring to a second topic people bring up when counterposing their church community to the specter of irreverence. This is the Second Vatican Council. Unlike many conservative (and schismatic) Catholics, they do not look upon Vatican II as a kind of *coup d'église* by which nearly two millennia of church tradition were overthrown by a conspiratorial cadre of liberal bishops.[65] That would be tantamount to denying the role of the Holy Spirit in guiding the church's magisterium and consequently undermining the sacredness of church tradition itself. They consider the council's efforts to update the church to have been both laudable and in accordance with God's will. Nonetheless, they also claim that many conciliar documents were misinterpreted and misapplied in the ensuing decades.

What they are opposed to is what they see as an alarming disrespect among Catholics for their own tradition. To a degree unparalleled by members of the other parishes, these people are profoundly attached to the sense of mystery and holiness they experience through the symbols, practices, and overall devotionalism associated with the pre–Vatican II church. Unparalleled, too, are their expressions of contempt for those who neglect to accord this the proper respect. Liturgical innovators; nuns espousing a feminist agenda; priests who do not seem especially pious or committed to expounding church dogma; the laity's ignorance of church teachings and history; a waning dedication to practices such as praying the Rosary, reciting traditional prayers, and participating in the Sacrament of Penance: All these and more are scornfully offered as examples of disrespect. Traditional roles and practices are not merely religious frills, parishioners contend (echoing the attitude of many within multicultural parishes toward ethnic-based customs). They are what it means to be Catholic. They create a distinctive way of being religious that, in their absence, would no longer be possible. "I have no objections to Vatican II, but I have objections to a lot of the abuses that came about in the name of Vatican II," says a member of the parish council. "I mean, if I build a bridge to San Francisco, and then people use that bridge, go to San Francisco, and burn it down, that doesn't make the bridge builders responsible. It's the people who misused it when they had the chance. I guess what I'm trying to say," she concludes, "is that church leaders wanted to embrace the modern world, but instead people have decided they want to *become* the modern world. I don't think you can do that and truly be Catholic at the same time."

One of the reasons for parishioners' wariness is that the modern world itself is often portrayed in an unfavorable light at Saint Margaret Mary. Here irreverence is manifest in the immorality presumed to be rampant in what one parishioner termed "our debauched society." One need not wait long to hear this view corroborated, with the same examples cited again and again. Americans have accepted what Pope John Paul II called a "culture of death," they claim, typically supporting this view with references to legalized abortion and initiatives to legalize euthanasia. They use homosexuality, pornography, and graphic television and movie content to illustrate an indecency that is creeping into everyday life. Corporate and government corruption are cited as indicative of the moral impoverishment of public institutions. Teenagers—how they speak, what they wear, whom they emulate—are held up (as they have to some extent since time immemorial) as "exhibit A" of an ever-increasing moral permissiveness. Their exasperation is nearly palpable when they speak of such matters. "How do you end something like pornography?" sighs one parishioner. "How about bad language or all these strip clubs? What do you do? Sometimes I'll go to a movie and then walk out because it's horrible; every joke has to be dirty. It's hard to know what to do. I don't like it, so I often think I'll just have to be like my mother and stay home praying the Rosary."

The distinction between what is deemed reverent and castigated as irreverent is based upon community-specific symbols and norms. According to the great sociologist Emile Durkheim, the classification of some things as sacred and others as profane is fundamental to all religious worldviews.[66] These classifications, he also astutely contends, can be quite arbitrary. For instance, Saint Margaret Mary's parishioners are not always clear why one style of worship is more reverential than another or why devotionalism, itself an innovative departure from forms of Catholic piety that preceded it, is more sacred (or, as they usually put it, "more Catholic") than what has come after. Nor do they generally prepare careful arguments about matters such as why some societal practices represent a morally repugnant "culture of death," whereas others—capital punishment, preemptive war, inaction in the face of deadly famines—do not. The creation of such categories and people's acceptance of them is not something that is unique to Saint Margaret Mary, of course. Other parishes have similar dos and don'ts, ideas about what is sacred and profane, and a sense of what is reverential and what is not. It is simply that these oppositions are most glaring within oppositional parish communities.

Gay Pride within a Homophobic Church and Society

This is certainly true at Most Holy Redeemer. Rather than reverence and irreverence, the primary opposition here is between seeing homosexuality as an authentic feature of self-identity (sacred) and perpetuating homophobia (profane). For the predominantly gay and lesbian members of this parish, to partake of the sacred is to acknowledge one's self-worth. It is to experience a power that transcends the human and thus disrupts the presumption of heteronormativity, which parishioners generally think of as a cultural construction. "Representing morality" by opposing this presumption, one should note, is very different from opposing irreverence. Irreverence, in the minds of people at Saint Margaret Mary, is something "out there" beyond the walls of their church, undermining the integrity of the Mass, religious tradition, and social mores. Homophobia, on the other hand, is experienced by GLBT (gay, lesbian, bisexual, transgendered) people at Most Holy Redeemer as a more personalized affront that undermines their very humanity.

This is why, contrary to resistance narratives told at Saint Margaret Mary, parishioners here are effusive about just how important the sociability they experience at church is to them. Some say it is the main way they get connected to volunteer opportunities or first became acquainted with people who have since become role models for them. Most give the church very high marks for fellowship, and they claim it to be a valuable part of their social lives. More than all of this, nearly everyone says it provides them with much-needed feelings of "acceptance." With the possible exception of "inclusive," no word is used more liberally when describing the parish. "Society so often rejects us," informs one parishioner, "but we're accepted here. When we've been put down, when we're sick, even in death. In the front of the church we have a scroll with nearly nine hundred names of people from this parish who've died of AIDS. Even in death, we accept them. Even then we say, 'You belong here.'"

Other people compare their feelings of belonging at Most Holy Redeemer with the ostracism they face from their own families. "A lot of us are alienated from our families, our true blood families," explains one newcomer who serves on various church committees. "We come to San Francisco from Boston or Atlanta or wherever, and this becomes our family. When you can be part of a family you've chosen, then I think there's a lot more openness and love and acceptance." Finally, parishioners typically claim to have found a level of acceptance they could not get in other religious contexts. Even though they are apt to rail vehemently against Vatican officials, whom they typically deride for perpetuating simplistic understandings of sexuality, as well as harmful stereotypes of gays and lesbians, they seldom have "previous parish" tales to tell. Instead of angrily disparaging other churches for overtly rejecting homosexuals, most say these churches simply did not allow them to be as open about their lives as they would have liked. Lacking any real meaning to them, they just stopped attending. "It's different here because people are much more accepting," explains a member of the choir who had stopped going to church for nearly fifteen years before discovering Most Holy Redeemer. "Somebody with spiked hair or somebody into leather or somebody in church wearing chaps with their butt showing: We don't get into other people's business. But at the same time, I get to be who I really am—my whole self, my gay self—without needing to hide or apologize for that."

In addition to freeing gay Catholics *from* doing certain things—like hiding or apologizing—this acceptance provides a social space *for* doing the kind of religious negotiation necessary to oppose those attitudes that make hiding and apologizing compulsory in the first place. Negotiating with the tradition is not nearly as critical for parishioners at Saint Margaret Mary. They can oppose the irreverence they see around them by drawing upon the church's official teachings, which they consider quite sufficient "as is" for formulating their narratives of resistance. Not so at Most Holy Redeemer. Because official church teachings portray homosexuality as a "trial" and homosexual behavior as "intrinsically disordered," they cannot be as readily deployed in opposing homophobia. They require careful reflection and often significant reworking.[67]

Few parishioners put the matter in these terms, yet this kind of negotiation is ubiquitous. The most frequent example of it is parishioners' religious revalorization of what it means to be gay. Here, people tend to envision gay identity as a religious asset of sorts. Unlike a "middle-class Catholic" or a "Filipino Catholic" or a "conservative Catholic," the gist of this contention suggests, the "gay Catholic" is generally perceived by the wider public as a contradiction in terms. It is an identity that lacks the presumed legitimacy of those others. As a result, many parishioners say, for a homosexual to choose to become or remain Catholic is a matter of particular gravity and a sign of greater conviction than it would be if, as one put it, "the religion were just handed down to them like a birthright." "Being a lesbian has forced me to earn a place on the planet," says one Eucharistic minister evoking this theme, "and, with respect to Catholicism, I've had to do pretty much the same—you know, think it through, grapple with it, stake a claim when many people would rather I didn't." Among those preferring that she not stake this claim, one would certainly *not* include the straight members of the parish. Time and again they make a point of agreeing with this line of thinking, and they are often inspired by the seriousness and tenacity with which they see "gay Catholics" clinging to this identity. "I was born Catholic," explains one older woman who recalls attending church at Most Holy Redeemer with her now deceased husband as early as the mid-1950s. "But those people," she continues, referring to her gay fellow parishioners, "they're *choosing* to be in that building and worship even though the institution, eight times out of ten, has said, 'We don't want you.' But they continue to come back because of their faith in Christ. That takes a lot of guts, and it's very powerful to see that. It touches me very deeply."

Another way gay identity gets revalorized is through the generalized sense that the challenges associated with being homosexual and Catholic can lead one to a closer relationship with God. This point is made very frequently, but no one states it more compellingly than Aaron Coffin, a member of the parish's finance committee and a teacher at a local Catholic high school:

> God is in people's experiences of suffering and more profoundly in the joy that is brought forth in spite of it. That is a real element at Most Holy Redeemer, a real part of the community. We always say that God hears the cry of the poor. Well, the poor are not just materially poor; they can be

brutalized in other ways, too. Even though most of us share the experience of discrimination, we know as Catholics that that is not the end of the story. When we come together, we see that everything is going to be all right because we have this community that upholds us. We have this community that represents God for us and is God for us, so we know it'll be okay in the end.

Instead of discussing homosexuality from the perspective of the church's moral theology, Coffin looks to its social justice teachings. God is not some neutral arbiter, according to this body of teaching, but indeed "hears the cry of the poor" and wills a respect for the dignity of all to erode the sin of discrimination visited upon some. Coffin, like many of his fellow parishioners, also explains that being gay has actually enabled him to be a better Catholic than he might otherwise have become:

Again, I think God is very near to people's pain. I'd say this brings an opportunity to enter into a more profound relationship with God because of the experience of being put down. Not because God is more available to me than to anyone else but because I feel I'm more available to God.

How has that affected your experience as a Catholic?

I think it has helped both of us [Coffin and his partner] enter more deeply into the reality of what Catholicism is all about. We went there with our faith; we went there with our relationship. We asked the tough questions, investigated, studied, prayed. We got lost, we got found again, we got help. We took the risk and continue to take the risk of being in relationship with God. I think a lot of people don't do all this because I think they're afraid to. That's okay, but you're not going to get anywhere if you're afraid. You'll just stay on the ritual level.

And being gay has helped you to move beyond that level?

Absolutely. Because you have to surrender all your defenses when you realize you can't make it in the world by yourself, when society says you're so awful. You have to look at yourself more deeply and say, "This is how God made me." You really have to trust that your sexuality is also a gift from God and appreciate it as a gift.

Coffin has reworked many things. The suffering and pain wrought by what he sees as a heterosexist church and society are actually opportunities for becoming more open to God's grace. A predominantly gay church community and a longtime relationship with his lover are not contrary to his identity as a Catholic; they are actually means for him to understand his faith more deeply. And, while it might seem "awful" to many, he experiences his sexuality not as stigma but as nothing short of a divine gift. It is not a lifestyle choice that must be defended as such or, as official teaching purports, a "trial" that must be withstood. Coffin is quite representative in understanding his homosexuality not as something added to his identity but as something at his very core and, in light of his hard-won realization that "this is how God made me," something to embrace.

All of this puts the community in an oppositional stance. By describing their church as a place of acceptance, parishioners subvert dominant norms by creating an alternative way of talking about the world and refusing to retreat to the margins.[68] This alternative discourse rings out loud and clear. "The most important thing about this community is that it gives you a different soundtrack for your life," says one parishioner who is also a former seminarian. "The other soundtrack—by far the loudest one—is that we're sinners or a bunch of deviants. It can drown everything else out. But here you realize it's only one soundtrack. You can change the channel and eventually change how you see your life." Changing the channel means talking back to what in American culture is frequently accepted as one of life's realities: namely, that homosexuality is sinful and deviant.[69] It means puncturing this reality by defying the grip of social stigma. "The person with a shameful differentness can break with what is called reality," wrote social theorist Erving Goffman, "and obstinately attempt to employ an unconventional interpretation of the character of his social identity."[70]

Narratives of resistance envision church community as a space where just this sort of obstinacy can be collectively sustained. In addition to revalorizing homosexuality, parishioners do this by drawing upon highly traditional religious language and using it in a nontraditional fashion. Their resistance narratives are typically not based on secular human rights discourse or on what sociologists often refer to as "queer theory" or, contra Goffman, on wholly "unconventional" interpretations of what it means to be Catholic today. Instead, they rely upon very traditional Catholic symbols and norms, which are reworked in ways parishioners perceive as more consonant with Jesus's message and more attentive to their own experience.[71]

Maureen Graeber, a member of the liturgy committee, is a good example. After some conversation about the debate over same-sex marriage in San Francisco, she offers the following reflection:

This whole debate has unearthed a lot of stereotypes about gay and lesbian people, and it's made me appreciate my church even more. Really. Most Holy Redeemer has kept me close to my own truth and given me words to express that.

What do you mean exactly?

I'm accountable for living the life God gave me; God's will is truly what I want to be. So, if I follow the teachings of Christ, I know I'll be true to who I am. No human being can see this. And I know that to be who I am, to be authentic, that's a higher calling than what the church tells me to do. God knows what God is doing! God doesn't make people with defective souls. How do I know this? Well, one of the main reasons has been because of my relationship with Karen [her partner]. . . . Meeting her at that point in my life was like a resurrection for me. . . . It's been life giving. I know in my heart that the source of this is God. And now it's blossoming in new ways. Now we're in the process of becoming foster parents. That's a kind of proof of our love, our life. We know lots of people think that we're totally inappropriate, that we shouldn't be parents. But I feel that God is with me on this one. I really feel called to this despite what anyone or even the church itself thinks about it.

How do you know God is with you on this one?

Well, scripture says that you'll be known by the fruits of the spirit. And, as I said, our relationship has done nothing but bear fruit. Also, I'm not some little girl. My disagreement with the church is based on my well-informed conscience. And it's based on Christ. As I read scripture more and more, it seems pretty clear to me that Christ came and said, "Out with all these rules!" and, in the temple, "Get rid of all this stuff; it's so hypocritical!" You know what I mean? But all the rules keep getting made, which is easier for keeping people in line than staying true to Christ's spirit. I'm at the place where I can see that for what it is—the desire for control. I used to get angry and feel hurt by church statements and such. But I'm at the point now where I forgive my church.

Community for Graeber is *both* oppositional and resoundingly Catholic. Reappropriated Catholic symbols appear throughout her reflections. She is part of God's creation ("God doesn't make people with defective souls"), she refers to her relationship with Karen as a kind of "resurrection" and firmly believes that "the source of this is God." Given that it is the only majority gay and lesbian parish in this study, much of this theological reinterpretation is unique to Most Holy Redeemer. Nonetheless, it is abetted significantly by parishioners' reliance upon some of the more pervasive themes within American Catholic culture. Graeber picks up the "my faith" conversational shard described earlier. She wants to be "authentic" and "true to who I am," and she discerns signs that she and Karen are on the right track because, she reports, "our faith has only grown more and more." Commensurate with the "good person" shard, she indeed connects her Catholicism with being good and finds "proof" of this in a relationship that, in her estimation, "has done nothing but bear fruit" and promises to continue doing so as they begin the process of becoming foster parents. Moreover, similar to the people we heard in chapter 4, she is reflexive about the institutional dilemmas of the larger church. She understands the "dilemma of delimitation" and thus differentiates between theological baby and bathwater by relying on her "well-informed conscience" and on what she knows about the person and message of Jesus. Nor is she naïve about the "desire for control" that often accompanies the establishment of "administrative order." In forgiving her church, she reveals her awareness that, while often causing anger and emotional pain, the church's focus on "keeping people in line" is ultimately a product of human beings' often clumsy attempts to institutionalize "Christ's spirit."

More Conceptual Complexities

This communal narrative, like the other two introduced in this chapter, are examples of what sociologist Max Weber referred to as "ideal types," analytical constructs that function to both isolate a specified feature of social life—images of church community, for instance—and allow for comparative examination of the different ways in which that feature becomes manifest in everyday life.[72] There is much to commend in this methodological tool. For one thing, when ideal types are not simply imposed upon reality but are instead constructed from the ground up, they truly reveal how one parish culture can vary from the next.

At the same time, ideal types necessarily simplify real life. Take the ideal type "oppositional parish." Without doubt, narratives of resistance are the dominant means through which community is imagined within Saint Margaret Mary and Most Holy Redeemer, but this is not to say they are nonexistent within other parishes. Multicultural parishes, for example, are oppositional toward patterns of exclusion and the wider society's misrecognition. And while multicultural parishes expressly address issues of racial and ethnic identity, other (predominantly white) parishes are not wholly divorced from such matters. As studies of "whiteness" often reveal, even institutions that try to disregard race often inadvertently perpetuate existing patterns of racialization by occluding the connection between white identity and social privilege.[73] Likewise, whereas a personalist ethos is most prominent in shaping hometown parishes, it has clearly seeped into the other parishes as well. All of this is to say that, even though each parish has a dominant communal narrative, real life defies easy categorization.

What is true of these parishes in general is equally true of a particular feature of oppositional parishes. Some people within these two churches think of their communities as protecting them from what is perceived as profane (irreverence, homophobia), while others see the church as empowering them to pursue a more transformational agenda.[74] This protect-transform dichotomy is also defied in real life. Most of the parishioners at Saint Margaret Mary seem to lean more toward the protection end of this continuum. Yet, as people like Kevin Murray demonstrate, their parish community can also energize them and connect them with like-minded others. His and his wife's pro-life activism, premarital counseling, and decision to first have and then homeschool their six children may not fit some people's definition of working toward societal transformation, but these things are clearly in keeping with the Murrays' own definition. Similarly, at Most Holy Redeemer, most of the people speak of their parish and of themselves as making some contribution toward the steady transformation of a heterosexist society. On the other hand, they are also quite candid in saying they want acceptance from the parish; they want to feel protected. Some of the more transformation-minded among them actually regret this, saying that with fewer parishioners now dying of AIDS, too many church members have become less socially mobilized and simply want the church to be a place where they can be gay and Catholic without feeling out of place.

Lots of people at both churches envision their resistance in a more protective mode, whereas some of the more vocal leaders want to see people become more active and assume a more transformational attitude. Such is the nature of activists, after all. More than that, though, this attitude also coincides with some of the more prophetic elements of the Christian tradition and with the Catholic Church's teachings on social justice. Given all of this, one wonders why this outlook is not more commonplace. We turn to this question in the next chapter.

6

Civil Society

Private and Public Good

"Our Best-Kept Secret"

Developing the Commons: A Public Forum at Saint Augustine

When I arrived at the public forum to discuss an upcoming ballot measure, I was initially surprised by the size of the crowd. But it turned out that the parish community center was hosting two events that night, and a baptism preparation meeting was by far the bigger draw. Fewer than thirty people made their way into the gymnasium, where a small stage, podium, and far too many rows of folding chairs had been set up. Four seats were occupied by the evening's speakers. Others were taken up by either their loyal supporters from outside the parish or about a dozen or so parishioners interested in educating themselves about what had lately become a contentious political issue in their growing city.

At issue was what to do with the so-called Bernal Property recently acquired from the City of San Francisco. Phase I of the development plan was already under way. A 198-acre portion of this land was rapidly filling up with residential and commercial units. How best to develop the remaining 318 acres—Phase II—had long been a topic of discussion at city council meetings and in the numerous and increasingly heated editorial sections of Pleasanton's local newspapers. Measure V, the ballot initiative that would decide the matter, was complicated. Yet, in most partisans' eyes, it could be boiled down to a basic choice. A vote for it would mean building more housing on this land, 15 percent of which would be much-needed affordable housing. A vote against it, on the other hand, would set this land aside as open space. This would preserve certain woodlands and ponds and make some parcels available for the development of recreational facilities such as sports fields, a community center, and an outdoor amphitheater. Supporters typically framed the issue as a matter of welcoming the lower-income "have nots" into the community rather than hoarding land to provide greater amenities for the "haves." Opponents viewed the measure as irresponsibly filling the valley with sprawl instead of preserving space for families to recreate and enjoy nature.

However uncharitably each group depicted the other, things were to be different at this event. "Incivility has no place at a church function," warned the first speaker, who would also serve as moderator. "This is not a debate," he continued, "so one of the ground rules is that speakers should speak to the audience and should *not* direct their comments to any of the other speakers." After delineating additional ground rules (e.g., no "personal attacks," no "political speeches") and identifying the event's main speakers—an ethics professor from a nearby Catholic seminary, a local businessman (against the measure), and a member of the city's planning board (for it)—he then introduced the professor by explaining the reason for the latter's presence. "The saying that the church's social teachings have been, for Catholics and non-Catholics alike, 'our best kept secret' is unfortunately very true," he opined. "But I'm optimistic that, if we pay attention to the core values that are embedded within these teachings, they'll help us to clarify our moral thinking on even this divisive issue and then help us to discern together what is best for our community."[1]

With that and amid a smattering of polite applause, the professor stepped onto the stage and took his place behind the podium. He explained that, rather than attempting to tell people what to think or how to vote, he preferred to highlight certain themes within the tradition of Catholic social thought in order to assist those assembled in "bringing those values to bear on the important decisions that affect your community." To emphasize this point, he read from the National Conference of Catholic Bishops' pamphlet, typically published before election years, titled *Faithful Citizenship*:

> Let me read to you something that our Catholic bishops said just a few years ago that I think explains why we're here tonight *at a church* talking about *political* issues: "As members of the Catholic community, we enter the public forum to act on our moral convictions, share our experience in serving the poor and vulnerable, and add our values to the dialogue over our community's future. Catholics are called to be a community of conscience within the larger society and to test public life by the moral wisdom anchored in Scripture and consistent with the best of our nation's founding ideals. Our moral framework does not easily fit the categories of right or left, Democrat or Republican. Our responsibility is to measure every party and platform by how its agenda touches human life and dignity."[2]

The professor then proceeded to do this very sort of measuring. He addressed various themes within the church's social teachings and, in the hope of carving out a common language for the ensuing discussion, demonstrated how people on each side of Measure V might use those themes to think through the issue and the way in which their position on it might affect the public good. He looked at how a vote for or against the measure could be justified in terms of protecting the sacred dignity of human beings. Then he did the same with respect to the idea that human beings are inherently social in nature. This was followed by a discussion of how each position might conform to the church's "preferential option for the poor." Finally, he took up the matter of stewardship and looked at the measure through the lens of Catholics' obligation to care for the gift of creation.

It was likely obvious to all that they had witnessed an extremely nuanced and even-handed presentation. As the professor spoke, many people scribbled notes, and, perhaps because he did so with such eloquence, even the moderator, who had promised to "strictly enforce the time limits," did not seem to mind that he went on for nearly twenty-five minutes. "Those are a few of the many principles expressed within the tradition of Catholic social thought," he finally concluded, sharing the moderator's optimism about what he assumed would be the group's ensuing collective discernment, "but they're the ones I believe will best sharpen our conversation and inform the decision that's before you."

For such a competent presentation, it was surprising to discover how mistaken this conclusion would prove to be. The much briefer comments the next two speakers offered were, while repeatedly interrupted by enthusiastic applause from partisan supporters, neither sharpened nor informed by anything that preceded them. The professor's comments were never mentioned. Arguing against Measure V, the second speaker informed the audience that there were already more than twelve hundred subsidized residential units within the city, that adding more housing in the proposed location would stress the city's infrastructural capacities, and that open spaces and parks benefit lower-income families as much as or more than they do richer ones. He also insisted upon basing such decisions on what citizens actually want and mentioned the results of a recent poll that indicated that 71 percent of Pleasanton's citizens felt that unrestrained growth was among the city's biggest problems. When her turn came, the third speaker devoted most of her time to presenting her own statistics. These pointed to the city's growing population, rising housing costs, and the need for additional affordable housing so that teachers, firefighters, and other human service professionals "can actually live where they work."

Just as there was no indication that the principles addressed by the professor informed these other speakers' thinking on this issue, there was also scant evidence that they contributed much by way of conversational sharpening. Lasting less than fifteen minutes, the questions (not conversation) from the audience were at first entirely directed toward the second and third speakers and concerned only the logistical details of land development. How many houses could be built on this land? Would additional soccer fields count as open space? How long would each of the contending development plans take to complete? Then, with just minutes to go, the moderator reminded the audience that they could also direct questions to the professor. But even these were not at all focused on sharpening the issue's ethical implications. "Isn't the Catholic Church the largest landowner in the world?" asked a supporter of the second speaker. "Why does the Catholic Church always base its teachings on trying to instill guilt into people?" inquired a member of the parish. The professor tried earnestly to address this second question, but, when the moderator announced that the allotted time had elapsed, he simply could not hide the look of relief that came over him. He had apparently planned for a different sort of conversation.

Giving and Getting: An Advent Fair at Saint Monica

Saint Monica does a great deal of outreach ministry during the holiday season. It held a Thanksgiving dinner for senior citizens in the parish. People were encouraged to participate in a blood drive sponsored by the local Red Cross. In coordination with the annual Bay Area–based One Warm Coat Drive, the parish collected coats and sweatshirts and then delivered them to Oakland's Department of Human Services. The Women's Faithsharing Group helped them by making fleece scarves and writing holiday notes, both of which were included with the clothing. For its part, the Men's Club sponsored a food drive and set up boxes and barrels at the church's entrances to hold, respectively, people's donations of money and nonperishable food. Working with a local crisis center, the Outreach Committee asked that parishioners "adopt" a family by signing up to purchase food and at least two gifts per family member to ensure that about one hundred needy households from a neighboring town would experience a pleasant Christmas.

From 3:30 PM to 5:30 PM on the first Sunday of Advent, the newly constructed Parish Education and Activities Center (PEACe) was, true to its name, the center of all of this seasonal activity. At the height of the annual Advent fair, the largest room was filled with about fifty high schoolers and many of their parents for a dinner and then a raucous game of bingo. The proceeds from this help support the Service Immersion thru Education N' Action (SIENA) program, which connects high school students with week-long service experiences both within the Bay Area and as far away as Mexico. In one of the classrooms a group of about twenty-five children and parents were making Advent wreaths, while a similar group decorated Christmas cookies in the classroom next door. Two other classrooms each held groups of about a dozen: one busy making Christmas cards; the other decorating framed representations of Our Lady of Guadalupe for use as Christmas tree ornaments.

Without a doubt, the primary focus of this whole event was on giving. In the main hallway, two sets of tables were set up to help convey this message. On the first set were all of the accoutrements for the alternative gifts fair sponsored by the fifth-graders in the parish's faith-formation program. Working with the inter-faith nonprofit organization Alternative Gifts International, they and their teachers selected gifts that parishioners could purchase and then give—in the form of written descriptions placed inside Christmas cards—to loved ones. Twenty dollars, these descriptions announce to the people in whose name they are given, purchases one share of emergency relief service either for people in New Orleans displaced by Hurricane Katrina or for those in the Darfur region of the Sudan suffering from famine and political violence. Twenty-five dollars pays for either one sleeping bag to be distributed to homeless people by the Berkeley Catholic Worker or one share of groceries purchased to restock the shelves of food banks throughout the United States. For $39 parishioners can pay for one month of a literacy teacher's salary in Haiti. For $49 they can provide a free wheelchair for a Cambodian in need of one. One hundred dollars is enough to supply medicine for ten people in Tijuana, Mexico. These were certainly not the kinds of gifts most Americans have grown accustomed to giving or receiving.

Nor were the ones arranged on the tables across the hallway. Sponsored by the parish's eighth-graders, this assortment of fair trade handcrafts was supplied by Work of Human Hands, a Catholic Relief Services program that helps artisans from thirty-three nations to receive fair prices (mostly from U.S. consumers) for their products. They do this primarily by establishing direct relationships with local producers, which keeps intermediaries such as brokers and retailers from cutting into profit margins. As with the alternative gift fair across the way, it was made clear to parishioners that, by buying, they were helping, too. "When you purchase one of these items, everyone wins," read the pastor's explanation in the parish bulletin. "You get a high-quality handcraft, and the people who created them get hope for a better future for themselves and their families." Hair barrettes and hummingbird ornaments from Argentina; silk scarves and snowflake-shaped trivets from Bangladesh; embroidered purses and sculpted nativity scenes from Chile—reasonably priced gifts from one nation after another appear in the catalogue. Available for closer examination were necklaces and earrings, decorated crosses and candles, wool handbags and straw baskets, and free trade chocolate bars and coffee beans ("Hope and Justice Blend," a particular favorite), all strewn across these tables and representing to parishioners their own salubrious blend of buying and helping.

The highlight of this event (not surprising within Catholic circles) was the 5:30 PM Mass. Dubbed the "Church of Rock," this Mass, as is usually the case, was attended mostly by teenagers and featured contemporary music supplied by electric instruments, as well as a full drum set with accompanying conga drums and a few teenagers singing into microphones. Although the music was certainly different and a larger proportion of young people was evident among the nearly two hundred people seated in the pews, almost everything else was similar to what occurred at the other masses that had been celebrated earlier that day. This included the lighting of a single Advent candle. It was also true of the readings for the day, which, in keeping with the overall theme of Advent, exhorted believers to live righteously and remain faithful in expectation of Christ's arrival at Christmas and, ultimately, at the end of time. It was true, too, of the basic message conveyed by the pastor's homily, which encouraged parishioners to resist giving into the busyness, stressfulness, and inordinate fixation upon achievement that purportedly mark the culture of "Lamorinda" (a colloquialism that denotes the adjoining and relatively affluent towns of Lafayette, Moraga, and Orinda).

Reminiscent of the numerous talk-show hosts one commonly sees on daytime television, the pastor began by walking between and then into the pews with a handheld microphone and asking, "Who's busy?" "I sure am," announced the parish's coordinator of high school youth ministry, who then proceeded to provide the requisite evidence—an upcoming retreat, planning Bible-study classes, and so on. "Me, too," blurted out a high schooler, who went on a bit about upcoming final exams, French camp, and the trepidations of Christmas shopping. "I'm really, really busy," claimed one of the fifth-graders, who, amusing to many, actually seemed a bit overwhelmed by academic, social, and household chore obligations. "That's right," the pastor explained into the mike summarily. "The busyness of the holiday season parallels the busyness of our lives. We go and go and go and go until we don't even have time to breathe." After making vague references to "the rat race," hours spent commuting to work, taxiing kids from one activity to another, and "being held hostage by the holiday season," he informed the faithful, using phrases captured from the day's gospel reading, that they are called to "stand up straight" and "hold your head high." While not explaining precisely what these might mean, he informed those gathered that Advent was the proper time for Christians to recommit themselves to this task:

> People sometimes ask me why the inside of the church is so bare this time of year. I tell them because it's not Christmas yet. This is a time for taking stock. It's about the need to stop, to be deliberate, and to have the patience to wait for Christ to come. That's why, when you think about it, Advent really is quite countercultural. All around us we hear, "Hurry up," "Go, go, go," but the church asks us to slow down, to be willing to wait, to prepare ourselves for Our Lord. That's what Saint Monica's is all about. It's about slowing down and paying attention to the people around us and being in relationship with them. It's about, as the Gospel tells us, standing up and

walking with head held high. This is against the norm. But if we can do this—if we're willing to watch and wait for the Lord—this example will be a true gift to the people throughout Lamorinda.

With that, the pastor concluded his homily, and the band began playing the offertory song that accompanied the collection of people's gifts and their presentation before the altar. Because I was in the "crying room" at the back of the church with my young son at the time, I could hear a man standing a few feet from me with an infant in his arms say, "That's such an important message!" "How do you do it, though?" responded the woman, likely his wife, standing next to him and plucking a bill from her purse just in time for the arrival of the collection basket. "It's hard to know what that would look like," she said until, perhaps catching me listening in, she leaned in closer and continued in a whisper.

Promise and Peril

Saint Augustine and Saint Monica do not, like oppositional parishes, draw upon civil society discourse as their primary means for imagining church community. Nevertheless, these hometown parishes, like Catholic parishes generally, are connected to civil society in important ways.[3] Without them, some of the people described earlier in this chapter might not have known or cared much about Measure V or have found a venue as inviting as an Advent fair to direct their energies and money toward serving the broader public. In return, participation within civil society enhances their members' sense of fellowship and common purpose, thus making religious belonging more meaningful for them.

Yet, it is critical to keep in mind that the connection between civil society and parishes has a "yes, but" quality to it, exemplified by three tendencies I explore in this chapter. Yes, parishes do get people involved in civil society, but they also demonstrate a tendency toward *civic underachieving.* Only about fifteen parishioners attended the public forum on Measure V, for example. Moreover, the families who volunteered or simply showed up at the Advent fair were, as one parish staff member groused, the "usual suspects," who always seem to do most of what needs doing at the church.

Second, parishes provide people with ready-made opportunities they might otherwise not have for serving others. But, at the same time, this service is marked by a *civic narrowing,* whereby parishes tend to be much better at steering people toward charitable endeavors than at undertaking long-term projects to fulfill the Catholic Church's social justice mission. People at Saint Monica generally considered their Advent fair to be a success. They enjoyed one another's company, they worshipped together, and, in the process of giving to friends and family, they also got the satisfaction of helping needy people throughout the world. This kind of giving and getting defines relationships based on charity, which are easier to maintain than longer-term initiatives. Meanwhile, even though nearly all of the parishioners in attendance at the public forum were in favor of the additional affordable housing they hoped Measure V would bring, that goal was much harder to achieve. It was overwhelmingly voted down at the polls the following month.

Third, parishes can be important sites for public discourse. They are often where people hear political cues, learn humane values, and challenge their own suppositions or biases in dialogue with other parishioners. However, they can also succumb to *civic silencing,* the tendency for those cues, values, and challenges to go relatively unheard within church settings. This occurs, as we saw in the first vignette, when the values embedded in the church's social teachings are competently presented but then not discussed or actually used to do the work of ethical reflection for which they are intended. It also occurs when these values are simply not presented to push people beyond the self-satisfactions of charity or when, in the face of platitudes, the difficult discussions about how to actually live them out are relegated to "crying room" whispers.

Thinking through all of this requires some nuance. Like other American congregations, most Catholic parishes have not totally withdrawn into the sphere of private concerns ranging from salvation to self-realization as some observers, bemoaning their public irrelevance, have contended. Nor are they capable of nearly single-handedly reviving civic life, which many neoconservatives who uncritically herald faith-based initiatives seem to think. Neither privatized sinners nor civic saints, parishes have a "yes, but" connection to civil society marked by much promise, as well as the aforementioned three tendencies that threaten to keep the church's "best-kept secret" a well-kept one.

Participation, but Also Civic Underachieving

The wide array of community-building activities and other programs sponsored by parishes seems to provide their members with plenty of opportunities to get involved in the goings-on of their churches and wider communities. Nearly all parishes in the United States provide religious education for children under fourteen, about eight in ten do so for high school–aged youth, and about seven in ten have adult education programs. Four-fifths of all parishes sponsor a ministry to shut-ins, three-fifths sponsor one to the elderly, and two-fifths have a ministry to the bereaved. About half of all parishes sponsor faith-sharing groups, and charismatic prayer groups and twelve-step groups each can be found within one-quarter of them. Nearly nine in ten parishes have at least one choir, more than eight in ten sponsor social events, about four in ten sponsor sports programs, and about two in ten periodically put on some kind of cultural event. Catholic associational staples like bingo and "night at the races" are still alive and well in about a third of all parishes.[4]

This sense of community often extends beyond the church in the form of outreach services within the surrounding area. The average parish sponsors four service programs and supports—with money, volunteers, or both—about four more. Almost every parish does at least some social service, and nearly one-third sponsor or support ten or more programs. These typically attend to the needs of the most vulnerable populations. For instance, four-fifths of all parishes offer some sort of cash or voucher assistance, and about the same number sponsor or support a food pantry or soup kitchen. Substance abuse recovery, community organizing, low-income housing, and prison ministry programs are each sponsored or supported by about one-third of all parishes. Finally, about one-quarter of them sponsor or support counseling services, tutoring programs, and voter registration initiatives.[5]

Evidence that opportunities like these make a difference in people's civic engagement is easy to come by. Close to one-half (44 percent) of all Catholic parishioners are members of at least one civic group, but this is true of only one-quarter of those Catholics without a parish affiliation.[6] Parishioners' greater involvement with church-based groups accounts for much of the disparity. Yet, they are more likely than nonparishioners to become active in specifically secular groups as well.

Some of the people and events with which we are now familiar offer still more evidence of parish membership's civic benefit. Given Elizabeth Weiland's confession that she "never volunteered for anything," it is hard to imagine she would have become so active if she had not gotten plugged into her church's recruitment network. Even among the especially active interviewees for this study, it is striking just how many, often after some initial foot dragging, first became more involved at their church after simply being asked to do so by their pastor or some other parishioner they respect.[7] Similarly, Natalia Acuña is quick to credit her church with helping her to acquire the civic skills and confidence she once lacked. Kevin Murray gets most of his information about issues related to home schooling and pro-life activism from his church. Without Saint Augustine's public forum on the matter, at least some of the modest number in attendance would not have known as much about Measure V or about how Catholic social teachings might assist them in thinking through its ethical implications. The alternative gifts portion of Saint Monica's Advent fair could not have occurred without the parish's partnerships with both Alternative Gifts International and Work of Human Hands.

All of this doing does something to parishioners. Again and again they claim that getting involved in their churches changes them in meaningful ways. Many, like this longtime member and dependable volunteer at Saint Louis Bertrand, say their participation helps to reinforce their religious identity: "Prayer is important, and so is going to Mass, receiving the sacraments, and believing the Gospel. It's all important. But for me, the best way to be a follower of Jesus—and to really *feel* like a follower of Jesus—is to act like Jesus, which is what I'm trying to do here."

Others say their parish participation continually reminds them of what Abraham Lincoln, in his first inaugural address, called the "better angels of our nature." This is the view of a Saint Monica parishioner who spoke about a prayer service conducted in the aftermath of the attacks on September 11, 2001: "It seems that everywhere you turned, someone was talking about bringing terrorists to justice, vengeance, getting ready for war. It would have been so easy to have gotten caught up in that. . . . At that service we prayed for the victims, and we also prayed for forgiveness and for world peace. So that's just one example of what I'm talking about. Saint Monica's is good in the sense that it steers people in the right direction and helps them focus on what's most important, most humane."

Broadening one's vision of the world frequently gets mentioned. A parishioner at Saint Mary–Saint Francis, puts the matter this way: "We have presentations on the church's social teachings after Mass a few times each year. Or we hear that we're now drinking free trade coffee from Guatemala at the coffee hour. Or, you know, we'll write letters with Amnesty International throughout the year. So there's always these reminders of how we're connected to the larger world and how we're called to live differently because of that awareness."

Having the feeling that one is doing at least something positive in the face of countless and potentially paralyzing social problems is yet another thing people's doing purportedly does for them. "You don't have to feel so helpless," says a member of Saint Monica's Pax Christi group, who then elaborates: "The AIDS epidemic, the violence and desperation in inner cities, the incredible suffering in Iraq, everything that's going on in Darfur: Seriously, everywhere you look, there's so much need. You could easily give yourself over to despair, which is something I've really experienced in my own life. But you can do something good at a place like Saint Monica's. It's often something small, but you can at least say, 'I'm on the side of making the world a little bit better.'" It would be extremely easy to provide many more examples. Catholics who take advantage of parish-based opportunities for community involvement report that these open them to at least the possibility of being more Christ-like, humane, globally aware, hopeful, and many more qualities they claim would otherwise remain beyond their reach.

However, we might also ask questions of these people. What sociopolitical benefit accrues when people try to act more like Jesus? When they get steered in the vaguely specified "right direction"? When they feel a connection with others who are in many ways quite distant from them? When they feel content just doing "something small" in response to problems that are anything but small in scope? These questions–and the suspicions they reflect–are legitimate ones. They are especially warranted in light of the "yes, but" reality that, even if we take these people at their word, such highly active parishioners are simply not representative of Catholics in general.

Public policy scholar Mary Jo Bane admits to feeling perplexed by what she dubs the "Catholic puzzle." She summarizes this as "a strong set of official teachings on social justice and faithful citizenship alongside Catholic participation in various realms of civic life that is no higher than that of other denominations, and in a number of areas, lower."[8] This is indeed puzzling. American Catholics are currently well above national averages with respect to educational attainment, occupational status, and family income, which are all factors that typically correlate with greater levels of volunteerism, associational membership, and charitable giving. Also, in light of the seemingly endless stream of papal encyclicals and bishops' pastoral letters denouncing social maladies such as economic inequality, racism, consumerism, militarism, and family disruption, one could reasonably expect Catholics' contributions to civil society to be roused beyond those made by the rank and file of other denominations.

Other factors make this expectation only more feasible. The Catholic Church is unique in having a unified body of social teachings disseminated through a single authority structure and presumed to be taken seriously by all of the faithful. Long an "immigrant church," it has a laudable history of community assistance to newcomers.[9] Unrivaled in scope, the so-called Catholic philanthropic tradition encompasses initiatives that range from the social concerns committee at the local parish to Catholic Charities, the nation's single largest social service provider.[10] Socially activist icons like Dorothy Day, the Berrigan brothers, Cesar Chavez, and Mother Teresa still have a place in many Catholics' imaginations. And Catholicism is widely perceived as promoting a distinctive communitarian ethic that, according to a 2002 book on the topic, "emphasizes connectivity, loyalty, and involvement."[11] How, then, does this square with the reality that Catholics are no more civically active on most counts than those of different religions?

Size is a key factor. The average Catholic parish has approximately twenty-five hundred registered members, more than eight times that of the average Protestant congregation.[12] Therefore, even though the percentages of *parishes* that sponsor or support various community-building groups and social service programs is generally not much different from that of other congregations, when measured per capita, things look very different. To account for this, Bane looked at only those congregations with at least one thousand members and discovered some surprising discrepancies. With fourteen worship services per week, parishes far exceed the number offered in both the more liberal "mainline" (3 per week) and conservative

(3.5 per week) Protestant churches. They are well behind, however, with respect to getting members involved in nonworship activities. Their average of three choirs and seven groups per parish is about half the number in both mainline and conservative churches (each averaging six choirs and 13.5 groups). The fourteen classes per parish is just more than half the number sponsored by mainline (23.5 classes) and conservative (25 classes) churches. Perhaps more startling are the differences in the number of people who actually participate in these activities. Keeping in mind that some people are likely to be active in more than one context, parishes involve an average of 200 adult participants in their choirs, groups, and classes. Mainline congregations, on the other hand, involve an average of 525 adults, and, for conservative congregations, the average is an impressive 920 adults.[13]

According to one study, fewer than one-fifth of all American Catholics participate weekly in nonworship activities at their parishes, whereas twice as many mainline Protestants and three times as many evangelicals report this much participation.[14] Another discovered that fewer than one-third of all parishioners had volunteered at their parish in the past month, but about half of all Lutheran, Presbyterian, and Assemblies of God congregants had done so.[15] Furthermore, if stewardship counts as participation, Catholics are now somewhat notorious for their lower levels of giving to their churches. Hovering at about 1 percent of household income, Catholics' annual contributions to their collection baskets are roughly half of those by Protestants. This is why Catholic churches, despite being eight times larger than Protestant ones, have annual revenues only twice as high.[16] No doubt this goes a long way toward explaining the staff and program deficiencies in many parishes, which likely result in less vibrant parishes, less overall participation, and, as a consequence, even less impetus to give in the future.

Catholics' contributions to civic life outside their churches likewise do not look much different from those of other Christians. About two in five Catholics say they have done some sort of volunteering in the past month, and nearly half have volunteered in the past year, which is what Protestants also report.[17] Focusing on different Protestant families shows that the percentage of Catholics who volunteer outside their churches (48 percent) is modestly higher than the rates for evangelical (44 percent) and African American (39 percent) Protestant churches but lower than that of mainline ones (55 percent). Moreover, when it comes to explicitly political activities, Catholics tend to participate at appreciably lower rates than members of these other churches. They score the lowest with respect to the percentages of people who claim to have, in the past year, given money to a political candidate or party (12 percent), attended a political rally or meeting (12 percent), and worked for a political campaign (6 percent). And, they score second lowest when asked whether they, in the past year, contacted an elected official (27 percent) or attended a class or lecture about sociopolitical issues (20 percent).[18]

Catholics' political attitudes have shifted considerably in the past few decades. Since the 1970s, the percentage affiliated with the Democratic Party has dropped 40 percent, and the number of Catholic Republicans has risen 80 percent.[19] As they move toward increased political conservatism, they also seem to be moving away from their longstanding affinity for their church's social teachings. Parish affiliation seems to do very little to remedy this. Catholics who are members of parishes are much more likely than nonmembers to accept traditional beliefs and practices, as well as church teachings on matters of sexuality. But they are not significantly more accepting of its social teachings.[20] Thus, Catholics' attitudes on political issues depart little from those of the average American. Whether closely connected to parishes or not, they are neither *more* likely than the rest of the country to agree that "government should do more for the needy" (about 48 percent) nor *less* likely to agree that "the best way to ensure peace is through military strength" (about 36 percent).[21] Meanwhile, neither the four in ten Catholics who would like to see churches put "a lot" more emphasis on services for poor people nor the half who think about their responsibility for the poor a "great deal" or a "fair amount" stand out. These percentages are the same for the nation as a whole.[22]

As Bane and others have also contended, the key to solving the Catholic puzzle is to pay attention to certain institutional features of the church in the United States.[23] As mentioned, relative to other churches of comparable size, Catholic parishes provide members with fewer opportunities to get involved. This means that parishioners become connected to fewer church-based social networks than do other congregants; as a result, they are less likely to be recruited into various forms of civic engagement.[24] Closely related is the argument made by political scientist Sidney Verba and his colleagues that parishes are also less likely to equip their members with the portable civic skills that increase their chances of becoming socially engaged.[25] They contend that the fact that Catholics are only about one-third as likely as Protestants to write a letter to a political representative, plan or attend a meeting, and deliver a speech in conjunction with some church initiative means they are likely to possess fewer of the skills learned by doing such things and are that much less capable of participating within civil society as a result.

The church's impressive institutional differentiation is another organizational reason for Catholics' civic underachievement. There are more than eleven hundred Catholic hospitals and health care centers in the United States. Catholic Charities has developed a network of fourteen hundred social service agencies. The Catholic Campaign for Human Development currently helps organize and fund two hundred local antipoverty groups throughout the country. Moreover, one-third of all Catholic parishes in the United States support a parochial school.[26] These institutions, while remarkably successful, have also succeeded in allocating a sense of responsibility for social action toward the professionals who run them and, in the minds of many, away from the people in the pews.

Finally, the fact that the church is a hierarchical institution led by a celibate, exclusively male clergy has taken a civic toll in a couple of ways. First, it has created a generalized habit of deference to priestly authority with respect to social action that, in turn, has frequently deterred lay initiative and participation. Second, the dramatic decline (and aging) of Catholic priests since the 1960s has left a leadership vacuum within many parishes. Two-thirds of all parishes in the United States have only one, typically overworked, priest, whose main focus tends to be sacramental ministry.[27] There are now approximately thirty thousand professional lay ministers working in parishes, but because this averages out to only about 1.5 per parish, more leaders will be necessary in order to create the networks, teach the classes, facilitate the groups, and deliver the inspiring homilies needed to stir the energies of the faithful.[28]

Serving Others, but Also Civic Narrowing

The examples of Saint Augustine's public forum and Saint Monica's Advent fair also tell us something about the direction in which those energies are most often and most successfully pointed—charity. Despite magisterial documents' countless exhortations to Catholics to focus on the underlying causes of social injustice, parishes overwhelmingly sponsor projects that are short-term, small-scale, and ameliorative. One study after another has demonstrated that this is also true of American congregations in general. Take, for example, a national survey conducted by the research institute Independent Sector. It found that, while nearly three-quarters of all congregations provide recreation or camp programs for youth and marriage counseling for adults, fewer than one in five are involved in either more extensive after-school programs for those same youngsters or more rigorous economic-development and job-training programs for those adults.[29] A more focused study of the Washington, D.C., metropolitan area discovered that an impressive 95 percent of all congregations support at least one social service program. But a closer look indicated that three-quarters of these congregations were active in some sort of emergency assistance, whereas fewer than 5 percent were involved in initiatives that require greater expertise or capital, such as foster care, job training, and legal, medical, and mental health services.[30]

Many American congregations are part of religious traditions with more "other-worldly" orientations, which lead them to steer their outreach in the direction of saving souls, practicing charity, and, in the main, devaluing rather than attempting to change society. This is not the case with the Catholic tradition. Turning our attention to parishes, we learn that the tendency for their outreach to become narrowed into charitable endeavors is not a function of theological otherworldliness, but of both institutional and cultural causes.

Institutionally, as suggested earlier, parishes generally lack the resources to undertake more long-term, complex, and costly community-serving ventures. Parish budgets are very tight, largely due to Catholics' exceptionally modest level of giving. The average parish income is about $426 annually per regularly participating adult, which is significantly lower than that of African American ($637 per adult), mainline ($1,143), and evangelical ($1,286) congregations.[31] Quite tellingly, only about one in five parishes in the United States has a staff member who devotes more than one-quarter of his or her time to church-based service or community-development programs of any kind.[32]

Parish volunteers find it understandably difficult to pick up the slack. Typically they have numerous work and family commitments and so do not always have the requisite discretionary time for grappling with and doggedly pursuing more long-term approaches to social problems. They generally lack expertise in such matters as well and thus would not know how to go about solving intractable social problems even if they had the time. And, since they are usually at church to help themselves and their families to better connect with God, their commitment to service usually flows from, not substitutes for, this primary interest. Given all of this, it is not surprising that, within the past year, groups, meetings, classes, or events focused on prayer, training religious education teachers, and welcoming new members were each sponsored by about four-fifths of all U.S. parishes, and those dedicated to parenting issues and cleaning the church were each sponsored by about two-thirds of all parishes. On the other hand, groups, meetings, classes, or events on race relations and lobbying elected officials were each sponsored by only one-quarter of all parishes, and those dedicated to registering voters and addressing environmental issues were each sponsored by only one in five.[33] "The projects we take on here aren't going to solve the world's problems," says Elaine McBride, one of the volunteers at Saint Monica's Advent fair, in apparent explanation of these de facto priorities. "But they truly do derive from our desire to be church together," she continues, "and, at the same time, they're doable for busy people, and they're much, much better than doing nothing."

One would be hard pressed to disagree with her. Even though giving people an opportunity to purchase a wheelchair in Cambodia in the name of a loved one or a bar of free trade chocolate for oneself contributes little to solving the world's problems, it is without doubt "better than doing nothing." Like charitable efforts in general, McBride is also correct in stating that getting involved at the Advent fair is something "doable" for busy people with multiple personal commitments. And, in noting that the contributions she and her fellow parishioners make to civil society come from their primary "desire to be church together," she also suggests a second institutional cause of parishes' inability to move beyond the charitable. This is the reality that the minority of Catholics who actually are active parishioners actually devote most of their volunteer time to sustaining their churches as institutions. National surveys have demonstrated that Catholics' parish membership correlates with greater than average rates of three types of volunteering. It is weakly correlated with volunteering for educational institutions (especially schools attended by one's own children) and with "informal" volunteering such as babysitting, visiting the elderly, and helping friends. On the other hand, it is strongly correlated with "religion-related" activities, especially volunteering within one's parish.[34] As table 6.1 shows, for example, parishioners in this study are far more active within their parishes (Items 1 through 5) than they are within their wider communities (Items 6 and 7).

Even though "other volunteer work in the parish" (Item 5) often includes various social service projects, and "parish committees" (Item 4) can include the occasionally vital social justice committee (which, at Catholic parishes, tends to focus on short-term service projects), the preponderance of parishioners' volunteering is done to support fellowship, liturgy, and catechesis at their churches. True of interviewees in this study, this trend is also reflected in an important national survey of parish-registered Catholics conducted in the 1980s. More than half of these parishioners, it discovered, were the proverbial "people in the pews" who attended Mass but participated in no other activity at church. Twenty-two percent of them, however, were involved in fellowship activities, 19 percent volunteered with liturgy, and 14 percent helped with catechesis, all of which steers people's energies in the direction of sustaining the institution. Meanwhile, only 4 percent participated in anything that would fall under the rubric of "social action, welfare, justice."[35] What this suggests is that, for even their most active members, local parishes often become what sociologist Lewis Coser refers to as "greedy institutions."[36] They consume the

TABLE 6.1. "About how often do you participate in each of the following church and community activities?" (in %).

	Weekly or more	At Least Monthly
1. Mass attendance	81	97
2. Mass participation (reader, choir member, greeter, etc.)	40	66
3. Parish fellowship activities	30	64
4. Parish committees	16	48
5. Other volunteer work in the parish	27	56
6. Civic, school, political, or community groups	14	37
7. Other volunteer work in the community	12	37

skills and discretionary time of the people most personally invested in them and, in doing so, render their most committed members less available for promoting some of the more outward-looking goals expressed in the church's social teachings.

McBride's mention of her own and her fellow parishioners' "desire to be church together" points to the first cultural cause of civic narrowing. For good or for ill, doing good and remedying society's ills are simply not at the forefront of people's thinking about why they are religious and why they participate at church. When asked what they believe to be Christians' primary duty, three-fifths of all American Catholics say it is following the teachings of Jesus as the basis for spiritual growth, and nearly one-quarter say it is participating in the church's tradition and sacraments. In contrast, only 6 percent identify their primary duty as "helping to change unjust social structures."[37] Similarly, about nine in ten of the Bay Area parishioners in this study state that spirituality and personal growth are "very important" to them as Catholics, and the same proportion say this about receiving the sacraments. More revealing, though, is the fact that six in ten report that getting involved in parish groups and activities is "very important" to them, whereas only four in ten say the same for participating in groups and activities in their local communities. Thus, along with lacking the requisite resources, McBride reports that the various projects sponsored at Saint Monica "aren't going to solve the world's problems" because she also knows that attempting to do so is not the reason she and even the most active of her fellow parishioners come to church. "To be close to God," "I want a feeling of holiness in my life," "Growing in faith and being true to myself," "Saying 'yes' to God by following Christ's example"—these are the things they, in fact, do say. They want to be connected to religious symbols, narratives, and experiences that, in turn, connect them to the sacred. Other things—experiences of community, opportunities for service, feelings of personal efficacy, and so forth—"derive," as McBride puts it, from this more fundamental desire. Sociologist Mark Chaves has also made this central point in the aftermath of his massive National Congregations Study. "The core purpose for which congregations gather people," he writes, "the purpose to which congregations devote most of their resources and involve most of their members, is producing and reproducing religious meanings through ritual and religious education."[38]

Moreover, even if we agree that this constitutes parishes' core purpose, the reality is that they are still not particularly successful in "reproducing" among their members the religious meanings carried by the church's justice tradition. This is the second cultural reason for Catholics' narrowed approach to social betterment, and indications of it are numerous. For instance, only about half of all Catholics in the United States consider "seeking justice" to be a Christian virtue.[39] More than half (55 percent) disapprove of their bishops' speaking out on "political issues" such as war and the economy.[40] Close to two-thirds (62 percent) agree with the statement that "Religion is a private matter that should be kept out of public debates over social and political issues."[41] Compounding this problem is the subtler reality that Catholics are not only unconvinced that they *should* bring their religious values to bear on specifically public matters. Evidence also suggests that, even if so inclined, they are not at all sure *how* to do this. Consider a 1996 national survey that provided people with a list of social issues and then asked them to state which of six specified sources of information "had the biggest influence on your thinking on this issue."[42] Approximately three in ten Catholics cited their religious beliefs as their most influential source of information on the issues of both abortion and same-sex marriage. Much lower percentages, though, said this about more overtly sociopolitical issues such as the death penalty (14.6 percent), government assistance to the needy (4.8 percent), the deployment of U.S. troops to Bosnia (2.5 percent), the role of women in the workforce (2.3 percent), and environmental protection (0.8 percent). Somewhat startlingly, with the exception of abortion, Catholics relied on their religious beliefs significantly less than the American population as a whole on each of these issues.

This indicates that some ethical teachings are accessible to Catholics as they think about the world around them, and others simply are not. Helpful for understanding this is sociologist Gene Burns's analysis of the "ideological reconstruction of Catholicism," which accompanied the church's loss of political authority in the modern era.[43] No longer able to control the social order, Burns argues, church leaders have come to focus their authority on matters that pertain to faith and morals. Magisterial pronouncements on these issues tend to be very specific and are presumed to be binding on the faithful. Over time, these have effectively subordinated the church's more general, often vague, and thus far less binding social justice teachings. The result is the creation of what Burns calls a "hierarchy of issues," which renders Catholics much less familiar with the ethical tools at their disposal for dealing with political issues not related to personal morality and sexuality. As a consequence, even if trying to solve the world's problems were one of the chief motivations for Catholics to affiliate with their parishes, most would be insufficiently fluent in an ethical language that could assist them in expressing and discerning together how best to go about this.

Public Discourse, but Also Civic Silencing

Keeping "Our Best-Kept Secret" a Secret

Like learning a foreign language, becoming more fluent in the church's social justice tradition can occur only when one is immersed in it. This is why public discourse within parishes is so important. Catholics gain access to these idioms— concepts such as the "priority of labor over capital," human dignity, subsidiarity, the common good, a "preferential option for the poor," distributive and social justice, stewardship of the earth's resources, and "just war" criteria—when they hear them used repeatedly. They learn how to deploy these concepts only by doing so in actual conversation. What is more, encouraging such conversations is probably the best hope of honestly identifying and addressing various problems associated with civic underachieving and narrowing.

Unbridled optimism about such prospects would mean neglecting the "yes, but" quality of parish cultures. As the account of Saint Augustine's public forum reminds us, even when parish-based events, groups, and classes attend to sociopolitical matters, they are seldom designed to make Catholicism's justice language more accessible to and deployable by parishioners. The few people who ordinarily attend these are more often audience members listening to "experts" than interlocutors who are expected to actually engage with one another. Such events tend to be one-time rather than ongoing affairs, which would be more challenging, formative experiences. These occasions are also likely to succumb to a kind of centripetal force, whereby they seem inevitably to converge upon more individual concerns. What am I learning from this? How does this relate to my family? How does this help me to be a better person? How can I incorporate this into my busy life? While often large hearted and well intentioned, queries of this sort reflect the reality that people are infrequently encouraged or equipped to think in terms broader than those pertaining to the self. As at the public forum, rarely are biblical principles or the church's social teachings actually used as ethical sources that enable people to more critically examine political ideologies, public policies, social problems, and especially the underlying societal structures that parishioners themselves generally assist in perpetuating.

Encouragement to think in these terms is also unlikely to come regularly from the pulpit. Homilies during the Mass are renowned for their brevity and, especially when it comes to complicated social issues, for their very general, often platitudinous character. This is partly because, like lay leaders, many priests simply do not feel they have the expertise to make public pronouncements on matters of social concern. Even when they do, they often refrain from making them because, knowing that Catholics normally resent a "Father knows best" approach to such subjects and are apt to express that resentment by "voting with their feet," priests are generally reticent to alienate parishioners by speaking out. Perhaps this is why, although the U.S. bishops wrote highly regarded pastoral letters on both economic justice and issues concerning war and peace during the 1980s, by the early 1990s fewer than one in five Catholics claimed to have heard of them.[44]

So, yes, public discourse is occurring in parishes. But it is often undermined by a tendency toward civic silencing, whereby the idioms of the church's social justice tradition are expressed less interactively, less incisively, and less regularly.

As a consequence, they are unfamiliar to many Catholics, and, thus, they truly do constitute the tradition's "best-kept secret."

A minority of the three hundred parishioners interviewed for this book are quite knowledgeable about this component of their tradition, and a few say they take some pride in it. Nevertheless, when discussing their views on issues such as people's and governments' obligations to poor people and the U.S. war in Iraq, almost no one says these were significantly informed or shaped by their church involvement. "I guess I've always believed in my heart that you should give people a helping hand when they're down," said one Saint Louis Bertrand parishioner in expressing her agreement with the church. "In my opinion, if someone's a threat, then we're justified in taking care of it," said a Saint Margaret Mary parishioner when asked why he paid no attention to the pope's disapproval of America's pre-emptive war with Iraq. Their minds, they both emphatically declared, had already been made up. Interestingly, parishioners commonly cite their connection to family, schools, and workplaces as having a significant effect on how they see various social issues. Not so their churches, though. Broadly speaking, they appreciate any convergence of church teaching and their personal views, but they are not especially aggrieved when this does not occur. In either case, they are consistently dismissive of suggestions that their church involvement might have altered their views.

One way to understand this is to think in terms of cultural allocation. Much of the last chapter illustrates what we can call a *differentiated* cultural allocation. Different parishes allocate distinctive community ideologies. As we saw, not all cultural meanings of community—expressed by distinctive communal narratives— are emphasized within each type of parish. Similarly, there are also cultural meanings that cannot be effectively emphasized in most any parish—we can term this a *blocked* cultural allocation.

Just as the presence of any given community ideology is produced when people actively appropriate the religious meanings that best relate to their lives, so too is the relative silencing of other religious meanings a contextualized, collective production. This may sound counterintuitive. It might be easier to think of civic silencing as a glitch in the supply or demand of previously produced religious meanings. If that were the case, then one could say that the dearth of public discourse on sociopolitical concerns within parishes is due to parish leaders' reluctance, for whatever reason, to supply both the church's social teachings and opportunities for seriously engaging them among the faithful. On the other hand, one could point to parishioners' purported civic apathy or to the many distractions in their busy lives as evidence of their suboptimal demand for those teachings. But this supply-and-demand formulation is too trite. Civic silencing—the absence of sustained and challenging public discourse concerning the common good—is not simply a function of inadequate supply or demand with respect to already produced cultural meanings. It is itself a cultural production that, to various extents, is maintained in each of the parishes in this study.[45] As we will see next, the mechanisms that produce this silencing are of the interpretive and discursive varieties.

Interpretive Mechanisms: The Irony of Religious Agency and Institutional Reflexivity

In the place of civic discourse, parishes frequently instill in people a sense that there is nothing to talk about when it comes to sociopolitical issues. This permeating sensibility is largely an unintended consequence of the religious agency that is now ubiquitous among American Catholics. Because all parishioners are entitled to their own interpretation of church doctrines, biblical principles, and even what constitutes a Catholic in good standing, the fundamental attitude goes, then whether or how such individualized understandings inform one's social consciousness is overwhelmingly considered a private affair. The prevailing axiom seems to be that, "in matters of public concern, there can be no dispute." The upshot of this is a notable hushing of moral deliberation. In the absence of much ideological contention or even much considered dialogue at all, people are typically left to interpret aspects of their religious tradition in ways that, if not self-serving, are certainly less challenging to them than might otherwise be the case.

Of course, some see the increasing disparity in wealth both domestically and globally in terms of the Catholic principle of subsidiarity and accordingly speak about the government's obligation to help rectify this and their own responsibility to pressure it to do so. Much more common, though, are those people who talk about putting extra money in the collection basket or volunteering each month at a local soup kitchen. Some counterpoise our society's rampant consumerism with their conviction of being in solidarity with the poor, which is reflected in their decisions about subjects ranging from where they live to the kind of car they drive to their choice of profession. However, most people say they do their best not to become overly materialistic or, as one parishioner put it, they "try to resist giving the kids *everything* they want this Christmas." Some use social justice language to describe how institutions perpetuate racial inequality and therefore envision institution-level remedies. But, again, the majority of people (of all races) simply insist that they "treat everybody the same way," a practice they typically suggest would, if universalized, suffice to solve this problem. Such exceptions notwithstanding, left to their own interpretive devices, most people come to terms with these issues to the best of their ability and, as this pattern indicates, tend to neglect or domesticate their church's social teachings in the process.

This widespread pattern is especially noticeable when parishioners are asked to consider certain Bible passages. A well-known and particularly difficult one (Mt. 19:16–26) tells about a rich young man who asks Jesus what he must do "to have eternal life." After hearing that he should keep the commandments and responding with assurances that he has done so, the man asks what he still lacks. "If you would be perfect," Jesus tells him, "go, sell what you possess and give to the poor, and you will have treasure in heaven; and come, follow me." After the man, now described as "sorrowful," hears this, he goes away, which prompts Jesus to turn to his disciples and offer them instruction. It will be hard for a rich man to enter heaven, he explains to them and then amplifies: "It is easier for a camel to go through the eye of a needle than for a rich man to enter the kingdom of God." "Greatly astonished" by this, when the disciples inquire "Who then can be saved?" Jesus informs them that "with God all things are possible."

Like various other "hard sayings" attributed to Jesus in the Bible, this one is understandably difficult for many to hear. Frank Morgan, a long-time Saint Margaret Mary parishioner who proudly labels himself a "traditional Catholic," found this to be the case. "You have to understand this one metaphorically," he began—until reminded that this metaphorical approach was precisely the one he had rejected with respect to the Last Judgment. "People who soft-pedal what Jesus says about an actual heaven and an actual hell are just deluding themselves so they can feel better," he asserted, reflecting on that other passage. When asked whether he might be doing some soft-pedaling of his own, he began to truly struggle with this text:

I often wonder [long pause] . . . that's a toughie. I would hope that, if Jesus was standing in front of me and he told me to sell what I have, I would have done it. But, on the other hand, maybe this person was really greedy or lacked understanding of who Jesus was and so couldn't do it. What would I have done in that situation? I think I would have gone ahead and sold everything. But I think as people today accumulate more stuff and more wealth, this is harder to do because you can get so used to having more. You have to be on guard against becoming too attached to things.

How does this coincide with what you said before? When we discussed the Last Judgment passage, you said Jesus's message applies to everyone, and people need to take its difficult message literally. Are you now saying something else?

That's a good point. If you take the passage to its fullest extent, you would sell everything. But what would you do then? Would you take a vow of poverty? I think priests should do this, but I don't think I have the right mental discipline to be a priest. I have to support myself. I try to share what I have, but I'm certainly not following that commandment, *if* it is a commandment. Maybe later on in life I'll do a better job of it. Maybe when I'm dead I'll give it all to charity. Practically speaking, though, if everyone sold their possessions, the world would grind to a halt. It would be interesting to see [pause]. . . . Maybe we should all try this. I am willing to try it. It'd be hard, though; I'll say that.

To his credit, Morgan kept on struggling. He seemed to try on one interpretation after another. At first he suggested that Jesus directed his comments only to this particular young man. However, this construal conflicted with his earlier contention that Jesus's commands apply to all serious Christians. As many exegetes point out, this individualized reading also neglects the fact that "the poor," the people who are in need of what the rich man possesses, are an important part of the story as well. They remain an object of Jesus's concern regardless of what this man or anyone else decides to do with their resources. Morgan then cast the scene in a more metaphorical light (i.e., the need to be detached from material things) until he was rereminded of his earlier prohibition against "soft-pedaling." Next he relied on the traditional Catholic distinction between two grades of discipleship: the faithful masses who follow the commandments to the best of their ability and the "perfect," who enter religious life and abide by the so-called evangelical counsels of poverty, chastity, and obedience. Once again, though, his explanation foundered upon the shoals of a closer examination of the text. Rather than denoting religious superiority, most exegetes agree that the word "perfect" is better interpreted as "mature" or "whole" and that it—like the phrases "have eternal life," "enter life," "enter the kingdom of heaven," and "be saved"—designates a single goal pertaining to all of Jesus's followers. Then, in rapid succession, Morgan wondered how seriously to take Jesus's words ("*if* it is a commandment"), whether his own future self might be better able to live up to them ("Maybe later on in life I'll do a better job of it"), and what the practical results would be if they were taken as something of a categorical imperative binding upon everyone ("the world would grind to a halt"). Finally, he ended where he had begun. His concluding "It'd be hard, though" is an honest, hard-won recapitulation of his prefacing "that's a toughie."

Others agree with Morgan's assessment of the passage's difficulty but, when interpreting it for themselves, rely more on some of the themes we have frequently heard. For example, Janice Gray, a catechism teacher at Saint Monica, confided that she sometimes feels guilty about things such as living in a million-dollar home ("although we did get it at 10 percent off market value"), driving a new-model BMW, and golfing "probably more than I should." While many people consider this scripture passage too unambiguous for their own comfort, its primary difficulty for her centers upon understanding precisely what Jesus meant. She summed it up by using the omnipresent "good person" theme:

> Yeah, that's a hard one to figure out. It says to be perfect you have to give everything away. And it says it's difficult for people with great possessions to enter heaven. But then it gives a little bit of hope by saying that all things are possible with God. So there's a lot in that passage to digest, and I really wouldn't claim to understand it yet. But in a nutshell, I'd say it's a passage calling us to reach out and give as much as you can and to be the best person you can be. . . . I think that will be a goal I'll continue to strive for. It makes me think of that children's book *The Giving Tree*. Some people hate it because the tree ends up a mere stump at the end, but it's one of my favorite books because its message is similar to Jesus's—that you have to use your blessings to do God's work. If you hoard it all, you'll never be happy.

Equally common is the use of the spiritual growth theme, which, as we have seen, is also commonplace. No one illustrates this better than Cindy Mahoney, a Eucharistic minister at Saint Mary–Saint Francis. "I've always said that Jesus was an enlightened being," she said. "And so he's really telling us what the Buddha taught his disciples." When pushed on this point, she explained:

> I think he's really talking about a preoccupation with material things and how this sort of affects all of us. . . . It's also about not getting caught up in all the concerns of daily life. What he's talking about here is taking time every day to grow spiritually. And when he says it's easier for a camel to go through the eye of a needle than for a rich man to enter the kingdom of God, I think he really meant that you shouldn't get caught up in all the everyday stuff of, you know, making money, being stressed all the time, being preoccupied with the complexities of things, and not thinking about your spiritual life, your inner life. I don't think Christ thought it was bad to be rich. I think he thought it was bad to be preoccupied with making money and endless striving, which is something poor people can get caught up in, too.

Like Morgan, these two women seem to negotiate with a text that both claim is familiar to them. For a relatively brief and straightforward story, its meaning, they say, is not easy to discern. Interestingly, both feel the need to "go off the board" by supplementing the text with meanings imported from a children's book and from another religious tradition. One wonders, of course, about the distorting effects of this interpretive strategy. Consider Gray's response. Even if one is not a biblical scholar, a close reading of this passage raises the question of just how closely Jesus's message coincides with that of *The Giving Tree* and how concerned he truly was with what might make the rich young man happy. Likewise, contrary to Mahoney's interpretation, one could make a strong argument that Jesus was actually quite interested in taking "the concerns of daily life" seriously and indeed regarded the differences between "the everyday stuff" with which rich and poor are forced to contend as being highly problematic.

Such concerns notwithstanding, the main point is that people do struggle with challenging biblical texts like this one with greater and lesser degrees of seriousness. Yet, they tend to do this struggling on their own. Almost none of the parishioners interviewed could recall an instance when their reading of scripture or their position on a social issue was actually challenged at the parish or when they engaged someone in a critical-minded conversation about such matters. This, incidentally, is also true of participants in Bible-study and other small groups. Even the gentle prodding about people's biblical interpretations or their views on various social issues that occurred during interviews was generally met with little appreciation. For example, when questioned about the validity of their interpretations of the rich young man passage or about whether they should take the story more literally (thus with more radical implications for them personally), people almost uniformly referred to the near sacrosanct nature of their religious agency as a means of forestalling further inquiry. "This is where I am with this passage right now," said one person, confidently anticipating further growth and understanding in the years ahead. "This is how it speaks to me," said another. "You have to take something from scripture, a message of some kind, and move on," said a third, testifying to the Bible's assistance in helping him to be a good person. Such statements each seemingly end with a resounding "Case closed!" They are conversation stoppers because they elevate the interpretive authority of the self over the possibility that they could achieve further insights by engaging other people's perspectives in sustained dialogue.

One additional source of perspective on issues as such discipleship, disparities in wealth, and the common good are the church's official teachings. But these too are conversation stoppers. Many parishioners see their church as a flawed institution rife with the dilemmas discussed in chapter 4. This standpoint contributes to the production of civic silence because it tends to deprecate the instructional value of church teachings and therefore people's felt need to take them seriously as a source of both ethical wisdom and personal challenge. People consistently say the church's social teachings give them "something to think about." Almost no one, though, says they ever trump their own thinking or cause them to question their complacency or even complicity in the face of pressing social problems. They fail to do so, parishioners say, because the church's focus on institutional maintenance has greatly undermined its moral authority.

Jennifer Witte, one of the coordinators of Saint Augustine's small faith communities, exemplifies this pervasive tendency. When asked why she does not feel the need to follow or discuss Catholic social teachings with other parishioners, she mentions the hierarchy's position on women's ordination, the single most frequently cited issue used to explain (or simply justify) people's unwillingness to take these teachings seriously:

> If you think through this issue [women's ordination], at a certain point you realize how stupid it is, and then you get to thinking to yourself, "Wait a minute, my moral authority is just as valid as theirs." You know, you look at the history, and you realize that women did do ministry and did lead worship in people's homes. You look at the gospels, and it becomes obvious that our becoming a male-dominated church had nothing to do with Jesus. So, when you recognize that, you can't help but recognize that it's all about keeping the organization going, you know? And because of that reality, it's not long before you're thinking, "I'm as important a part of the church as the pope is. I know things he doesn't." All of a sudden all bets are off. I'll listen to church teachings on political issues, but I'm the one deciding from now on.

Rather than speaking so generally of "political issues," other people depreciate the church's authority when specific issues come to the fore. A longtime member of Most Holy Redeemer's liturgy committee, David Tronto is a good example. Interviewed in the spring of 2004, he says he has never been "pro-war," but, unlike most of his fellow parishioners, he felt that the United States was justified in going to war against Iraq. Asked how he squared this with the fact that the pope and the U.S. bishops declared this morally questionable, he replied, "I just ignored it really." "Well, they also condemn gays, so I take everything they say with a grain of salt," he continued in response to further inquiry. "Sometimes I think the hierarchy thinks of itself less as a church and more of a government dispossessed of power. But they need to get over it! They're so addicted to wielding power over people that they end up abdicating their spiritual authority and ruining their moral credibility."

Tronto's concluding reference to power is appropriate for highlighting a central irony concerning people's approach to the church's teaching authority. By privileging their religious agency as individuals and offering their institutional understanding of the church as grounds for neglecting it as a source of ethical insight, parishioners deprive themselves of a shared moral language for deliberating upon social problems. They resist the power of the church to tell them what to think and do. Yet, ironically, this can be disempowering in that it silences public discourse within parishes, which limits members' capacity to wrestle with societal issues in ways that are at once both intellectually rigorous and informed by the wisdom of their faith tradition.

When people can interpret various teachings and biblical passages as they see fit, a sense emerges that there is really nothing much to talk about. Thus, the conversations that might disclose to people that they are indeed "soft-pedaling," they are not as good as they think they are, or their individual lives are inescapably connected to the life of the broader community end up being far less likely to occur. Similarly, transforming a healthy dose of institutional skepticism into a license for pursuing a moral "go it alone" strategy can also be disempowering. Witte's declaration that she is "the one deciding from now on" and Tronto's decision to take church leaders "with a grain of salt" may ultimately render them impervious to teachings that might make them uncomfortable or push them to live in a manner more consonant with gospel values. What's more, this disempowerment only serves to perpetuate the ways in which power is presently exercised in that world. Civic silencing, in other words, is not without consequences within civil society. "There can be no escape for public Catholicism," writes historian David O'Brien, "for even a religion that professes to confine itself to spiritual matters by that very stance influences the larger society."[46]

Discursive Mechanisms: The Hushing Effect of Affective Commitment

Accompanying the prevailing sense that there is really nothing to talk about when it comes to politics, parishes also send their members the underlying message that there is no one to talk to. Public discourse within parishes is constrained by tacit discursive rules that govern the kinds of communication that are typically deemed appropriate.[47] Why do such rules function to deprive people of interlocutors when it comes to their church's social teachings? The answer becomes clear when we consider the three main types of commitment people have to religious institutions: commitment to the other people in the group (affective commitment), to the group itself (instrumental commitment), and to the group's norms and teachings (moral commitment).[48] Moral commitment, as we have already seen, has become significantly undermined by the normalization of religious individualism. Something similar can be said of instrumental commitment. Parishioners have become wary of expressing their undying allegiance to the broader institution, and their individual-expressive style of attachment to a particular parish means that this can be quite provisional as well. Even most of these active Catholics say they were less active at (or disaffiliated from) church during at least one period in their lives, and most of them could imagine that something might cause them to reduce their involvement in the future.

In the wake of these trends, the affective—or interpersonal—type of commitment has taken up much of the slack. In the last chapter, we saw that parishes could be differentiated according to the distinctive "communal narratives." What those ties all have in common, regardless of parish type, is that people feel they are strongly supported by others who care about them. In return, even though they seldom say either that they know most of their fellow parishioners or that most of their closest friends are counted among their ranks, people still speak about them in the most affective of terms. They say they "love" their fellow parishioners, they "feel close" to them, and they consider them to be "a blessing," like a "second family," or a "true Godsend." These parish ties are imagined differently, in other words, but they are quite uniform in binding their members to one another. Along with these undoubtedly numerous personal benefits come considerable civic costs. Relying so heavily on this type of commitment has meant that the discursive rules engendered within these parishes are geared more toward maintaining parishioners' interpersonal ties and therefore minimizing the kinds of interactions—especially discussions or disagreements on sociopolitical concerns—that could potentially disrupt them.[49] Examining three of these implicit rules will illustrate this point.

ONE SIZE DOESN'T FIT ALL. This is shorthand for the discursive rule that says that having an interest in the social ramifications of their religious tradition is not a requirement but simply one way among many of being Catholic. Thus, parishioners should accord equal respect to each of these ways. For many, to transgress this rule by assuming that all parishioners must tailor their religious identities to fit the mold of the socially engaged Catholic is to give short shrift to the multidimensionality of the faith. "There is a kind of endlessness in the Catholic tradition," observes one Most Holy Redeemer parishioner. "You know, a spirituality has developed over the millennia; then there is the intellectual tradition; then there is the artistic tradition; then the entire liturgical form slowly, organically developed; and then there's the whole social justice tradition, which interests me, too. There are just so many different things for different people." Like Gregorian chant or systematic theology or Baroque painting, he suggests, an affinity for the social dimension of the faith may rightly appeal to some people but not necessarily to others. To lose sight of this widespread presumption is to risk raising the ire of some of these others. David Tronto once again is a good example. He is one of a growing cadre of parishioners who appreciate Most Holy Redeemer's Wednesday night suppers and other ministries to the local homeless population while also contending that people take things too far when they insist that homeless people be included in the social hour after the main Sunday morning Mass, as well as other parish events. He finds this disruptive to parishioners' valuable fellowship time and reflective of an overly restrictive understanding of what it means to be Catholic. "Most of the people who are involved in causes like this one seem to think *everything* is that," he complains. "But there's a hell of a lot more to life and to the Catholic faith than just that. So, because it can get so shrill, I tend to shy away from the social justice angle of the church."

Many base their conformity to the "one size doesn't fit all" rule on what they see as the nonconforming nature of the authentic self. Challenging or often even entering into conversation with other people on a variety of issues, such people claim, is tantamount to disrespecting their religious agency. The topic of abortion is the best example. There are exceptions, especially at Saint Margaret Mary, but the basic attitude of Saint Augustine's Jill McCloskey is commonplace. "I feel that for me abortion would be wrong because of my personal beliefs," she says. "I do not think that I can tell you whether abortion is wrong for you or not. So I absolutely believe a woman should follow her own conscience, but I can only answer for my own." If McCloskey's reservations seem excessive, consider the response of her friend and fellow Eucharistic minister to the question of whether she is amenable to having discussions about abortion and other social issues within the parish: "Yes, as long as people don't try to enforce their opinions on me," she explains. "I accept people for who they are, so other people shouldn't try to get me to change."

Parishes themselves inadvertently perpetuate this sense of the individual conscience as unchallengeable. They actually enhance the plausibility of the "one size doesn't fit all" rule by offering a broad menu of groups that enable parishioners to carve out their religious identities on their own terms. In doing so, they often give the impression that the various dimensions of the Catholic tradition are indeed selectable. If some people choose to take the church's social teachings seriously, then that entails their joining a usually quite small group of people who feel this kind of faith best fits them. In the process, thoughtful discussion of sociopolitical concerns often becomes the province of a sequestered clique of likeminded people rather than something incumbent upon all. "We don't get into a lot of political discussions here," says one Saint Louis Bertrand parishioner, "but if you're interested in that, we have a group that's into community organizing and that kind of thing. And there are groups for other things, too. That way, people's different perspectives don't come to the fore all the time, and we don't get into disagreements."

DON'T ROCK THE BOAT. This parishioner's concluding sentence is a fair encapsulation of a second discursive rule. Rocking the boat means upsetting the otherwise tranquil waters of community by bringing one's own political perspectives, especially unpopular ones, to the fore. Prohibitions against doing so are deeply ingrained in people's sense of tact, which greases the wheels of social interaction.[50] They also likely reflect Americans' well-known propensity for avoiding disagreement. Some scholars attribute this inclination to the fact that much community association in the United States—like parish involvement, for instance—is voluntary and thus can easily become fragmented should differences of opinion be allowed to surface.[51] Others have argued that Americans' (particularly suburbanites') looser and more fluid social ties make it possible for them to sidestep the kind of interpersonal conflict that would be unavoidable in more highly integrated societies. This situation pur- portedly results in what one sociologist calls "moral minimalism," which character- izes many people's "live and let live" attitude toward their fellow citizens.[52]

Whether ultimately due to tact, voluntarism, moral minimalism, or, most likely, an amalgam of all of these, compliance with the "don't rock the boat" rule is usually framed in terms of parishioners' affective commitment. As one of many examples, consider Susan Masotti's discussion of her pro-choice position. A teacher in Saint Monica's faith-formation program for middle schoolers, Masotti talks to her students about respecting other people's opinions on various religious and social issues. At the same time, she would never dream of sharing her views on abortion with these young people, nor, interestingly, would she do so even with the other adults at her parish:

> I sometimes feel I'm on the hush about this one. I mean, I don't go out
> of my way ever to discuss my pro-choice feelings or ideas with the pro-
> lifers in the parish. I don't think it's constructive or particularly condu-
> cive to the feeling of community that's here. There's nothing wrong with
> their convictions, and there's nothing wrong with mine. But I don't think
> there's anything to be gained by saying, "Hey, I'm not a pro-lifer. I'm not
> on the team with you!" So it's a bit hushed. I don't go out of my way, and
> yet I don't shy away from it either. If someone came up and challenged me
> on it, I would have to probably explain my point of view.

This is a nice reprise of the themes presented earlier. Being "on the hush" is essen- tially being tactful. A focus on what is "constructive" is to have an eye toward build- ing up a community that, because it is based on voluntary participation, could easily be demolished by discord. Moreover, one would be hard pressed to find a better definition for moral minimalism than Masotti's seemingly contradictory assertion that "There's nothing wrong with their convictions, and there's nothing wrong with mine." She wants to protect the "feeling of community" she cherishes at Saint Monica. This is not an overriding concern, she insists, because, if someone were to confront her on her views, she would certainly stand up for herself. When asked about this, though, she could not recall a single time when this had actually happened. Nor would one expect it to happen soon. The importance of community to Christianity means that a desire to protect it can be justified by the tradition itself. "Raising a bunch of divisive issues and making sure people are all on the same page is really unnecessary," says Saint Augustine's Natalie Poston, exemplifying this approach. "I think it was Saint Augustine who said, 'In essential things, unity; in doubtful things, freedom; and in all things, love.' That's basically my view."

Not everyone agrees with Poston's implied view that the church's social teachings are "doubtful" or that people's positions on them should enjoy quite so much "freedom" from being challenged by others. Some think that rocking the boat on occasion is important. Linda Zaller, a member of Saint Margaret Mary's choir, is a good example. She recalls that, at the outbreak of the Iraq War, another parishioner (who was not in the choir) would sing "God Bless America" before the 8:30 AM Mass until Zaller insisted that the pastor tell her to stop. She also says she was upset by people's "grumblings" when the pastor read the pope's letter criticizing the United States' initiation of war and by the surreptitious and repeated removal of a peace banner that had been placed at the entrance to the church. "People will do passive-aggressive crap like that," she says angrily, "but they won't take the church's position against war seriously enough to actually discuss it with one another."

As a conservative member of more liberal Saint Mary–Saint Francis, Stephen Debray might seem to be in a situation exactly opposite to Zaller, a self-described liberal person at conservative Saint Margaret Mary. His complaint is basically the same as hers, however. "All you hear is, 'Of course, everybody is a Democrat,' 'Of course, everybody is against the war with Iraq,' 'Of course, we're against tax cuts that mean less money for social services,'" he says. "You see, it's that 'of course' that troubles me. We demonize the other side so we don't have to talk to 'those people.' As a result, we never have those hard conversations that might get us to really think through these major issues."

NEITHER THE TIME NOR THE PLACE. A third discursive rule goes a long way in explaining why boat-rocking advocates like Zaller and Debray are relatively rare and, even when they are sufficiently angered or troubled to make waves, they are usually unsuccessful in initiating the kinds of conversations they seek. The "neither the time nor the place" rule mandates vigilance in maintaining the imagined boundary between sacred and profane. Set off from ordinary time and reserved for prayer and worship, church is envisioned by many as an inappropriate venue for the prosaic, nitty-gritty, and likely contentious conversations to which Zaller and Debray refer. Restricting such conversations thus becomes a subtle means of enhancing the sense of sacredness in church. In her book on the homosexuality debate within two United Methodist congregations, sociologist Dawne Moon nicely describes how this widely accepted divide between sacred and profane is indeed effective in convincing congregants to repudiate anything that seems unduly politicized in their churches. "If politics is rooted in current events and concerns, the opposite is timeless," she writes. "If politics is self-interested, the opposite is selfless. If politics is base, the opposite is lofty. If politics is isolating and combative, the opposite is about togetherness and caring."[53]

Given the importance of affective commitment, the sacred is truly about experiencing the "togetherness and caring" most parishioners both prize and seem intent on protecting. "Church is neither the time nor the place for a lot of political-type discussions and being at loggerheads with other people," declares Saint Louis Bertrand's Delores Chapman, providing this discursive rule with its nomenclature. "What we're strong at is presenting the church's teachings about these issues and then hoping people will learn from them—that they'll take what they've learned out in the world with them. The best part of the Mass is when the priest says, 'Go in peace to serve the Lord.' Church really begins when people leave and apply what they've learned in everyday life." Not wanting to be at loggerheads with her fellow parishioners, Chapman seems to have a strong preference for airily "hoping" they will learn and apply church teachings "in the world" or "in everyday life" rather than braving the messiness of engaging them for certain within the parish itself. Since most parishioners' everyday lives are unavailable for scrutiny, she really has no way of knowing whether they have indeed learned much or what precisely they have elected to "take" from church teaching. Such matters, however, seem less important than preserving a sense of sacredness within her church.

Chapman is not alone in this regard. In fact, preserving this feeling of sacredness is also a preoccupation of those people who take the social justice tradition very seriously and also carry it into the world with them. Consider, for instance, Jared Wilkes, a lector at Saint Augustine's parish. He is active in a number of progressive political causes outside of church but is also quite resistant to addressing these same causes within it. Accounting for this disparity, he is candid about expressing a feeling that many other people only hint at:

> I never talk about social justice or the kinds of political issues that are important to me at church. To be perfectly honest, it's because I don't want to disappoint myself. I don't want to know when people think we [the United States] should "nuke 'em" or poor people should just "pull themselves up by their bootstraps." I get into all this stuff at work, though. I have a couple of colleagues with those kinds of attitudes. We go at it sometimes. I have to admit I really lay into them. They're so focused on the individual, they just eat up Bush's simplistic rhetoric, they have no appreciation for the common good, you know? So it's no holds barred, but they've told me they like to have these debates or discussions—whatever—because it challenges them. . . . That's at work, though. I just can't bring myself to get into all this at Saint Augustine's because I really need to feel like I'm part of a religious community.

Wilkes really does bring the church's social messages into his everyday life. On the other hand, he and Chapman agree that this kind of work should take place outside of church. Theirs is not simply a desire to avoid conflict, as it is among those for whom the boat-rocking rule is most salient. Rather, in order to preserve feelings of sacredness, as well as affection, for their fellow parishioners, people who conform to this rule sequester profane sociopolitical matters into what sociologist Erving Goffman calls the "back region" of social interaction.[54] Having access to this dimension of other parishioners' lives, Wilkes reveals, would likely be disappointing and make his church participation feel less religious, less sacred than he would like. He instead has access to their "front region"—as they do his—in which their performance of self seems unencumbered by worldly concerns and biases, and thus more attuned to the sacred. "Neither the time nor the place," in other words, functions as a reminder to many that their churches are, among other things, also sites of synchronized performance whereby people jettison those aspects of themselves that seem less religious in order to engender a shared sense of transcendence.

"Our Best-Kept Secret" as a Cultural Product

When people complain that the church's social teachings are Catholics' "best-kept secret," they usually do so on the basis of their belief that, if the people in the pews actually knew those teachings, they would inspire them to become more active participants in civil society. Greater familiarity with the tradition of Catholic social thought, this logic suggests, produces better citizens. There is much to recommend this line of thinking. No doubt it has proven true in innumerable cases. The problem is that thinking only in these terms risks being inattentive to the reality that the very opposite occurs at the same time. Parish cultures also produce tendencies toward noncivicness. When a culture of sociopolitical quiescence is produced within parishes (civic silencing), few people acquire an appreciation for their church's social tradition that comes from their habitual use of its idioms. Similarly, when parishes normalize both a relatively scant level of involvement among their memberships (civic underachieving) and an approach to outreach mostly confined to charity (civic narrowing), a self-satisfied complacency about the wider world can emerge that is seldom rendered problematic. As a result, people may see little need to interrogate that world at a deeper level and, in doing so, rely upon the critical tools bequeathed to them by the church's social justice tradition. Complacency's platitudes and well-worn pieties may come to seem perfectly sufficient.

In the course of his own deliberations about American Catholics in his Jacksonian-era classic, *Democracy in America*, Alexis de Tocqueville displayed a rare moment of confusion. Trying to reconcile their purported doctrinal submissiveness with the democratic opinions and habits he claimed they honed as a result of their minority and lower-class status, he threw up his hands in surrender to what seemed to him a strange duality. "American Catholics are both the most obedient of the faithful *and*," he added summarily, "the most independent of citizens."[55] More than one and a half centuries later, this situation appears to have reversed. Given their insistence on making their own religious choices, Catholics are now anything but submissive to official church doctrine. And, despite having traveled far beyond their minority and lower-class origins, we have seen that there is no longer any justification for deeming them especially independent with respect to how they think and act as citizens.

Nonetheless, their "yes, but" duality remains. Yes, their religious affiliation assists them in being more civically engaged than they otherwise might, but not nearly so much as what one would reasonably expect in light of official church teachings. Many of the concepts expressed in these teachings are articulated during events like Saint Augustine's public forum, but participants do not actually use them to do the ethical work for which they were intended. People may authentically grapple with a social message they hear from the pulpit, but frequently do so in hushed tones, whispering in the "crying room" at the back of the church. Finally, while most parishioners do not share Tocqueville's acute sensitivities toward tensions such as these, they are still affected by them. In other words, if the "yes, but" character of Catholics' civic lives is not addressed by them, this will almost certainly mean that the most incisive conceptual resources at their disposal for doing so will go largely untapped. In that event, this duality will become a real debacle in that the social dimension of their tradition existing to help Catholics be more critical about such matters will be shrouded in greater secrecy then they can know, well-kept even from themselves.

PART III

Stepping Back: Thinking about the Big Picture

7

Paradox

Tradition in a Posttraditional Society

Ending and Beginning: Easter Morning

Easter at Saint Monica

Despite their best efforts to fit in, most sociologists will readily admit to feeling out of place when conducting participant observation. Arriving at Saint Monica's for an Easter morning Mass, I was no exception. The old clunker I drove could not have been more conspicuous among the sporty and elegant new-model cars that filled the church parking lot. Although the ballpoint pen in my breast pocket and the spiral notebook discretely tucked within my jacket drew no attention, they still reinforced my outsider status. I was an analytical gazer, a sociological onlooker out of sync with the spirit of the occasion. I had anticipated these feelings. What came as a surprise was how quickly they were gently assuaged by the smiles and cooing directed at my sixteen-month-old son. As I carried him past the overflow seating (which was packed to capacity) and into the "crying room" filled with toys, more kids, and other parents seemingly just like me, I began to feel, rather surprisingly, just like them. I could see parents and children in every pew in the church.

There was much to command one's attention. The semicircular pews and, above them, the enormous beams that, like the spokes of a wheel, converged upon the altar were all made of beautifully polished wood. So, too, was the figure of the crucified Jesus on one side of the altar, the figure of the glorified Christ on the other side, and, behind it, a huge cross upon which a piece of white linen was draped. The wall-to-wall light-blue carpet, ornate banners, and Easter lilies provided color. Before long a pianist and a soloist, both extremely skilled, filled the church with music, while hymn lyrics were electronically projected above the altar to encourage the congregation's participation.

Even as some adults took advantage of this and raised their voices in song, the main participants that Sunday morning were undoubtedly the youngsters. A large children's choir sang Easter hymns both at the opening of the Mass and, to much exuberant applause, at its conclusion. During the offertory, the children walked up the center aisle and presented the presiding priest, the pastor, with the bread and wine. Rather than being proclaimed from the pulpit, the gospel was actually enacted by the children. Some were dressed as Roman guards, and some as the women—Mary Magdalene; Mary, the mother of James; and Salome—who are remembered for discovering the empty tomb. They all fell in awe before one of their third-grade classmates who was dressed in a flowing white robe. "Do not be amazed," he commanded them as authoritatively as his eight-year-old voice would allow. "You seek Jesus of Nazareth, the crucified. He has been raised; he is not here." Then, as his classmates looked upon some linen placed upon a faux stone, another similarly clad third-grader asked them, "Why do you seek the living among the dead?"

As the applause dissipated and the last camera flashed, the pastor bounded to the altar and invited still more children, close to one hundred of them, to join him for question-and-answer time. He asked them whether they could explain the meaning of the nearby baptismal font (or "Jesus's Jacuzzi," as he playfully nicknamed it). After receiving no response, he explained that it symbolized their entrance into "God's family," which is commemorated on Easter. "Where is Jesus anyway?" he asked them next. This time he got an answer. "In heaven, but kinda here, too," offered one soft voice. "That's right," exclaimed a second child. "He's up there and in here at the same time!" "Up there and in here," repeated the pastor poignantly, his head nodding exaggeratedly in agreement. "Ladies and gentlemen," he announced to those assembled, many of whom were also nodding to one another. "They just nailed the whole thing!" The ensuing applause indicated a consensus.

The pastor nevertheless sought further elaboration from the children. "Then what do you think Jesus wants you to do?" he prodded and was met with a of flurry suggestions: "Be good to your friends!" "Do good in school!" "Love everybody!" "Do your chores!" "That's right, that's right," he said to them, raising his hands to signal that they had said enough. "Jesus thinks you're special, and he wants you to do things to make yourself happy and your friends happy and your parents happy." He was wrapping up the session. But, he seemed surprised when one child retorted quizzically, "How can doing chores make us happy?" Everyone laughed or smiled. "Well," he said, deferring to the children, "why does this make us happy?" "Because it makes Jesus happy," asserted one of the Roman guards, "and doing chores can make God's kingdom come closer to us."

Then followed still more applause, more head nodding, a few more camera flashes, and no further commentary. It seemed that the children had indeed sufficiently nailed it for everyone else. "Let's listen to the wisdom of these children and recommit ourselves to the new life we received at baptism," the pastor declared before walking up and down the aisles while casting holy water onto parishioners with a tree branch. In the meantime, the soloist sang the Apostles' Creed, while, after each section, the people responded by singing "Amen, amen, amen, we do believe." From there, the Mass continued as usual with only minor alterations. At the final prayer, the pastor challenged the people to exclaim "Alleluia!" louder than he. "Because Jesus is risen, I say 'Alleluia!'" he yelled. The parishioners responded and, on their third try, managed to yell louder than the pastor. Then, as people streamed through the two main exits, they, to the children's delight, were greeted by two furry Easter bunnies dispensing candy while silently waving and shaking hands.

Easter at Saint Louis Bertrand

Easter at Saint Louis Bertrand was a very different experience. When my son (now twenty-eight months old) and I pulled into this church parking lot, my car, now a year clunkier, did not look so out of place. Greeting us were not Moraga's rolling hills, evergreen and pear trees, and chorus of songbirds. This was an urban scene. Concrete-paved and frenetically teeming and commercialized, Oakland's flatlands pulsed with clamor and traffic. Mariachi music emanated from the portable radios, and the scent of tacos and tamales wafted from the grills of sidewalk vendors. Unlike Saint Monica's assemblage of architecturally coordinated and impeccably maintained buildings on neatly manicured grounds, this imposing church building could not hide its chipped paint, rusty gutters, and decaying roof under the glare of the late morning sun. Also unlike Saint Monica's, where I eventually felt somewhat at home, it was when I entered this church that I most felt like an outsider.

The church was filled with several hundred people, many standing along the sides of the pews and overflowing into the outer colonnade. My son and I were among only a handful of non-Latinos. Behind the altar was a life-sized, lifelike, and, for being beaten and bloodied, nearly lifeless Jesus hanging from a cross draped in white linen. To the side, as always, was a large pictorial representation of Our Lady of Guadalupe, before which those who had offered prayers to her had also placed flower arrangements of various kinds. Rather than concluding the Mass with shouting as at Saint Monica's, here the outcries began about fifteen minutes before the beginning of Mass, when a lay leader took the pulpit and began to exhort the assembled in Spanish. "A few days ago there was a story on the news that said Jesus's tomb has been found along with his remains," he announced and then declared emphatically, "But I say that's impossible because Jesus rose from the dead! Jesus's tomb was empty because he rose!" Arms raised, he then asked in a booming voice, "How is the tomb?" To this the people, nearly all standing and many with eyes closed and arms waving, yelled back to him, "Empty!" "How is the tomb?" he asked again. "Empty!" "Louder: How is the tomb?" "Empty!" they bellowed. On and on this went. Then, as the sounds of maracas and guitars filled the church, people began to sing:

> God is alive; he is not dead.
> God is alive; he is not dead

"The tomb is empty because he has conquered death; he is risen," continued the leader, who then asked, "Why is it empty?" "Because he is risen!" the parishioners replied, interrupting the song. "Why is it empty?" "Because he is risen!" "Why are there really no remains?" "Because he is risen!" they insisted and continued singing:

> I feel him in my hands; I feel him in my feet.
> I feel him in my soul; I feel him in my entire being.

"How is the tomb?" "Empty!" "Why is it empty?" "Because he is risen!" "Jesus Christ was dead, and now he's alive. Alleluia!" "Alleluia!" "He is powerful!" "Alleluia!" "He conquered death!" "Alleluia!" they responded again as they sang:

> We should be born of the water; we should be born of God's spirit.
> We need to be born of the water and God's spirit; we should be born
>   of the Lord.

The exhortations and singing continued until the pastor, accompanied by a deacon and an acolyte, moved in procession up the main aisle, incensed the altar and the people, and then began the Mass, which was conducted entirely in Spanish.

The readings for this day center on remembering Christ's resurrection and bearing witness to it as Christians. Lest anyone in attendance miss this message, Father Sandoval, the pastor, stated it in no uncertain terms during his homily. "As Saint Peter said in the first reading, we are approved witnesses before God," he said. "We do not seek the living among the dead; we seek Christ here because he is alive among this parish of the faithful." He explained further:

> There are testimonies all around us. We see it in those who seek a more
> complete life within the church through the sacraments of Confirma-
> tion and the Eucharist. It's evident in the couples who want to get mar-
> ried but desire to include Christ in their marriage. Each and every one of
> us have testimonies from our mothers and fathers, our godmothers and
> godfathers, who took us and baptized us in the name of the Father, the

Son, and the Holy Spirit. On Good Friday, when people came to vener-
ate Christ on the cross, there was a man in a wheelchair who stayed by
the image of Christ, and then, as a faithful child, he yelled, "Father Tony,
I know he's going to make me walk again!" This is a testimony that gives
life to our faith. For that reason, we should always trust in our past. We
have to remember the apostles of Jesus Christ. We have to remember our
predecessors, our parents, and our godparents, who took us to be baptized
and who made that bond of trust. Now it's our turn.

With that, he led the people in a profession of faith and afterward walked among
the pews blessing everyone with holy water.

After nearly two hours, the Mass came to a close. A parishioner whom I had
interviewed about a year earlier went to the pulpit to make two announcements.
The first was to inform the congregation that facilitators were available to those
who were interested in forming a Bible-study group to meet regularly in their
home. The second was to invite them to participate in a May Day march from the
church to downtown Oakland as a public demonstration of the parish's support
for immigration reform. The undocumented are "just like us," he reminded the
assembled. And the assembled, in turn, are very much like their "predecessors in
faith," Father Sandoval told the congregation when he returned to the pulpit and
then urged them once again to give testimony to the risen Christ within their daily
lives. As he finished making the sign of the cross, the sound of maracas and guitars
filled the church as everyone sang and chatted and laughed their way to the exits.

In Appreciation of the Paradoxical

As these accounts of two very different Easter celebrations remind us, a paradox
exists at the core of the faith professed by those we have met in this book. This, of
course, is the conviction that in death there is life. The original disciples confronted
this paradox just as American Catholics and other Christians do today. And, just
as the early Jesus movement was transformed after that first Easter, so too is the
American church continually transformed as its witness to this mystery takes on
new forms within new cultural contexts. Indeed, because the paradoxical is central
to parishioners' understanding of the sacred, it seems appropriate to frame this
concluding chapter in similar terms.

Stated simply, religious traditions are paradoxical in that they both conserve
and change. They preserve a particular conception of the sacred across time and
space, but, in doing so, they ultimately alter that conception. At Saint Monica's,
for example, much effort is directed toward transmitting the faith in an easy-to-use
manner to families with young children. At the same time, the parish's incorporation

of therapeutic culture can change the tradition when entry into the Christian community is equated with being part of "God's family," Jesus's message is distilled into feeling special and being happy, and a group of third-graders can nail the whole meaning of Easter with some off-the-cuff reflections. Something analogous occurred at Saint Louis Bertrand. Here the emphasis was placed not on the children in attendance but on remembering past generations of the faithful. This does not mean the tradition went unchanged, though. The Mass also served as a means for ritualizing Latino identity, which is itself a fairly recent ethnic innovation. The opening (and raucous) exhortation by the lay leader is an example of the church's incorporation of elements from a chief religious competitor for the Latino faithful, Pentecostalism. Even Father Sandoval's examples of "testimonies" are illuminating in this respect. Of all of the possible examples he could have given, the fact that he explicitly focused on the reception of sacraments demonstrates a subtle reaction to what he and others see as the problem of many Latino parishioners' reticence to partake of the church's sacramental life.

In the remaining pages of this book I step back a bit. I delve into the paradoxical nature of tradition in general and then explore three specific interpretive practices—negotiating, reframing, and innovating—through which Catholics have been instrumental in changing their religious tradition. I then conclude by showing that an appreciation for what is most paradoxical about religious traditions prods one toward a skeptical depreciation of rigid analytical categories, which are ultimately confounded when applied to the messiness of people's lived faith.

Stasis and Flux: How Traditions Are Lived

Living through Living Traditions

Conceived since its founding as a *novus ordo seclorum,* a new order of the ages, the United States has always been a distinctly "posttraditional" society. Many of its earliest European settlers made their way to these shores precisely in the hopes of slipping the iron-clad bonds of Old World tradition. Escaping the divine rights of the mighty, they sought individual rights for the many. Escaping the privileges of aristocracy, they sought a measure of egalitarianism. And escaping social statuses fixed by steely custom, they sought possibilities for social mobility affected less by pedigree than by one's readiness, as Adam Smith once phrased it, "to truck, barter and exchange."[1] Celebrating the "new lands, new men, new thoughts" that distinguished the still-young nation from others, Ralph Waldo Emerson, America's first truly renowned public intellectual, joined his fellow citizens in registering his refusal to "grope among the dry bones of the past."[2] This refusal is amplified today. Perhaps the best evidence of this, as discussed in chapter 2, is the reality that the nation's dominant societal institutions operate with nary a nod to traditional norms or to the "this-is-the-way-it-has-always-been-done" pretensions of convention. They instead abide by their own internal logic in pursuing their respective ends.

Beyond secular institutions, many scholars now see little tradition within the realm of culture. Suggesting that Americans suffer from "tradition deprivation," one critic points to their long-noticed penchant for attending more to the promise of an anticipated future than to the lessons of a remembered past. "Living in the daylight of the present moment," William Dean writes, "if Americans listen to anything, they listen to the intermittent crackle of transmissions from the future, and they forget the steady hum of crickets from the previous night."[3] Another scholar argues that, even if Americans were to listen to the wisdom of the past, they would discover three sets of once-powerful cultural codes—based on widely held conceptions of Puritan piety, democratic citizenship, and class solidarity—that are simply no longer up to the task of providing people with a set of shared meanings. In the "loosely bounded" culture of the United States, Richard Merelman reflects with some consternation, "Americans are now forced to make something of themselves without much help from traditional cultural codes."[4] This inevitable task of self-making, as observers of contemporary religion are apt to insist, applies also to matters of the spirit. Among the more provocative is literary critic Harold Bloom, who, dubbing the United States a "post-Christian nation," characterizes Americans' faith as a creedless, inner-seeking Gnosticism focused primarily on plumbing the depths of the atomized self. "We are a religiously mad culture, furiously searching for the spirit," he concedes, adding a caveat, "but each of us is subject and object of the one quest, which must be for the original self, a spark or breath in us that we are convinced goes back to before the Creation."[5]

Such reflections on American culture warrant at once serious thought and considerable reservation. One wonders whether all things traditional truly melt into air. This general claim seems excessive, and, like Shakespeare's Gertrude, scholars who subscribe to some version of it "doth protest too much, methinks." Posttraditional in the above-mentioned institutional sense, the United States is not a traditional society per se. Yet, to coin a term, it remains profoundly "traditioned" with respect to the main sources of cultural meanings available to people.

Known for their historical and cultural amnesia, Americans may indeed forget what happened last night. Nevertheless, their attitudes are still shaped by the recent and the remote past, and whatever "transmissions from the future" they might receive are filtered through perceptual categories they have inherited. Likewise, Americans do seem "forced to make something of themselves," but this project must be undertaken with the cultural tools that have been handed down to them. And, though Bloom is correct in pointing to the religiously autonomous individual as the *subject* of the spiritual quest, becoming an *object* to oneself is truly possible only by assuming a perspective from outside oneself. "To be a being that is an object to itself is possible genetically and actually," explains theologian H. Richard Niebuhr with great acuity, "only as I take toward myself the attitude of other selves, see myself as seen, hear myself as heard, speak to myself as spoken to."[6] To be an object of one's own evaluation or, in other words, to experience oneself as seen, heard, and spoken to is to experience oneself as "traditioned." It is to gauge oneself, even when acting in an intentionally non- or antitraditional manner, with respect to standards and expectations that, while continually adjusted to the present context, are largely derived from the past.[7]

Just as thinking is a kind of conversation with oneself, becoming an object to oneself opens up that conversation to others, including one's forebears, who initially set the symbolic terms of this conversation. True, Americans are religiously enfranchised to an unprecedented degree. No longer tightly held by their traditions, it is they who hold on to whichever components of those traditions they consider most worthwhile. Nevertheless, when making such judgments, they still rely upon cultural meanings and modes of organizing experience that are more tied to the past than they typically realize. "Tradition means giving votes to the most obscure of all classes, our ancestors," once wrote G. K. Chesterton of the still-heard voices of those who came before us: "It is the democracy of the dead."[8]

Coming to a fuller appreciation of the enduring place of tradition in a posttraditional society is to acknowledge a central paradox. Like a confluence of two rivers, the flow of tradition is fed by both stasis and flux.[9] The expression "living tradition" is commonly used, but, because traditions are organic, ongoing conversations with the past, it is actually redundant. Making this point with exceptional panache is historian Jaroslav Pelikan. "Tradition is the living faith of the dead," he declares, whereas "traditionalism is the dead faith of the living."[10] Although some people might mistake them as such, traditionalism's calcified dogmas, outdated symbols, and quaint moralisms are in reality not the stuff of tradition at all. These are the as yet uninterred remains of moribund tradition. They are the dissipating echoes of a conversation long since completed.

In contrast, tradition is by definition alive. This is because people, who themselves are very much alive, converse with traditions, pay attention to the cultural meanings they carry, and enlist them in the reflexive project of making something of themselves. They rely upon these preexisting narratives for scripting themselves and thus for constructing a sense of personal coherence. When doing so, they appropriate some of the features of any given tradition, modify others, and reject still others in light of the needs and dilemmas that coincide with the ever-shifting circumstances of their lives. As these change, so too does their conversation with tradition. They find themselves drawn to and conversant in some beliefs, some norms, and some symbols, whereas others no longer speak to them. The latter, as suggested earlier, begin to ring hollow, like a distant echo from a place they have long since abandoned. As life circumstances and individual selves change, so too do the traditions that shape and, in turn, are shaped by the people who take them seriously. This is why traditions are not only crucially important, collectively shared narratives but, in the words of philosopher Alasdair MacIntyre, always "not-yet-completed" ones as well.

"A living tradition then," contends MacIntyre in offering what has become a highly influential account, "is an historically extended, socially embedded argument, and an argument precisely in part about the goods which constitute that tradition."[11] Capturing the quality of stasis, he tells us that a given tradition remains intact as it extends through history. Moreover, the goods it transmits—whether they be certain dispositions, moral virtues, ritual practices, or doctrinal teachings, for instance—display a degree of constancy as well. He also captures tradition's fluid side by calling it an "argument." Consider, for example, the goods transmitted by a specifically religious tradition. As "living," it is embodied by different people who manifest its core dispositions in a number of ways, who seldom reach consensus about how certain virtues should be applied, who find particular rituals resonant and others rote, and who interminably disagree about the meaning or salience of various doctrines. Where is the line between reverence and irreverence? How should a desire to be hopeful, faithful, and charitable redound into one's family or career choices? Which rituals have withered into ritualism? How do we distinguish teachings that are essential to the tradition from those that are peripheral? If answers to questions such as these were set in stone, they would ultimately become that tradition's headstone. For a tradition to remain alive, such questions must be expressed as an ongoing argument among—or simply answered in a variety of ways by—those who live it. It is they who, in coming to new answers better suited to new circumstances, enable the larger narrative of the tradition to unfold continually.

Catholicism as a Living Tradition

That the Catholic tradition is marked by this same confluence of stasis and flux is clear. For two millennia it has persisted in handing on certain "goods" to the faithful. Expectations of personal holiness, admonitions to love others, and the ritual of a commemorative meal recalling the life and abiding presence of Jesus are all good examples. So, too, are certain teachings. While their theological interpretations have varied over time, the hope of eternal life and the conviction that Jesus is both fully human and fully divine have long been stable and authoritative teachings within Christian communities. Not unexpectedly, this tradition evinces a fluid quality as well. The manner in which such dispositions, rituals, and virtues have actually been enacted has varied considerably throughout history and from one social context to another. Nineteenth-century theologians like John Henry Newman and Johann Adam Möhler examined the development of church doctrine, yet it is not until the Second Vatican Council that one finds the first official articulation of this reality.[12] "This tradition which comes from the apostles develops in the church with the help of the Holy Spirit," reads a previously cited passage from the "Dogmatic Constitution on Divine Revelation," "for there is a growth in the understanding of the realities and the words which have been handed down."[13]

Sometimes the result of this developing understanding—or, as MacIntyre envisions it, this historically extended argument—is that certain beliefs and practices no longer have a place in the larger tradition. Official church teachings that once lent support to the institution of slavery and condemned religious freedom are good examples of this. At other times, beliefs and practices not previously considered part of church teaching are held up for acceptance by theologians and the rank and file as authentic tradition. Here the examples are quite numerous. The use of the Greek word *homoousios* [one in being] to describe Christ's relationship to God the Father, the doctrines of original sin and transubstantiation, and the practice of venerating saints are all important additions to the life of the church. This, incidentally, is also true of the Catholic understanding of tradition as a source of revelation distinct from scripture, a development that occurred during the Protestant Reformation in reaction to many reformers' teaching of *sola scriptura* [scripture alone].

At still other times, it is simply too soon to tell what will become of various beliefs and practices. At such points it is apparent to even the most cursory observer that this historically extended argument and indeed this tradition remain very much "works in progress." For instance, it is not yet clear whether the notion of a "preferential option for the poor," a product of the theological reflection of church leaders throughout Latin America since the 1960s, will ultimately become a widely accepted component of the tradition. The same can be said of the still fledgling practice of using gender-inclusive language in liturgical settings. Nor do we know whether, in light of widespread disagreement among the faithful, magisterial teachings on matters such as birth control, an exclusively male priesthood, and papal infallibility will one day no longer bear the authority proper to tradition. We have no way of knowing because this living tradition is a "not-yet-completed" reality. It is a narrative still being told in different accents, lived in different contexts, and argued about in different ways. In short, it remains open ended. "On this side of the eschaton, tradition is not finished," reflects theologian John Thiel. "It is always being configured. Its continuity is always developing."[14]

Helpful for understanding Thiel's nexus of continuity and development, of tradition's stasis and flux, is to note two derivatives of the Latin verb *tradere*, meaning "to transmit" or "to hand on," both of which are central to the Catholic understanding of tradition.[15] The first, *tradita*, refers to the things transmitted or handed on. These are things (goods) that have already been mentioned: dispositions, virtues, rituals, and doctrinal teachings handed on to successive generations of Catholics. Essentially synonymous with what is often referred to as the "deposit of faith," this is what comes to most Catholics' minds when they think of tradition. However, another aspect of Catholic tradition is *traditio,* the actual process of transmitting or handing on. This more active, relational aspect of tradition tends to be overlooked in much the same way as does the "socially embodied" or institutionalized nature of the argument MacIntyre describes. This oversight is likely a function of what has been called Americans' "culture of individualism," which makes them widely dismissive about the role of institutions in passing on tradition.[16]

We tend to give short shrift to the fact that, for the transmission of meanings or discourse to be culturally possible, they must be embodied within institutions that make them accessible to the people "traditioned" by them. An exception to this tendency is theologian Dorothy Bass, who sees local churches as indispensable institutional spaces in and through which *traditio,* or the cultural transmission of religious goods, happens. In the midst of this localized process, she insists, religious traditions are both sustained and changed. "Congregations impart to individuals and families a place in a tradition," she writes, "and conversely, those same individuals and families, through congregations, give back to a tradition its own being and vitality, constituting and reconstituting it through time."[17]

This is exactly what occurs in Catholic parishes. Without doubt they help transmit the goods constitutive of the Catholic tradition to the individuals and families active within them. As a consequence, the tradition persists. But Catholics are hardly passive consumers of those goods. Every engagement with cultural meanings is tantamount to a reinterpretation of those meanings, a reformulation of them for changing selves. In short, it is always a new cultural production.[18] Catholics, then, do not simply receive or consume their religious tradition inviolably. They disrupt it, reappropriate it, and in doing so produce it anew with each successive generation. As critical as this point is, it is also important to again balance it with a sense of tradition's persistence. Parishioners take part in the creative process of cultural production, but they do not create ex nihilo. The tradition itself has a specific "story line," a determinative interpretive history, and a finite set of symbols and goods that impose limits upon what can be conceived by those attempting to remain faithful to it in their own way. *Traditio* (the process of handing on) reproduces *tradita* (the things handed on), but *tradita* also places constraints on *traditio.*

With American Catholics' newfound propensity for religious agency and reflexivity, *traditio,* the transmission of religious meanings, happens very differently than in times past. Simply equating modernity with an inexorable "detraditionalization," as many do, is overwrought and underappreciative of just how traditioned modern people, Catholics included, truly are.[19] What is different about contemporary American life is not a wholesale rejection of religious and other traditions. Rather, it is that people relate to traditions differently from how they did in the past. American Catholics relate to their tradition more self-consciously. They engage it with a greater insistence on their own autonomy and with an acute sense of responsibility for their connection to the sacred. They have been handed a tradition that has persisted for two thousand years. Yet how they go about actually interpreting and drawing upon that tradition keeps it alive at the very moment that it also modifies it. Three interpretive practices are key to this process.

Negotiating

The most common of the three, negotiation actually subsumes the other two since they are simply more specific types of negotiating. An outcropping of what Michele Dillon calls the enhanced "interpretive authority" among Catholics (officially legitimated by Vatican II), negotiating with the broader tradition basically means appropriating those meanings proper to it in ways that best coincide with one's own sense of self. People speak of "my faith" because, aware of the religious agency they have grown accustomed to exercising, they think of their religious identity as a product of their past choices and future goals, both of which can be quite individualized. Cognizant that others have made different choices and mapped out dissimilar life goals, they highlight their nonjudgmentalism and religious unknowing by refusing to enter the tabernacle of ultimate "Truth" and preferring instead to linger within the outer portico of what is true "for me." Less sure of what they know, they tend to focus on how they act as a means of identifying themselves as Catholic, and they then monitor their actions to determine whether they are (or are likely to become) a "good person." Finally, they undertake this negotiation process in conjunction with—and often in resistance to—an institutional church that, while generally setting the parameters of their religious agency, most parishioners understand as simultaneously necessary and fraught with serious shortcomings.

These themes appear again and again as Catholics go about rooting themselves within their tradition in a way that feels authentic to them. By way of briefly reviewing these themes, consider parishioners' discussions of the well-known Bible story of Peter's confession of faith in Jesus (Lk. 9:18–26). Immediately following the story of the loaves and fishes, it begins with Jesus asking his disciples how people identify him. As John the Baptist, as Elijah, as one of the prophets, they declare, indicating the people's prophetic interpretation of him. "But," Jesus inquires of them further, "who do you say that I am?" To this, Peter responds, "The Christ of God." Rather than simply following in a venerable line of prophets, Peter acknowledges that, as the anointed one, God is doing something new in the person of Jesus.

Though it shows his great faith, even this deeper understanding is incomplete; thus Jesus informs him of his own impending suffering, death, and resurrection. Yet Peter still does not seem to grasp the difficulties that accompany true discipleship. Now addressing "all"—the disciples, the previously fed people, and presumably the gospel readers themselves—Jesus announces, "If any man would come after me, let him deny himself and take up his cross daily and follow me." Amplifying this, he continues, "For whoever would save his life will lose it; and whoever loses his life for my sake, he will save it." When he comes into his glory, he states, the Son of man will be ashamed of "whoever is ashamed of me and of my words."

When people are presented with this passage, two things become immediately clear. One is that the parishioner who exclaimed she has heard or read it "close to a gazillion times!" is not alone. Second, it serves as a particularly clear prism through which to see the practice of negotiation in action. For instance, when Tim Reznick, a lector at Saint Augustine, was asked to reflect on this passage, he responded this way:

Jesus was a man who was able to give us an example of how life should be lived. He was a living example of what we strive for, of what we try to be as people. He shows me how I can hopefully learn to put my ego and my needs aside, to look to others first and become the kind of person I know I can be. I think that's who he is for me: you know, that person, that goal I'd like to become.

Okay. What about later in the passage when Jesus talks about taking up one's cross? Is that meaningful to you or something you've thought about?

I think about taking up my cross as acknowledging my personal failings, seeing where I haven't been 100 percent honest with myself or haven't done right by other people. The grudges I might hold, the pain I might feel, bad feelings, and things like that: Those are the crosses I carry. And, hopefully, by following his example, slowly but surely, I can work through those things along the way.

Overall, do you think you're doing a good job working on these things?

Little by little, you know? It's a journey. It's hard. I know I don't want to face some of the shortcomings I have, some fears I have, some of my issues with family that are hard. Those are the kinds of things that I, you know, slowly but surely, have to work on and bring to the surface. I know I'm not going to feel as good as I should until I work on these things. Umm [pause] . . . that's what it [the cross] is for me.

When Reznick thinks about Jesus's question, "But who do you say that I am?" he draws upon the "good person" theme. Jesus is a kind of moral lodestar for Reznick, helping him to navigate the often choppy waters that stretch between who he is currently and, off in the distance, "the kind of person I know I can be." This theme is prevalent among parishioners. So too are the quotidian examples Reznick offers when explaining how he actually takes up his cross. Interestingly, unlike in the gospel of Mark, where taking up one's cross undoubtedly implies actual martyrdom, Luke adds to Jesus's injunction to take up one's cross the word "daily," which gives his call to discipleship an enduring quality. Many people talk about this more day-to-day construal as resisting an ethos of consumerism, trying to balance career and family obligations, dealing with physical and mental health issues, or, especially at Saint Margaret Mary, taking a stand against what parishioners perceive as the immorality of the surrounding culture. That said, Reznick is in no way unusual in equating discipleship with overcoming everyday challenges such as those related to "personal failings," "grudges," and "bad feelings." Nor, consonant with the "my faith" shard, is he alone in explaining the meaning of taking up one's cross with respect to making good on a commitment to individual growth and discernment. Creating a sense of religious identity, he reveals, does not come easily. It requires "work." He sees it as a "hard" process that requires that he "strive" and continue to "try." He is only "hopefully" optimistic about the final outcome. Nonetheless, he experiences himself as being on the move toward becoming the kind of self he perceives on the temporal horizon. "It's a journey," he says. And whatever progress he makes is likely to come "little by little," "slowly but surely."

At the conclusion of his comments, Reznick also touches upon the "for me" shard. Andrew Boone, a choir member at Most Holy Redeemer, joins the chorus of people who pick up this theme when addressing the question of Jesus's identity. "Different people are going to answer it in their own way," he says. Moreover, at the same time as Reznick interprets Jesus's instructions on discipleship in a way that makes sense to him, it is Boone's reflexivity about the church as an institution that brings him to an entirely different conclusion:

> It's not an easy question. Different people are going to answer it in their own way. I'd say that my relationship with Jesus is constantly changing. At one time I saw him as a God who was just out there. And now I see him more like a companion, an old friend, a confidant. Someone I have known for a long time and who has known me. . . . That first part of the gospel makes sense to me. I really can't say the same about the rest of it, though.

Why is that?

Because when you hear that God is going to be ashamed of you if you don't do certain things, that is fear and that is guilt. We [gay Catholics] have to be really careful when we hear that because Catholicism has used that card to the detriment of a lot of people. They feel guilty for not playing into the hierarchy's idea of what it means to be Catholic. That can be detrimental. Because the hierarchy has played this huge guilt trip on people, a lot of them have not been able to grow beyond that. . . . If you try to bring people to faith through fear and guilt, you don't really have faith. God is not part of that. God is not part of that sort of control. Christ has shown us clearly that God is a God of freedom. And this is a freedom to live in this world with God present to you. The good news is that I think that the people at Most Holy Redeemer get that message. If they don't come knowing that already, they will learn it within the community because we're not going to base our faith on fear, on being told what to do. You know, basing it on "This is right and this is wrong."

Within Catholicism, do you think there are limits on freedom that people should consider?

Yes, the institutional church puts incredible limits on one's freedom in the form of its written documents and its interpretation of morality and of life in general. There are a lot of restrictions there. And I don't think they're restrictions that the gospels necessarily reinforce.

Are there restrictions that the gospels actually do reinforce?

Oh, yes: Love one another. If that can be called a restriction, then the gospels definitely reinforce it. But when you think about it, that really is not a restriction. That is a freedom to love one another. Love your enemies, your persecutors—that cross, if you will, is really a freedom, not a restriction.

For Boone, Jesus is someone with whom one can have a personal relationship that changes over time and likely varies from person to person. What is more, for him, the portion of the scripture passage on discipleship makes little sense, a fact he explains by relying on his awareness of some of the institutional dilemmas addressed in chapter 4. Subscribing to neither "the hierarchy's idea of what it means to be Catholic" nor an unduly controlling image of God, Boone sees these as outdated symbols and counters them with what he envisions as a "God of freedom" (the symbolic dilemma). Understanding that church teachings can burden believers by becoming, in O'Dea's words, a "vast intellectual structure," he finds the mandate to "Love one another" as central to the gospel, which in his estimation makes many other teachings merely peripheral (the dilemma of delimitation). He regrets the fact that the church places "a lot of restrictions" on people and worries that this may impinge upon their growth as Catholics (the dilemma of administrative order). Finally, like many parishioners, he demonstrates a less nuanced understanding of the dilemma of power. He is adamant about resisting whatever influence the church might have in controlling people through fear and guilt, and he will not abide being "told what to do." However, this comes with a difficulty he and most others seldom acknowledge. That is, if the "good news" truly is simply a freedom to reject even the most carefully discerned judgments that conclude "this is right and this is wrong," then this may ultimately prove disempowering to church communities by undermining their capacity for meaningful ethical deliberation and consensus building.[20] In any case, people's discussions of this scriptural passage are a particularly clear illustration of how Catholics negotiate with their tradition and in the process both sustain and alter it considerably.

Reframing

Reznick thinks of Jesus as a moral exemplar, and Boone sees him in somewhat more intimate terms as a confidant with whom he has had a longstanding relationship. Such images do not exhaust their understanding of Jesus, though. These men privilege Jesus's humanity in order to better relate to him, but they also affirm his divinity. As discovered through further conversation with each of them, Peter's confession is essentially their own. They both wholeheartedly agree with the traditional Catholic teaching that Jesus is indeed the Christ, the Son of God who became incarnate in order to bring salvation to humanity. What this tells us is that, when parishioners like Reznick and Boone negotiate with religious symbols, they do not necessarily disbelieve or disregard the traditional understanding of those symbols. They simply appropriate them in ways that render them more consonant with the ways in which modern people generally think about the world and consequently make their religious tradition more relevant to their lives.

This is not the case with a second interpretive practice: reframing. Reframing is the process of using evocative symbols, unmoored from their traditional meanings, to essentially create religious truths rather than looking on them as signifying some objective religious truth. In other words, even when people do not subscribe to the traditional interpretations of those symbols, they still have much spiritual value. They are reinterpreted *as symbols,* which opens up new possibilities for conceptualizing and connecting to the sacred.[21]

Because this practice separates religious symbols from the transcendent truths to which they purportedly refer, one would expect it to be common among Catholics (or former ones) who have fallen away from the institutional church. Yet, it is a common practice among active parishioners as well. Most of them believe, for example, that Jesus was raised from the grave and that they too will be bodily resurrected after death. However, even among these very serious Catholics, some interpret this core teaching in a more reflexively symbolic fashion. "I really don't take it literally," said one just a few weeks after Easter. "It [Jesus's resurrection] basically represents this hope we all have that someday, somehow our spirit will continue on after we're gone. To me, it says we should live hopefully." Most also believe in the Real Presence of Jesus in the Eucharist. Others understand this sacrament less in terms of transubstantiation and more as a means of linking them to a tradition that extends across time. "What's most meaningful to me," another parishioner explained, "is that I'm doing what Jesus's disciples did and then what the early church did and what's been done through all these centuries."

Next, the topic of Mary, the mother of Jesus, arose during only a minority of conversations. When it did, though, it was not rare for people to reframe teachings such as those on her Immaculate Conception and perpetual virginity. As one respondent reflected about her virginity, "I actually like the symbolism of it because it's simply a way of saying that, with Jesus's birth, God was breaking into history in a totally new way. I understand feminists' qualms that it's antibody or antiwomen's sexuality, but I have to say that that image really touches me." Finally, even the meaning of the church itself is frequently reframed. "I'm not part of the church because, as the leadership seems to think, it's the only or it's the best way to be saved," stated yet another parishioner. "Being part of this particular church isn't as important as being part of any spiritual community. The idea that I'm on this search that other people are on and we need each other to keep going—that's the idea that most grabs me."

People like these and many others may not express the "official" interpretations of the Resurrection, the Eucharist, the Virgin, and the church, but this does not mean that these matters are therefore unimportant. Untethered from their traditional referents, these symbols are highly charged, and, when successfully reframed, they assist parishioners in creating new religious meanings for themselves. It also does not mean that these symbols have lost their power to transmit a sense of sacredness. Reoriented symbols may very well continue to orient people as Catholics. After all, to live hopefully, to situate oneself within a far-reaching and meaningful history, to harbor expectations of God's novel action in the world, and to inculcate a sense of shared spiritual mission are no mean religious feats.

Especially ripe for reframing are depictions of the miraculous. The account of Jesus walking on the water (Mt. 14:22–33) is an excellent example. It begins on a lakeshore with Jesus, who wishes to pray in solitude, telling his disciples to take their boat to the distant shore, which they attempt to do. With their boat "beaten by waves" since evening, at long last Jesus appears to them "in the fourth watch of the night" (i.e., 3–6 AM) walking on the water. "It is a ghost!" the terrified disciples cry out until they hear Jesus's assuring words: "Take heart, it is I; have no fear." Peter is quickest to speak. "Lord," he says, "if it is you, bid me to come to you on the water." When Jesus does so, Peter walks toward him on the water until, struck by great fear, he begins to sink and beseeches, "Lord, save me." Jesus again responds, this time reaching out to snatch him from the tumultuous waves and ruefully asking, "O man of little faith, why did you doubt?" At this, they both enter the boat, the wind dies down, and together the disciples knowingly confess, "Truly you are the Son of God."

Only a minority of parishioners say they think Jesus may have actually walked across the sea. On the other hand, hardly anyone teased out the various themes that have long interested biblical scholars. No one, for instance, drew a comparison between the anguished disciples in the boat "beaten" by waves and the early church, which, at the time the gospels were written, likely struggled with remaining faithful in the face of violent persecution. Nor did many suggest that in Jesus's doing only what God can do (walking on water) and, reminiscent of Yahweh's "I am" (Ex. 3:14), in his speaking as God speaks ("it is I"), the story functions as a symbol of Jesus's divinity. This notwithstanding, we should not underestimate people's ability to make use of their religious tradition. That such literal, ecclesiastical, and Christological interpretations are no longer important to most parishioners does not mean the passage itself has ceased to be. Familiar to all and described by more than a few as one of their favorites, people still encounter new meanings in this old story. They may be dubious about Jesus walking on water ("unless they had a pretty deep freeze in Galilee," one parishioner guffawed) and not especially drawn to biblical exegesis, but they often describe this passage as simply too resonant and too useful to them to discard.

When they reframe it, they overwhelmingly do so in one of two ways. The first is to denote—and thus in some ways to engender—their openness to the miraculous. Saint Mary–Saint Francis's Alicia Clayton insists she is "totally dubious" about the likelihood that Jesus walked across the water. At the same time, her world is certainly not characterized by, to use a term from sociologist Max Weber, the "disenchantment" that many take to be a definitive feature of modern life.[22] In fact, she insists that this passage remains an especially salient one for her:

> I actually think about that passage quite a bit. It's really a good reminder that miracles happen all the time, usually when you least expect it. I'm talking about tons of little miracles. You know what I mean? It can be something you've been praying for for a long time that doesn't happen, and then

all of a sudden it does. Or it can be something somebody says that you just needed to hear. Or it can be one of the many, many coincidences—or what might seem like coincidences—that, again, happen all the time.

Can you give me an example?

I can give you lots. Just the other day, I was in this really bad mood. So, I had a bunch of things to do, but instead I decided to drop by a friend's house, which is something I never do in the middle of the day. It's weird, but, as I came to this intersection, I could just tell that a car coming up next to me didn't see the red light, and the lady wasn't going to stop. So I just laid on my horn, and she and this SUV both came to a screeching stop. They were like four feet apart. Okay. If I wasn't going to my friend's, who knows what would have happened? The point is that weird things like that seem to happen all the time.

Clayton's faith is not about a particular miracle. It is about the "tons of little miracles" that, for those without eyes to see, *appear* to be things that simply happen, something somebody says, or just so many coincidences. This, moreover, is not a one-time thing. Learning from Peter's watery trepidation and seemingly countering his later denials of Jesus, she three times professes her faith in a world in which miracles "happen all the time." This openness to the miraculous is not marked by the same devotionalist sensibilities as it was for, say, her grandparents. A part-time teacher, wife, mother of three small children, and an avid jogger, Clayton does not include saying a daily Rosary on her list of priorities. She seems to prefer wearing smart-looking jewelry to religious medals. And, as a member of the parish council, she spends time at church making sure the finances are in order and the buildings are in good shape, which leaves her little time for lighting votive candles, even if she is so inclined. Nonetheless, her thinking about this passage "quite a bit" is one of a variety of ways in which she orients herself to the sacred and ensures that her world remains every bit as enchanted for her as it was for Catholics of previous generations.

A second way in which people typically reframe this passage is as a reminder of God's providence and, in light of this, one's own ability to act in the world with confidence. It has been said that ours is a "risk society" characterized by the creation of new threats to human well-being and especially by an unprecedented level of popular awareness and thus fear of the harms that can befall anyone.[23] But this would be news to Kyle Ostner, a parishioner at Most Holy Redeemer. The passage helps him see the world as less risky, more orderly, and, in short, a place where the seemingly unmanageable is in fact manageable. As is the case with many other parishioners, these are the themes he touches upon when asked to reflect on the story:

> It's kind of funny that, when we recognize our powerlessness, we end up getting power from that.

What do you mean?

> Well, I have this friend in AA [Alcoholics Anonymous], who, like lots of other people in AA, has a stronger sense of a higher power than we do as Catholics. As a result—unlike many people who think they can do everything themselves until hard times come around and they find themselves sinking fast—he really knows he needs this higher power to be successful, stay sober, whatever.

How does that translate into being more powerful?

> It gives you confidence that things are going to be okay. That you can face things head on. That story [the scripture passage] made me think of a scare we had about a year ago. They thought there was a problem with my pancreas. They never said it, but, of course, I thought [I had] pancreatic cancer, with which you only last two or three weeks. Initially I was really devastated. You know, dying, leaving Doug [his partner for nearly twenty years]. But then I thought God would see him through it, and I'd be with God. And if that was the diagnosis, everything would be okay. So, as I waited the next couple of days to hear from the doctor, I didn't run away from that experience. I didn't, you know, drown in it. I really faced up to it and knew I could trust that, whatever was going to happen, God was somehow allowing it to unfold for a reason.

Again, this kind of stance before the world, this capacity to "face things head on," is no mean feat. Like Clayton, Ostner demythologizes this Bible passage and reframes it so that it takes on a new, yet wholly religious, set of meanings that make sense to him. He alters its meaning but does not divest it of its impact. Generations of Catholics have been captivated by Jesus's actual ability to walk on water, which further convinced them of God's power in the world. Yet, though Ostner does not believe Jesus did this, his determination to resist running away from an emotionally tempestuous situation and then his own ability to calmly walk above the fearful squall of the moment and toward his final diagnosis demonstrates for him that very same power.

Innovating

Parishioners' third interpretive practice is a longstanding and especially interesting feature of American religion. "There is no conservative tradition in America because God is not a conservative," ruminates historian William McLoughlin in his classic book on the nation's series of religious awakenings. Rather, "God is an innovator."[24] Or, if not God, certainly many people with faith in God are religious innovators. Religious entrepreneurs who have consolidated unique worldviews and thus spawned what have become known as "new religious movements" have appeared with some regularity throughout U.S. history.[25] Leaders of more mainstream religious groups have also innovated on occasion, often by "inventing traditions" in an attempt to respond to novel social situations by devising largely fictitious accounts of the past.[26] The Vatican's resistance to gender-inclusive translations of scripture, for instance, is largely based on an invented account of how biblical scholarship has been undertaken in the past.[27]

Rather than forming new religious movements or inventing traditions, the main way in which the people in the pews innovate is to fuse specifically Catholic symbols with other cultural symbols and scripts available to them. This process is at least somewhat theologically legitimated in the Catholic understanding that religious teachings and practices must be properly "inculturated" within specific local contexts. We have already seen examples of this. Saint Monica's emphasis on children and Saint Augustine's expansive offering of small groups correlate with (predominantly white) middle-class understandings of child rearing and self-improvement. Both Saint Louis Bertrand's focus on Latino and African American identity and Saint Mary–Saint Francis's more multicultural ethos rely heavily on distinctly American conceptualizations of race and its ensuing power relations, which they then reimagine or problematize. In addition, Most Holy Redeemer's efforts to revalorize gay identity, as well as Saint Margaret Mary's project of retraditionalizing Catholic identity, would be incoherent apart from their close connection to those aspects of American culture—namely, homophobia and irreverence—that summon their opposition.

Any interaction with the surrounding culture, these examples illustrate, inevitably results in religious innovation. In fact, parishioners' proclivity for appropriating symbols and ideas from other cultural repertoires to better configure themselves as Catholics is seemingly evident wherever one looks. Describing all of the ways they do this would likely require another entire book. For that reason, let us focus on two of the most important sources of religious innovation among laypeople: the mass media and other religions.

The cultural symbols and scripts I have mentioned are examples of what in chapter 2 were labeled *extra*religious cultural meanings, to which people have access when thinking religiously. Others are Americans' well-known individualism, guardedness toward institutions, and therapeutic sensibility, all of which are enormously influential in shaping the ways in which Catholics understand their faith. More surprising is the role the mass media seem to play. As suggested by parishioners' references to works such as Dante's *Divine Comedy* and *The Giving Tree*, the books they read supply them with ideas and tropes that they can intermix with what they know of their tradition. During the interviews, for example, a few people mentioned that recent scholarship on the historical Jesus had influenced them, while another parishioner discussed theological insights she had gleaned from reading the far less theologically hearty *Chicken Soup for the Expectant Mother's Soul*. Others mentioned things they had seen on television. One devoted *Oprah* viewer talked about the program's lessons on self-esteem as a kind of revelation for her. Another pointed to the denizens of the small Alaskan town depicted in the show *Northern Exposure* as exemplars of respectful interreligious dialogue and cooperation. They cited celebrities ranging from pop diva Britney Spears to rock singer Bono as evidence of, respectively, society's increasing moral decay and the power of a single person to make a positive contribution to the world. These are just a smattering of examples. However else one might describe the religiously pertinent ideas communicated through the mass media—simplified, commoditized, incoherent, and so on—one thing is certainly true: Entirely unregulated by official religious authority, they are available to people to appropriate at will.[28]

To get just a sense of this, consider the reflections of Saint Margaret Mary's Rebecca Barber on Mel Gibson's much-talked-about film *The Passion of the Christ*. With great enthusiasm, she describes it as "an extremely good tool to bring people back to religion" and reports that she herself had seen it four times. Detecting a surprised reaction to this, she explains that she viewed it the last two times mostly in order to take her twelve- and thirteen-year-old nephews to see it. Queried about whether such a graphic film is appropriate for youngsters, she responded:

> My nephews are altar boys who serve at the traditional Mass. When we talked about it, we decided that they serve at Mass, so they should know about the passion of Jesus. I mean, they already know it. They know it from Bible verses; they know if from the Stations of the Cross; they know it from the Sorrowful Mysteries. But we figured they should know it at this more visceral level, too.

> *What do you think they gained from knowing it at that level?*

> I think they got a deeper sense of God's love. The fact that Jesus would go through what he did for our salvation is just amazing. You know, it

begins in the garden of Gethsemane with Satan trying to tempt Jesus from going through with it. But Jesus just keeps on resisting him, the way we all should. He knows he has to die for our salvation. And so they saw that and just came to that deeper understanding that he went through it all for their sins. . . . I think the hardest thing for one of my nephews was that it was the first time he ever saw his father cry, and we talked about that afterward. I basically said it's a fine thing; there's nothing wrong with crying, you know, and my brother talked about experiencing Jesus as his Savior and how moved he was. And I think they got the message that the fact that he cried only demonstrated how important faith is.

Notice that innovations abound. Added to what Barber's nephews know about Jesus's passion through the Mass, the Stations of the Cross, and the Rosary, they now have a "more visceral" experience. Despite the rich history of scholarship and popular reflection on the meaning of the Atonement, here they encounter a far simpler scenario. In other words, rather than Jesus's role in salvation history becoming clearer over time, here Jesus is depicted as being extremely knowledgeable about such theological matters insofar as he "knows he has to die for our salvation." He is concerned with resisting Satan in a scene that, while deeply meaningful to Barber, is nowhere mentioned in the Bible itself. In going "through it all for their sins," Jesus, through his crucifixion, is connected to these boys as individuals.

Finally, if still not convinced of the importance of faith, Barber's brother demonstrates this to them by his emotional reaction, which functions as a rather dramatic confirmation of belief for both him and presumably for his young son. This medium, in other words, enables this family to experience and then to discuss Jesus's passion in a fashion that is more theologically sparse, descriptively embellished, personalized, and emotionally compelling than would likely otherwise be the case. It simplifies the event for them and enables them to attach meanings to it more easily than if their access to the crucifixion were only through gospel accounts, theological affirmations, or ritual reenactments.

Along with such *extra*religious meanings, parishioners also appropriate symbols and practices *inter*religiously. As discussed, their sensitivity toward religious difference is reflected in their nonjudgmentalism and widely shared conviction that other faiths are indeed legitimate ways of conceiving and worshipping God. Also noteworthy is their tendency to import ideas from some of these religious traditions and integrate them into their own. When Barber recounts her brother's emotionally charged conviction that Jesus is "his Savior," it is easy to hear the same chords of evangelical piety struck by many other parishioners as well. Some also claim to believe in reincarnation. A few others describe Jesus as "enlightened" and compare him favorably to the Buddha. Every so often, one also detects vestiges of so-called New Age spirituality.

This tendency is especially pronounced within multireligious households. One parishioner, for example, recounted the lively Thanksgiving dinner she and her husband recently had with their five grown children, four of whom now practice a different religion. Another stated that the holidays are particularly busy given that their family celebrates both Christmas and, because her husband is Jewish and their three young children are as yet "undecided," the eight days of Chanukah. A third woman, Saint Augustine's Kay Paxton, provides a particularly good example of how ideas that are borrowed from other traditions can become wedded with Catholicism. Paxton is very active at her parish and is raising her two elementary school–aged children Catholic. But her husband is a practicing Muslim who, while they are at Mass, attends a Farsi class each Sunday. This arrangement can be difficult. When Ramadan occurs during the Christmas season or, more commonly, when he is at prayer during a time when the kids need attention, Paxton can find herself getting frustrated. Still, she truly admires her husband's convictions and even concedes that "he's much farther along the path in cultivating a relationship with God than I am." As for her own path, while undoubtedly Catholic, it winds its way among various Muslim ideas as well. This becomes apparent when she explains why she no longer believes in hell: "I guess I've sort of gotten the proverbial second opinion regarding that doctrine. There's this one passage in the Koran where this person—who was evil his entire life—eventually died, and all his sins were piled up on one side of a scale. But there was this one instance during his life when this guy said one small prayer to God. So God places that single act on the other side, which causes the whole scale to tip to that side—to the side of forgiveness. So I guess I've outsourced that one. It's a good thing because it reminds me that God is ultimately merciful." Dissatisfied with what the Bible tells her about the final judgment, Paxton innovates. She seeks a second opinion and fuses it to her own eminently revisable religious understanding. Unable to do the cultural work with the tools her own tradition has bequeathed to her, in other words, she simply looks elsewhere within the largely unregulated economy of religious meanings to which she has access.

This Category and That: How Traditions Are Investigated

Much of the preceding section (and indeed much of this entire book) has been devoted to challenging categorizations that, although commonly cast as such, are not really in contradistinction to one another. For instance, as delineated in chapter 2, the terms *sacred* and *secular* are often counterpoised regardless of the more nuanced reality that American society is profoundly secular at the same time that it remains, as historian Jon Butler has noted of the nation's early decades, "awash in a sea of faith."[29] Something similar can be said of the simultaneous constancy and fluidity that are characteristic of religious traditions. Just as the parishioners we have met in this book can be both thoroughly modern and religious, so too can they accept the two-millennia-old tradition handed on to them while, through the interpretive practices discussed earlier, doing their part to both enliven and change it.

In demonstrating such nuances, these Catholics also challenge us to more critically consider some of the analytical categories through which scholars have come to investigate lived religion. These categories, of course, assist "outsiders" in interpreting the ways in which religious "insiders" actually go about the business of relating to the sacred. However, insiders can also teach outsiders a thing or two. Analytical categories are helpful for organizing the manner in which we see reality, but then that reality bites back. The varied and complicated ways people carry out their faiths frequently defy the rigid nature of certain categorizations and thus compel us to adjust or abandon them. Unable to be sufficiently captured by them, lived religion tends to puncture many of the this-or-that categorizations widely employed by analytical outsiders.

Substantive versus Functional Definitions of Religion?

At the most rudimentary level, this study pushes us to reconsider even how things become defined as religious. Scholars have generally preferred one of two basic definitional strategies.[30] Some have leaned toward what are often called substantive definitions of religion. These establish what religion is by delineating the specific components without which any given phenomenon would not qualify as religion. An excellent example is found in the work of anthropologist Melford Spiro, who defines religion as "an institution consisting of culturally patterned interaction with culturally postulated superhuman beings."[31] Like all substantive definitions, this one is relatively straightforward and easy to employ. Religion entails both an institution and an interaction with superhuman beings presumed to exist. Absent these components, the thing in question is not religion. With the virtue of clarity, however, comes the vice of neglecting manifestations of religiosity that do not fit in such neat definitional packaging. What about forms of personal or even group spirituality that are not carried by "an institution"? What about Eastern traditions such as Confucianism and various strands of Buddhism that do not postulate "superhuman beings" and yet are without question important religions?

These misgivings have convinced other scholars to favor functional definitions that, rather than specifying what religion *is*, focus instead on what religion *does* for believers. The problem with this strategy is the very opposite of the first approach. Functional definitions can be so inclusive as to depict religion as indistinguishable from other pursuits. For instance, Robert Bellah's conception of religion as "a set of symbolic forms and acts which relate man to the ultimate conditions of his existence" could include activities that most people (even those who engage in these very activities) do not ordinarily think of as religious.[32] While prayer and group worship would certainly qualify as symbolic forms and acts that function as Bellah suggests, the same could be said of "functional equivalents" of religion such as political activism, intellectual pursuits, family life, psychotherapy, and extreme sports.

The distinction between these two types of definition breaks down when one focuses less on grand theorizing and more on how different people actually try to live out a single religious tradition.[33] This book on active parishioners has obviously been predicated on a substantive understanding of religion—religion defined as Catholicism. Yet, as we have seen, things become more complicated in light of the religious agency that Catholics typically exercise in appropriating only certain aspects of their tradition. Switching definitions, one could say that, rather than Catholicism per se, religion for these parishioners is actually that individual-specific amalgam of religious symbols and practices that *function* to render reality meaningful to them. But this is also too simple. Parishioners do not access such symbols and practices willy-nilly. They do so by interacting with the meanings embedded in the substantive religious tradition with which they are most familiar: Catholicism. In defiance of these two equally distorting definitional strategies, these Catholics live out their faiths in what we might dub a "substantively functionalist" mode. They relate to the religious symbols that function to render life personally meaningful. However, even when innovating, they do this by interacting with symbolic representations that are both provided and significantly delimited by a particular religious tradition.

Religion versus Spirituality?

Lived religion also resists the neat categories of religion and spirituality, which observers often use in a mutually exclusive fashion. Religion usually denotes institutionalization, group affiliation, and adherence to official doctrines and practices. In contrast, one presumably looks in vain for these religious accoutrements when it comes to spirituality. To reference categories that theologian Ernst Troeltsch used nearly a century ago, rather than highly institutionalized "sects" or especially "churches," here one finds the more free-floating and often atomized "mysticism" type of meaning making.[34] In place of forming strong ties to faith communities, one associates spirituality with enhancing individuals' experience of the sacred and meeting personal needs. Instead of officially defined orthodoxy, here what one scholar calls the "democratization of religious opinion" holds sway, and religious questioning is seen as indicative of inner depth, as is steadfast belief.[35]

These spirituality-related themes are becoming increasingly familiar as an expanding stock of religious meanings becomes ever more culturally available to Americans intent on tailoring their religious preferences. An analytical problem arises when spirituality is construed as set apart from religion. Religion, in this rigid view, is synonymous with church participation, whereas spirituality is assumed to be something "out there," completely severed from church communities. But this view is deficient in two respects. First, even the most free-floating, individualized spirituality has some relation to religious institutions. These serve as carriers of meanings that contribute significantly to the broader religious culture from which even the most unchurched of spiritual practitioners draws. Religious institutions also function as relevant out-groups. In other words, they commonly help consolidate the identities of the unchurched by providing them with (often exaggerated) exemplars of certain religious traits—dogmatic, hypocritical, boring, and so forth—that they see as being in contrast to how they connect to the sacred.[36]

Second, if spirituality is typically reliant upon the cultural tooling and contrast example supplied by religious institutions, these in turn are frequently infused with a generalized quest for the spiritual. One of this study's more unambiguous findings is that, instead of being something "out there," the use of spirituality language and the sensibilities it signifies are very much "in here"—within Catholic parishes. The parishioners we interviewed are avowedly Catholic and strongly invested in the life of their church communities, and they generally approach church teachings and ritual practices with great seriousness. They are, in a word, religious. Yet, they relate to their tradition in ways that are usually very different from how their parents and grandparents did. They are not loath to announce "I'm not religious, I'm more spiritual" to describe their commitment to personal growth. And they are not afraid to reclaim the expression "cafeteria Catholic" as a marker of their capacity for discernment and continued seeking. They are, in short, overwhelmingly religious *and* spiritual, a fact that should compel us to seriously reconsider the analytical value of this distinction.

Reason versus Tradition?

Finally, it seems that no set of oppositions enjoys quite the same broad-based acceptance among scholars as does the one that pits reason against religious tradition. On one side of the hypothetical ledger is an adherence to the Enlightenment's project of thinking critically, investigating the world empirically, and justifying one's convictions by rational deliberation. On the other side are the deeply grooved patterns of life formed by collective habit. Whereas we generally take the ideas and norms we derive from reason to be universally applicable, those born of tradition are said to bear the mark of parochialism and thus pertain only to specific people within specific locales. Reason's gaze presumably looks forward, connecting the present with expectations of future progress. Tradition, on the other hand, presumably looks backward, connecting the present with examples remembered from the past. In one-word summations, living rationally requires reflexivity, while living through traditions mandates conformity.

Seeming to work from this ledger is influential social theorist Anthony Giddens. Modernity, for him, is tantamount to "rolling social life away from the fixities of tradition."[37] Deprived of such fixities, people must establish them reflexively. In other words, they must do their best to formulate their own ways of life by continuously monitoring and revising their beliefs and practices in light of new experiences. This crucial use of reason, he further contends, is a stranger to religious traditions. "Tradition can be justified," writes Giddens, "but only in the light of knowledge which is not itself authenticated by tradition."[38] Indeed, because he presumes them to be contrary to one another, he argues that any tradition justified or interrogated through reflexive reasoning would actually be a tradition in appearance only. In reality, he posits, it would be merely a "sham" tradition.[39]

There are two problems with this view, both of which become obvious upon once again recalling how Catholics actually live through their religious tradition. First, at the same time as reason can be marshaled to interrogate tradition, the opposite is also true. Seventeenth- and eighteenth-century Enlightenment thinkers' assault on tradition was largely a reaction to what they saw as its undue power, which inevitably encumbered individuals with the yoke of conformism. Now, ironically, it is often religious tradition that assists in forging an ideological resistance to those derivatives of modern rationality—consumerism, careerism, radical individualism, nationalism, and so on—to which many people now readily conform.[40] Parishioners do not always make use of their religious tradition with great verve or consistency, but it nonetheless provides them with a countervailing language for talking back to the instrumental rationality of the modern age. It goads them to prefer, at least occasionally, God to Mammon. It connects them to the sacred in ways that can set them at odds with mainstream culture. It provides them with idioms for resisting social injustices and embracing whichever versions of community that most resonate with them. In short, it enables them to think, to say, and ultimately to be the things they otherwise could not.

Secondly, Giddens overlooks religious traditions' capacity for interrogating themselves and then adapting when necessary. He understands tradition as essentially invariable and undynamic. This is unfortunate because closer examination reveals that, like impulses toward conformity, those toward reflexivity are hardly strangers to religious traditions. A major role of Catholic "elites" such as priests, bishops, liturgists, and theologians is precisely to think reflexively with respect to how best to relate the wisdom of their religious tradition to contemporary contexts.

This obligation is shared by the laity. It is officially sanctioned in Vatican II's account of one's conscience as "the most secret core and sanctuary" of the person, who is thereby enjoined to consult it unimpeded by coercion from outside.[41]

Add to this the council's retrieval of the centuries-old notion of the *sensus fidei*. The more subjective dimension of this teaching is that individual believers possess a "sense of faith (*sensus fidei*), an inner capacity to discern both religious truth and what is contrary to it. In its more objective dimension, it is expressed as the "sense of the faithful" (*sensus fidelium*), which refers to those religious truths upon which, in light of believers' concrete experience of living out their faith, the church as a whole has come to some agreement and about which it cannot err. As subjective, it is a "supernatural sense," while, when considered as an objective body of beliefs, it represents a "universal agreement in matters of faith and morals."[42]

Theologians, not surprisingly, have long grappled with this notion.[43] Subjectively speaking, if a sense of faith is broadly extant among earnestly discerning Catholics, how then does one account for their many theological differences? Objectively speaking, is a consensus ever possible within a church that so elevates individual conscience and is so variable in its localized forms around the globe? These questions naturally elicit a wide spectrum of responses. Beyond contention, though, is the overriding conceptualization of the Catholic tradition as inherently reflexive. Both dimensions of *sensus fidei* presume that so-called ordinary Catholics have a capacity for engaging in careful discernment with regard to their faith and that the fruits of their discernment should be taken seriously as a source of theological insight by the church as a whole.

If, according to official teaching, Catholics *ought* to be reflexive about their faith, this book has demonstrated that they unquestionably are. The parishioners we have met are not what Giddens would likely dub "sham" Catholics, who interrogate and come to grips with their religious tradition on the basis of knowledge not authenticated by it. In other words, they usually do not import scientific discourse to explain the empirical validity of their beliefs or use utilitarian arguments about the greatest good for the greatest number to make a case for whatever moral positions they stake out. Instead, they employ modes of reasoning that are clearly engendered and authenticated by the tradition.

They rely heavily on the cultural tools handed down to them by their tradition when reflecting on the world around them. They draw from the Bible, church teachings, priests' homilies, and conversations with people they trust in order to think through what it means to be Catholic. Their judgments about which doctrines are central or peripheral to the faith, which symbols seem meaningful or calcified, which features of the institutional church merit their devotion or disdain, and which aspects of the surrounding world are sacred or profane are based on neither a lock-step conformism nor a purely rationalistic gaze. They arrive at these decisions through a reasoning that is at once highly critical and very much situated within the tradition. This kind of reason is directed toward attaining what MacIntyre calls "the goods which constitute that tradition," and toward helping parishioners to critically interpret and revise their faith in ways that make sense to them.

Reflexivity, Tradition, and Lived Catholicism

If nothing else, the people observed and interviewed for this book have demonstrated that the term *reflexive tradition* is not an oxymoron. In defiance of the tendency to see critical reason and religious faith as mutually exclusive, parishioners bring these together when living out their Catholicism, an integration that Vatican II's emphasis on *sensus fidei* officially sanctions. In fact, one of the most notable themes within the conciliar documents is a resistance to the longstanding habit of characterizing the church hierarchy and magisterium as the teaching church (*ecclesia docens*) and the laity as the learning church (*ecclesia discens*). Envisioning rank-and-file Catholics' lives and religious discernment as authentic sources of theological insight necessarily confounds such categories. Like church leaders themselves, the laity are both learners and teachers when it comes to arriving at new understandings about the mystery of God and the meaning of faith in an ever-changing world. Thus, given that the focus here is on laypeople, it is worth pondering what might result from taking their sense of the faith seriously, which is precisely what this book has endeavored to do.

The first thing to note is that laypeople indeed have some things to learn. First, when thinking about their identities as Catholics, they tend to appropriate religious symbols self-consciously and with a critical stance toward their church as an institution. However, as discussed in chapters 5 and 6, their capacity to think both *about* and *with* these symbols has its limits. They are not particularly adept, in other words, at seeing how their images of religious community are less discerningly formulated and more dependent upon (as well as considerably narrowed by) the preexisting conceptualizations of community in American culture that happen to resonate with their own social locations. Connection, difference, and resistance are important ways of imagining community but, when unquestioned, can keep people from reflecting upon other dimensions of what it means to be part of a specifically religious community. Nor are parishioners usually aware of the degree to which their churches can fail to allocate to them aspects of Catholic culture that are essential to allowing their sense of social concern to, as one scholar put it, "spiral outward" into civil society.[44] Parishes (some more intentionally than others) do take some steps to instruct them how to incorporate the church's social teachings into their lives. But there is still much to accomplish with respect to helping parishioners become more participatory, giving them a more expansive understanding of justice, and providing them with opportunities to engage one another on social issues, as well as the larger topic of how to integrate their faith with their responsibilities as citizens.

Second, they also have much to learn about what philosopher Friedrich Nietzsche called the "genealogy" of their beliefs and dispositions.[45] For instance, parishioners exercise their religious agency while frequently ignoring the reality that their doing so is the product of a particular social formation in which individualized quests for authenticity have become increasingly normative. This, as we have seen, can pose a problem when it comes to arriving at some consensus on their convictions as Catholics. Also, akin to what one scholar calls "tolerant traditionalists," they cling to their faith while refraining from passing judgment on others of different or no faiths.[46] Again, though, they seldom seem to recognize this attitude as a product of Catholics' moving out of their religious ghetto, as well as of other social transformations that have made the ideological boundaries among faiths less salient to more and more Americans.[47] In short, learning to plumb the sociocultural roots of their beliefs and dispositions could assist parishioners in more clearly seeing how their religious lives are influenced by important changes within American culture more broadly. This, in turn, would likely help them as Catholics to more purposively discern which societal trends to embrace and which to resist.

Even in light of all of this, it is likewise true—and usually far less acknowledged—that the laypeople we have met in the preceding pages have much to teach the wider church. For one thing, they demonstrate that Catholics are much less passive than they might appear when seated quietly in rows of neatly arranged pews. On the contrary, they are actively reflexive about their own religious selves. They take responsibility for their connections to the sacred by appropriating elements of the tradition based on what they feel is most authentic to them. Some undertake the project of negotiating, reframing, and innovating with great nimbleness, and, of course, some do so less adeptly. None of the parishioners interviewed, however, relate to their tradition as passive bystanders. Second, Catholics are equally reflexive about their church as an institution. This is a good reminder to those who need it that, although important, the institutional carrier of Christ's presence and message is generally less important to parishioners than their own efforts to experience that presence and live out that message. Third, in their emphasis on being good and avoiding religious hypocrisy, parishioners teach a practical lesson. That is, even though they do not always think through all of the complexities of doing so and even though they are often no strangers to complacency, parishioners insist that faith must be reflected in (and in some ways made real by engaging in) some kind of service to others. Fourth, though they may not always be sure of its genealogy, parishioners demonstrate tolerance or, more positively, much openness to other ways of seeking holiness. Seldom are they experts on the historical and theological details of other faiths. Instead, they are simply willing to take them seriously and refrain from writing them off as somehow inferior. They let these alternative paths signify to themselves the unboundedness of the sacred and, just as importantly, the limits of their own religious knowing.

This suggests a final lesson, one that is related to each of the others. After engaging nearly three hundred active Catholics in conversation about some of the things that matter most to them, it is remarkable just how consistently forthcoming they are in acknowledging their unknowing. Even when echoing the four very clear lessons delineated above, they unfailingly express at least some tinge of equivocation. How does one determine what is most authentic to oneself? How can one come to some certainty when adjudicating between what the institution should carry on and what it should cast aside? How good does one have to be to be good? In addition to cultivating tolerance, how does one truly understand the value of being Catholic and devoted to Christ in a religiously pluralistic world? To such nagging questions, they display precious little theological certainty and perhaps even less self-recrimination.

Their theological uncertainty might well serve as a lesson for sociologists in particular. The quantitative data generated by surveys are useful, it seems to say, but examining their responses to closed-ended questions can make Catholics seem more assured in their convictions than they actually are. Within the context of prolonged discussion, they demonstrate further complexity, considerable grayness, and, of course, far less certainty when addressing matters as nuanced as religious faith.

Their overall lack of self-recrimination about this, on the other hand, is a lesson or perhaps even a challenge likely to be germane to other Catholics, especially the ones reading this book. It suggests that their faith is less about answering questions—as was the case in the era of the *Baltimore Catechism*—than it is about questioning the answers articulated and handed down to them by previous generations. They generally seem to experience this as a distinctly precarious, uncertain undertaking. Yet what is most striking is that it does not at all seem to undermine the value of the religious tradition, and by no means does it render it a sham. Reflexively interrogating their tradition instead reveals to many parishioners that it is actually the fixation with knowing itself that is the real sham. It seems to bring them into a more intimate awareness of reason's limitations and thus reminds them that their religious tradition is, in the end, a historically extended conversation about faith in things unseen and indefinite. Time and again, rather than apologizing for it, they seem to embrace the real poverty of their religious understanding. Like the sprightly donning of a tattered suit, they seem to wear the rags of their unknowing with a measure of satisfaction in its fit. For it is indeed fitting, their dearth of self-recrimination implies, that even the most earnest of believers should stutter before the sacred. They are not especially bothered by this because they generally interpret a lack of religious cocksureness as a fuller appreciation of God's holiness and inscrutability. They frequently couple this with the lesson that theological propositions are not God and that being honest about how little people actually know about God is helpful in reducing religious discord, drawing closer to the divine mystery, and learning to accept the life of faith as one fraught with paradox.

Rome and California: How an End Is Also a Beginning

It is impossible to know whether or to what extent church leaders might seriously consider the sensibilities of the American faithful as a source of religious insight. Only time will tell whether they will abide by Vatican II's call for honestly "scrutinizing the signs of the times" and respond accordingly.[48] Such a response would entail church leaders' greater awareness of how the surrounding culture affects Catholics' understanding of their faith, as well as a firm commitment to assist laypeople in seeing this more clearly for themselves. It would also require them to scrutinize the various lessons offered to them by the laity concerning their individual and institutional reflexivity, their openness to service and to other faiths, and their sense of theological humility before the divine mystery. Of course, the burden of responding to this challenge is not that of church leaders alone. It is likewise impossible to know whether or to what extent laypeople might react to such instruction from church leaders and to the very real possibility that their own religious insights and lives might make important contributions to the unfolding of the Catholic tradition.

I greet such possibilities in the same spirit as I have tried to present key aspects of parishioners' sense of faith throughout this book—that is, with neither excessive celebration nor consternation. In keeping with the aforementioned image of the art lover, I have instead examined the intricate brushstrokes and complicated hues of American Catholics' religious lives in an appreciative temper. I have looked carefully at the manner in which they go back again and again to a shared palette of religious symbols to produce a connection to the sacred that changes with each added touch. There are limits to this art metaphor, though. This symbolic production, lived religion, is not actually roped off and exhibited in some cultural museum. Instead, it is produced in the everyday world. It is being worked on and constantly reinterpreted as new circumstances require. This is a messy process that takes place at the interstices of stasis and flux, flouts rigid analytical categories, and, when explored in actual conversation rather than trite presumptions, challenges any notion that it is less religious than what has come before.

Such old notions die hard primarily because shifts in the topography of people's religious lives tend to outpace our efforts to chart them. I recall, for instance, a 1990 letter to the editors of *Commonweal* in which the great Catholic novelist Walker Percy upbraided them for what he saw as their increasing obeisance to an "obligatory hostility" toward the church hierarchy. "If the magisterium and the sacramental orthodoxy of the church are compromised in the name of 'creative pluralism' or suchlike, there may be a lot of hugging and kissing and good feeling going on," he complained. But there will no longer be any room for people attracted to the church's traditional claims, which are "breathtaking in their singularity and exclusivity."[49] Not one to mince words, Percy further pointed out that unabated criticism of the hierarchy within the magazine's pages could be "destructive and divisive to the Catholic people." He then ended his letter rather abruptly. "Get rid of 'Rome,'" he brooded, "and what will be left in the end is California."

Although rhetorically evocative, we have good reason to doubt that Percy provides us with the only two choices at our disposal. His is a religious mapping, the voices heard in this book seem to declare in unison, that is in dire need of revision. Neither solely Rome nor solely California, these parishioners have become acclimated to a less familiar spiritual clime. In the everyday practicing of their faiths, they reside in the expansive meaning-making spaces between Rome and California that, while populous, remain scarcely charted. In this religious landscape they look toward the magisterium and sacramental orthodoxy of the church while believing that these are enhanced, not compromised, by creative pluralism and perhaps even by occasional hugging and kissing. Here they remain very attracted to the church's traditional claims. It is simply that they also claim for themselves considerable latitude in interpreting these, and they are not entirely convinced of their singularity and exclusivity. They are also more apt to equate criticizing the church hierarchy with evidence of the Catholic people's spiritual maturity than with a tendency likely to prove destructive and divisive.

This religious landscape, some have argued, is almost sure to be increasingly inhabited by Catholics with little inclination to participate in church life.[50] Historian Jay Dolan, the thoughtful interpreter of the devotional Catholicism of a bygone era, echoes this point. Reflecting on the present era of American Catholicism, he distinguishes between a "people's church," which continually interacts with the cultural changes that shape it, and a "bureaucratic church," which, in recent decades, seems ever more intent on imposing discipline and exerting control over the faithful. These two expressions of Catholicism, he notes, "are like two ships passing in the night, each traveling in a different direction."[51] This is a real possibility. Perhaps this mutual distancing will continue. After all, even the exceptionally active parishioners introduced in this book are much more likely to locate their commitment to the institutional church within their local parish than within the wider church bureaucracy.

Yet, whatever the future holds, the people we have met here caution us against writing them off as less Catholic than their predecessors. Their critiques of the church hierarchy are usually not blithely made but are formulated on the basis of what they contend is central to the Catholic faith. They, to summon Percy's metaphor, are very acquainted with Rome in the sense that, when conceptualizing and revering the sacred, they deploy cultural symbols profoundly shaped by Catholic tradition. Rather than drawing upon just *any* cultural tools, they rely on those that assist them in coming to grips with a world in which the risen Christ, a merciful God, sacramentalism, and expectations of life where death abounds are all realities (albeit variously interpreted). They also know California in both the literal sense and, more metaphorically, in the sense that their identities as Catholics have been dramatically altered by broader transformations in American culture and religion. Residing somewhere in the unnamed outskirts of Rome and California, then, they are both resoundingly Catholic and American. Like the Easter story, the narrative of their identities as Catholic is one in which an ending ultimately turns out to be a beginning. One iteration of American Catholicism has clearly ended, but another has begun. Less dogmatic, exclusive, and institutionally dependent, as well as typically far less sure of its own bearings, it is hardly less religious than what has preceded it.

This book has looked more deeply into Catholics' lived religion by engaging people in conversation. Lived religion is messy, and it exists in between the familiar coordinates on which people's approach to the sacred is often plotted. It is worth the effort to explore it, however, because it demonstrates how religious traditions are reinterpreted, rethought, and, even if not always recognized as such, revivified by the very people whose lives they render meaningful. Some readers, especially those who prefer to simplify complicated matters, might respond warily to this interpretation. Some might cling to this or that analytical category and not want to see them discarded. Some may persist in envisioning the faith as being wholly of Rome or California. And some might very well respond by relying on an understanding of tradition as, to use Bill McNamara's memorable words, "some monolithic, unchanging thing." To answers such as these, I offer the question reportedly posed by the two angels outside of Jesus's empty tomb and then reasked by one of Saint Monica's third-graders more than two thousand Easter mornings later: "Why do you seek the living among the dead?"

APPENDIX A

Sense of the Faithful

A Sociological Snapshot

THE DATA HERE REPRESENT THE 301 PARISHIONERS SURVEYED FOR THIS study. With the exception of fourteen people at Saint Augustine and thirty at Saint Louis Bertrand, each parishioner also agreed to an in-depth interview. Due to rounding off, not all of the percentages add up to 100.

	#	%
Parish membership		
St. Mary–St. Francis	44	15
St. Louis Bertrand	72	24
St. Monica	45	15
St. Augustine	59	20
St. Margaret Mary	40	13
Most Holy Redeemer	41	14
Sex		
Female	184	61
Male	117	39
Age		
Under 40	57	19
40–59	142	47
60 and over	102	34

	#	%
Race/Ethnicity		
White	168	56
Hispanic	62	21
African American	35	12
Asian/Pacific Islander	33	11
Other	3	1
Marital status		
Married	181	60
Never married	49	16
Partnered	22	7
Divorced/separated	24	8
Widowed	22	7
No response	3	1
Educational level		
Some high school or less	24	8
High school diploma	27	9
Some college/vocational school	52	17
College degree	88	29
Some graduate school	23	8
Graduate/professional degree	87	29
Employment status		
Full-time	122	41
Part-time	58	19
Unemployed	33	11
Retired	85	28
No response	3	1
Socioeconomic status		
Under $50,000	105	35
$50,000–$99,999	89	30
$100,000–$149,999	46	15
$150,000 and over	43	14
No response	18	6

APPENDIX B

Sense of the Faithful

An Interview Schedule

PERSONAL BACKGROUND

1. Were you raised Catholic? If not, from which other religion did you switch to Catholicism and why?
2. How long have you been a member/attending this parish?
3. Why did you choose this particular parish? What has attending/being a member of this parish meant to you personally?

PARISH INVOLVEMENT

1. What types of parish activities are you involved in?
2. Why are you so involved in the parish? Has your involvement increased or decreased at any specific time? If so, why?
3. You seem to *give* a lot to the parish, but what do you think you *get* from your membership and involvement within the parish?

INVOLVEMENT WITHIN THE WIDER COMMUNITY

1. In what types of activities are you involved outside of the parish? [Prompt: volunteering, political activism, etc.]
2. Why do you give your time and money to causes within the wider community? When did you begin to do this? Has this involvement increased or decreased at any specific time? If so, why?
3. To what extent does your religious faith influence your involvement within the wider community?

PARISH COMMUNITY

1. To what extent does this parish provide you with a sense of community?
2. What, in your estimation, is the meaning of the term "community"?
3. Have you provided some kind of support to other people within the parish community? Can you give me a specific example of this?
4. Have you received support from people within the parish community? Can you give me a specific example of this?
5. What does this parish do particularly well? [Prompt: What are some of the things you highlight when describing the parish to an outsider?]
6. What does this parish not do quite so well? [Prompt: What are some areas where there's room for improvement?]
7. Do you consider the mass to be important to you? Why or why not? Other sacraments? Other rituals at the parish? Why or why not?

CATHOLIC IDENTITY

1. Why are you Catholic? Would you ever consider switching to another religion? Why or why not?
2. Do you consider yourself to be a good/strong Catholic? What, in your opinion, makes someone a good/strong Catholic? Why do you think you mentioned these things? Why do you think you didn't mention . . . ? [Prompt: Various items discussed by other parishioners but not discussed by the respondent]
3. Do you get to disagree with church teachings? If so, then what is the role of religious authority in your opinion?
4. Do you think that the Catholic faith is better or truer than other Christian or even non-Christian faiths? If so, why do you say this? If not, then why be specifically Catholic?
5. Do you think there's anything about your particular identity [Prompt: marital status, sex, race/ethnicity, class, sexual orientation, recent immigrant, etc.] that has shaped how you understand your faith?

VARIOUS THEMES AND STORIES

1. The Catholic Church has a long tradition of instructing Catholics in matters pertaining to religious faith and ethical behavior. What are some of the things [Prompt: lessons, values, etc.] you've learned from church teaching about how to live an ethical life?
   - For each lesson/value, ask the following:
     - How have you tried to live in accordance with this lesson/value/theme?
     - To what extent is your parish community helpful in assisting you to live out this lesson/value more fully?

2. Read the Golden Rule passage (Matthew 22:34–40):
   - Is this passage meaningful to you personally? If so, what does it mean to you? [Prompt: Ask about the meaning of commandments, what it means to love God and to love others, etc.]
3. Read the Last Judgment passage (Matthew 25:31–46):
   - Is this passage meaningful to you personally? If so, what does it mean to you? [Prompt: Ask about interviewee's views on heaven and hell, about how and whether people should live in accordance with this passage, etc.]
4. Read the "walking on water" passage (Matthew 14:22–33):
   - Is this passage meaningful to you personally? If so, what does it mean to you? [Prompt: Ask about miracles, the meaning of having faith today, etc.]
5. Read the Petrine confession passage (Luke 9:18–26):
   - Is this passage meaningful to you personally? If so, what does it mean to you? [Prompt: Ask who Jesus is for them, what it means to take up one's cross and follow Jesus today, etc.]
6. Read the "rich young man" passage (Matthew 19:16–26):
   - Is this passage meaningful to you personally? If so, what does it mean to you? [Prompt: Ask if this "hard" commandment is really necessary, whether they consider themselves to be among the rich, etc.]
7. Are there any other Bible passages/stories/images that are particularly meaningful to you and that you perhaps hold close to your heart? If so, why?

VARIOUS ISSUES
1. The Catholic Church teaches that individual Catholics—and even governments as a whole—have a moral obligation to care for poor people and to help bring about social justice.
   - Do you agree with the church's teaching?
   - Does church teaching influence your own thinking on this issue? Why or why not?
2. The Catholic Church teaches that abortion is wrong. [Repeat the bulleted questions above.]
3. The Catholic Church teaches that homosexual relations are immoral and that gay marriages should not be permitted. [Repeat the bulleted questions above.]
4. The Catholic Church teaches that only men—not women—can be ordained as priests. [Repeat the bulleted above.]
5. Before the United States went to war with Iraq, the Catholic Church publicly declared this action to be immoral. [Repeat the bulleted above.]

6. The Catholic Church in the United States has been affected by the so-called sex scandal in which numerous priests have been accused of sexually abusing children and numerous bishops have neglected to address this forcefully enough.
   - Has this situation affected either your faith or your attitude toward the Catholic Church? Why or why not?

CONCLUSION

1. Is there anything else you would like to add?
2. Conclude interview:
   - Ask them to sign consent form.
   - Ask them to fill out survey.
   - Provide them with Prof. Baggett's contact information, and remind them that they are free to contact him with whatever additional information, questions, and so on they might have.

Notes

CHAPTER 1

1. Herbert J. Gans, *The Urban Villagers: Group and Class in the Life of Italian-Americans* (New York: Free Press of Glencoe, 1962).

2. I use the Vatican's translation of this encyclical, which appears on the Vatican's "Papal Encyclicals Online" website at www.papalencyclicals.net.

3. Walter Elliot, *Le père Hecker, foundateur des "Paulistes" Americains* (Paris, 1897).

4. Again, see the "Papal Encyclicals Online" website.

5. José Casanova, *Public Religions in the Modern World* (Chicago: University of Chicago Press, 1994), 168.

6. John Tracy Ellis, *American Catholicism*, 2d ed., rev. (Chicago: University of Chicago Press, 1969), 119–23.

7. Catherine L. Albanese, *America: Religion and Religions* (Belmont, Calif.: Wadsworth, 1992), 94.

8. Quoted in Sydney E. Ahlstrom, *A Religious History of the American People* (New Haven, Conn.: Yale University Press, 1972), 835.

9. See "Papal Encyclicals Online."

10. This 1907 encyclical was titled *Pascendi Dominici Gregis* (*On the Doctrine of the Modernists*). For excellent explorations of this period see R. Scott Appleby, *Church and Age Unite! The Modernist Impulse in American Catholicism* (Notre Dame, Ind.: Notre Dame University Press, 1992), and Lester R. Kurtz, *The Politics of Heresy: The Modernist Crisis in Roman Catholicism* (Berkeley: University of California Press, 1986).

11. Michael W. Cuneo, *The Smoke of Satan: Conservative and Traditionalist Dissent in Contemporary American Catholicism* (New York: Oxford University Press, 1997), 8.

12. See William M. Halsey, *The Survival of American Innocence: Catholicism in an Era of Disillusionment* (Notre Dame, Ind.: Notre Dame University Press, 1980).

13. Gerhard Lenski, *The Religious Factor: A Sociological Study of Religion's Impact on Politics, Economics, and Family Life* (Garden City, N.Y.: Doubleday, 1961).

14. Ibid., 52.

15. Ibid., 150.

16. Quoted in Mark S. Massa, *Catholics and American Culture: Fulton Sheen, Dorothy Day, and the Notre Dame Football Team* (New York: Crossroad, 1999), 158.

17. See Clifford Geertz, "Ethos, World View, and the Analysis of Sacred Symbols," in *The Interpretation of Cultures: Selected Essays* (New York: Basic Books, 1973), 126–41.

18. See Jay P. Dolan, *The American Catholic Experience: A History from Colonial Times to the Present* (New York: Doubleday, 1985), 221–40. I am also indebted to Patrick H. McNamara's discussion of Dolan's devotionalist ethos in his *Conscience First, Tradition Second: A Study of Young American Catholics* (Albany, N.Y.: SUNY Press, 1992), 22–24.

19. Gene Burns, *The Frontiers of Catholicism: The Politics of Ideology in a Liberal World* (Berkeley: University of California Press, 1992), especially chapter two.

20. John Mahoney, *The Making of Moral Theology: A Study of the Roman Catholic Tradition* (New York: Oxford University Press, 1987), 28.

21. I have found historian Robert A. Orsi's work to be particularly helpful in exploring this devotionalist trait. For the importance of the devotion to Our Lady of Mount Carmel, see his *The Madonna of 115th Street: Faith and Community in Italian Harlem, 1880–1950* (New Haven, Conn.: Yale University Press, 1985), and, for a nuanced investigation of the devotion to Saint Jude, see his *Thank You, St. Jude: Women's Devotion to the Patron Saint of Hopeless Causes* (New Haven, Conn.: Yale University Press, 1996).

22. Dorothy Day, *The Long Loneliness: The Autobiography of Dorothy Day* (San Francisco: Harper and Row, 1952), 62–63.

23. James D. Davidson, "Religion among America's Elite: Persistence and Change in the Protestant Establishment," *Sociology of Religion* 55 (1994): 419–40.

24. Will Herberg, *Protestant, Catholic, Jew: An Essay in American Religious Sociology* (Garden City, N.J.: Doubleday, 1960), 225.

25. Jay P. Dolan, *In Search of an American Catholicism: A History of Religion and Culture in Tension* (New York: Oxford University Press, 2002), 133.

26. John T. McGreevy, *Parish Boundaries: The Catholic Encounter with Race in the Twentieth-century Urban North* (Chicago: University of Chicago Press, 1996), 79.

27. See Philip Jenkins, *The New Anti-Catholicism: The Last Acceptable Prejudice* (New York: Oxford University Press, 2003), 23–45.

28. Charles R. Morris, *American Catholic: The Saints and Sinners Who Built America's Most Powerful Church* (New York: Vintage, 1997), 141, 162.

29. Bryan T. Froehle and Mary L. Gautier, *Catholicism USA: A Portrait of the Catholic Church in the United States* (Maryknoll, N.Y.: Orbis, 2000), 72–73, 79, 90–91.

30. Morris, *American Catholic*, 160–61.

31. Garry Wills, *Bare Ruined Choirs: Doubt, Prophecy, and Radical Religion* (Garden City, N.Y.: Doubleday, 1972), 15–16. No doubt a testimony to his special eloquence, Wills's description is frequently quoted and appears also in Cuneo's *Smoke of Satan* (10) and McNamara's *Conscience First, Tradition Second* (17).

32. Doris Kearns Goodwin, *Wait Till Next Year: A Memoir* (New York: Simon and Schuster, 1997), 93.

33. Dolan, *In Search of an American Catholicism*, 181.

34. Alan Ehrenhalt, *The Lost City: The Forgotten Virtues of Community in America* (New York: Basic Books, 1995), 280. Dolan also discusses Ehrenhalt's book and uses this same quotation in *In Search of an American Catholicism*, 184.

35. Casanova, *Public Religions in the Modern World*, 177.

36. See J. John Palen, *The Suburbs* (New York: McGraw-Hill, 1995), and, with a more explicit focus on religion, James Hudnut-Beumler, *Looking for God in the Suburbs: The Religion of the American Dream and Its Critics, 1945–1965* (New Brunswick, N.J.: Rutgers University Press, 1994).

37. James Hennesey, S.J., *American Catholics: A History of the Roman Catholic Community in the United States* (New York: Oxford University Press, 1981), 280.

38. Ehrenhalt, *Lost City*, 118.

39. Two excellent examples of this are Thomas F. O'Dea's *American Catholic Dilemma: An Inquiry into the Intellectual Life* (New York: Sheed and Ward, 1958) and John Tracy Ellis's essay "American Catholics and the Intellectual Life," *Thought* 30 (Autumn 1955): 351–88.

40. Joseph H. Fichter, S.J., *Social Relations in the Urban Parish* (Chicago: University of Chicago Press, 1954), 119. McNamara also draws upon the work of Fichter and Herberg to illustrate various changes in postwar American Catholicism in his *Conscience First, Tradition Second* (18–21).

41. Ibid., 59–60, 62.

42. Herberg, *Protestant, Catholic, Jew*, 151.

43. Ibid., 271.

44. Ibid., 267.

45. Ibid., 160.

46. For this sense of the ideological impact of Vatican II on American Catholics' self-understanding I am especially indebted to Michele Dillon's *Catholic Identity: Balancing Reason, Faith, and Power* (New York: Cambridge University Press, 1999), 48–53. Worth quoting in full, she states the matter quite well: "As I will elaborate, Vatican II institutionalized the doctrinal-intellectual resources for an emancipatory agenda grounded in rational-critical discussion. Vatican II affirmed the values of equality, religious freedom, and diversity; recognized the importance of social movements in achieving change; emphasized culture as a human and social product; validated the legitimacy of diverse interpretive stances; stated explicitly that disagreements were to be resolved by dialogue rather than official authority; and argued for consistency between egalitarian values and institutional practices" (48). Other important scholarly works I draw on in this section are: Avery Dulles, *Models of the Church* (Garden City, N.Y.: Doubleday, 1974); Paul Lakeland, *The Liberation of the Laity: In Search of an Accountable Church* (New York: Continuum, 2003); Richard P. McBrien, *Catholicism* (Minneapolis: Winston Press, 1980), especially vol. 2, 657–90; John W. O'Malley, S.J., *Tradition and Transition: Historical Perspectives on Vatican II* (Lima, Ohio: Academic Renewal Press, 2002); and T. Howland Sanks, *Salt, Leaven, and Light: The Community Called Church* (New York: Crossroad, 1992).

47. "Dogmatic Constitution on the Church" *(Lumen gentium)*, in Walter M. Abbott, S.J., ed., *The Documents of Vatican II* (Chicago: Follett, 1966), no. 23, 44; also quoted in McBrien, *Catholicism*, 672.

48. "Pastoral Constitution on the Church in the Modern World" *(Gaudium et spes)*, in Abbott, ed., *Documents of Vatican II*, no. 58, 264.

49. Ibid.

50. See Sanks, *Salt, Leaven, and Light,* 136.

51. Ibid., no. 43, 245; also quoted in Dillon, *Catholic Identity,* 50.

52. "Pastoral Constitution," no. 4, 201.

53. Ibid., no. 2, 200; also quoted in McBrien, *Catholicism,* 678.

54. "Declaration on the Relationship of the Church to Non-Christian Religions" *(Nostra aetate)* in Abbott, ed., *Documents of Vatican II,* no. 2, 662.

55. "Pastoral Constitution," no. 21, 220; also quoted in McBrien, *Catholicism,* 674.

56. Ibid., no. 3, 201; also quoted in Sanks, *Salt, Leaven, and Light,* 130.

57. "Dogmatic Constitution on the Church," no. 10, 27.

58. "Decree on the Apostolate of the Laity" *(Apostolicam actuositatem),* in Abbott, ed., *Documents of Vatican II,* no. 3, 492.

59. "Pastoral Constitution," no. 43, 243.

60. Ibid., no. 16, 213; also quoted in Dillon, *Catholic Identity,* 48.

61. Dillon, *Catholic Identity,* 48.

62. Ibid., 52.

63. "Dogmatic Constitution on Divine Revelation" *(Dei verbum)* in Abbott, ed., *Documents of Vatican II,* no. 8, 116; also quoted in McBrien, *Catholicism,* 677.

64. For a helpful investigation see John Seidler and Katherine Meyer, *Conflict and Change in the Catholic Church* (New Brunswick, N.J.: Rutgers University Press, 1989).

65. Sanks, *Salt, Leaven, and Light,* 143.

66. Andrew Greeley has made this point most strongly in his *The American Catholic: A Social Portrait* (New York: Basic Books, 1977), 126–50, and also in his *The Catholic Myth: The Behavior and Beliefs of American Catholics* (New York: Scribner's, 1990), 90–105.

67. Peter L. Berger, *A Far Glory: The Quest for Faith in an Age of Credulity* (New York: Free Press, 1992), 44.

68. James D. Davidson, Andrea S. Williams, Richard A. Lamanna, Jan Stenftenagel, Kathleen Maas Weigert, William J. Whalen, and Patricia Wittberg, S.C., *The Search for Common Ground: What Unites and Divides American Catholics* (Huntington, Ind.: Our Sunday Visitor, 1997).

69. William V. D'Antonio, James D. Davidson, Dean R. Hoge, and Mary L. Gautier, *American Catholics Today: New Realities of Their Faith and Their Church* (New York: Rowman and Littlefield, 2007), 27.

70. Peter Steinfels, *A People Adrift: The Crisis of the Roman Catholic Church in America* (New York: Simon and Schuster, 2003), 29–30.

71. Laurence R. Iannaccone, "Why Strict Churches Are Strong," *American Journal of Sociology* 99 (1994): 1180–1211.

72. Much less knowledgeable than both mainline and evangelical Protestants, fewer than one-third of American Catholics, according to one study, can name all four gospels, and fewer than two in five can identify the person who delivered the Sermon on the Mount as Jesus. See George Gallup Jr. and Jim Castelli, *The American Catholic People: Their Beliefs, Practices, and Values* (Garden City, N.Y.: Doubleday, 1987), 35.

73. Dean R. Hoge, William D. Dinges, Mary Johnson, and Juan L. Gonzales, *Young Adult Catholics: Religion in the Culture of Choice* (Notre Dame, Ind.: Notre Dame University Press, 2001), 59.

74. D'Antonio et al., *American Catholics Today*, 175, 174, 177.

75. Dillon, *Catholic Identity*, 81–82.

76. Marie Therese Winter, Adair Lummis, and Alison Stokes, *Defecting in Place: Women Claiming Responsibility for Their Own Spiritual Lives* (New York: Crossroad, 1994), 114–15.

77. Gallup and Castelli, *American Catholic People*, 15, 193.

78. Davidson et al., *Search for Common Ground*, 26; George Gallup Jr. and D. Michael Lindsay, *Surveying the Religious Landscape: Trends in U.S. Beliefs* (Harrisburg, Penn.: Morehouse, 1999), 55.

79. D'Antonio et al., *American Catholics Today*, 177.

80. Ibid., 60.

81. Jim Castelli and Joseph Gremillion, *The Emerging Parish: The Notre Dame Study of Catholic Life since Vatican II* (San Francisco: Harper and Row, 1987), 145.

82. This insight is informed by Peter Berger's well-known argument concerning religion and modernity in his *The Heretical Imperative: Contemporary Possibilities of Religious Affirmation* (Garden City, N.Y.: Doubleday, 1979).

83. See Wade Clark Roof and William McKinney, *American Mainline Religion: Its Changing Shape and Future* (New Brunswick, N.J.: Rutgers University Press, 1992), 40–71.

84. See Paul Wilkes, *The Good Enough Catholic: A Guide for the Perplexed* (New York: Ballantine, 1996).

85. See Andrew M. Greeley, *The Communal Catholic: A Personal Manifesto* (New York: Seabury, 1976).

86. See, for example, David D. Hall, ed., *Lived Religion in America: Toward a History of Practice* (Princeton, N.J.: Princeton University Press, 1997). Another insightful collection on this theme is Nancy T. Ammerman, ed., *Everyday Religion: Observing Modern Religious Lives* (New York: Oxford University Press, 2006).

87. See the fourth chapter, titled "Official and Nonofficial Religion," in Meredith B. McGuire, *Religion: The Social Context*, 5th ed. (Belmont, Calif.: Wadsworth, 2002), 97–148.

88. Lawrence W. Neuman, *Social Research Methods: Qualitative and Quantitative Approaches*, 4th ed. (Boston: Allyn and Bacon, 2000).

89. I have been alert to possible interactive effects associated with parishioners' being interviewed by a professor at a Catholic theologate. However, after carefully comparing my interview data with those collected by my research assistants, I see no evidence that the interviewees were unduly influenced by my status as a professor. The things parishioners told me and my research assistants (men and women, Catholic and non-Catholic) are remarkably similar.

90. On occasion I also draw upon earlier surveys conducted by D'Antonio and his research teams. Their 1993 survey is discussed in William V. D'Antonio, James D. Davidson, Dean R. Hoge, and Ruth A. Wallace, *Laity, American and Catholic: Transforming the Church* (Kansas City, Mo.: Sheed and Ward, 1996), and their 1999 survey is presented in William V. D'Antonio, James D. Davidson, Dean R. Hoge, and Katherine Meyer, *American Catholics: Gender, Generation, and Commitment* (Walnut Creek, Calif.: AltaMira, 2001). A couple of other charts draw upon a 1995 national survey reported on in Davidson et al., *Search for Common Ground*.

91. See "Dogmatic Constitution on the Church," no. 12, 29.

CHAPTER 2

1. Matthew Arnold, "Culture and Anarchy," in Lionel Trilling, ed., *The Portable Matthew Arnold* (New York: Viking, 1949), 499.

2. I am indebted to William H. Sewell Jr. for clarifying the distinction between these last two conceptions of culture (although he does not label them as I do); see his essay "The Concept(s) of Culture," in Victoria E. Bonnell and Lynn Hunt, eds., *Beyond the Cultural Turn: New Directions in the Study of Society and Culture* (Berkeley: University of California Press, 1999), 35–61.

3. My understanding of culture as a "repertoire" or "tool kit" has been greatly informed by Ann Swidler's work. Along with her important article, "Culture in Action: Symbols and Strategies," *American Sociological Review* 51 (1986): 273–86, I have also learned much from her extremely insightful book *Talk of Love: How Culture Matters* (Chicago: University of Chicago Press, 2001).

4. Pierre Bourdieu, *Distinction: A Social Critique of the Judgment of Taste,* trans. Richard Nice (Cambridge, Mass.: Harvard University Press, 1984).

5. See, for example, Ann Arnett Ferguson, *Bad Boys: Public Schools in the Making of Black Masculinity* (Ann Arbor: University of Michigan Press, 2001).

6. H. Richard Niebuhr, *Radical Monotheism and Western Culture* (1943; reprint, New York: Harper and Brothers, 1960), 35.

7. William James, *Some Problems of Philosophy: A Beginning of an Introduction to Philosophy* (1911; reprint, Lincoln: University of Nebraska Press, 1996), 50.

8. See Harold Garfinkel's use of "breaching experiments" to uncover the tacit rules governing social interaction in his *Studies in Ethnomethodology* (Englewood Cliffs, N.J.: Prentice-Hall, 1967), 35–75.

9. William H. Sewell Jr., "A Theory of Structure: Duality, Agency, and Transformation," *American Journal of Sociology* 98 (July 1992): 1–29.

10. This is essentially the strategy undertaken by David Yamane, who compellingly advocates examining secularization on the three levels—individual, organizational, and societal—that I also address in this chapter. See his incisive article "Secularization on Trial: In Defense of the Neosecularization Paradigm," *Journal for the Scientific Study of Religion* 36 (January 1997): 109–22.

11. See, for example, David Martin, *A General Theory of Secularization* (New York: Harper and Row, 1978), and Talal Asad, *Formations of the Secular: Christianity, Islam, and Modernity* (Stanford, Calif.: Stanford University Press, 2003).

12. For a thoughtful and provocative statement of how this occurs, utilizing the lens of social movement theory, see Christian Smith, "Introduction: Rethinking the Secularization of American Public Life," in Christian Smith, ed., *The Secular Revolution: Power, Interests, and Conflict in the Secularization of American Public Life* (Berkeley: University of California Press, 2003), 1–96.

13. Martin Riesebrodt, *Pious Passion: The Emergence of Modern Fundamentalism in the United States and Iran,* trans. Don Reneau (Berkeley: University of California Press, 1993).

14. Stephanie Coontz, *The Way We Never Were: American Families and the Nostalgia Trap* (New York: Basic Books, 1992).

15. Rodney Stark, "Secularization, R.I.P.," *Sociology of Religion* 60 (1999): 249–73.

16. George Gallup Jr. and D. Michael Lindsay, *Surveying the Religious Landscape: Trends in U.S. Beliefs* (Harrisburg, Penn.: Morehouse, 1999), 24. Note that, while using different categories, the recent national survey conducted by the Pew Research Center found that things have not changed much since 1999. It discovered that 92 percent of Americans believe in God; disaggregating, it found that 71 percent are "absolutely certain," 17 percent are "fairly certain," 5 percent are "not certain," and 5 percent "don't believe in God" (3 percent fell in the "other / don't know" category. See *U.S. Religious Landscape Survey: Religious Beliefs and Practices: Diverse and Politically Relevant* (Washington, D.C.: Pew Forum on Religion and Public Life, 2008), 28.

17. *U.S. Religious Landscape Survey,* 45, 23.

18. Quoted in Martin E. Marty, "The Spirit's Holy Errand: The Search for a Spiritual Style in Secular America," *Daedalus* 96(1) (Winter 1967): 99–115.

19. Gallup and Lindsay, *Surveying the Religious Landscape,* 79.

20. The sociological term for this process is differentiation. For fuller explication see Niklas Luhmann, *The Differentiation of Society* (New York: Columbia University Press, 1982). Also important for making the case that, rather than religious privatization or decline, differentiation is the "structural trend" that defines "secular" society is José Casanova's *Public Religions in the Modern World* (Chicago: University of Chicago Press, 1994), 11–39. Finally, according to one sociologist who examined and compared the most influential theories of secularization, "differentiation, in one form or another, is absolutely central to all the secularization theories, without exception." See Olivier Tschannen, "The Secularization Paradigm: A Systemization," *Journal for the Scientific Study of Religion* 30(4) (1991): 395–415.

21. To put the matter in the tripartite categories used by social theorist Daniel Bell, religion now seems far less at home within both the "polity" and "techno-economic" order and more connected to "culture." See his *The Cultural Contradictions of Capitalism* (New York: Basic Books, 1976), 3–30.

22. This is one of the chief characteristics of modern religion, according to Robert N. Bellah, as described in his important essay, "Religious Evolution" in *Beyond Belief: Essays on Religion in a Post-traditionalist World* (Berkeley: University of California Press, 1970), 20–50.

23. See, for example, Peter L. Berger, *The Sacred Canopy: Elements of a Sociological Theory of Religion* (New York: Doubleday, 1967), 127–53. In his typical, thoughtful response to new developments, however, Berger no longer holds this view; see Peter Berger, "Epistemological Modesty: An Interview with Peter Berger," *Christian Century* 114 (Oct. 29, 1997): 972–75, 978.

24. Christian Smith, et al., *American Evangelicalism: Embattled and Thriving* (Chicago: University of Chicago Press, 1998), 102–104.

25. Roger Finke and Rodney Stark, *The Churching of America: Winners and Losers in Our Religious Economy, 1776–1990* (New Brunswick, N.J.: Rutgers University Press, 1992).

26. Garfinkel, *Studies in Ethnomethodology,* 68; "By 'cultural dope,'" Garfinkel writes, "I refer to the man-in-the-sociologist's-society who produces the stable features of the society by acting in compliance with preestablished and legitimate alternatives of action that the common culture provides."

27. See especially Swidler, *Talk of Love,* chapter two.

28. Robert Wuthnow, *The Restructuring of American Religion: Society and Faith since World War II* (Princeton, N.J.: Princeton University Press, 1988), 88–89.

29. Gallup and Lindsay, *Surveying the Religious Landscape,* 68, 32.

30. See, most famously, Clifford Geertz, "Religion as a Cultural System," in *The Interpretation of Cultures* (New York: Basic, 1973), 87–125.

31. James A. Beckford, *Religion and Advanced Industrial Society* (London: Unwin Hyman, 1989), 171–72. For an extremely sophisticated account of what she calls "the myth of cultural integration," see also Margaret S. Archer, *Culture and Agency: The Place of Culture in Social Theory,* rev. ed. (New York: Cambridge University Press, 1996), especially chapter one.

32. Again, Michele Dillon's analysis in *Catholic Identity: Balancing Reason, Faith, and Power* (New York: Cambridge University Press, 1999) is a notable exception; see especially her chapter titled "Pluralism in Community" (194–220).

33. Robert N. Bellah, Richard Madsen, William M. Sullivan, Ann Swidler, and Steven M. Tipton, *Habits of the Heart: Individualism and Commitment in American Life* (Berkeley: University of California Press, 1985), 227.

34. Here my argument is informed by Michèle Lamont's explanation of "symbolic boundaries" in her *Money, Morals, and Manners: The Culture of the French and American Upper-middle Class* (Chicago: University of Chicago Press, 1992), 1–14.

35. Robert Wuthnow explores these and other institutional forms in *Producing the Sacred: An Essay on Public Religion* (Chicago: University of Illinois Press, 1994).

36. Michael O. Emerson, *People of the Dream: Multiracial Congregations in the United States* (Princeton, N.J.: Princeton University Press, 2006), 7.

37. Mark Chaves, *Congregations in America* (Cambridge, Mass.: Harvard University Press, 2004), 3, 23.

38. David O. Moberg, *The Church as a Social Institution* (Englewood Cliffs, N.J.: Prentice-Hall, 1962), chapter six. See also a recounting of these themes in David A. Roozen, William McKinney, and Jackson W. Carroll, *Varieties of Religious Presence: Mission in Public Life* (New York: Pilgrim, 1984), 26–27.

39. Here I am informed by Ulf Hannerz's understanding of the "social distribution" of culture; see his *Cultural Complexity: Studies in the Social Organization of Meaning* (New York: Columbia University Press, 1992).

40. Gary Alan Fine, *With the Boys: Little League Baseball and Preadolescent Culture* (Chicago: University of Chicago Press, 1987), 124–61. Penny Edgell Becker uses Fine's notion of idioculture with great nuance in her *Congregations in Conflict: Cultural Models of Local Religious Life* (New York: Cambridge University Press, 1999), 8–12.

41. Here I am drawing upon the concepts of "institutional retention" and cultural "retrievability" as astutely explained in Michael Schudson's essay "How Culture Works: Perspectives from Media Studies on the Efficacy of Symbols," *Theory and Society* 18 (1989): 153–80.

42. R. Stephen Warner, "The Place of the Congregation in Contemporary American Religious Configuration," in James P. Wind and James W. Lewis, eds., *American Congregations.* Vol. 2: *New Perspectives in the Study of Congregations* (Chicago: University of Chicago Press, 1994), 54–99.

43. Even though all the parishes in this study have changed at least somewhat since I began my research more than five years ago, but none have changed more than this parish. Within the past year or so, it has experienced an influx of worshipers from nearby and

recently closed St. Andrew-St. Joseph parish. And, in fall 2008, this church will also be closed and its members will be encouraged to begin worshipping at the newly constructed cathedral in downtown Oakland, which will be called The Cathedral Parish of Christ the Light.

44. Ernst Cassirer, *An Essay on Man* (New Haven, Conn.: Yale University Press, 1944), 32–35. Using the term *homo credens,* Christian Smith makes a similar argument in his *Moral, Believing Animals: Human Personhood and Culture* (New York: Oxford University Press, 2003), 46–55.

45. Kenneth Burke, *Permanence and Change: An Anatomy of Purpose,* 3rd ed. (Berkeley: University of California Press, 1984), 49.

CHAPTER 3

1. See, for example, Gustavo Gutiérrez, *A Theology of Liberation: History, Politics, and Salvation* (Maryknoll, N.Y.: Orbis, 1973), 83–105.

2. Kenneth J. Gergen, *The Saturated Self: Dilemmas of Identity in Contemporary Life* (New York: Basic Books, 1991), 13.

3. See Erik H. Erikson, *Identity: Youth and Crisis* (New York: Norton, 1968).

4. Robert Wuthnow makes this point in *After Heaven: Spirituality in America since the 1950s* (Berkeley: University of California Press, 1998), 148.

5. Peter Berger, Brigitte Berger, and Hansfried Kellner, *The Homeless Mind: Modernization and Consciousness* (New York: Vintage, 1973), 63–82.

6. Sociologist Erving Goffman makes this point insightfully. "The self in this sense is not a property of the person to whom it is attributed," he writes, "but dwells rather in the pattern of social control that is exerted in connection with the person by himself and those around him. This special kind of institutional arrangement does not so much support the self as constitute it." See *Asylums: Essays on the Social Situation of Mental Patients and Other Inmates* (New York: Anchor, 1961), 168.

7. Jean-Paul Sartre, *Being and Nothingness: An Essay on Phenomenological Ontology,* trans. Hazel E. Barnes (New York: Philosophical Library, 1956), 30.

8. Zygmunt Bauman, *Intimations of Postmodernity* (New York: Routledge, 1992), 35.

9. Charles Taylor, *The Ethics of Authenticity* (Cambridge, Mass.: Harvard University Press, 1991).

10. Anthony Giddens, *Modernity and Self-identity: Self and Society in the Late Modern Age* (Stanford, Calif.: Stanford University Press, 1991), 32.

11. Michele Dillon makes a similar point concerning the "doctrinal reflexivity" evident among the "pro-change" *Catholics in Catholic Identity: Balancing Reason, Faith, and Power* (New York: Cambridge University Press, 1999), especially 24–31 and 164–93.

12. Margaret R. Somers and Gloria D. Gibson, "Reclaiming the Epistemological 'Other': Narrative and the Social Constitution of Identity," in *Social Theory and the Politics of Identity,* ed. Craig Calhoun (Malden, Mass.: Blackwell, 1994), 37–99.

13. Charles Taylor, *Sources of the Self: The Making of Modern Identity* (Cambridge, Mass.: Harvard University Press, 1989), 47.

14. Pierre Bourdieu, *The Logic of Practice,* trans. Richard Nice (Stanford, Calif.: Stanford University Press, 1990), 66.

15. See especially Wuthnow's chapter titled "From Dwelling to Seeking," in *After Heaven*, 1–18.

16. Wuthnow recognizes the hybridity of many people's religious lives and accordingly explains a third type, which he calls "practice-orientated spirituality." See *After Heaven*, 168–98.

17. I borrow the term "experientialism" from theologian Harvey Cox's analysis of Pentecostalism in his *Fire from Heaven: The Rise of Pentecostal Spirituality and the Reshaping of Religion in the Twenty-first Century* (New York: Addison-Wesley, 1995), 304–20.

18. Dean R. Hoge, Benton Johnson, and Donald A. Luidens, *Vanishing Boundaries: The Religion of Protestant Baby Boomers* (Louisville, Ky.: Westminster/John Knox Press, 1994), 112–15.

19. Alan Wolfe, *One Nation after All: What Middle-class Americans Really Think about God, Country, Family, Racism, Welfare, Immigration, Homosexuality, Work, the Right, the Left, and Each Other* (New York: Viking, 1998), 54.

20. Robert N. Bellah, Richard Madsen, William M. Sullivan, Ann Swidler, and Steven M. Tipton, *Habits of the Heart: Individualism and Commitment in American Life* (Berkeley: University of California Press, 1985), 221.

21. Congregation for the Doctrine of the Faith, *Declaration "Dominus Jesus" on the Unicity and Salvific Universality of Jesus Christ and the Church* (2000), no. 22.

22. G. F. W. Hegel, *Philosophy of Right*, trans. T. M. Knox (1821; reprint, New York: Oxford University Press, 1967), 13.

23. Robert S. Lynd and Helen Merrell Lynd, *Middletown: A Study in Modern American Culture* (1929; reprint, New York: Harcourt Brace Jovanovich, 1957), chapter 20.

24. Theodore Caplow, Howard M. Bahr, and Bruce A. Chadwick, *All Faithful People: Change and Continuity in Middletown's Religion* (Minneapolis: University of Minnesota Press, 1983), 91–95.

25. Wade Clark Roof, *Spiritual Marketplace: Baby Boomers and the Remaking of American Religion* (Princeton, N.J.: Princeton University Press, 1999), 75.

26. I borrow this term from Robert Wuthnow; see his *Christianity in the Twenty-first Century: Reflections on the Challenges Ahead* (New York: Oxford University Press, 1993), 108.

27. Robert Wuthnow, *America and the Challenges of Religious Diversity* (Princeton, N.J.: Princeton University Press, 2005), 190–98.

28. See Leonardo Boff and Clodovis Boff, *Introducing Liberation Theology* (Maryknoll, N.Y.: Orbis, 1989), 49–50.

29. Nancy T. Ammerman, "Golden Rule Christianity: Lived Religion in the American Mainstream," in *Lived Religion in America: Toward a History of Practice*, ed. David D. Hall (Princeton, N.J.: Princeton University Press, 1997), 196–216.

30. For a fascinating account of pragmatism's birth in the United States see Louis Menand's *The Metaphysical Club: A Story of Ideas in America* (New York: Farrar, Straus, and Giroux, 2001).

31. One recent poll found that 72 percent of American adults believe in heaven, while a more modest 56 percent believe in hell; see George Gallup Jr. and D. Michael Lindsay, *Surveying the Religious Landscape: Trends in U.S. Beliefs* (Harrisburg, Penn.: Morehouse, 1999), 30.

32. See Immanuel Kant, *Foundations of the Metaphysics of Morals,* trans. Lewis White Beck (1785; reprint, New York: Macmillan, 1990), 58–63.

CHAPTER 4

1. James Davison Hunter, *Culture Wars: The Struggle to Define America* (New York: Basic, 1991).

2. For example, see the insightful essays in Rhys H. Williams, ed., *Culture Wars in American Politics: Critical Reviews of a Popular Myth* (New York: Aldine de Gruyter, 1997).

3. Congregation for the Doctrine of the Faith, "The Pastoral Care of Homosexual Persons," *Origins* 16 (November 1986): 377, 379–82.

4. My argument that Bay Area parishioners are reflexive about their church as an institution builds upon the "institutional reflexivity" that Michele Dillon attributes to the church as a whole (manifested in Vatican II reforms, for example) and to the "pro-change" Catholics she studied. See her *Catholic Identity: Balancing Reason, Faith, and Power* (New York: Cambridge University Press, 1999), especially 24–31.

5. Thomas F. O'Dea, "Five Dilemmas of the Institutionalization of Religion," *Journal for the Scientific Study of Religion* 1(1) (October 1961): 30–41. These same dilemmas are also presented in a somewhat different version in Thomas F. O'Dea and Janet O'Dea Aviad, *The Sociology of Religion* (Englewood Cliffs, N.J.: Prentice-Hall, 1983), 56–64. For the sake of simplicity and because all five dilemmas were first articulated in O'Dea's 1961 article, I discuss both versions of this work in the body of the text as simply "O'Dea's dilemmas." The strategy of employing O'Dea's categories in this manner has been informed by a similar one that Margaret M. Poloma used in her study of the Assemblies of God denomination; see her *The Assemblies of God at the Crossroads: Charisma and Institutional Dilemmas* (Knoxville: University of Tennessee Press, 1989).

6. O'Dea's institutional dilemmas builds upon Max Weber's notion of the "routinization of charisma," especially as depicted in Weber's work on the transition of religious charisma and understanding from the prophetic to the priestly form. See especially Weber's chapter titled "The Religious Congregation, Preaching, and Pastoral Care," in *The Sociology of Religion*, trans. Ephraim Fischoff (Boston: Beacon, 1963), 60–79.

7. Andrew Greeley, *The Catholic Revolution: New Wine, Old Wineskins, and the Second Vatican Council* (Berkeley: University of California Press, 2004), 99–119.

8. "A religious symbol can die only if the correlation of which it is an adequate expression dies," wrote the influential theologian Paul Tillich more than a half century ago. "This occurs whenever the revelatory situation changes and former symbols become obsolete. The history of religion, right up to our own time, is full of dead symbols which have been killed not by scientific criticism of assumed superstitions but by a religious criticism of religion." See his *Systematic Theology*, vol. 1 (Chicago: University of Chicago Press, 1951), 240.

9. O'Dea and Aviad, *Sociology of Religion*, 59.

10. Jean Seguy, "L'approche wébérienne des phénomènes religieux," in *Omaggio a Ferrarotti*, ed. R. Cipriani and M. Macioti (Rome: Siares, Studi e Richerche, 1989), 180.

11. See Peter Steinfels, "Future of Faith Worries Catholic Leaders," *New York Times*, June 1, 1994, A1, B8.

12. James Davidson points to three other 1990s' surveys that suggest that American Catholics' belief in the Real Presence is actually much stronger and argues that the "either-or" formulation of the *New York Times* survey is problematic. He posits that if this survey offered a "both-and" response, which is consonant with church teaching (i.e., that the bread

and wine are both symbols and become the body and blood of Christ), then belief in the Real Presence would not appear to be so eviscerated. See James D. Davidson, *Catholicism in Motion: The Church in American Society* (Liguori, Mo.: Liguori/Triumph, 2005), 164–65.

13. For a classic statement about this see David Tracy, *The Analogical Imagination* (New York: Crossroad, 1982).

14. For important scholarly examples of a constructivist approach to God, see Gordon D. Kaufman, *The Theological Imagination: Constructing the Concept of God* (Philadelphia: Westminster, 1981), and Sallie McFague, *Models of God: Theology for an Ecological, Nuclear Age* (Philadelphia: Fortress, 1987).

15. Winifred Gallagher, *Working on God* (New York: Modern Library, 1999).

16. Adam B. Seligman, *Modernity's Wager: Authority, the Self, and Transcendence* (Princeton, N.J.: Princeton University Press, 2000), 5.

17. O'Dea and Aviad, *Sociology of Religion*, 61.

18. Eugene Kennedy, *Tomorrow's Catholics, Yesterday's Church: The Two Cultures of American Catholicism* (New York: Harper and Row, 1988), 21.

19. John Henry Newman, *An Essay in Aid of a Grammar of Assent* (1870; reprint, New York: Oxford University Press, 1985).

20. George Gallup Jr. and D. Michael Lindsay, *Surveying the Religious Landscape: Trends in U.S. Beliefs* (Harrisburg, Penn.: Morehouse, 1999), 83. This statistic correlates with four-fifths of American adults who agree that "an individual should arrive at his or her own religious beliefs independent of any churches or synagogues"; see George Gallup Jr., *The Unchurched American: 10 Years Later* (Princeton, N.J.: Princeton Religion Research Center, 1988).

21. George Gallup Jr. and George O'Connell, *Who Do Americans Say That I Am?* (Philadelphia: Westminster, 1986), 69, 102.

22. Stephen Prothero, *American Jesus: How the Son of God Became a National Icon* (New York: Farrar, Straus, and Giroux, 2003), 301.

23. Dillon, *Catholic Identity,* 164–93.

24. O'Dea, "Five Dilemmas," 36.

25. O'Dea and Aviad, *Sociology of Religion,* 60.

26. W. Richard Scott, *Organizations: Rational, Natural, and Open Systems* (Englewood Cliffs, N.J.: Prentice Hall, 1992), 4.

27. Robert Michels, *Political Parties: A Sociological Study of the Oligarchical Tendencies of Modern Democracy* (1915; reprint, Glencoe, Ill.: Free Press, 1962); see his part V, chapter two, which is titled "Democracy and the Iron Law of Oligarchy."

28. For extremely considered reflections on this see Eugene C. Bianchi and Rosemary Radford Ruether, eds., *A Democratic Catholic Church: The Reconstruction of Roman Catholicism* (New York: Crossroad, 1992).

29. William V. D'Antonio, James D. Davidson, Dean R. Hoge, and Mary L. Gautier, *American Catholics Today: New Realities of Their Faith and Their Church* (New York: Rowman and Littlefield, 2007), 120.

30. George Ritzer, *The McDonaldization of Society* (Thousand Oaks, Calif.: Pine Forge, 2000).

31. See James D. Davidson and Dean R. Hoge, "Catholics after the Scandal: A New Study's Major Findings," *Commonweal* (Nov. 19, 2004): 13–19.

32. O'Dea and Aviad, *Sociology of Religion,* 58.

33. O'Dea, "Five Dilemmas," 36.

34. Michele Dillon summarizes and analyzes these very ably in her book *Catholic Identity*, 60–64.

35. Pope John Paul II, "Ordinatio Sacerdotalis," *Origins* 24 (June 9, 1994): 49–52.

36. Jürgen Habermas, *Legitimation Crisis*, trans. Thomas McCarthy (Boston: Beacon, 1975). Michele Dillon uses this term in her analysis of the sex-abuse scandal in her essay "The Struggle to Preserve Religious Capital: A Sociological Perspective on the Catholic Church in the United States," which appears in *Church Ethics and Its Organizational Context: Learning from the Sex Abuse Scandal in the Catholic Church*, ed. Jean M. Bartunek, Mary Ann Hinsdale, and James F. Keenan (Lanham, Md.: Rowman and Littlefield, 2006), 43–56.

37. See Frank Parkin, *Marxism and Class Theory: A Bourgeois Critique* (New York: Columbia University Press, 1979), 44–73.

38. O'Dea and Aviad, *Sociology of Religion*, 58.

39. Ibid., 63.

40. O'Dea, "Five Dilemmas," 37.

41. Davidson, *Catholicism in Motion*, 166–7.

42. James D. Davidson, Andrea S. Williams, Richard A. Lamanna, Jan Stenftenagel, Kathleen Maas Weigert, William J. Whalen, and Patricia Wittberg, S.C., *The Search for Common Ground: What Unites and Divides American Catholics* (Huntington, Ind.: Our Sunday Visitor, 1997), 48.

43. Mark Chaves, "Secularization as Declining Religious Authority," *Social Forces* 72 (March 1994): 749–74.

44. Steven Lukes uses the language of power's three dimensions with great analytical effectiveness in his important book *Power: A Radical View*, 2d ed. (New York: Palgrave Macmillan, 2005).

45. Michel Foucault, *Power/Knowledge: Selected Interviews and Other Writings, 1972–1977*, ed. Colin Gordon (New York: Pantheon, 1980), 119.

46. Robert Wuthnow, *American Mythos: Why Our Efforts to Be a Better Nation Fall Short* (Princeton, N.J.: Princeton University Press, 2006), 24–35.

47. Here I am instructed by Pierre Bourdieu's important notion of "habitus," which, in his *Logic of Practice* (Stanford, Calif.: Stanford University Press, 1990), he defines as "a system of durable, transposable dispositions, structured structures predisposed to function as structuring structures, that is, as principles which generate and organize practices and representations that can be objectively adapted to their outcomes without presupposing a conscious aiming at ends or an express mastery of the operations necessary in order to attain them" (53).

48. Jean-Jacques Rousseau, *The Social Contract and Discourse on the Origin of Inequality*, ed. Lester G. Crocker (1767; reprint, New York: Washington Square, 1967), book I, chapter 7, 22.

49. These parishioners would look very favorably upon Michele Dillon's depiction of what she calls a "deliberative church," which is "one in which people reason about contested differences with a view toward reaching understanding about a future course of action." See her book, *Catholic Identity*, 247–51.

50. Alasdair MacIntyre, *After Virtue: A Study in Moral Theory* (Notre Dame, Ind.: University of Notre Dame Press, 1981), 2.

51. See Albert O. Hirschman, *Exit, Voice, and Loyalty: Responses to Decline in Firms, Organizations, and States* (Cambridge, Mass.: Harvard University Press, 1970).

52. For his classic discussion of manifest and latent functions see Robert K. Merton, *Social Theory and Social Structure* (New York: Free Press, 1968), 73–138.

53. Phillip E. Hammond, *Religion and Personal Autonomy: The Third Disestablishment in America* (Columbia: University of South Carolina Press, 1992).

CHAPTER 5

1. I derive this term from Andrew Greeley's *Denominational Society: A Sociological Approach to Religion in America* (Glenview, Ill.: Scott, Foresman, 1972), 31–70.

2. For the small-group movement see Robert Wuthnow, *Sharing the Journey: Support Groups and America's New Quest for Community* (New York: Free Press, 1994); for seeker churches, see Kimon Howland Sargeant, *Seeker Churches: Promoting Traditional Religion in a Nontraditional Way* (New Brunswick, N.J.: Rutgers University Press, 2000); and, for an examination of how one well-known parachurch organization adapts to people's religious needs, see my book titled *Habitat for Humanity: Building Private Homes, Building Public Religion* (Philadelphia: Temple University Press, 2001).

3. Michael P. Hornsby-Smith, *The Changing Parish: A Study of Parishes, Priests, and Parishioners after Vatican II* (New York: Routledge, 1989), 66.

4. Froehle and Gautier estimated that in 1998 about one in five Catholic K–8 students and about one in seven high school students were enrolled in parochial schools; see Bryan T. Froehle and Mary L. Gautier, *Catholicism USA: A Portrait of the Catholic Church in the United States* (Maryknoll, N.Y.: Orbis, 2000), 72–3.

5. For an excellent assessment of how parishes are defined in canon law and how this has changed over time see James A. Coriden, *The Parish in Catholic Tradition: History, Theology, and Canon Law* (Mahwah, N.J.: Paulist Press, 1997).

6. William V. D'Antonio, James D. Davidson, Dean R. Hoge, and Mary L. Gautier, *American Catholics Today: New Realities of Their Faith and Their Church* (New York: Rowman and Littlefield, 2007), 46.

7. The classic, perhaps overly influential, statement here is Ferdinand Tönnies's late nineteenth-century depiction of modernity as tantamount to a shift from *Gemeinschaft* to *Gesellschaft* forms of social organization. Roughly translated as "community," this first "ideal type" was, in his view, characterized by its small scale, close affective bonds, and a strong sense of in-group solidarity, which results from a shared language and a set of commonly held traditions. Whereas here Tönnies envisioned the rural village, the model for *Gesellschaft* or "society" was the bustling metropolis. Fragmented by a multiplicity of self-interests and individual identities based on "achieved" social statuses, fast-growing and fast-paced modern urban life seemed to him inimical to feelings of intimacy and belonging. See Ferdinand Tönnies, *Community and Society*, trans. Charles P. Loomis (1887; reprint, New York: Harper and Row, 1963).

8. R. Stephen Warner, *New Wine in Old Wineskins: Evangelicals and Liberals in a Small-town Church* (Berkeley: University of California Press, 1988), 201–208. See also Nancy Ammerman's thoughtful exploration of this theme in her *Congregation and Community*, with Arthur E. Farnsley II and Tammy Adams (New Brunswick, N.J.: Rutgers University Press, 1997), 352–353.

9. For instance, if all of the most important past scholarship on community break-down in the United States is to be believed, claims historian Thomas Bender, then this soci-etal calamity occurred serially in the 1650s, 1690s, 1740s, 1780s, 1820s, 1850s, 1880s, and 1920s. See Thomas Bender, *Community and Social Change in America* (Baltimore: Johns Hopkins University Press, 1978), 51.

10. Cited in Robert Wuthnow, *Loose Connections: Joining Together in America's Frag-mented Communities* (Cambridge, Mass.: Harvard University Press, 1998), 68.

11. George A. Hillery Jr., "Definitions of Community: Areas of Agreement," *Rural Soci-ology* 20 (1955): 779–91.

12. See Justice Potter Stewart's concurring opinion in *Jacobellis v. Ohio* (1964).

13. Kai T. Erikson, *Everything in Its Path: Destruction of Community in the Buffalo Creek Flood* (New York: Simon and Schuster, 1976), 193–94.

14. The term "community of memory" comes from Robert N. Bellah, Richard Madsen, William M. Sullivan, Ann Swidler, and Steven M. Tipton, *Habits of the Heart: Individual-ism and Commitment in American Life* (Berkeley: University of California Press, 1985); see especially 152–63.

15. My thinking on the matter has been informed by David M. Hummon's exploration of "community ideologies" in his book *Commmonplaces: Community Ideology and Identity in American Culture* (Albany, N.Y.: SUNY Press, 1990).

16. It is in this sense that I agree with international studies scholar Benedict Anderson, who advises that "communities are to be distinguished, not by their falsity/genuineness, but by the style in which they are to be imagined." See Benedict Anderson, *Imagined Communi-ties: Reflections on the Origin and Spread of Nationalism,* rev. ed. (New York: Verso, 1991), 6.

17. Georg Simmel, "The Metropolis and Mental Life," in *The Sociology of Georg Simmel,* ed. Kurt H. Wolff (1905; reprint, New York: Free Press, 1964), 409–24.

18. Robert E. Park, "The City: Suggestions for the Investigation of Human Behavior in the Urban Environment," in *The City,* ed. Robert E. Park and E. W. Burgess (Chicago: Uni-versity of Chicago Press, 1967), 40.

19. See especially William Kornhauser, *The Politics of Mass Society* (New York: Free Press, 1959).

20. Vance Packard, *A Nation of Strangers* (New York: McKay, 1972).

21. Lyn H. Lofland, *A World of Strangers: Order and Action in Urban Public Space* (Pros-pect Heights, Ill.: Waveland, 1973), 179.

22. See Claude S. Fischer's very illuminating work, especially Claude S. Fischer, Rob-ert Max Jackson, C. Ann Stueve, Kathleen Gerson, and Lynne McCallister Jones, with Mark Baldassare, *Networks and Places: Social Relations in the Urban Setting* (New York: Free Press, 1977), and Fischer's *To Dwell among Friends: Personal Networks in Town and City* (Chicago: University of Chicago Press, 1982).

23. See Juliet B. Schor, *The Overworked American: The Unexpected Decline of Leisure* (New York: Basic, 1991).

24. Wuthnow, *Loose Connections,* 223. In addition, J. A. English-Lueck touches on some of these themes in her ethnographic study of Silicon Valley, *Cultures@SiliconValley* (Stan-ford, Calif.: Stanford University Press, 2002).

25. Robert M. MacIver and Charles H. Page, *Society: An Introductory Analysis* (New York: Rinehart, 1949), 192–93.

26. See Robert Redfield, *The Little Community and Peasant Society and Culture* (Chicago: University of Chicago Press, 1960), 1–16.

27. This term comes from Margaret Harris, "Quiet Care: Welfare Work and Religious Congregations," *Journal of Social Policy* 24 (1995): 53–71.

28. Seeing these parishes as havens has been facilitated by Gerardo Marti's use of this concept in describing Mosaic, a multiethnic church in Los Angeles; see his *Mosaic of Believers: Diversity and Innovation in a Multiethnic Church* (Bloomington: Indiana University Press, 2005).

29. The term *personalist* has various meanings. However, my use of it follows Paul Lichterman's conceptualization of "personalism as a cultural trend" as incisively articulated in his book *The Search for Political Community: American Activists Reinventing Commitment* (New York: Cambridge University Press, 1996), 5–9.

30. See Wade Clark Roof, *A Generation of Seekers: The Spiritual Journeys of the Baby Boom Generation* (San Francisco: HarperCollins, 1993), 32–60.

31. Ronald Inglehart, *Culture Shift in Advanced Industrial Society* (Princeton, N.J.: Princeton University Press, 1990).

32. Daniel Yankelovich, *New Rules: Searching for Self-fulfillment in a World Turned Upside Down* (New York: Random, 1981), 5.

33. Philip Rieff, *The Triumph of the Therapeutic: Uses of Faith after Freud* (Chicago: University of Chicago Press, 1966), 252.

34. Ibid., 261.

35. Lichterman, *Search for Political Community*, 7.

36. Quoted in Arthur M. Schlesinger Jr., *The Disuniting of America: Reflections on a Multicultural Society*, rev. ed. (New York: Norton, 1998), 38.

37. Peter C. Phan, "Introduction: The New Faces of the American Catholic Church," in *Many Faces, One Church: Cultural Diversity and the American Catholic Experience*, ed. Peter C. Phan and Diana Hayes (Lanham, Md.: Rowman and Littlefield, 2005), 3.

38. For important explorations of religion and the "new immigrants," see R. Stephen Warner and Judith G. Wittner, eds., *Gatherings in Diaspora: Religious Communities and the New Immigration* (Philadelphia: Temple University Press, 1998); Helen Rose Ebaugh and Janet Saltzman Chafetz, eds., *Religion and the New Immigrants: Continuities and Adaptation in Immigrant Congregations* (Walnut Creek, Calif.: AltaMira, 2000); Karen I. Leonard, Alex Stepick, Manuel A. Vasquez, and Jennifer Holdaway, eds., *Immigrant Faiths: Transforming Religious Life in America* (Lanham, Md.: Rowman and Littlefield, 2005); Fred Kniss and Paul David Numrich, *Sacred Assemblies and Civic Engagement: How Religion Matters for America's Newest Immigrants* (New Brunswick, N.J.: Rutgers University Press, 2007); and Michael W. Foley and Dean R. Hoge, *Religion and the New Immigrants: How Faith Communities Form Our Newest Citizens* (New York: Oxford University Press, 2007).

39. R. Stephen Warner, "Religion and New (Post-1965) Immigrants: Some Principles Drawn from Field Research," in *A Church of Our Own: Disestablishment and Diversity in American Religion* (New Brunswick, N.J.: Rutgers University Press, 2005), 232–33.

40. R. Stephen Warner, "The De-Europeanization of American Christianity," in *A Nation of Religions: The Politics of Pluralism in Multireligious America*, ed. Stephen Prothero (Chapel Hill: University of North Carolina Press, 2006), 236.

41. For instance, historian Jay Dolan finds that church leaders are extremely accommodating. In his *In Search of an American Catholicism,* he determines that, "by endorsing a cultural pluralism that recognized the unique richness of each ethnic group, the church and its leaders have acknowledged the importance of the ethnic dynamic in defining what it means to be Catholic in the United States." See Jay P. Dolan, *In Search of an American Catholicism: A History of Religion and Culture in Tension* (New York: Oxford University Press, 2002), 224. On the other hand, sociologists Barry A. Kosmin and Seymour P. Lachman seem far less convinced of the church's endorsement of cultural pluralism in their book *One Nation under God: Religion and Contemporary American Society* (New York: Harmony, 1993). Seeing initiatives such as offering Mass in various languages to be relatively superficial efforts, they conclude that "For its part, the church demonstrates skepticism toward attempts to divide its flock in the interests of 'cultural empowerment' and so divert its followers' attention away from the church's own religious agenda" (128).

42. Barry A. Kosmin and Ariela Keysar, *Religion in a Free Market: Religious and Non-religious Americans* (Ithaca, N.Y.: Paramount Market, 2006), 236.

43. Peter C. Phan, *Vietnamese-American Catholics* (Mahwah, N.J.: Paulist Press, 2005).

44. Steffi San Buenaventura, "Filipino Religion at Home and Abroad: Historical Roots and Immigrant Transformations," in *Religions in Asian America: Building Faith Communities,* ed. Pyong Gap Min and Jung Ha Kim (Walnut Creek, Calif.: AltaMira, 2002), 143–83.

45. Kosmin and Keysar, *Religion in a Free Market,* 236.

46. I draw many of the distinctive themes delineated in this paragraph from R. Stephen Warner's essay, "The De-Europeanization of American Christianity," 233–55.

47. See James C. Cavendish, Michael R. Welch, and David C. Leege, "Social Network Theory and Predictors of Religiosity for Black and White Catholics: Evidence of a 'Black Sacred Cosmos'?" *Journal for the Scientific Study of Religion* 37(3) (1998): 397–410, and also James D. Davidson, Andrea S. Williams, Richard A. Lamanna, Jan Stenftenagel, Kathleen Maas Weigert, William J. Whalen, and Patricia Wittberg, S.C., *The Search for Common Ground: What Unites and Divides American Catholics* (Huntington, Ind.: Our Sunday Visitor, 1997), 158–61.

48. Judith N. Shklar, *American Citizenship: The Quest for Inclusion* (Cambridge, Mass.: Harvard University Press, 1991), 3.

49. Charles Taylor, "The Politics of Recognition," in Amy Gutmann, ed., *Multiculturalism: Examining the Politics of Recognition* (Princeton, N.J.: Princeton University Press, 1994), 25.

50. George Herbert Mead, *Mind, Self, and Society* (Chicago: University of Chicago Press, 1934).

51. See Michael A. Hogg and Dominic Abrams's description of "categorization" in *Social Identifications: A Social Psychology of Intergroup Relations and Group Processes* (New York: Routledge, 1998), 19–21.

52. See Jennifer L. Hochschild, *Facing Up to the American Dream: Race, Class, and the Soul of the Nation* (Princeton, N.J.: Princeton University Press, 1995).

53. See Russell Jeung, *Faithful Generations: Race and New Asian American Churches* (New Brunswick, N.J.: Rutgers University Press, 2005).

54. Quoted in Nathan O. Hatch, *The Democratization of American Christianity* (New Haven, Conn.: Yale University Press, 1989), 58.

55. Sociologists often denote this more complicated process as "segmented assimilation." See especially Min Zhou and Carl L. Bankston III, *Growing Up American: How Vietnamese Children Adapt to Life in the United States* (New York: Russell Sage Foundation, 1998).

56. See especially Jürgen Habermas, *The Structural Transformation of the Public Sphere: An Inquiry into a Category of Bourgeois Society* (Cambridge, Mass.: MIT Press, 1989), as well as the important collection of essays on his work, Craig Calhoun, ed., *Habermas and the Public Sphere* (Cambridge, Mass.: MIT Press, 1992).

57. Seyla Benhabib, "Judgment and the Moral Foundations of Politics in Hannah Arendt's Thought" in *Situating the Self: Gender, Community and Postmodernism in Contemporary Ethics* (New York: Routledge, 1992), 141.

58. Leon Wieseltier, "Against Identity," *New Republic* (Nov. 28, 1994): 30.Quoted in Todd Gitlin, *The Twilight of Common Dreams: Why America Is Wracked by Culture Wars* (New York: Metropolitan, 1995), 207.

59. See William Cenkner, ed., *The Multicultural Church: A New Landscape in U.S. Theologies* (Mahwah, N.J.: Paulist Press, 1996).

60. Edmund Burke, *Reflections on the Revolution in France* (1790; reprint, New York: Penguin, 1969), 135.

61. Adam Ferguson, *An Essay on the History of Civil Society* (Philadelphia: William Fry, [1782] 1819), 365.

62. Peter L. Berger and Richard John Neuhaus, *To Empower People: The Role of Mediating Structures in Public Policy* (Washington, D.C.: American Enterprise Institute, 1977), 6.

63. See, for example, Hank Johnston and Bert Klandermans, eds., *Social Movements and Culture* (Minneapolis: University of Minnesota Press, 1995).

64. Sara M. Evans and Harry C. Boyte, *Free Spaces: The Sources of Democratic Change in America* (New York: Harper and Row, 1986), 189.

65. See Joseph A. Komonchak, "Interpreting the Council: Catholic Attitudes toward Vatican II," in *Being Right: Conservative Catholics in America,* ed. Mary Jo Weaver and R. Scott Appleby (Bloomington: Indiana University Press, 1995), 21.

66. In his classic *The Elementary Forms of Religious Life,* trans. Karen E. Fields (1912; reprint, New York: Free Press, 1995), Durkheim writes: "Whether simple or complex, all known religious beliefs display a common feature: They presuppose a classification of the real or ideal things that men conceive of into two classes—two opposite genera—that are widely designated by two distinct terms, which the words *profane* and *sacred* translate fairly well. The division of the world into two domains, one containing all that is sacred and the other all that is profane—such is the distinctive trait of religious thought" (34).

67. *Catechism of the Catholic Church* (Liguori, Mo.: Liguori Publications, 1994), nos. 2357–58.

68. In this way, the community functions as what political philosopher Nancy Fraser calls a "subaltern counterpublic." See Nancy Fraser, "Rethinking the Public Sphere: A Contribution to the Critique of Actually Existing Democracy," in *Habermas in the Public Sphere,* ed. Craig Calhoun (Cambridge, Mass.: MIT Press, 1992), 109–42.

69. One frequently cited *Washington Post*/Kaiser Family Foundation/Harvard University national poll has found that, while tolerant of difference, 72 percent of respondents said that "gay sex" was "unacceptable." See Hanna Rosin and Richard Morin, "As Tolerance Grows, Acceptance Remains Elusive," *Washington Post,* Dec. 26, 1998, A1.

70. Erving Goffman, *Stigma: Notes on the Management of Spoiled Identity* (New York: Simon and Schuster, 1963), 10.

71. An excellent illustration of this is Michele Dillon's account of pro-change Catholics "using doctrine to critique doctrine." See her *Catholic Identity: Balancing Reason, Faith, and Power* (New York: Cambridge University Press, 1999), especially chapter six.

72. According to Weber, "an ideal type is formed by the one-sided accentuation of one or more points of view and by the synthesis of a great many diffuse, discrete, more or less present and occasionally absent concrete individual phenomena, which are arranged according to those one-sidedly emphasized viewpoints into a unified analytical construct." See Max Weber, *The Methodology of the Social Sciences,* ed. and trans. Edward A. Shils and Henry A. Finch (New York: Free Press, 1949), 90.

73. See, for example, Ruth Frankenberg, *White Women, Race Matters: The Social Construction of Whiteness* (Minneapolis: University of Minnesota Press, 1993).

74. A classic exploration of these themes is found in Charles Y. Glock, Benjamin B. Ringer, and Earl R. Babbie, *To Comfort and to Challenge: Dilemma of the Contemporary Church* (Berkeley: University of California Press, 1967).

CHAPTER 6

1. See, for example, Peter J. Henriot, Edward P. DeBerri, and Michael J. Schultheis, *Catholic Social Teaching: Our Best Kept Secret* (Maryknoll, N.Y.: Orbis, 1992).

2. *Faithful Citizenship* (Washington, D.C.: National Conference of Catholic Bishops, 1999), 4.

3. Parts of this chapter draw upon two articles I have written. They are "Congregations and Civil Society: A Double-edged Connection," *Journal of Church and State* 44 (Summer 2002): 425–54, and "The Catholic Citizen: Perennial Puzzle or Emergent Oxymoron?" *Social Compass* 53 (2006): 291–309.

4. Philip J. Murnion and David DeLambo, *Parishes and Parish Ministers: A Study of Parish Lay Ministry* (New York: National Pastoral Life Center, 1999), 16–18.

5. Mary Beth Celio, *Celebrating Catholic Parishes: A Study Done in Conjunction with the Cooperative Congregational Studies Project, Faith Communities Today (FACT)—A Preliminary Report on Roman Catholic Parishes* (Seattle: Catholic Archdiocese of Seattle, March 2001), 11.

6. James D. Davidson, "Civic Engagement among American Catholics, Especially the post–Vatican II Generation," paper presented at the Commonweal Winter 2001 Colloquium; see the colloquium website, http://www.catholicsinthepublicsquare.org.

7. This is commensurate with sociologist David Leege's finding that two-thirds of all active parishioners had to be specifically asked to become more involved within their churches; see his essay titled "The American Parish," in *American Catholic Identity: Essays in an Age of Change,* ed. Francis J. Butler (Kansas City, Mo.: Sheed and Ward, 1994), 80.

8. Mary Jo Bane, "The Catholic Puzzle: Parishes and Civic Life," in *Taking Faith Seriously,* ed. Mary Jo Bane, Brent Coffin, and Richard Higgins (Cambridge, Mass.: Harvard University Press, 2005), 62–93.

9. See, for example, James T. Fischer, *Communion of Immigrants: A History of Catholics in America* (New York: Oxford University Press, 2000), chapter three.

10. See Mary J. Oates, *The Catholic Philanthropic Tradition in America* (Indianapolis: Indiana University Press, 1995), and Dorothy M. Brown and Elizabeth McKeown, *The Poor Belong to Us: Catholic Charities and American Welfare* (Cambridge, Mass.: Harvard University Press, 1997).

11. John E. Tropman, *The Catholic Ethic and the Spirit of Community* (Washington, D.C.: Georgetown University Press, 2002), 15. See also Andrew Greeley, *The Catholic Imagination* (Berkeley: University of California Press, 2000).

12. Murnion and DeLambo, *Parishes and Parish Ministers,* 11.

13. Bane, "Catholic Puzzle," 24.

14. Christian Smith, et al., *American Evangelicalism: Embattled and Thriving* (Chicago: University of Chicago Press, 1998), 34.

15. Dean Hoge, Charles Zech, Patrick McNamara, and Michael J. Donahue, "The Value of Volunteers as Resources for Congregations," *Journal for the Scientific Study of Religion* (1998) 37(3): 470–80. This information came in response to the following question: "How many hours, if any, during the last month have you given in volunteer time at your church to teach, lead, serve on a committee, or help with some program, event, or task?"

16. Dean R. Hoge, Charles Zech, Patrick McNamara, and Michael J. Donahue, *Money Matters: Personal Giving in American Churches* (Louisville, Ky.: Westminster John Knox, 1996), 31. See also Charles E. Zech, *Why Catholics Don't Give and What Can Be Done about It* (Huntington, Ind.: Our Sunday Visitor, 2000).

17. Virginia A. Hodgkinson and Murray S. Weitzman, *Giving and Volunteering in the United States* (Washington, D.C.: Independent Sector, 1996), 54.

18. Robert Wuthnow, "Beyond Quiet Influence? Possibilities for the Protestant Mainline," in *The Quiet Hand of God: Faith-based Activism and the Public Role of Mainline Protestantism,* ed. Robert Wuthnow and John H. Evans (Berkeley: University of California Press, 2002), 392.

19. William B. Prendergast, *The Catholic Voter in American Politics: The Passing of the Democratic Monolith* (Washington, D.C.: Georgetown University Press, 1999), 219.

20. James D. Davidson, Andrea S. Williams, Richard A. Lamanna, Jan Stenftenagel, Kathleen Maas Weigert, William J. Whalen, and Patricia Wittberg, S.C., *The Search for Common Ground: What Unites and Divides American Catholics* (Huntington, Ind.: Our Sunday Visitor, 1997), 181.

21. Andrew Kohut, John C. Green, Scott Keeter, and Robert C. Toth, *The Diminishing Divide: Religion's Changing Role in American Politics* (Washington, D.C.: Brookings Institution Press, 2000), 143–45.

22. Robert Wuthnow, *God and Mammon in America* (New York: Free Press, 1994), 197, 219.

23. Bane very helpfully explores seven different "structural and organizational features of the American Catholic Church," which she labels as (1) hierarchical structures; (2) specialization by national and regional structures; (3) human resource constraints; (4) financial constraints; (5) constraints on preaching and proclaiming the message; (6) constraints on dialogue; and (7) challenges to credibility. In the same collection of essays, Nancy Ammerman focuses more on the relative deficiency in Catholic parishes for interaction and participation; see her essay titled "Religious Narratives in the Public Square," in *Taking Faith Seriously,* ed. Bane, Coffin, and Higgins, 146–74.

24. Here I am instructed by Robert D. Putman's important exploration of "social capital" in the United States as presented in his widely read *Bowling Alone: The Collapse and Revival of American Community* (New York: Simon and Schuster, 2000).

25. Sidney Verba, Kay Lehman Schlozman, Henry E. Brady, *Voice and Equality: Civic Voluntarism in American Politics* (Cambridge, Mass.: Harvard University Press, 1995), 382.

26. Bryan T. Froehle and Mary L. Gautier, *Catholicism USA: A Portrait of the Catholic Church in the United States* (Maryknoll, N.Y.: Orbis, 2000), 72, 87–106.

27. Ibid., 59; see also Richard A. Schoenherr and Lawrence A. Young, *Full Pews and Empty Altars: Demographics of the Priest Shortage in United States Catholic Dioceses* (Madison: University of Wisconsin Press, 1993).

28. Murnion and DeLambo, *Parishes and Parish Ministers,* iii.

29. Virginia A. Hodgkinson, Murray S. Weitzman, Arthur D. Kirsch, Stephen M. Noga, and Heather A. Gorski, *From Belief to Commitment: The Community Service Activities and Finances of Religious Congregations in the United States* (Washington, D.C.: Independent Sector, 1993).

30. Tobi Jennifer Printz, "Faith-based Service Providers in the Nation's Capital: Can They Do More?" (Washington, D.C.: Urban Institute, 1998), 3.

31. Bane, "Catholic Puzzle," 89.

32. This is according to Mark Chaves's National Congregations Study, the results of which are available at the American Religion Data Archive (ARDA) at http://www.thearda.com/Archive/Files/Descriptions/NCS.asp.

33. Ibid.

34. See Robert Wuthnow, "Mobilizing Civic Engagement: The Changing Impact of Religious Involvement," in *Civic Engagement in American Democracy,* ed. Theda Skocpol and Morris P. Fiorina (Washington, D.C.: Brookings Institution Press, 1999), 331–63.

35. David C. Leege and Thomas A. Trozzolo, "Religious Values and Parish Participation: The Paradox of Individual Needs in a Communitarian Church," Report No. 4, Notre Dame Study of Catholic Parish Life (Notre Dame, Ind.: University of Notre Dame, 1985), 5.

36. Lewis A. Coser, *Greedy Institutions: Patterns of Undivided Commitment* (New York: Free Press, 1974). Relying on Coser's work, Hornsby-Smith makes a similar point; see Michael P. Hornsby-Smith, *The Changing Parish: A Study of Parishes, Priests, and Parishioners after Vatican II* (New York: Routledge, 1989), 89–92.

37. Hoge et al., *Money Matters,* 44.

38. Mark Chaves, *Congregations in America* (Cambridge, Mass.: Harvard University Press, 2004), 9.

39. Nancy Tatom Ammerman, *Pillars of Faith: American Congregations and Their Partners* (Berkeley: University of California Press, 2005), 126–27.

40. David C. Leege, "Catholics and the Civic Order: Parish Participation, Politics, and Civic Participation," *Review of Politics* 50 (Fall 1988): 704–36.

41. Smith, et al., *American Evangelicalism,* 134.

42. These data come from the 1996 Pew Religion and Politics Survey, which are available online at the American Religion Data Archive at http://www.thearda.com/Archive/Files/Descriptions/96KOHUT.asp. Along with "your religious beliefs," the other five response categories this survey provided were "a personal experience," "the views of your friends and family," "what you have seen or read in the media," "your education," and "something else."

43. Gene Burns, *The Frontiers of Catholicism: The Politics of Ideology in a Liberal World* (Berkeley: University of California Press, 1992); see especially chapter one.

44. William V. D'Antonio, James D. Davidson, Dean R. Hoge, and Mary L. Gautier, *American Catholics Today: New Realities of Their Faith and Their Church* (New York: Rowman and Littlefield, 2007), 92.

45. Michele Dillon explains and employs this "production of culture" approach very effectively in her *Catholic Identity: Balancing Reason, Faith, and Power* (New York: Cambridge University Press, 1999); see especially 22–31. See also Richard A. Peterson's influential edited volume titled *The Production of Culture* (Beverly Hills, Calif.: Sage, 1976), and, focusing explicitly on American religion, Robert Wuthnow's *Producing the Sacred: An Essay on Public Religion* (Chicago: University of Illinois Press, 1994).

46. David J. O'Brien, *Public Catholicism* (Maryknoll, N.Y.: Orbis, 1996), 252.

47. On discursive rules, see Stephen Hart, *Cultural Dilemmas of Progressive Politics: Styles of Engagement among Grassroots Activists* (Chicago: University of Chicago Press, 2001), 13–21. Also, for an understanding of how discourse is institutionally delimited, see C. Wright Mills's classic essay, "Situated Actions and Vocabularies of Motive," in Irving Louis Horowitz, ed., *Power, Politics, and People: The Collected Essays of C. Wright Mills* (New York: Oxford University Press, 1963), 439–52.

48. Rosabeth Moss Kanter, *Commitment and Community: Communes and Utopias in Sociological Perspective* (Cambridge, Mass.: Harvard University Press, 1972), 61–74.

49. My analysis of the "hushing effect" operative in these parishes has been greatly informed by Nina Eliasoph's exploration of the "political evaporation" that occurs among the activist groups she investigates in her book *Avoiding Politics: How Americans Produce Apathy in Everyday Life* (New York: Cambridge University Press, 1998).

50. Erving Goffman, *Behavior in Public Places* (New York: Free Press, 1966).

51. See, for example, Hervé Varenne, *Americans Together: Structured Diversity in a Midwestern Town* (New York: Teachers College Press, 1977).

52. M. P. Baumgartner, *The Moral Order of a Suburb* (New York: Oxford University Press, 1988).

53. Dawne Moon, *God, Sex, and Politics: Homosexuality and Everyday Theologies* (Chicago: University of Chicago Press, 2004), 144.

54. Erving Goffman, *The Presentation of Self in Everyday Life* (New York: Doubleday, 1959). I am also indebted to Nina Eliasoph's use of Goffman's front and back regions in *Avoiding Politics*, 97–100.

55. Alexis de Tocqueville, *Democracy in America*, ed. J. P. Mayer and trans. George Lawrence (1835-40; reprint, Garden City, N.Y.: Doubleday, Anchor Books, 1969), 289. Jay Dolan also draws on Tocqueville in noting this paradox in his book *In Search of an American Catholicism: A History of Religion and Culture in Tension* (New York: Oxford University Press, 2002), 83–84.

CHAPTER 7

1. Adam Smith, *The Wealth of Nations* (1776; reprint, New York: Penguin, 1982), 117.

2. Ralph Waldo Emerson, "Nature," in *Emerson: Selected Essays*, ed. Larzer Ziff (1836; reprint, New York: Penguin Classics, 1982), 35.

3. William Dean, *The American Spiritual Culture: And the Invention of Jazz, Football, and the Movies* (New York: Continuum, 2002), 55.

4. Richard M. Merelman, *Making Something of Ourselves: On Culture and Politics in the United States* (Berkeley: University of California Press, 1984), 26.

5. Harold Bloom, *The American Religion: The Emergence of the Post-Christian Nation* (New York: Touchstone, 1992), 22.

6. H. Richard Niebuhr, *The Responsible Self: An Essay in Christian Moral Philosophy* (San Francisco: HarperCollins, 1963), 72.

7. For an important investigation of the construction of communal memory, see Maurice Halbwachs, *On Collective Memory,* ed. and trans. Lewis A. Coser (Chicago: University of Chicago Press, 1992), especially chapter six. For a more contemporary account inspired by Halbwachs's work, see Paul Connerton, *How Societies Remember* (New York: Cambridge University Press, 1989).

8. Gilbert K. Chesterton, *Orthodoxy* (New York: John Lane, 1908), 84–85.

9. Or, to lift a phrase from sociologist Edward Shils's watershed book on the topic, traditions represent "particular configurations of persistence and disruption." Their persistence, he argues, is due to people's need to coordinate with one another both the meanings they discern and the actions they undertake collectively. "As long as human beings need rules and categories and institutions and as long as they cannot create these for themselves just when the occasion arises and for that occasion only," he writes, "they will cling to traditions, even when they proudly think that they are not doing so. As long as the separate actions of separate individuals do not suffice to achieve all the ends which any human being can want, enduring arrangements of the actions of many human beings will be necessary, organizations will be necessary; where there is organization, there will be authority and authority will become enmeshed in traditions." See Edward Shils, *Tradition* (Chicago: University of Chicago Press, 1981), 321–22.

10. Jaroslav Pelikan, *The Vindication of Tradition* (New Haven, Conn.: Yale University Press, 1984), 65.

11. Alasdair MacIntyre, *After Virtue: A Study in Moral Theory* (Notre Dame, Ind.: University of Notre Dame Press, 1981), 207.

12. See John Henry Newman, *An Essay on the Development of Christian Doctrine* (1878; reprint, Notre Dame, Ind.: Notre Dame University Press, 1989), and Johann Adam Möhler, *Unity in the Church or the Principle of Catholicism: Presented in the Spirit of the Church Fathers of the First Three Centuries* (1825; reprint, Washington, D.C.: Catholic University of America Press, 1995).

13. "Dogmatic Constitution on Divine Revelation" (*Dei verbum*) in Walter M. Abbott, S.J., ed., *The Documents of Vatican II* (Chicago: Follett, 1966), no. 8, 116.

14. John E. Thiel, *Senses of Tradition: Continuity and Development in Catholic Faith* (New York: Oxford University Press, 2000), 210. The material used in this paragraph was culled largely from Thiel's thorough presentation of what he calls the "literal," "development-in-continuity," "dramatic development," and "incipient development" senses of Catholic tradition. See also John T. Noonan Jr., *A Church That Can and Cannot Change: The Development of Catholic Moral Teaching* (Notre Dame, Ind.: Notre Dame University Press, 2005).

15. See Robert J. Schreiter, *Constructing Local Theologies* (Maryknoll, N.Y.: Orbis, 1985), 109–13, and Max Radin, "Tradition," in *Encyclopaedia of the Social Sciences,* vol. 15, ed. Edwin Seligman (New York: Macmillan, 1937), 62–67.

16. Robert N. Bellah, Richard Madsen, William M. Sullivan, Ann Swidler, and Steven M. Tipton, *The Good Society* (New York: Vintage, 1991), 6.

17. Dorothy C. Bass, "Congregations and the Bearing of Traditions," in *American Congregations,* Vol. 2: *New Perspectives in the Study of Congregations,* ed. James P. Wind and James W. Lewis (Chicago: University of Chicago Press, 1994), 169–91.

18. Again, Michele Dillon makes this point with great care and nuance in *Catholic Identity: Balancing Reason, Faith, and Power* (New York: Cambridge University Press, 1999), 24–31.

19. For a wide-ranging collection of essays on this topic see Paul Heelas, Scott Lash, and Paul Morris, eds., *Detraditionalization: Critical Reflections on Authority and Identity* (Cambridge, Mass.: Blackwell, 1996).

20. For the classic statement on differentiating "negative" and "positive" freedom, see "Two Concepts of Liberty," in Isaiah Berlin's *Four Essays on Liberty* (New York: Oxford University Press, 1969), 118–72.

21. Reframing, according to Marsha Witten, "allows men and women to draw on the resonance of the symbols to create statements about the meaning of the whole of life." See Marsha G. Witten, *All Is Forgiven: The Secular Message in American Protestantism* (Princeton, N.J.: Princeton University Press, 1993), 29.

22. See especially his essay "Science as a Vocation," in *From Max Weber: Essays in Sociology,* ed. H. H. Gerth and C. Wright Mills (New York: Oxford University Press, 1946), 129–56.

23. Ulrich Beck, *Risk Society: Towards a New Modernity,* trans. Mark Ritter (Thousand Oaks, Calif.: Sage, 1992).

24. William G. McLoughlin, *Revivals, Awakenings, and Reform: An Essay on Religion and Social Change in America, 1607–1977* (Chicago: University of Chicago Press, 1978), 18.

25. For a very influential account of religious revival and innovation, which in their usage pertain to sect and cult formation respectively, see Rodney Stark and William Sims Bainbridge, *The Future of Religion: Secularization, Revival, and Cult Formation* (Berkeley: University of California Press, 1985).

26. See Eric Hobsbawm, "Introduction: Inventing Traditions," in *The Invention of Tradition,* ed. Eric Hobsbawm and Terence Ranger (New York: Cambridge University Press, 1983).

27. Theologian Terrence W. Tilley makes this argument in his *Inventing Catholic Tradition* (Maryknoll, N.Y.: Orbis, 2000), 36–43.

28. For a thoughtful exploration of the mass media's impact on religion, see David Lyon's *Jesus in Disneyland: Religion in Postmodern Times* (Malden, Mass.: Polity, 2000).

29. Jon Butler, *Awash in a Sea of Faith: Christianizing the American People* (Cambridge, Mass.: Harvard University Press, 1990).

30. Meredith B. McGuire, *Religion: The Social Context,* 5th ed. (Belmont, Calif.: Wadsworth, 2002), 5–12.

31. Melford Spiro, "Religion: Problems of Definition and Explanation," in *Anthropological Approaches to the Study of Religion,* ed. Michael Banton (London: Tavistock, 1966), 96.

32. Robert N. Bellah, "Religious Evolution," in *Beyond Belief: Essays on Religion in a Post-traditionalist World* (Berkeley: University of California Press, 1970), 21.

33. See Danièle Hervieu-Léger, *Religion as a Chain of Memory* (Malden, Mass.: Blackwell, 2000), 23–41.

34. Ernst Troeltsch, *The Social Teaching of the Christian Churches,* vol. II (Louisville, Ky.: Westminster/John Knox, 1992), especially 991–1013.

35. Wade Clark Roof, *Spiritual Marketplace: Baby Boomers and the Remaking of American Religion* (Princeton, N.J.: Princeton University Press, 1999), 71; I quote Roof here while also noting that he has a very nuanced understanding of the interplay between religion and spirituality.

36. For a sophisticated exploration of the creation of in-group identity through comparison with relevant out-groups, see Michael A. Hogg and Dominic Abrams, *Social Identifications: A Social Psychology of Intergroup Relations and Group Processes* (New York: Routledge, 1998), 6–30.

37. Anthony Giddens, *The Consequences of Modernity* (Stanford, Calif.: Stanford University Press, 1990), 53 See also Giddens's essay "Living in a Post-traditional Society," in *Reflexive Modernization: Politics, Tradition, and Aesthetics in the Modern Social Order,* ed. Ulrich Beck, Anthony Giddens, and Scott Lash (Stanford, Calif.: Stanford University Press, 1994), 56–109.

38. Ibid., 38.

39. For a fuller assessment of Giddens's understanding of tradition and one that has informed my own thinking about the reflexive nature of specifically religious traditions, see Philip A. Mellor, "Reflexive Traditions: Anthony Giddens, High Modernity, and the Contours of Contemporary Religiosity," *Religious Studies* 29 (March 1993): 111–27.

40. This irony is addressed brilliantly in David Gross's *The Past in Ruins: Tradition and the Critique of Modernity* (Amherst: University of Massachusetts Press, 1992), especially 40–61.

41. "Pastoral Constitution on the Church in the Modern World" (*Gaudium et spes*) in Abbott, ed., *Documents of Vatican II,* no. 16, 213.

42. These phrases come from the council's clearest treatment of *sensus fidei* in "Dogmatic Constitution on the Church" *(Lumen gentium),* in Abbott, ed., *Documents of Vatican II,* no. 12, 29–30. Related notions presented in conciliar documents are *sensus catholicus* in "Decree on the Ministry and Life of Priests" *(Apostolicam actuositatem),* no. 30; *sensus christianus fidelium* in "Pastoral Constitution on the Church in the Modern World" *(Gaudium et spes),* no. 52; *sensus christianus* in *Gaudium et spes,* no. 62; *sensus religiosus* in *Gaudium et spes,* no. 59, in "Declaration on the Relationship of the Church to Non-Christian Religions *(Notra aetate),* no. 2, and in "Declaration on Religious Freedom" *(Dignitatis humanae),* no. 4; *sensus Dei* in *Gaudium et spes,* no. 7, and in "Dogmatic Constitution on Divine Revelation" *(Dei verbum),* no. 15; and *sensus Christi et ecclesiae* in "Decree on the Church's Missionary Activity" *(Ad gentes),* no. 19.

43. Two classic texts are John Henry Newman's 1859 essay, *On Consulting the Faithful on Matters of Doctrine* (Kansas City, Mo.: Sheed and Ward, 1961), and Yves M. J. Congar, O. P., *Lay People in the Church: A Study for a Theology of the Laity* (London: Geoffrey Chapman, 1959). Some useful contemporary explorations of this general topic are Orlando O. Espín, *The Faith of the People: Theological Reflections on Popular Catholicism* (Maryknoll, N.Y.: Orbis, 1997); Daniel J. Finucane, *Sensus fidelium: The Use of a Concept in the Post–Vatican II Era* (San Francisco: International Scholars, 1996); Richard R. Gallardetz, *By What Authority? A Primer on Scripture, the Magisterium, and the Sense of the Faithful* (Collegeville, Minn.: Liturgical Press, 2003); and Paul Lakeland, *The Liberation of the Laity: In Search of an Accountable Church* (New York: Continuum, 2003).

44. I take this useful phrase from Paul Lichterman's important book, *Elusive Togetherness: Church Groups Trying to Bridge America's Divisions* (Princeton, N.J.: Princeton University Press, 2005).

45. See especially Friedrich Nietzsche, *The Genealogy of Morals* (New York: Modern Library, 1940), as well as his *Use and Abuse of History* (New York: Liberal Arts Press, 1949).

46. Alan Wolfe, *One Nation after All: What Middle-class Americans Really Think about God, Country, Family, Racism, Welfare, Immigration, Homosexuality, Work, the Right, the Left, and Each Other* (New York: Viking, 1998), especially chapter two.

47. Alan Wolfe addresses many of these cultural transformations affecting both American Catholics and other Americans in his highly informative *The Transformation of American Religion: How We Actually Live Our Faith* (New York: Free Press, 2003).

48. "Pastoral Constitution on the Church in the Modern World" *(Gaudium et spes),* in Abbott, ed., *Documents of Vatican II,* no. 4, 201.

49. Walker Percy, "Rome Isn't the Villain," *Commonweal* 67(2) (Jan. 26, 1990): 34.

50. This is one of the themes emphasized in William V. D'Antonio, James D. Davidson, Dean R. Hoge, and Mary L. Gautier, *American Catholics Today: New Realities of Their Faith and Their Church* (New York: Rowman and Littlefield, 2007).

51. Jay Dolan, *In Search of an American Catholicism: A History of Religion and Culture in Tension* (New York: Oxford University Press, 2002), 255.

Index